21

Part 1300 to End
Revised as of April 1, 2008

Food and Drugs

Containing a codification of documents
of general applicability and future effect

As of April 1, 2008

With Ancillaries

Published by
Office of the Federal Register
National Archives and Records
Administration

A Special Edition of the Federal Register

D1477999

Code of Federal Regulations

U.S. GOVERNMENT OFFICIAL EDITION NOTICE

Legal Status and Use of Seals and Logos

The seal of the National Archives and Records Administration (NARA) authenticates the Code of Federal Regulations (CFR) as the official codification of Federal regulations established under the Federal Register Act. Under the provisions of 44 U.S.C. 1507, the contents of the CFR, a special edition of the Federal Register, shall be judicially noticed. The CFR is prima facie evidence of the original documents published in the Federal Register (44 U.S.C. 1510).

It is prohibited to use NARA's official seal and the stylized Code of Federal Regulations logo on any republication of this material without the express, written permission of the Archivist of the United States or the Archivist's designee. Any person using NARA's official seals and logos in a manner inconsistent with the provisions of 36 CFR part 1200 is subject to the penalties specified in 18 U.S.C. 506, 701, and 1017.

Use of ISBN Prefix

This is the Official U.S. Government edition of this publication and is herein identified to certify its authenticity. Use of the 0–16 ISBN prefix is for U.S. Government Printing Office Official Editions only. The Superintendent of Documents of the U.S. Government Printing Office requests that any reprinted edition clearly be labeled as a copy of the authentic work with a new ISBN.

 U.S. GOVERNMENT PRINTING OFFICE

U.S. Superintendent of Documents • Washington, DC 20402–0001

http://bookstore.gpo.gov

Phone: toll-free (866) 512-1800; DC area (202) 512-1800

Table of Contents

Cite this Code: **CFR**

To cite the regulations in this volume use title, part and section number. Thus, 21 CFR 1300.01 *refers to title 21, part 1300, section 01.*

Explanation

The Code of Federal Regulations is a codification of the general and permanent rules published in the Federal Register by the Executive departments and agencies of the Federal Government. The Code is divided into 50 titles which represent broad areas subject to Federal regulation. Each title is divided into chapters which usually bear the name of the issuing agency. Each chapter is further subdivided into parts covering specific regulatory areas.

Each volume of the Code is revised at least once each calendar year and issued on a quarterly basis approximately as follows:

Title 1 through Title 16...as of January 1
Title 17 through Title 27 ....as of April 1
Title 28 through Title 41 ....as of July 1
Title 42 through Title 50 ....as of October 1

The appropriate revision date is printed on the cover of each volume.

LEGAL STATUS

The contents of the Federal Register are required to be judicially noticed (44 U.S.C. 1507). The Code of Federal Regulations is prima facie evidence of the text of the original documents (44 U.S.C. 1510).

HOW TO USE THE CODE OF FEDERAL REGULATIONS

The Code of Federal Regulations is kept up to date by the individual issues of the Federal Register. These two publications must be used together to determine the latest version of any given rule.

To determine whether a Code volume has been amended since its revision date (in this case, April 1, 2008), consult the "List of CFR Sections Affected (LSA)," which is issued monthly, and the "Cumulative List of Parts Affected," which appears in the Reader Aids section of the daily Federal Register. These two lists will identify the Federal Register page number of the latest amendment of any given rule.

EFFECTIVE AND EXPIRATION DATES

Each volume of the Code contains amendments published in the Federal Register since the last revision of that volume of the Code. Source citations for the regulations are referred to by volume number and page number of the Federal Register and date of publication. Publication dates and effective dates are usually not the same and care must be exercised by the user in determining the actual effective date. In instances where the effective date is beyond the cut-off date for the Code a note has been inserted to reflect the future effective date. In those instances where a regulation published in the Federal Register states a date certain for expiration, an appropriate note will be inserted following the text.

OMB CONTROL NUMBERS

The Paperwork Reduction Act of 1980 (Pub. L. 96–511) requires Federal agencies to display an OMB control number with their information collection request.

Many agencies have begun publishing numerous OMB control numbers as amendments to existing regulations in the CFR. These OMB numbers are placed as close as possible to the applicable recordkeeping or reporting requirements.

OBSOLETE PROVISIONS

Provisions that become obsolete before the revision date stated on the cover of each volume are not carried. Code users may find the text of provisions in effect on a given date in the past by using the appropriate numerical list of sections affected. For the period before January 1, 1986, consult either the List of CFR Sections Affected, 1949–1963, 1964–1972, 1973–1985, or 1986–2001 published in seven separate volumes. For the period beginning January 1, 2001, a "List of CFR Sections Affected" is published at the end of each CFR volume.

INCORPORATION BY REFERENCE

What is incorporation by reference? Incorporation by reference was established by statute and allows Federal agencies to meet the requirement to publish regulations in the Federal Register by referring to materials already published elsewhere. For an incorporation to be valid, the Director of the Federal Register must approve it. The legal effect of incorporation by reference is that the material is treated as if it were published in full in the Federal Register (5 U.S.C. 552(a)). This material, like any other properly issued regulation, has the force of law.

What is a proper incorporation by reference? The Director of the Federal Register will approve an incorporation by reference only when the requirements of 1 CFR part 51 are met. Some of the elements on which approval is based are:

(a) The incorporation will substantially reduce the volume of material published in the Federal Register.

(b) The matter incorporated is in fact available to the extent necessary to afford fairness and uniformity in the administrative process.

(c) The incorporating document is drafted and submitted for publication in accordance with 1 CFR part 51.

Regulations containing properly approved incorporations by reference in this volume are listed in the Finding Aids at the end of their CFR volume.

What if the material incorporated by reference cannot be found? If you have any problem locating or obtaining a copy of material listed in the Finding Aids of this volume as an approved incorporation by reference, please contact the agency that issued the regulation containing that incorporation. If, after contacting the agency, you find the material is not available, please notify the Director of the Federal Register, National Archives and Records Administration, Washington DC 20408, or call 202-741-6010.

CFR INDEXES AND TABULAR GUIDES

A subject index to the Code of Federal Regulations is contained in a separate volume, revised annually as of January 1, entitled CFR INDEX AND FINDING AIDS. The CFR Index also contains the parallel table of statutory authorities and agency rules. A list of CFR titles, chapters, subchapters, and parts and an alphabetical list of agencies publishing in the CFR.

An index to the text of "Title 3—The President" is carried within 3 CFR.

The Federal Register Index is issued monthly in cumulative form. This index is based on a consolidation of the "Contents" entries in the daily Federal Register.

A List of CFR Sections Affected (LSA) is published monthly, keyed to the revision dates of the 50 CFR titles.

REPUBLICATION OF MATERIAL

There are no restrictions on the republication of material appearing in the Code of Federal Regulations.

INQUIRIES

For a legal interpretation or explanation of any regulation in this volume, contact the issuing agency. The issuing agency's name appears at the top of odd-numbered pages.

For inquiries concerning CFR reference assistance, call 202–741–6000 or write to the Director, Office of the Federal Register, National Archives and Records Administration, Washington, DC 20408 or e-mail fedreg.info@nara.gov.

SALES

The Government Printing Office (GPO) processes all sales and distribution of the CFR. For payment by credit card, call toll-free, 866-512-1800, or DC area, 202-512-1800, M-F 8 a.m. to 4 p.m. e.s.t. or fax your order to 202-512-2250, 24 hours a day. For payment by check, write to: US Government Printing Office – New Orders, P.O. Box 979050, St. Louis, MO 63197-9000. For GPO Customer Service call 202-512-1803.

ELECTRONIC SERVICES

The full text of the Code of Federal Regulations, the LSA (List of CFR Sections Affected), The United States Government Manual, the Federal Register, Public Laws, Public Papers, Weekly Compilation of Presidential Documents and the Privacy Act Compilation are available in electronic format at *www.gpoaccess.gov/ nara* ("GPO Access"). For more information, contact Electronic Information Dissemination Services, U.S. Government Printing Office. Phone 202-512-1530, or 888-293-6498 (toll-free). E-mail, *gpoaccess@gpo.gov.*

The Office of the Federal Register also offers a free service on the National Archives and Records Administration's (NARA) World Wide Web site for public law numbers, Federal Register finding aids, and related information. Connect to NARA's web site at *www.archives.gov/federal-register.* The NARA site also contains links to GPO Access.

RAYMOND A. MOSLEY,
Director,
Office of the Federal Register.
April 1, 2008.

THIS TITLE

Title 21—FOOD AND DRUGS is composed of nine volumes. The parts in these volumes are arranged in the following order: Parts 1–99, 100–169, 170–199, 200–299, 300–499, 500–599, 600–799, 800–1299 and 1300–end. The first eight volumes, containing parts 1–1299, comprise Chapter I—Food and Drug Administration, Department of Health and Human Services. The ninth volume, containing part 1300 to end, includes Chapter II—Drug Enforcement Administration, Department of Justice, and Chapter III—Office of National Drug Control Policy. The contents of these volumes represent all current regulations codified under this title of the CFR as of April 1, 2008.

For this volume, Elmer Barksdale and Kenneth R. Payne were Chief Editors. The Code of Federal Regulations publication program is under the direction of Michael L. White, assisted by Ann Worley.

Title 21–Food and Drugs

(This book contains part 1300 to End)

CHAPTER II—DRUG ENFORCEMENT ADMINISTRATION, DEPARTMENT OF JUSTICE

PART 1300—DEFINITIONS

Sec.
1300.01 Definitions relating to controlled substances.
1300.02 Definitions relating to listed chemicals.

AUTHORITY: 21 U.S.C. 802, 871(b), 951, 958(f)

SOURCE: 62 FR 13941, Mar. 24, 1997, unless otherwise noted.

§ 1300.01 Definitions relating to controlled substances.

(a) Any term not defined in this part shall have the definition set forth in section 102 of the Act (21 U.S.C. 802), except that certain terms used in part 1316 of this chapter are defined at the beginning of each subpart of that part.

(b) As used in parts 1301 through 1308 and part 1312 of this chapter, the following terms shall have the meanings specified:

(1) The term *Act* means the Controlled Substances Act, as amended (84 Stat. 1242; 21 U.S.C. 801) and/or the Controlled Substances Import and Export Act, as amended (84 Stat. 1285; 21 U.S.C. 951).

(2) The term *Administration* means the Drug Enforcement Administration.

(3) The term *Administrator* means the Administrator of the Drug Enforcement Administration. The Administrator has been delegated authority under the Act by the Attorney General (28 CFR 0.100).

(4) The term anabolic steroid means any drug or hormonal substance, chemically and pharmacologically related to testosterone (other than estrogens, progestins, corticosteroids, and dehydroepiandrosterone), and includes:

(i) 3β,17-dihydroxy-5a-androstane

(ii) 3α,17β-dihydroxy-5a-androstane

(iii) 5α-androstan-3,17-dione

(iv) 1-androstenediol (3β,17β-dihydroxy-5α-androst-1-ene)

(v) 1-androstenediol (3α,17β-dihydroxy-5α-androst-1-ene)

(vi) 4-androstenediol (3β,17β-dihydroxy-androst-4-ene)

(vii) 5-androstenediol (3β,17β-dihydroxy-androst-5-ene)

(viii) 1-androstenedione ([5α]-androst-1-en-3,17-dione)

(ix) 4-androstenedione (androst-4-en-3,17-dione)

(x) 5-androstenedione (androst-5-en-3,17-dione)

(xi) bolasterone (7α,17α-dimethyl-17β-hydroxyandrost-4-en-3-one)

(xii) boldenone (17β-hydroxyandrost-1,4,-diene-3-one)

(xiii) calusterone (7β,17α-dimethyl-17β-hydroxyandrost-4-en-3-one)

(xiv) clostebol (4-chloro-17β-hydroxyandrost-4-en-3-one)

(xv) dehydrochloromethyltestosterone (4-chloro-17β-hydroxy-17α-methyl-androst-1,4-dien-3-one)

(xvi) Δ1-dihydrotestosterone (a.k.a. '1-testosterone') (17β-hydroxy-5α-androst-1-en-3-one)

(xvii) 4-dihydrotestosterone (17β-hydroxy-androstan-3-one)

(xviii) drostanolone (17β-hydroxy-2α-methyl-5α-androstan-3-one)

(xix) ethylestrenol (17α-ethyl-17β-hydroxyestr-4-ene)

(xx) fluoxymesterone (9-fluoro-17α-methyl-11β,17β-dihydroxyandrost-4-en-3-one)

(xxi) formebolone (2-formyl-17α-methyl-11α,17β-dihydroxyandrost-1,4-dien-3-one)

(xxii) furazabol (17α-methyl-17β-hydroxyandrostano[2,3-c]-furazan)

(xxiii) 13β-ethyl-17β-hydroxygon-4-en-3-one

(xxiv) 4-hydroxytestosterone (4,17β-dihydroxy-androst-4-en-3-one)

(xxv) 4-hydroxy-19-nortestosterone (4,17β-dihydroxy-estr-4-en-3-one)

(xxvi) mestanolone (17α-methyl-17β-hydroxy-5-androstan-3-one)

(xxvii) mesterolone (1αmethyl-17β-hydroxy-[5α]-androstan-3-one)

(xxviii) methandienone (17α-methyl-17β-hydroxyandrost-1,4-dien-3-one)

(xxix) methandriol (17α-methyl-3β,17β-dihydroxyandrost-5-ene)

(xxx) methenolone (1-methyl-17β-hydroxy-5α-androst-1-en-3-one)

(xxxi) 17α-methyl-3β, 17β-dihydroxy-5a-androstane

(xxxii) 17α-methyl-3α,17β-dihydroxy-5a-androstane

(xxxiii) 17α-methyl-3β,17β-dihydroxyandrost-4-ene

(xxxiv) 17α-methyl-4-hydroxynandrolone (17α-methyl-4-hydroxy-17β-hydroxyestr-4-en-3-one)

(xxxv) methyldienolone (17α-methyl-17β-hydroxyestra-4,9(10)-dien-3-one)

5

(xxxvi) methyltrienolone (17α-methyl-17β-hydroxyestra-4,9-11-trien-3-one)

(xxxvii) methyltestosterone (17α-methyl-17β-hydroxyandrost-4-en-3-one)

(xxxviii) mibolerone (7α,17α-dimethyl-17β-hydroxyestr-4-en-3-one)

(xxxix) 17α-methyl-Δ1-dihydrotestosterone (17bβ-hydroxy-17α-methyl-5α-androst-1-en-3-one) (a.k.a. '17-α-methyl-1-testosterone')

(xl) nandrolone (17β-hydroxyestr-4-en-3-one)

(xli) 19-nor-4-androstenediol (3β, 17β-dihydroxyestr-4-ene)

(xlii) 19-nor-4-androstenediol (3α, 17β-dihydroxyestr-4-ene)

(xliii) 19-nor-5-androstenediol (3β, 17β-dihydroxyestr-5-ene)

(xliv) 19-nor-5-androstenediol (3α, 17β-dihydroxyestr-5-ene)

(xlv) 19-nor-4-androstenedione (estr-4-en-3,17-dione)

(xlvi) 19-nor-5-androstenedione (estr-5-en-3,17-dione

(xlvii) norbolethone (13β, 17α-diethyl-17β-hydroxygon-4-en-3-one)

(xlviii) norclostebol (4-chloro-17β-hydroxyestr-4-en-3-one)

(xlix) norethandrolone (17α-ethyl-17β-hydroxyestr-4-en-3-one)

(l) normethandrolone (17α-methyl-17β-hydroxyestr-4-en-3-one)

(li) oxandrolone (17α-methyl-17β-hydroxy-2-oxa-[5α]-androstan-3-one)

(lii) oxymesterone (17α-methyl-4,17β-dihydroxyandrost-4-en-3-one)

(liii) oxymetholone (17α-methyl-2-hydroxymethylene-17β-hydroxy-[5α]-androstan-3-one)

(liv) stanozolol (17α-methyl-17β-hydroxy-[5α]-androst-2-eno[3,2-c]-pyrazole)

(lv) stenbolone (17β-hydroxy-2-methyl-[5α]-androst-1-en-3-one)

(lvi) testolactone (13-hydroxy-3-oxo-13,17-secoandrosta-1,4-dien-17-oic acid lactone)

(lvii) testosterone (17β-hydroxyandrost-4-en-3-one)

(lviii) tetrahydrogestrinone (13β, 17α-diethyl-17β-hydroxygon-4,9,11-trien-3-one)

(lix) trenbolone (17β-hydroxyestr-4,9,11-trien-3-one)

(lx) Any salt, ester, or ether of a drug or substance described in this paragraph. Except such term does not include an anabolic steroid that is expressly intended for administration through implants to cattle or other nonhuman species and that has been approved by the Secretary of Health and Human Services for such administration. If any person prescribes, dispenses, or distributes such steroid for human use, the person shall be considered to have prescribed, dispensed, or distributed an anabolic steroid within the meaning of this paragraph.

(5) The term *basic class* means, as to controlled substances listed in Schedules I and II:

(i) Each of the opiates, including its isomers, esters, ethers, salts, and salts of isomers, esters, and ethers whenever the existence of such isomers, esters, ethers, and salts is possible within the specific chemical designation, listed in § 1308.11(b) of this chapter;

(ii) Each of the opium derivatives, including its salts, isomers, and salts of isomers whenever the existence of such salts, isomers, and salts of isomers is possible within the specific chemical designation, listed in § 1308.11(c) of this chapter;

(iii) Each of the hallucinogenic substances, including its salts, isomers, and salts of isomers whenever the existence of such salts, isomers, and salts of isomers is possible within the specific chemical designation, listed in § 1308.11(d) of this chapter;

(iv) Each of the following substances, whether produced directly or indirectly by extraction from substances of vegetable origin, or independently by means of chemical synthesis, or by a combination of extraction and chemical synthesis:

(A) Opium, including raw opium, opium extracts, opium fluid extracts, powdered opium, granulated opium, deodorized opium and tincture of opium;

(B) Apomorphine;

(C) Codeine;

(D) Etorphine hydrochloride;

(E) Ethylmorphine;

(F) Hydrocodone;

(G) Hydromorphone;

(H) Metopon;

(I) Morphine;

(J) Oxycodone;

(K) Oxymorphone;

(L) Thebaine;

(M) Mixed alkaloids of opium listed in Section 1308.12(b)(2) of this chapter;

(N) Cocaine; and

(O) Ecgonine;

(v) Each of the opiates, including its isomers, esters, ethers, salts, and salts of isomers, esters, and ethers whenever the existence of such isomers, esters, ethers, and salts is possible within the specific chemical designation, listed in § 1308.12(c) of this chapter; and

(vi) Methamphetamine, its salts, isomers, and salts of its isomers;

(vii) Amphetamine, its salts, optical isomers, and salts of its optical isomers;

(viii) Phenmetrazine and its salts;

(ix) Methylphenidate;

(x) Each of the substances having a depressant effect on the central nervous system, including its salts, isomers, and salts of isomers whenever the existence of such salts, isomers, and salts of isomers is possible within the specific chemical designation, listed in § 1308.12(e) of this chapter.

(6) The term *commercial container* means any bottle, jar, tube, ampule, or other receptacle in which a substance is held for distribution or dispensing to an ultimate user, and in addition, any box or package in which the receptacle is held for distribution or dispensing to an ultimate user. The term commercial container does not include any package liner, package insert or other material kept with or within a commercial container, nor any carton, crate, drum, or other package in which commercial containers are stored or are used for shipment of controlled substances.

(7) The term *compounder* means any person engaging in maintenance or detoxification treatment who also mixes, prepares, packages or changes the dosage form of a narcotic drug listed in Schedules II, III, IV or V for use in maintenance or detoxification treatment by another narcotic treatment program.

(8) The term *controlled substance* has the meaning given in section 802(6) of Title 21, United States Code (U.S.C.).

(9) The term *customs territory* of the United States means the several States, the District of Columbia, and Puerto Rico.

(10) The term *detoxification treatment* means the dispensing, for a period of time as specified below, of a narcotic drug or narcotic drugs in decreasing doses to an individual to alleviate adverse physiological or psychological effects incident to withdrawal from the continuous or sustained use of a narcotic drug and as a method of bringing the individual to a narcotic drug-free state within such period of time. There are two types of detoxification treatment: Short-term detoxification treatment and long-term detoxification treatment.

(i) Short-term detoxification treatment is for a period not in excess of 30 days.

(ii) Long-term detoxification treatment is for a period more than 30 days but not in excess of 180 days.

(11) The term *dispenser* means an individual practitioner, institutional practitioner, pharmacy or pharmacist who dispenses a controlled substance.

(12) The term *export* means, with respect to any article, any taking out or removal of such article from the jurisdiction of the United States (whether or not such taking out or removal constitutes an exportation within the meaning of the customs and related laws of the United States).

(13) The term *exporter* includes every person who exports, or who acts as an export broker for exportation of, controlled substances listed in any schedule.

(14) The term *hearing* means:

(i) In part 1301 of this chapter, any hearing held for the granting, denial, revocation, or suspension of a registration pursuant to sections 303, 304, and 1008 of the Act (21 U.S.C. 823, 824 and 958).

(ii) In part 1303 of this chapter, any hearing held regarding the determination of aggregate production quota or the issuance, adjustment, suspension, or denial of a procurement quota or an individual manufacturing quota.

(iii) In part 1308 of this chapter, any hearing held for the issuance, amendment, or repeal of any rule issuable pursuant to section 201 of the Act (21 U.S.C. 811).

(15) The term *import* means, with respect to any article, any bringing in or introduction of such article into either the jurisdiction of the United States or the customs territory of the United States, and from the jurisdiction of the United States into the customs territory of the United States (whether or

not such bringing in or introduction constitutes an importation within the meaning of the tariff laws of the United States).

(16) The term *importer* includes every person who imports, or who acts as an import broker for importation of, controlled substances listed in any schedule.

(17) The term *individual practitioner* means a physician, dentist, veterinarian, or other individual licensed, registered, or otherwise permitted, by the United States or the jurisdiction in which he/she practices, to dispense a controlled substance in the course of professional practice, but does not include a pharmacist, a pharmacy, or an institutional practitioner.

(18) The term *institutional practitioner* means a hospital or other person (other than an individual) licensed, registered, or otherwise permitted, by the United States or the jurisdiction in which it practices, to dispense a controlled substance in the course of professional practice, but does not include a pharmacy.

(19) The term *interested person* means any person adversely affected or aggrieved by any rule or proposed rule issuable pursuant to section 201 of the Act (21 U.S.C. 811).

(20) The term *inventory* means all factory and branch stocks in finished form of a basic class of controlled substance manufactured or otherwise acquired by a registrant, whether in bulk, commercial containers, or contained in pharmaceutical preparations in the possession of the registrant (including stocks held by the registrant under separate registration as a manufacturer, importer, exporter, or distributor).

(21) (i) *The term isomer* means the optical isomer, except as used in § 1308.11(d) and § 1308.12(b)(4) of this chapter. As used in § 1308.11(d) of this chapter, the term "isomer" means any optical, positional, or geometric isomer. As used in § 1308.12(b)(4) of this chapter, the term "isomer" means any optical or geometric isomer.

(ii) As used in § 1308.11(d) of this chapter, the term "positional isomer" means any substance possessing the same molecular formula and core structure and having the same functional group(s) and/or substituent(s) as those found in the respective schedule I hallucinogen, attached at any position(s) on the core structure, but in such manner that no new chemical functionalities are created and no existing chemical functionalities are destroyed relative to the respective schedule I hallucinogen. Rearrangements of alkyl moieties within or between functional group(s) or substituent(s), or divisions or combinations of alkyl moieties, that do not create new chemical functionalities or destroy existing chemical functionalities, are allowed i.e., result in compounds which are positional isomers. For purposes of this definition, the "core structure" is the parent molecule that is the common basis for the class; for example, tryptamine, phenethylamine, or ergoline. Examples of rearrangements resulting in creation and/or destruction of chemical functionalities (and therefore resulting in compounds which are not positional isomers) include, but are not limited to: ethoxy to *alpha*-hydroxyethyl, hydroxy and methyl to methoxy, or the repositioning of a phenolic or alcoholic hydroxy group to create a hydroxyamine. Examples of rearrangements resulting in compounds which would be positional isomers include: *tert*-butyl to *sec*-butyl, methoxy and ethyl to isopropoxy, N,N-diethyl to N-methyl-N-propyl, or *alpha*-methylamino to N-methylamino.

(22) The term *jurisdiction of the United States* means the customs territory of the United States, the Virgin Islands, the Canal Zone, Guam, American Samoa, and the Trust Territories of the Pacific Islands.

(23) The term *label* means any display of written, printed, or graphic matter placed upon the commercial container of any controlled substance by any manufacturer of such substance.

(24) The term *labeling* means all labels and other written, printed, or graphic matter:

(i) Upon any controlled substance or any of its commercial containers or wrappers, or

(ii) Accompanying such controlled substance.

(25) The term *Long Term Care Facility* (*LTCF*) means a nursing home, retirement care, mental care or other facility or institution which provides extended health care to resident patients.

(26) The term *maintenance treatment* means the dispensing for a period in excess of twenty-one days, of a narcotic drug or narcotic drugs in the treatment of an individual for dependence upon heroin or other morphine-like drug.

(27) The term *manufacture* means the producing, preparation, propagation, compounding, or processing of a drug or other substance or the packaging or repackaging of such substance, or the labeling or relabeling of the commercial container of such substance, but does not include the activities of a practitioner who, as an incident to his/her administration or dispensing such substance in the course of his/her professional practice, prepares, compounds, packages or labels such substance. The term *manufacturer* means a person who manufactures a drug or other substance, whether under a registration as a manufacturer or under authority of registration as a researcher or chemical analyst.

(28) The term *mid-level practitioner* means an individual practitioner, other than a physician, dentist, veterinarian, or podiatrist, who is licensed, registered, or otherwise permitted by the United States or the jurisdiction in which he/she practices, to dispense a controlled substance in the course of professional practice. Examples of mid-level practitioners include, but are not limited to, health care providers such as nurse practitioners, nurse midwives, nurse anesthetists, clinical nurse specialists and physician assistants who are authorized to dispense controlled substances by the state in which they practice.

(29) The term *name* means the official name, common or usual name, chemical name, or brand name of a substance.

(30) The term *narcotic drug* means any of the following whether produced directly or indirectly by extraction from substances of vegetable origin or independently by means of chemical synthesis or by a combination of extraction and chemical synthesis:

(i) Opium, opiates, derivatives of opium and opiates, including their isomers, esters, ethers, salts, and salts of isomers, esters, and ethers whenever the existence of such isomers, esters, ethers and salts is possible within the specific chemical designation. Such term does not include the isoquinoline alkaloids of opium.

(ii) Poppy straw and concentrate of poppy straw.

(iii) Coca leaves, except coca leaves and extracts of coca leaves from which cocaine, ecgonine and derivatives of ecgonine or their salts have been removed.

(iv) Cocaine, its salts, optical and geometric isomers, and salts of isomers.

(v) Ecgonine, its derivatives, their salts, isomers and salts of isomers.

(vi) Any compound, mixture, or preparation which contains any quantity of any of the substances referred to in paragraphs (b)(31)(i) through (v) of this section.

(31) The term *narcotic treatment program* means a program engaged in maintenance and/or detoxification treatment with narcotic drugs.

(32) The term *net disposal* means, for a stated period, the quantity of a basic class of controlled substance distributed by the registrant to another person, plus the quantity of that basic class used by the registrant in the production of (or converted by the registrant into) another basic class of controlled substance or a noncontrolled substance, plus the quantity of that basic class otherwise disposed of by the registrant, less the quantity of that basic class returned to the registrant by any purchaser, and less the quantity of that basic class distributed by the registrant to another registered manufacturer of that basic class for purposes other than use in the production of, or conversion into, another basic class of controlled substance or a noncontrolled substance or in the manufacture of dosage forms of that basic class.

(33) The term *pharmacist* means any pharmacist licensed by a State to dispense controlled substances, and shall include any other person (e.g., pharmacist intern) authorized by a State to dispense controlled substances under

the supervision of a pharmacist licensed by such State.

(34) The term *person* includes any individual, corporation, government or governmental subdivision or agency, business trust, partnership, association, or other legal entity.

(35) The term *prescription* means an order for medication which is dispensed to or for an ultimate user but does not include an order for medication which is dispensed for immediate administration to the ultimate user. (e.g., an order to dispense a drug to a bed patient for immediate administration in a hospital is not a prescription.)

(36) The term *proceeding* means all actions taken for the issuance, amendment, or repeal of any rule issued pursuant to section 201 of the Act (21 U.S.C. 811), commencing with the publication by the Administrator of the proposed rule, amended rule, or repeal in the FEDERAL REGISTER.

(37) The term *purchaser* means any registered person entitled to obtain and execute order forms pursuant to §§ 1305.04 and 1305.06.

(38) The term *readily retrievable* means that certain records are kept by automatic data processing systems or other electronic or mechanized record-keeping systems in such a manner that they can be separated out from all other records in a reasonable time and/or records are kept on which certain items are asterisked, redlined, or in some other manner visually identifiable apart from other items appearing on the records.

(39) The terms *register* and *registration* refer only to registration required and permitted by sections 303 or 1007 of the Act (21 U.S.C. 823 or 957).

(40) The term *registrant* means any person who is registered pursuant to either section 303 or section 1008 of the Act (21 U.S.C. 823 or 958).

(41) The term *reverse distributor* means a registrant who receives controlled substances acquired from another DEA registrant for the purpose of—

(i) Returning unwanted, unusable, or outdated controlled substances to the manufacturer or the manufacturer's agent; or

(ii) Where necessary, processing such substances or arranging for processing such substances for disposal.

(42) The term *supplier* means any registered person entitled to fill order forms pursuant to § 1305.08 of this chapter.

(43) The term *freight forwarding facility* means a separate facility operated by a distributing registrant through which sealed, packaged controlled substances in unmarked shipping containers (i.e., the containers do not indicate that the contents include controlled substances) are, in the course of delivery to, or return from, customers, transferred in less than 24 hours. A distributing registrant who operates a freight forwarding facility may use the facility to transfer controlled substances from any location the distributing registrant operates that is registered with the Administration to manufacture, distribute, or import controlled substances, or, with respect to returns, registered to dispense controlled substances, provided that the notice required by § 1301.12(b)(4) of Part 1301 of this chapter has been submitted and approved. For purposes of this definition, a distributing registrant is a person who is registered with the Administration as a manufacturer, distributor, and/or importer.

(44) The term *central fill pharmacy* means a pharmacy which is permitted by the state in which it is located to prepare controlled substances orders for dispensing pursuant to a valid prescription transmitted to it by a registered retail pharmacy and to return the labeled and filled prescriptions to the retail pharmacy for delivery to the ultimate user. Such central fill pharmacy shall be deemed "authorized" to fill prescriptions on behalf of a retail pharmacy only if the retail pharmacy and central fill pharmacy have a contractual relationship providing for such activities or share a common owner.

(45) The term automated dispensing system means a mechanical system that performs operations or activities,

other than compounding or administration, relative to the storage, packaging, counting, labeling, and dispensing of medications, and which collects, controls, and maintains all transaction information.

[62 FR 13941, Mar. 24, 1997, as amended at 65 FR 44678, July 19, 2000; 68 FR 37409, June 24, 2003; 68 FR 41228, July 11, 2003; 70 FR 25465, May 13, 2005; 70 FR 74656, Dec. 16, 2005; 71 FR 60427, Oct. 13, 2006; 72 FR 67852, Dec. 3, 2007]

§1300.02 Definitions relating to listed chemicals.

(a) Any term not defined in this part shall have the definition set forth in section 102 of the Act (21 U.S.C. 802), except that certain terms used in part 1316 of this chapter are defined at the beginning of each subpart of that part.

(b) As used in parts 1309, 1310, and 1313 of this chapter, the following terms shall have the meaning specified:

(1) The term *Act* means the Controlled Substances Act, as amended (84 Stat. 1242; 21 U.S.C. 801) and/or the Controlled Substances Import and Export Act, as amended (84 Stat. 1285; 21 U.S.C. 951) as amended.

(2) The term *Administration* means the Drug Enforcement Administration.

(3) The term *Administrator* means the Administrator of the Drug Enforcement Administration. The Administrator has been delegated authority under the Act by the Attorney General (28 CFR 0.100).

(4) The terms *broker* and *trader* mean any individual, corporation, corporate division, partnership, association, or other legal entity which assists in arranging an international transaction in a listed chemical by—

(i) Negotiating contracts;

(ii) Serving as an agent or intermediary; or

(iii) Fulfilling a formal obligation to complete the transaction by bringing together a buyer and seller, a buyer and transporter, or a seller and transporter, or by receiving any form of compensation for so doing.

(5) The term *chemical* export means transferring ownership or control, or the sending or taking of threshold quantities of listed chemicals out of the United States (whether or not such sending or taking out constitutes an exportation within the meaning of the Customs and related laws of the United States).

(6) The term *chemical exporter* is a regulated person who, as the principal party in interest in the export transaction, has the power and responsibility for determining and controlling the sending of the listed chemical out of the United States.

(7) The term *chemical import* means with respect to a listed chemical, any bringing in or introduction of such listed chemical into either the jurisdiction of the United States or into the Customs territory of the United States (whether or not such bringing in or introduction constitutes an importation within the meaning of the tariff laws of the United States).

(8) The term *chemical importer* is a regulated person who, as the principal party in interest in the import transaction, has the power and responsibility for determining and controlling the bringing in or introduction of the listed chemical into the United States.

(9) The term *chemical mixture* means a combination of two or more chemical substances, at least one of which is not a listed chemical, except that such term does not include any combination of a listed chemical with another chemical that is present solely as an impurity or which has been created to evade the requirements of the Act.

(10) The term *customs territory of the United States* means the several States, the District of Columbia, and Puerto Rico.

(11) The term *encapsulating machine* means any manual, semi-automatic, or fully automatic equipment which may be used to fill shells or capsules with any powdered, granular, semi-solid, or liquid material.

(12) The term *established business relationship* means the regulated person has imported or exported a listed chemical at least once within the past six months, or twice within the past twelve months from or to a foreign manufacturer, distributor, or end user of the chemical that has an established business with a fixed street address. A person or business that functions as a broker or intermediary is not a customer for purposes of this definition.

(13) The term *established record as an importer* means that the regulated person has imported a listed chemical at least once within the past six months, or twice within the past twelve months from a foreign supplier.

(14) The term *hearing* means any hearing held for the granting, denial, revocation, or suspension of a registration pursuant to sections 303, 304, and 1008 of the Act (21 U.S.C. 823, 824 and 958).

(15) The term *international transaction* means a transaction involving the shipment of a listed chemical across an international border (other than a United States border) in which a broker or trader located in the United States participates.

(16) The term *jurisdiction of the United States* means the customs territory of the United States, the Virgin Islands, the Canal Zone, Guam, American Samoa, and the Trust Territories of the Pacific Islands.

(17) The term *listed chemical* means any List I chemical or List II chemical.

(18) The term *List I chemical* means a chemical specifically designated by the Administrator in §1310.02(a) of this chapter that, in addition to legitimate uses, is used in manufacturing a controlled substance in violation of the Act and is important to the manufacture of a controlled substance.

(19) The term *List II chemical* means a chemical, other than a List I chemical, specifically designated by the Administrator in §1310.02(b) of this chapter that, in addition to legitimate uses, is used in manufacturing a controlled substance in violation of the Act.

(20) The term *name* means the official name, common or usual name, chemical name, or brand name of a substance.

(21) The term *person* includes any individual, corporation, government or governmental subdivision or agency, business trust, partnership, association, or other legal entity.

(22) The term *readily retrievable* means that certain records are kept by automatic data processing systems or other electronic or mechanized record-keeping systems in such a manner that they can be separated out from all other records in a reasonable time and/or records are kept on which certain items are asterisked, redlined, or in some other manner visually identifiable apart from other items appearing on the records.

(23) The terms *register* and *registration* refer only to registration required and permitted by sections 303 or 1007 of the Act (21 U.S.C. 823 or 957).

(24) The term *registrant* means any person who is registered pursuant to either section 303 or section 1008 of the Act (21 U.S.C. 823 or 958).

(25) The term *regular customer* means a person with whom the regulated person has an established business relationship for a specified listed chemical or chemicals that has been reported to the Administration subject to the criteria established in part 1313 of this chapter.

(26) The term *regular importer* means, with respect to a listed chemical, a person that has an established record as an importer of that listed chemical that is reported to the Administrator.

(27) The term *regulated person* means any individual, corporation, partnership, association, or other legal entity who manufactures, distributes, imports, or exports a listed chemical, a tableting machine, or an encapsulating machine, or who acts as a broker or trader for an international transaction involving a listed chemical, tableting machine, or encapsulating machine.

(28) The term *regulated transaction* means:

(i) A distribution, receipt, sale, importation, or exportation of a listed chemical, or an international transaction involving shipment of a listed chemical, or if the Administrator establishes a threshold amount for a specific listed chemical, a threshold amount as determined by the Administrator, which includes a cumulative threshold amount for multiple transactions, of a listed chemical, except that such term does not include:

(A) A domestic lawful distribution in the usual course of business between agents or employees of a single regulated person; in this context, agents or employees means individuals under the direct management and control of the regulated person;

(B) A delivery of a listed chemical to or by a common or contract carrier for carriage in the lawful and usual course of the business of the common or contract carrier, or to or by a warehouseman for storage in the lawful and usual course of the business of the warehouseman, except that if the carriage or storage is in connection with the distribution, importation, or exportation of a listed chemical to a third person, this paragraph does not relieve a distributor, importer, or exporter from compliance with parts 1309, 1310, 1313, and 1315 of this chapter;

(C) Any category of transaction or any category of transaction for a specific listed chemical or chemicals specified by regulation of the Administrator as excluded from this definition as unnecessary for enforcement of the Act;

(D) Any transaction in a listed chemical that is contained in a drug other than a scheduled listed chemical product that may be marketed or distributed lawfully in the United States under the Federal Food, Drug, and Cosmetic Act, subject to paragraph (b)(28)(i)(E) of this section, unless—

(1) The Administrator has determined pursuant to the criteria in §1310.10 of this chapter that the drug or group of drugs is being diverted to obtain the listed chemical for use in the illicit production of a controlled substance; and

(2) The quantity of the listed chemical contained in the drug included in the transaction or multiple transactions equals or exceeds the threshold established for that chemical;

(E) Any transaction in a scheduled listed chemical product that is a sale at retail by a regulated seller or a distributor required to submit reports under §1310.03(c) of this chapter; or

(F) Any transaction in a chemical mixture designated in §§1310.12 and 1310.13 of this chapter that the Administrator has exempted from regulation.

(ii) A distribution, importation, or exportation of a tableting machine or encapsulating machine except that such term does not include a domestic lawful distribution in the usual course of business between agents and employees of a single regulated person; in this context, agents or employees means individuals under the direct management and control of the regulated person.

(29) The term *retail distributor* means a grocery store, general merchandise store, drug store, or other entity or person whose activities as a distributor relating to drug products containing pseudoephedrine or phenylpropanolamine are limited almost exclusively to sales for personal use, both in number of sales and volume of sales, either directly to walk-in customers or in face-to-face transactions by direct sales. Also for the purposes of this paragraph, a grocery store is an entity within Standard Industrial Classification (SIC) code 5411, a general merchandise store is an entity within SIC codes 5300 through 5399 and 5499, and a drug store is an entity within SIC code 5912.

(30) The term *tableting machine* means any manual, semi-automatic, or fully automatic equipment which may be used for the compaction or molding of powdered or granular solids, or semi-solid material, to produce coherent solid tablets.

(31) The term combination ephedrine product means a drug product containing ephedrine or its salts, optical isomers, or salts of optical isomers, and therapeutically significant quantities of another active medicinal ingredient.

(32) The term *drug product means* an active ingredient in dosage form that has been approved or otherwise may be lawfully marketed under the Food, Drug, and Cosmetic Act for distribution in the United States.

(33) The term *valid prescription* means a prescription that is issued for a legitimate medical purpose by an individual practitioner licensed by law to administer and prescribe the drugs concerned and acting in the usual course of the practitioner's professional practice.

(34)(i) The term *scheduled listed chemical product* means a product that contains ephedrine, pseudoephedrine, or phenylpropanolamine and may be marketed or distributed lawfully in the United States under the Federal, Food, Drug, and Cosmetic Act as a nonprescription drug. Ephedrine, pseudoephedrine, and phenylpropanolamine include their salts, optical isomers, and salts of optical isomers.

(ii) Scheduled listed chemical product does not include any product that is a controlled substance under part 1308 of this chapter. In the absence of such scheduling by the Attorney General, a chemical specified in paragraph (b)(34)(i) of this section may not be considered to be a controlled substance.

(35) The term *regulated seller* means a retail distributor (including a pharmacy or a mobile retail vendor), except that the term does not include an employee or agent of the distributor.

(36) The term *mobile retail vendor* means a person or entity that makes sales at retail from a stand that is intended to be temporary or is capable of being moved from one location to another, whether the stand is located within or on the premises of a fixed facility (such as a kiosk at a shopping center or an airport) or whether the stand is located on unimproved real estate (such as a lot or field leased for retail purposes).

(37) The term *at retail*, with respect to the sale or purchase of a scheduled listed chemical product, means a sale or purchase for personal use, respectively.

[62 FR 13941, Mar. 24, 1997; 62 FR 15392, Apr. 1, 1997; 67 FR 14859, Mar. 28, 2002, as amended at 68 FR 23203, May 1, 2003; 68 FR 57803, Oct. 7, 2003; 71 FR 56023, Sept. 26, 2006; 72 FR 17406, Apr. 9, 2007; 72 FR 37448, July 10, 2007]

PART 1301—REGISTRATION OF MANUFACTURERS, DISTRIBUTORS, AND DISPENSERS OF CONTROLLED SUBSTANCES

1301.72 Physical security controls for non-practitioners; narcotic treatment programs and compounders for narcotic treatment programs; storage areas.
1301.73 Physical security controls for non-practitioners; compounders for narcotic treatment programs; manufacturing and compounding areas.
1301.74 Other security controls for non-practitioners; narcotic treatment programs and compounders for narcotic treatment programs.
1301.75 Physical security controls for practitioners.
1301.76 Other security controls for practitioners.
1301.77 Security controls for freight forwarding facilities.

EMPLOYEE SCREENING—NON-PRACTITIONERS

1301.90 Employee screening procedures.
1301.91 Employee responsibility to report drug diversion.
1301.92 Illicit activities by employees.
1301.93 Sources of information for employee checks.

AUTHORITY: 21 U.S.C. 821, 822, 823, 824, 871(b), 875, 877, 886a, 951, 952, 953, 956, 957.

SOURCE: 36 FR 7778, Apr. 24, 1971, unless otherwise noted. Redesignated at 38 FR 26609, Sept. 24, 1973.

GENERAL INFORMATION

§ 1301.01 Scope of this part 1301.

Procedures governing the registration of manufacturers, distributors, dispensers, importers, and exporters of controlled substances pursuant to sections 301–304 and 1007–1008 of the Act (21 U.S.C. 821–824 and 957–958) are set forth generally by those sections and specifically by the sections of this part.

[62 FR 13945, Mar. 24, 1997]

§ 1301.02 Definitions.

Any term used in this part shall have the definition set forth in section 102 of the Act (21 U.S.C. 802) or part 1300 of this chapter.

[62 FR 13945, Mar. 24, 1997]

§ 1301.03 Information; special instructions.

Information regarding procedures under these rules and instructions supplementing these rules will be furnished upon request by writing to the Registration Unit, Drug Enforcement Administration, Department of Justice, Post Office Box 28083, Central Station, Washington, DC 20005.

[36 FR 7778, Apr. 24, 1971. Redesignated at 38 FR 26609, Sept. 23, 1973, and amended at 51 FR 5319, Feb. 13, 1986]

REGISTRATION

§ 1301.11 Persons required to register.

(a) Every person who manufactures, distributes, dispenses, imports, or exports any controlled substance or who proposes to engage in the manufacture, distribution, dispensing, importation or exportation of any controlled substance shall obtain a registration unless exempted by law or pursuant to §§ 1301.22–1301.26. Only persons actually engaged in such activities are required to obtain a registration; related or affiliated persons who are not engaged in such activities are not required to be registered. (For example, a stockholder or parent corporation of a corporation manufacturing controlled substances is not required to obtain a registration.)

(b) [Reserved]

[62 FR 13945, Mar. 24, 1997]

§ 1301.12 Separate registrations for separate locations.

(a) A separate registration is required for each principal place of business or professional practice at one general physical location where controlled substances are manufactured, distributed, imported, exported, or dispensed by a person.

(b) The following locations shall be deemed not to be places where controlled substances are manufactured, distributed, or dispensed:

(1) A warehouse where controlled substances are stored by or on behalf of a registered person, unless such substances are distributed directly from such warehouse to registered locations other than the registered location from which the substances were delivered or to persons not required to register by virtue of subsection 302(c)(2) or subsection 1007(b)(1)(B) of the Act (21 U.S.C. 822(c)(2) or 957(b)(1)(B));

(2) An office used by agents of a registrant where sales of controlled substances are solicited, made, or supervised but which neither contains such substances (other than substances for display purposes or lawful distribution

as samples only) nor serves as a distribution point for filling sales orders; and

(3) An office used by a practitioner (who is registered at another location in the same State or jurisdiction of the United States) where controlled substances are prescribed but neither administered nor otherwise dispensed as a regular part of the professional practice of the practitioner at such office, and where no supplies of controlled substances are maintained.

(4) A freight forwarding facility, as defined in § 1300.01 of this part, provided that the distributing registrant operating the facility has submitted written notice of intent to operate the facility by registered mail, return receipt requested (or other suitable means of documented delivery) and such notice has been approved. The notice shall be submitted to the Special Agent in Charge of the Administration's offices in both the area in which the facility is located and each area in which the distributing registrant maintains a registered location that will transfer controlled substances through the facility. The notice shall detail the registered locations that will utilize the facility, the location of the facility, the hours of operation, the individual(s) responsible for the controlled substances, the security and record-keeping procedures that will be employed, and whether controlled substances returns will be processed through the facility. The notice must also detail what state licensing requirements apply to the facility and the registrant's actions to comply with any such requirements. The Special Agent in Charge of the DEA Office in the area where the freight forwarding facility will be operated will provide written notice of approval or disapproval to the person within thirty days after confirmed receipt of the notice. Registrants that are currently operating freight forwarding facilities under a memorandum of understanding with the Administration must provide notice as required by this section no later than September 18, 2000 and receive written approval from the Special Agent in Charge of the DEA Office in the area in which the freight for-

warding facility is operated in order to continue operation of the facility.

[62 FR 13945, Mar. 24, 1997, as amended at 65 FR 44678, July 19, 2000; 65 FR 45829, July 25, 2000; 71 FR 69480, Dec. 1, 2006]

§ 1301.13 Application for registration; time for application; expiration date; registration for independent activities; application forms, fees, contents and signature; coincident activities.

(a) Any person who is required to be registered and who is not so registered may apply for registration at any time. No person required to be registered shall engage in any activity for which registration is required until the application for registration is granted and a Certificate of Registration is issued by the Administrator to such person.

(b) Any person who is registered may apply to be reregistered not more than 60 days before the expiration date of his/her registration, except that a bulk manufacturer of Schedule I or II controlled substances or an importer of Schedule I or II controlled substances may apply to be reregistered no more than 120 days before the expiration date of their registration.

(c) At the time a manufacturer, distributor, reverse distributor, researcher, analytical lab, importer, exporter or narcotic treatment program is first registered, that business activity shall be assigned to one of twelve groups, which shall correspond to the months of the year. The expiration date of the registrations of all registrants within any group will be the last date of the month designated for that group. In assigning any of these business activities to a group, the Administration may select a group the expiration date of which is less than one year from the date such business activity was registered. If the business activity is assigned to a group which has an expiration date less than three months from the date of which the business activity is registered, the registration shall not expire until one year from that expiration date; in all other cases, the registration shall expire on the expiration date following the date on which the business activity is registered.

(d) At the time a retail pharmacy, hospital/clinic, practitioner or teaching institution is first registered, that business activity shall be assigned to one of twelve groups, which shall correspond to the months of the year. The expiration date of the registrations of all registrants within any group will be the last day of the month designated for that group. In assigning any of the above business activities to a group, the Administration may select a group the expiration date of which is not less than 28 months nor more than 39 months from the date such business activity was registered. After the initial registration period, the registration shall expire 36 months from the initial expiration date.

(e) Any person who is required to be registered and who is not so registered, shall make application for registration for one of the following groups of controlled substances activities, which are deemed to be independent of each other. Application for each registration shall be made on the indicated form, and shall be accompanied by the indicated fee. Fee payments shall be made in the form of a personal, certified, or cashier's check or money order made payable to the "Drug Enforcement Administration". The application fees are not refundable. Any person, when registered to engage in the activities described in each subparagraph in this paragraph, shall be authorized to engage in the coincident activities described without obtaining a registration to engage in such coincident activities, provided that, unless specifically exempted, he/she complies with all requirements and duties prescribed by law for persons registered to engage in such coincident activities. Any person who engages in more than one group of independent activities shall obtain a separate registration for each group of activities, except as provided in this paragraph under coincident activities. A single registration to engage in any group of independent activities listed below may include one or more controlled substances listed in the schedules authorized in that group of independent activities. A person registered to conduct research with controlled substances listed in Schedule I may conduct research with any substances listed in Schedule I for which he/she has filed and had approved a research protocol.

(1)

Business activity	Controlled substances	DEA application forms	Application fee (dollars)	Registration period (years)	Coincident activities allowed
(i) Manufacturing	Schedules I–V	New—225 Renewal—225a	2,293 2,293	1	Schedules I–V: May distribute that substance or class for which registration was issued; may not distribute or dispose any substance or class for which not registered. Schedules II–V: except a person registered to dispose of any controlled substance may conduct chemical analysis and preclinical research (including quality control analysis) with substances listed in those schedules for which authorization as a mfg. was issued.
(ii) Distributing	Schedules I–V	New—225 Renewal—225a	1,147 1,147	1	
(iii) Reverse distributing	Schedules I–V	New—225 Renewal—225a	1,147 1,147	1	

Business activity	Controlled substances	DEA application forms	Application fee (dollars)	Registration period (years)	Coincident activities allowed
(iv) Dispensing or instructing (includes Practitioner, Hospital/Clinic, Retail Pharmacy, Central fill pharmacy, Teaching Institution)	Schedules II–V	New—224 Renewal—224a	551 551	3	May conduct research and instructional activities with those substances for which registration was granted, except that a mid-level practitioner may conduct such research only to the extent expressly authorized under state statute. A pharmacist may manufacture an aqueous or oleaginous solution or solid dosage form containing a narcotic controlled substance in Schedule II–V in a proportion not exceeding 20% of the complete solution, compound or mixture. A retail pharmacy may perform central fill pharmacy activities.
(v) Research	Schedule I	New—225 Renewal—225a	184 184	1	A researcher may manufacture or import the basic class of substance or substances for which registration was issued, provided that such manufacture or import is set forth in the protocol required in § 1301.18 and to distribute such class to persons registered or authorized to conduct research with such class of substance or registered or authorized to conduct chemical analysis with controlled substances.
(vi) Research	Schedules II–V	New—225 Renewal—225a	184 184	1	May conduct chemical analysis with controlled substances in those schedules for which registration was issued; manufacture such substances if and to the extent that such manufacture is set forth in a statement filed with the application for registration or reregistration and provided that the manufacture is not for the purposes of dosage form development; import such substances for research purposes; distribute such substances to persons registered or authorized to conduct chemical analysis, instructional activities or research with such substances, and to persons exempted from registration pursuant to § 1301.24; and conduct instructional activities with controlled substances.
(vii) Narcotic Treatment Program (including compounder)	Narcotic Drugs in Schedules II–V	New—363 Renewal—363a	184 184	1	
(viii) Importing	Schedules I–V	New—225 Renewal—225a	1,147 1,147	1	May distribute that substance or class for which registration was issued; may not distribute any substance or class for which not registered.
(ix) Exporting	Schedules I–V	New—225 Renewal—225a	1,147 1,147	1	

Business activity	Controlled substances	DEA application forms	Application fee (dollars)	Registration period (years)	Coincident activities allowed
(x) Chemical Analysis	Schedules I–V	New—225 Renewal—225a	184 184	1	May manufacture and import controlled substances for analytical or instructional activities; may distribute such substances to persons registered or authorized to conduct chemical analysis, instructional activities, or research with such substances and to persons exempted from registration pursuant to §1301.24; may export such substances to persons in other countries performing chemical analysis or enforcing laws related to controlled substances or drugs in those countries; and may conduct instructional activities with controlled substances.

(2) DEA Forms 224, 225, and 363 may be obtained at any area office of the Administration or by writing to the Registration Unit, Drug Enforcement Administration, Department of Justice, Post Office Box 28083, Central Station, Washington, DC 20005.

(3) DEA Forms 224a, 225a, and 363a will be mailed, as applicable, to each registered person approximately 60 days before the expiration date of his/her registration; if any registered person does not receive such forms within 45 days before the expiration date of his/her registration, he/she must promptly give notice of such fact and request such forms by writing to the Registration Unit of the Administration at the foregoing address.

(f) Each application for registration to handle any basic class of controlled substance listed in Schedule I (except to conduct chemical analysis with such classes), and each application for registration to manufacture a basic class of controlled substance listed in Schedule II shall include the Administration Controlled Substances Code Number, as set forth in part 1308 of this chapter, for each basic class to be covered by such registration.

(g) Each application for registration to import or export controlled substances shall include the Administration Controlled Substances Code Number, as set forth in part 1308 of this chapter, for each controlled substance whose importation or exportation is to be authorized by such registration.

Registration as an importer or exporter shall not entitle a registrant to import or export any controlled substance not specified in such registration.

(h) Each application for registration to conduct research with any basic class of controlled substance listed in Schedule II shall include the Administration Controlled Substances Code Number, as set forth in part 1308 of this chapter, for each such basic class to be manufactured or imported as a coincident activity of that registration. A statement listing the quantity of each such basic class of controlled substance to be imported or manufactured during the registration period for which application is being made shall be included with each such application. For purposes of this paragraph only, manufacturing is defined as the production of a controlled substance by synthesis, extraction or by agricultural/horticultural means.

(i) Each application shall include all information called for in the form, unless the item is not applicable, in which case this fact shall be indicated.

(j) Each application, attachment, or other document filed as part of an application, shall be signed by the applicant, if an individual; by a partner of the applicant, if a partnership; or by an officer of the applicant, if a corporation, corporate division, association, trust or other entity. An applicant may authorize one or more individuals, who would not otherwise be authorized to do so, to sign applications for the applicant by filing with the Registration Unit of the Administration a power of attorney for each such individual. The power of attorney shall be signed by a person who is authorized to sign applications under this paragraph and shall contain the signature of the individual being authorized to sign applications. The power of attorney shall be valid until revoked by the applicant.

[62 FR 13946, Mar. 24, 1997, as amended at 68 FR 37409, June 24, 2003; 68 FR 41228, July 11, 2003; 68 FR 58598, Oct. 10, 2003; 71 FR 51112, Aug. 29, 2006]

§ 1301.14 Filing of application; acceptance for filing; defective applications.

(a) All applications for registration shall be submitted for filing to the Registration Unit, Drug Enforcement Administration, Department of Justice, Post Office Box 28083, Central Station, Washington, DC 20005. The appropriate registration fee and any required attachments must accompany the application.

(b) Any person required to obtain more than one registration may submit all applications in one package. Each application must be complete and should not refer to any accompanying application for required information.

(c) Applications submitted for filing are dated upon receipt. If found to be complete, the application will be accepted for filing. Applications failing to comply with the requirements of this part will not generally be accepted for filing. In the case of minor defects as to completeness, the Administrator may accept the application for filing with a request to the applicant for additional information. A defective application will be returned to the applicant within 10 days following its receipt with a statement of the reason for not accepting the application for filing. A defective application may be corrected and resubmitted for filing at any time; the Administrator shall accept for filing any application upon resubmission by the applicant, whether complete or not.

(d) Accepting an application for filing does not preclude any subsequent request for additional information pursuant to § 1301.15 and has no bearing on whether the application will be granted.

[62 FR 13948, Mar. 24, 1997]

§ 1301.15 Additional information.

The Administrator may require an applicant to submit such documents or written statements of fact relevant to the application as he/she deems necessary to determine whether the application should be granted. The failure of the applicant to provide such documents or statements within a reasonable time after being requested to do so shall be deemed to be a waiver by the applicant of an opportunity to present such documents or facts for consideration by the Administrator in granting or denying the application.

[62 FR 13948, Mar. 24, 1997]

§ 1301.16 Amendments to and withdrawal of applications.

(a) An application may be amended or withdrawn without permission of the Administrator at any time before the date on which the applicant receives an order to show cause pursuant to § 1301.37. An application may be amended or withdrawn with permission of the Administrator at any time where good cause is shown by the applicant or where the amendment or withdrawal is in the public interest.

(b) After an application has been accepted for filing, the request by the applicant that it be returned or the failure of the applicant to respond to official correspondence regarding the application, when sent by registered or certified mail, return receipt requested, shall be deemed to be a withdrawal of the application.

[62 FR 13949, Mar. 24, 1997]

§ 1301.17 Special procedures for certain applications.

(a) If, at the time of application for registration of a new pharmacy, the pharmacy has been issued a license from the appropriate State licensing agency, the applicant may include with his/her application an affidavit as to the existence of the State license in the following form:

Affidavit for New Pharmacy

I, _____, the _____ (Title of officer, official, partner, or other position) of _____ (Corporation, partnership, or sole proprietor), doing business as _____ (Store name) at _____ (Number and Street), _____ (City) _____ (State) _____ (Zip code), hereby certify that said store was issued a pharmacy permit No. _____ by the _____ (Board of Pharmacy or Licensing Agency) of the State of _____ on _____ (Date).

This statement is submitted in order to obtain a Drug Enforcement Administration registration number. I understand that if any information is false, the Administration may immediately suspend the registration for this store and commence proceedings to revoke under 21 U.S.C. 824(a) because of the danger to public health and safety. I further understand that any false information contained in this affidavit may subject me personally and the above-named corporation/partnership/business to prosecution under 21 U.S.C. 843, the penalties for conviction of which include imprisonment for up to 4 years, a fine of not more than $30,000 or both.

_____
Signature (Person who signs Application for Registration)
State of _____
County of _____
Subscribed to and sworn before me this _____ day of _____, 19___.

_____
Notary Public

(b) Whenever the ownership of a pharmacy is being transferred from one person to another, if the transferee owns at least one other pharmacy licensed in the same State as the one the ownership of which is being transferred, the transferee may apply for registration prior to the date of transfer. The Administrator may register the applicant and authorize him to obtain controlled substances at the time of transfer. Such registration shall not authorize the transferee to dispense controlled substances until the pharmacy has been issued a valid State license. The transferee shall include with his/her application the following affidavit:

Affidavit for Transfer of Pharmacy

I, _____, the _____ (Title of officer, official, partner or other position) of _____ (Corporation, partnership, or sole proprietor), doing business as _____ (Store name) hereby certify:

(1) That said company was issued a pharmacy permit No. _____ by the _____ (Board of Pharmacy of Licensing Agency) of the State of _____ and a DEA Registration Number _____ for a pharmacy located at _____ (Number and Street) _____ (City) _____ (State) _____ (Zip Code); and

(2) That said company is acquiring the pharmacy business of _____ (Name of Seller) doing business as _____ with DEA Registration Number _____ on or about _____ (Date of Transfer) and that said company has applied (or will apply on _____ (Date) for a pharmacy permit from the board of pharmacy (or licensing agency) of the State of _____ to do business as _____ (Store name) at _____ (Number and Street) _____ (City) _____ (State) _____ (Zip Code).

This statement is submitted in order to obtain a Drug Enforcement Administration registration number.

I understand that if a DEA registration number is issued, the pharmacy may acquire controlled substances but may not dispense them until a pharmacy permit or license is issued by the State board of pharmacy or licensing agency.

I understand that if any information is false, the Administration may immediately suspend the registration for this store and commence proceedings to revoke under 21 U.S.C. 824(a) because of the danger to public health and safety. I further understand that any false information contained in this affidavit may subject me personally to prosecution under 21 U.S.C. 843, the penalties for conviction of which include imprisonment for up to 4 years, a fine of not more than $30,000 or both.

_____
Signature (Person who signs Application for Registration)
State of _____
County of _____
Subscribed to and sworn before me this _____ day of _____, 19___.

_____
Notary Public

(c) If at the time of application for a separate registration at a long term care facility, the retail pharmacy has been issued a license, permit, or other form of authorization from the appropriate State agency to install and operate an automated dispensing system

21

for the dispensing of controlled substances at the long term care facility, the applicant must include with his/her application for registration (DEA Form 224) an affidavit as to the existence of the State authorization. Exact language for this affidavit may be found at the DEA Diversion Control Program Web site. The affidavit must include the following information:

(1) The name and title of the corporate officer or official signing the affidavit;

(2) The name of the corporation, partnership or sole proprietorship operating the retail pharmacy;

(3) The name and complete address (including city, state, and Zip code) of the retail pharmacy;

(4) The name and complete address (including city, state, and Zip code) of the long term care facility at which DEA registration is sought;

(5) Certification that the named retail pharmacy has been authorized by the state Board of Pharmacy or licensing agency to install and operate an automated dispensing system for the dispensing of controlled substances at the named long term care facility (including the license or permit number, if applicable);

(6) The date on which the authorization was issued;

(7) Statements attesting to the following:

(i) The affidavit is submitted to obtain a Drug Enforcement Administration registration number;

(ii) If any material information is false, the Administrator may commence proceedings to deny the application under section 304 of the Act (21 U.S.C. 824(a));

(iii) Any false or fraudulent material information contained in this affidavit may subject the person signing this affidavit and the above-named corporation/partnership/business to prosecution under section 403 of the Act (21 U.S.C. 843);

(8) Signature of the person authorized to sign the Application for Registration for the named retail pharmacy;

(9) Notarization of the affidavit.

(d) The Administrator shall follow the normal procedures for approving an application to verify the statements in the affidavit. If the statements prove to be false, the Administrator may revoke the registration on the basis of section 304(a)(1) of the Act (21 U.S.C. 824(a)(1)) and suspend the registration immediately by pending revocation on the basis of section 304(d) of the Act (21 U.S.C. 824(d)). At the same time, the Administrator may seize and place under seal all controlled substances possessed by the applicant under section 304(f) of the Act (21 U.S.C. 824(f)). Intentional misuse of the affidavit procedure may subject the applicant to prosecution for fraud under section 403(a)(4) of the Act (21 U.S.C. 843(a)(4)), and obtaining controlled substances through registration by fraudulent means may subject the applicant to prosecution under section 403(a)(3) of the Act (21 U.S.C. 843(a)(3)). The penalties for conviction of either offense include imprisonment for up to 4 years, a fine not exceeding $30,000 or both.

[62 FR 13949, Mar. 24, 1997, as amended at 70 FR 25465, May 13, 2005]

§ 1301.18 Research protocols.

(a) A protocol to conduct research with controlled substances listed in Schedule I shall be in the following form and contain the following information where applicable:

(1) Investigator:

(i) Name, address, and DEA registration number; if any.

(ii) Institutional affiliation.

(iii) Qualifications, including a curriculum vitae and an appropriate bibliography (list of publications).

(2) Research project:

(i) Title of project.

(ii) Statement of the purpose.

(iii) Name of the controlled substances or substances involved and the amount of each needed.

(iv) Description of the research to be conducted, including the number and species of research subjects, the dosage to be administered, the route and method of administration, and the duration of the project.

(v) Location where the research will be conducted.

(vi) Statement of the security provisions for storing the controlled substances (in accordance with § 1301.75 and for dispensing the controlled substances in order to prevent diversion.

(vii) If the investigator desires to manufacture or import any controlled substance listed in paragraph (a)(2)(iii) of this section, a statement of the quantity to be manufactured or imported and the sources of the chemicals to be used or the substance to be imported.

(3) Authority:

(i) Institutional approval.

(ii) Approval of a Human Research Committee for human studies.

(iii) Indication of an approved active Notice of Claimed Investigational Exemption for a New Drug (number).

(iv) Indication of an approved funded grant (number), if any.

(b) In the case of a clinical investigation with controlled substances listed in Schedule I, the applicant shall submit three copies of a Notice of Claimed Investigational Exemption for a New Drug (IND) together with a statement of the security provisions (as proscribed in paragraph (a)(2)(vi) of this section for a research protocol) to, and have such submission approved by, the Food and Drug Administration as required in 21 U.S.C. 355(i) and §130.3 of this title. Submission of this Notice and statement to the Food and Drug Administration shall be in lieu of a research protocol to the Administration as required in paragraph (a) of this section. The applicant, when applying for registration with the Administration, shall indicate that such notice has been submitted to the Food and Drug Administration by submitting to the Administration with his/her DEA Form 225 three copies of the following certificate:

I hereby certify that on _____ (Date), pursuant to 21 U.S.C. 355(i) and 21 CFR 130.3, I, _____ (Name and Address of IND Sponsor) submitted a Notice of Claimed Investigational Exemption for a New Drug (IND) to the Food and Drug Administration for:

_____
(Name of Investigational Drug).

_____
(Date)

_____
(Signature of Applicant).

(c) In the event that the registrant desires to increase the quantity of a controlled substance used for an approved research project, he/she shall submit a request to the Registration Unit, Drug Enforcement Administration, Post Office Box 28083, Central Station, Washington, DC 20005, by registered mail, return receipt requested. The request shall contain the following information: DEA registration number; name of the controlled substance or substances and the quantity of each authorized in the approved protocol; and the additional quantity of each desired. Upon return of the receipt, the registrant shall be authorized to purchase the additional quantity of the controlled substance or substances specified in the request. The Administration shall review the letter and forward it to the Food and Drug Administration together with the Administration comments. The Food and Drug Administration shall approve or deny the request as an amendment to the protocol and so notify the registrant. Approval of the letter by the Food and Drug Administration shall authorize the registrant to use the additional quantity of the controlled substance in the research project.

(d) In the event the registrant desires to conduct research beyond the variations provided in the registrant's approved protocol (excluding any increase in the quantity of the controlled substance requested for his/her research project as outlined in paragraph (c) of this section), he/she shall submit three copies of a supplemental protocol in accordance with paragraph (a) of this section describing the new research and omitting information in the supplemental protocol which has been stated in the original protocol. Supplemental protocols shall be processed and approved or denied in the same manner as original research protocols.

[62 FR 13949, Mar. 24, 1997]

EXCEPTIONS TO REGISTRATION AND FEES

§1301.21 Exemption from fees.

(a) The Administrator shall exempt from payment of an application fee for registration or reregistration:

(1) Any hospital or other institution which is operated by an agency of the United States (including the U.S. Army, Navy, Marine Corps., Air Force, and Coast Guard), of any State, or any political subdivision or agency thereof.

(2) Any individual practitioner who is required to obtain an individual registration in order to carry out his or her duties as an official of an agency of the United States (including the U.S. Army, Navy, Marine Corps, Air Force, and Coast Guard), of any State, or any political subdivision or agency thereof.

(b) In order to claim exemption from payment of a registration or reregistration application fee, the registrant shall have completed the certification on the appropriate application form, wherein the registrant's superior (if the registrant is an individual) or officer (if the registrant is an agency) certifies to the status and address of the registrant and to the authority of the registrant to acquire, possess, or handle controlled substances.

(c) Exemption from payment of a registration or reregistration application fee does not relieve the registrant of any other requirements or duties prescribed by law.

[62 FR 13950, Mar. 24, 1997]

§ 1301.22 Exemption of agents and employees; affiliated practitioners.

(a) The requirement of registration is waived for any agent or employee of a person who is registered to engage in any group of independent activities, if such agent or employee is acting in the usual course of his/her business or employment.

(b) An individual practitioner who is an agent or employee of another practitioner (other than a mid-level practitioner) registered to dispense controlled substances may, when acting in the normal course of business or employment, administer or dispense (other than by issuance of prescription) controlled substances if and to the extent that such individual practitioner is authorized or permitted to do so by the jurisdiction in which he or she practices, under the registration of the employer or principal practitioner in lieu of being registered him/herself.

(c) An individual practitioner who is an agent or employee of a hospital or other institution may, when acting in the normal course of business or employment, administer, dispense, or prescribe controlled substances under the registration of the hospital or other institution which is registered in lieu of

being registered him/herself, provided that:

(1) Such dispensing, administering or prescribing is done in the usual course of his/her professional practice;

(2) Such individual practitioner is authorized or permitted to do so by the jurisdiction in which he/she is practicing;

(3) The hospital or other institution by whom he/she is employed has verified that the individual practitioner is so permitted to dispense, administer, or prescribe drugs within the jurisdiction;

(4) Such individual practitioner is acting only within the scope of his/her employment in the hospital or institution;

(5) The hospital or other institution authorizes the individual practitioner to administer, dispense or prescribe under the hospital registration and designates a specific internal code number for each individual practitioner so authorized. The code number shall consist of numbers, letters, or a combination thereof and shall be a suffix to the institution's DEA registration number, preceded by a hyphen (e.g., APO123456–10 or APO123456–A12); and

(6) A current list of internal codes and the corresponding individual practitioners is kept by the hospital or other institution and is made available at all times to other registrants and law enforcement agencies upon request for the purpose of verifying the authority of the prescribing individual practitioner.

[62 FR 13950, Mar. 24, 1997]

§ 1301.23 Exemption of certain military and other personnel.

(a) The requirement of registration is waived for any official of the U.S Army, Navy, Marine Corps, Air Force Coast Guard, Public Health Service, or Bureau of Prisons who is authorized to prescribe, dispense, or administer, but not to procure or purchase, controlled substances in the course of his/her official duties. Such officials shall follow procedures set forth in part 1306 of this chapter regarding prescriptions, but shall state the branch of service or agency (e.g., "U.S. Army" or "Public

Health Service") and the service identification number of the issuing official in lieu of the registration number required on prescription forms. The service identification number for a Public Health Service employee is his/her Social Security identification number.

(b) The requirement of registration is waived for any official or agency of the U.S. Army, Navy, Marine Corps, Air Force, Coast Guard, or Public Health Service who or which is authorized to import or export controlled substances in the course of his/her official duties.

(c) If any official exempted by this section also engages as a private individual in any activity or group of activities for which registration is required, such official shall obtain a registration for such private activities.

[62 FR 13951, Mar. 24, 1997]

§ 1301.24 Exemption of law enforcement officials.

(a) The requirement of registration is waived for the following persons in the circumstances described in this section:

(1) Any officer or employee of the Administration, any officer of the U.S. Customs Service, any officer or employee of the United States Food and Drug Administration, and any other Federal officer who is lawfully engaged in the enforcement of any Federal law relating to controlled substances, drugs or customs, and is duly authorized to possess or to import or export controlled substances in the course of his/her official duties; and

(2) Any officer or employee of any State, or any political subdivision or agency thereof, who is engaged in the enforcement of any State or local law relating to controlled substances and is duly authorized to possess controlled substances in the course of his/her official duties.

(b) Any official exempted by this section may, when acting in the course of his/her official duties, procure any controlled substance in the course of an inspection, in accordance with § 1316.03(d) of this chapter, or in the course of any criminal investigation involving the person from whom the substance was procured, and may possess any controlled substance and distribute any such substance to any

other official who is also exempted by this section and acting in the course of his/her official duties.

(c) In order to enable law enforcement agency laboratories, including laboratories of the Administration, to obtain and transfer controlled substances for use as standards in chemical analysis, such laboratories shall obtain annually a registration to conduct chemical analysis. Such laboratories shall be exempted from payment of a fee for registration. Laboratory personnel, when acting in the scope of their official duties, are deemed to be officials exempted by this section and within the activity described in section 515(d) of the Act (21 U.S.C. 885(d)). For purposes of this paragraph, laboratory activities shall not include field or other preliminary chemical tests by officials exempted by this section.

(d) In addition to the activities authorized under a registration to conduct chemical analysis pursuant to § 1301.13(e)(1)(ix), laboratories of the Administration shall be authorized to manufacture or import controlled substances for any lawful purpose, to distribute or export such substances to any person, and to import and export such substances in emergencies without regard to the requirements of part 1312 of this chapter if a report concerning the importation or exportation is made to the Drug Operations Section of the Administration within 30 days of such importation or exportation.

[62 FR 13951, Mar. 24, 1997]

§ 1301.25 Registration regarding ocean vessels, aircraft, and other entities.

(a) If acquired by and dispensed under the general supervision of a medical officer described in paragraph (b) of this section, or the master or first officer of the vessel under the circumstances described in paragraph (d) of this section, controlled substances may be held for stocking, be maintained in, and dispensed from medicine chests, first aid packets, or dispensaries:

(1) On board any vessel engaged in international trade or in trade between ports of the United States and any merchant vessel belonging to the U.S. Government;

(2) On board any aircraft operated by an air carrier under a certificate of permit issued pursuant to the Federal Aviation Act of 1958 (49 U.S.C. 1301); and

(3) In any other entity of fixed or transient location approved by the Administrator as appropriate for application of this section (e.g., emergency kits at field sites of an industrial firm).

(b) A medical officer shall be:

(1) Licensed in a state as a physician;

(2) Employed by the owner or operator of the vessel, aircraft or other entity; and

(3) Registered under the Act at either of the following locations:

(i) The principal office of the owner or operator of the vessel, aircraft or other entity or

(ii) At any other location provided that the name, address, registration number and expiration date as they appear on his/her Certificate of Registration (DEA Form 223) for this location are maintained for inspection at said principal office in a readily retrievable manner.

(c) A registered medical officer may serve as medical officer for more than one vessel, aircraft, or other entity under a single registration, unless he/she serves as medical officer for more than one owner or operator, in which case he/she shall either maintain a separate registration at the location of the principal office of each such owner or operator or utilize one or more registrations pursuant to paragraph (b)(3)(ii) of this section.

(d) If no medical officer is employed by the owner or operator of a vessel, or in the event such medical officer is not accessible and the acquisition of controlled substances is required, the master or first officer of the vessel, who shall not be registered under the Act, may purchase controlled substances from a registered manufacturer or distributor, or from an authorized pharmacy as described in paragraph (f) of this section, by following the procedure outlined below:

(1) The master or first officer of the vessel must personally appear at the vendor's place of business, present proper identification (e.g., Seaman's photographic identification card) and a written requisition for the controlled substances.

(2) The written requisition must be on the vessel's official stationery or purchase order form and must include the name and address of the vendor, the name of the controlled substance, description of the controlled substance (dosage form, strength and number or volume per container) number of containers ordered, the name of the vessel, the vessel's official number and country of registry, the owner or operator of the vessel, the port at which the vessel is located, signature of the vessel's officer who is ordering the controlled substances and the date of the requisition.

(3) The vendor may, after verifying the identification of the vessel's officer requisitioning the controlled substances, deliver the control substances to that officer. The transaction shall be documented, in triplicate, on a record of sale in a format similar to that outlined in paragraph (d)(4) of this section. The vessel's requisition shall be attached to copy 1 of the record of sale and filed with the controlled substances records of the vendor, copy 2 of the record of sale shall be furnished to the officer of the vessel and retained aboard the vessel, copy 3 of the record of sale shall be forwarded to the nearest DEA Division Office within 15 days after the end of the month in which the sale is made.

(4) The vendor's record of sale should be similar to, and must include all the information contained in, the below listed format.

SALE OF CONTROLLED SUBSTANCES TO VESSELS

(Name of registrant)   _____

(Address of registrant)   _____

(DEA registration number)   _____

Line No.	Number of packages ordered	Size of packages	Name of product	Packages distributed	Date distributed
1	....	....	....	....	....
2	....	....	....	....	....
3	....	....	....	....	....

FOOTNOTE: Line numbers may be continued according to needs of the vendor.

Number of lines completed _____
Name of vessel _____
Vessel's official number _____
Vessel's country of registry _____
Owner or operator of the vessel _____
Name and title of vessel's officer who presented the requisition _____
Signature of vessel's officer who presented the requisition _____

(e) Any medical officer described in paragraph (b) of this section shall, in addition to complying with all requirements and duties prescribed for registrants generally, prepare an annual report as of the date on which his/her registration expires, which shall give in detail an accounting for each vessel, aircraft, or other entity, and a summary accounting for all vessels, aircraft, or other entities under his/her supervision for all controlled substances purchased, dispensed or disposed of during the year. The medical officer shall maintain this report with other records required to be kept under the Act and, upon request, deliver a copy of the report to the Administration. The medical officer need not be present when controlled substances are dispensed, if the person who actually dispensed the controlled substances is responsible to the medical officer to justify his/her actions.

(f) Any registered pharmacy that wishes to distribute controlled substances pursuant to this section shall be authorized to do so, provided:

(1) The registered pharmacy notifies the nearest Division Office of the Administration of its intention to so distribute controlled substances prior to the initiation of such activity. This notification shall be by registered mail and shall contain the name, address, and registration number of the pharmacy as well as the date upon which such activity will commence; and

(2) Such activity is authorized by state law; and

(3) The total number of dosage units of all controlled substances distributed by the pharmacy during any calendar year in which the pharmacy is registered to dispense does not exceed the limitations imposed upon such distribution by §1307.11(a)(4) and (b) of this chapter.

(g) Owners or operators of vessels, aircraft, or other entities described in this section shall not be deemed to possess or dispense any controlled substance acquired, stored and dispensed in accordance with this section. Additionally, owners or operators of vessels, aircraft, or other entities described in this section or in Article 32 of the Single Convention on Narcotic Drugs, 1961, or in Article 14 of the Convention on Psychotropic Substances, 1971, shall not be deemed to import or export any controlled substances purchased and stored in accordance with that section or applicable article.

(h) The Master of a vessel shall prepare a report for each calendar year which shall give in detail an accounting for all controlled substances purchased, dispensed, or disposed of during the year. The Master shall file this report with the medical officer employed by the owner or operator of his/her vessel, if any, or, if not, he/she shall maintain this report with other records required to be kept under the Act and, upon request, deliver a copy of the report to the Administration.

(i) Controlled substances acquired and possessed in accordance with this section shall not be distributed to persons not under the general supervision of the medical officer employed by the owner or operator of the vessel, aircraft, or other entity, except in accordance with §1307.21 of this chapter.

[62 FR 13951, Mar. 24, 1997]

§1301.26 Exemptions from import or export requirements for personal medical use.

Any individual who has in his/her possession a controlled substance listed in schedules II, III, IV, or V, which he/she has lawfully obtained for his/her personal medical use, or for administration to an animal accompanying him/her, may enter or depart the United States with such substance notwithstanding sections 1002–1005 of the Act (21 U.S.C. 952–955), provided the following conditions are met:

(a) The controlled substance is in the original container in which it was dispensed to the individual; and

(b) The individual makes a declaration to an appropriate official of the Bureau of Customs and Border Protection stating:

(1) That the controlled substance is possessed for his/her personal use, or

for an animal accompanying him/her; and

(2) The trade or chemical name and the symbol designating the schedule of the controlled substance if it appears on the container label, or, if such name does not appear on the label, the name and address of the pharmacy or practitioner who dispensed the substance and the prescription number.

(c) In addition to (and not in lieu of) the foregoing requirements of this section, a United States resident may import into the United States no more than 50 dosage units combined of all such controlled substances in the individual's possession that were obtained abroad for personal medical use. (For purposes of this section, a United States resident is a person whose residence (*i.e.*, place of general abode—meaning one's principal, actual dwelling place in fact, without regard to intent) is in the United States.) This 50 dosage unit limitation does not apply to controlled substances lawfully obtained in the United States pursuant to a prescription issued by a DEA registrant.

[69 FR 55347, Sept. 14, 2004]

§ 1301.27 Separate registration by retail pharmacies for installation and operation of automated dispensing systems at long term care facilities.

(a) A retail pharmacy may install and operate automated dispensing systems, as defined in § 1300.01 of this chapter, at long term care facilities, under the requirements of § 1301.17. No person other than a registered retail pharmacy may install and operate an automated dispensing system at a long term care facility.

(b) Retail pharmacies installing and operating automated dispensing systems at long term care facilities must maintain a separate registration at the location of each long term care facility at which automated dispensing systems are located. If more than one registered retail pharmacy operates automated dispensing systems at the same long term care facility, each retail pharmacy must maintain a registration at the long term care facility.

(c) A registered retail pharmacy applying for a separate registration to operate an automated dispensing system tem for the dispensing of controlled substances at a long term care facility is exempt from application fees for any such additional registrations.

[70 FR 25465, May 13, 2005]

§ 1301.28 Exemption from separate registration for practitioners dispensing or prescribing Schedule III, IV, or V narcotic controlled drugs approved by the Food and Drug Administration specifically for use in maintenance or detoxification treatment.

(a) An individual practitioner may dispense or prescribe Schedule III, IV, or V narcotic controlled drugs or combinations of narcotic controlled drugs which have been approved by the Food and Drug Administration (FDA) specifically for use in maintenance or detoxification treatment without obtaining the separate registration required by § 1301.13(e) if all of the following conditions are met:

(1) The individual practitioner meets the conditions specified in paragraph (b) of this section.

(2) The narcotic drugs or combination of narcotic drugs meet the conditions specified in paragraph (c) of this section.

(3) The individual practitioner is in compliance with either paragraph (d) or paragraph (e) of this section.

(b)(1) The individual practitioner must submit notification to the Secretary of Health and Human Services stating the individual practitioner's intent to dispense or prescribe narcotic drugs under paragraph (a) of this section. The notice must contain all of the following certifications:

(i) The individual practitioner is registered under § 1301.13 as an individual practitioner and is a "qualifying physician" as defined in section 303(g)(2)(G) of the Act (21 U.S.C. 823(g)(2)(G)).

(ii) The individual practitioner has the capacity to refer the patients to whom the individual practitioner will provide narcotic drugs or combinations of narcotic drugs for appropriate counseling and other appropriate ancillary services.

(iii) Where the individual practitioner is not a member of a group practice, the total number of such patients of the individual practitioner will not exceed 30 at any one time, unless regulations promulgated by the Secretary of Health and Human Services are modified.

(iv) Where the individual practitioner is a member of a group practice, the total number of such patients of the group practice will not exceed 30 at any one time, unless regulations promulgated by the Secretary of Health and Human Services are modified.

(2) If an individual practitioner wishes to prescribe or dispense narcotic drugs pursuant to paragraph (e) of this section, the individual practitioner must provide the Secretary of Health and Human Services the following:

(i) Notification as required under paragraph (b)(1) of this section in writing, stating the individual practitioner's name and DEA registration number issued under §1301.13.

(ii) If the individual practitioner is a member of a group practice, the names of the other individual practitioners in the group and the DEA registration numbers issued to the other individual practitioners under §1301.13.

(c) The narcotic drugs or combination of narcotic drugs to be dispensed or prescribed under this section must meet all of the following conditions:

(1) The drugs or combination of drugs have been approved for use in "maintenance treatment" or "detoxification treatment" under the Federal Food, Drug, and Cosmetic Act or section 351 of the Public Health Service Act.

(2) The drugs or combination of drugs have not been the subject of an adverse determination by the Secretary of Health and Human Services, after consultation with the Attorney General, that the use of the drugs or combination of drugs requires additional standards respecting the qualifications of practitioners or the quantities of the drugs that may be provided for unsupervised use.

(d)(1) After receiving the notification submitted under paragraph (b) of this section, the Secretary of Health and Human Services will forward a copy of the notification to the Administrator. The Secretary of Health and Human Services will have 45 days from the date of receipt of the notification to make a determination of whether the individual practitioner involved meets all requirements for a waiver under section 303(g)(2)(B) of the Act (21 U.S.C. 823(g)(2)(B)). Health and Human Services will notify DEA of its determination regarding the individual practitioner. If the individual practitioner has the appropriate registration under §1301.13, then the Administrator will issue the practitioner an identification number as soon as one of the following conditions occurs:

(i) The Administrator receives a positive determination from the Secretary of Health and Human Services before the conclusion of the 45-day review period, or

(ii) The 45-day review period has concluded and no determination by the Secretary of Health and Human Services has been made.

(2) If the Secretary denies certification to an individual practitioner or withdraws such certification once it is issued, then DEA will not issue the individual practitioner an identification number, or will withdraw the identification number if one has been issued.

(3) The individual practitioner must include the identification number on all records when dispensing and on all prescriptions when prescribing narcotic drugs under this section.

(e) An individual practitioner may begin to prescribe or dispense narcotic drugs to a specific individual patient under this section before receiving an identification number from the Administrator if the following conditions are met:

(1) The individual practitioner has submitted a written notification under paragraph (b) of this section in good faith to the Secretary of Health and Human Services.

(2) The individual practitioner reasonably believes that the conditions specified in paragraphs (b) and (c) of this section have been met.

(3) The individual practitioner reasonably believes that the treatment of an individual patient would be facilitated if narcotic drugs are prescribed or dispensed under this section before the sooner of:

(i) Receipt of an identification number from the Administrator, or

(ii) Expiration of the 45-day period.

(4) The individual practitioner has notified both the Secretary of Health

and Human Services and the Administrator of his or her intent to begin prescribing or dispensing the narcotic drugs before expiration of the 45-day period.

(5) The Secretary has not notified the registrant that he/she is not qualified under paragraph (d) of this section.

(6) The individual practitioner has the appropriate registration under § 1301.13.

(f) If an individual practitioner dispenses or prescribes Schedule III, IV, or V narcotic drugs approved by the Food and Drug Administration specifically for maintenance or detoxification treatment in violation of any of the conditions specified in paragraphs (b), (c) or (e) of this section, the Administrator may revoke the individual practitioner's registration in accordance with § 1301.36.

[70 FR 36342, June 23, 2005]

ACTION ON APPLICATION FOR REGISTRATION: REVOCATION OR SUSPENSION OF REGISTRATION

§ 1301.31 Administrative review generally.

The Administrator may inspect, or cause to be inspected, the establishment of an applicant or registrant, pursuant to subpart A of part 1316 of this chapter. The Administrator shall review the application for registration and other information gathered by the Administrator regarding an applicant in order to determine whether the applicable standards of section 303 (21 U.S.C. 823) or section 1008 (21 U.S.C. 958) of the Act have been met by the applicant.

[62 FR 13953, Mar. 24, 1997]

§ 1301.32 Action on applications for research in Schedule I substances.

(a) In the case of an application for registration to conduct research with controlled substances listed in Schedule I, the Administrator shall process the application and protocol and forward a copy of each to the Secretary of Health and Human Services (Secretary) within 7 days after receipt. The Secretary shall determine the qualifications and competency of the applicant, as well as the merits of the protocol (and shall notify the Administrator of his/her determination) within 21 days after receipt of the application and complete protocol, except that in the case of a clinical investigation, the Secretary shall have 30 days to make such determination and notify the Administrator. The Secretary, in determining the merits of the protocol, shall consult with the Administrator as to effective procedures to safeguard adequately against diversion of such controlled substances from legitimate medical or scientific use.

(b) An applicant whose protocol is defective shall be notified by the Secretary within 21 days after receipt of such protocol from the Administrator (or in the case of a clinical investigation within 30 days), and he/she shall be requested to correct the existing defects before consideration shall be given to his/her submission.

(c) If the Secretary determines the applicant qualified and competent and the research protocol meritorious, he/she shall notify the Administrator in writing of such determination. The Administrator shall issue a certificate of registration within 10 days after receipt of this notice, unless he/she determines that the certificate of registration should be denied on a ground specified in section 304(a) of the Act (21 U.S.C. 824(a)). In the case of a supplemental protocol, a replacement certificate of registration shall be issued by the Administrator.

(d) If the Secretary determines that the protocol is not meritorious and/or the applicant is not qualified or competent, he/she shall notify the Administrator in writing setting forth the reasons for such determination. If the Administrator determines that grounds exist for the denial of the application, he/she shall within 10 days issue an order to show cause pursuant to § 1301.37 and, if requested by the applicant, hold a hearing on the application pursuant to § 1301.41. If the grounds for denial of the application include a determination by the Secretary, the Secretary or his duly authorized agent shall furnish testimony and documents pertaining to his determination at such hearing.

(e) Supplemental protocols will be processed in the same manner as original research protocols. If the processing of an application or research protocol is delayed beyond the time limits imposed by this section, the applicant shall be so notified in writing.

[62 FR 13953, Mar. 24, 1997]

§ 1301.33 Application for bulk manufacture of Schedule I and II substances.

(a) In the case of an application for registration or reregistration to manufacture in bulk a basic class of controlled substance listed in Schedule I or II, the Administrator shall, upon the filing of such application, publish in the FEDERAL REGISTER a notice naming the applicant and stating that such applicant has applied to be registered as a bulk manufacturer of a basic class of narcotic or nonnarcotic controlled substance, which class shall be identified. A copy of said notice shall be mailed simultaneously to each person registered as a bulk manufacturer of that basic class and to any other applicant therefor. Any such person may, within 60 days from the date of publication of the notice in the FEDERAL REGISTER, file with the Administrator written comments on or objections to the issuance of the proposed registration.

(b) In order to provide adequate competition, the Administrator shall not be required to limit the number of manufacturers in any basic class to a number less than that consistent with maintenance of effective controls against diversion solely because a smaller number is capable of producing an adequate and uninterrupted supply.

(c) This section shall not apply to the manufacture of basic classes of controlled substances listed in Schedules I or II as an incident to research or chemical analysis as authorized in § 1301.13(e)(1).

[62 FR 13953, Mar. 24, 1997]

§ 1301.34 Application for importation of Schedule I and II substances.

(a) In the case of an application for registration or reregistration to import a controlled substance listed in Schedule I or II, under the authority of section 1002(a)(2)(B) of the Act (21 U.S.C. 952(a)(2)(B)), the Administrator shall, upon the filing of such application, publish in the FEDERAL REGISTER a notice naming the applicant and stating that such applicant has applied to be registered as an importer of a Schedule I or II controlled substance, which substance shall be identified. A copy of said notice shall be mailed simultaneously to each person registered as a bulk manufacturer of that controlled substance and to any other applicant therefor. Any such person may, within 30 days from the date of publication of the notice in the FEDERAL REGISTER, file written comments on or objections to the issuance of the proposed registration, and may, at the same time, file a written request for a hearing on the application pursuant to § 1301.43. If a hearing is requested, the Administrator shall hold a hearing on the application in accordance with § 1301.41. Notice of the hearing shall be published in the FEDERAL REGISTER, and shall be mailed simultaneously to the applicant and to all persons to whom notice of the application was mailed. Any such person may participate in the hearing by filing a notice of appearance in accordance with § 1301.43 of this chapter. Notice of the hearing shall contain a summary of all comments and objections filed regarding the application and shall state the time and place for the hearing, which shall not be less than 30 days after the date of publication of such notice in the FEDERAL REGISTER. A hearing pursuant to this section may be consolidated with a hearing held pursuant to § 1301.35 or § 1301.36 of this part.

(b) The Administrator shall register an applicant to import a controlled substance listed in Schedule I or II if he/she determines that such registration is consistent with the public interest and with U.S. obligations under international treaties, conventions, or protocols in effect on May 1, 1971. In determining the public interest, the following factors shall be considered:

(1) Maintenance of effective controls against diversion of particular controlled substances and any controlled substance in Schedule I or II compounded therefrom into other than legitimate medical, scientific research, or industrial channels, by limiting the

importation and bulk manufacture of such controlled substances to a number of establishments which can produce an adequate and uninterrupted supply of these substances under adequately competitive conditions for legitimate medical, scientific, research, and industrial purposes;

(2) Compliance with applicable State and local law;

(3) Promotion of technical advances in the art of manufacturing these substances and the development of new substances;

(4) Prior conviction record of applicant under Federal and State laws relating to the manufacture, distribution, or dispensing of such substances;

(5) Past experience in the manufacture of controlled substances, and the existence in the establishment of effective control against diversion;

(6) That the applicant will be permitted to import only:

(i) Such amounts of crude opium, poppy straw, concentrate of poppy straw, and coca leaves as the Administrator finds to be necessary to provide for medical, scientific, or other legitimate purposes; or

(ii) Such amounts of any controlled substances listed in Schedule I or II as the Administrator shall find to be necessary to provide for the medical, scientific, or other legitimate needs of the United States during an emergency in which domestic supplies of such substances are found by the Administrator to be inadequate; or

(iii) Such amounts of any controlled substance listed in Schedule I or II as the Administrator shall find to be necessary to provide for the medical, scientific, or other legitimate needs of the United States in any case in which the Administrator finds that competition among domestic manufacturers of the controlled substance is inadequate and will not be rendered adequate by the registration of additional manufacturers under section 303 of the Act (21 U.S.C. 823); or

(iv) Such limited quantities of any controlled substance listed in Schedule I or II as the Administrator shall find to be necessary for scientific, analytical or research uses; and

(7) Such other factors as may be relevant to and consistent with the public health and safety.

(c) In determining whether the applicant can and will maintain effective controls against diversion within the meaning of paragraph (b) of this section, the Administrator shall consider among other factors:

(1) Compliance with the security requirements set forth in §§ 1301.71–1301.76; and

(2) Employment of security procedures to guard against in-transit losses within and without the jurisdiction of the United States.

(d) In determining whether competition among the domestic manufacturers of a controlled substance is adequate within the meaning of paragraphs (b)(1) and (b)(6)(iii) of this section, as well as section 1002(a)(2)(B) of the Act (21 U.S.C. 952(a)(2)(B)), the Administrator shall consider:

(1) The extent of price rigidity in the light of changes in:

(i) raw materials and other costs and

(ii) conditions of supply and demand;

(2) The extent of service and quality competition among the domestic manufacturers for shares of the domestic market including:

(i) Shifts in market shares and

(ii) Shifts in individual customers among domestic manufacturers;

(3) The existence of substantial differentials between domestic prices and the higher of prices generally prevailing in foreign markets or the prices at which the applicant for registration to import is committed to undertake to provide such products in the domestic market in conformity with the Act. In determining the existence of substantial differentials hereunder, appropriate consideration should be given to any additional costs imposed on domestic manufacturers by the requirements of the Act and such other cost-related and other factors as the Administrator may deem relevant. In no event shall an importer's offering prices in the United States be considered if they are lower than those prevailing in the foreign market or markets from which the importer is obtaining his/her supply;

(4) The existence of competitive restraints imposed upon domestic manufacturers by governmental regulations; and

(5) Such other factors as may be relevant to the determinations required under this paragraph.

(e) In considering the scope of the domestic market, consideration shall be given to substitute products which are reasonably interchangeable in terms of price, quality and use.

(f) The fact that the number of existing manufacturers is small shall not demonstrate, in and of itself, that adequate competition among them does not exist.

[62 FR 13953, Mar. 24, 1997]

§ 1301.35 Certificate of registration; denial of registration.

(a) The Administrator shall issue a Certificate of Registration (DEA Form 223) to an applicant if the issuance of registration or reregistration is required under the applicable provisions of sections 303 or 1008 of the Act (21 U.S.C. 823 and 958). In the event that the issuance of registration or reregistration is not required, the Administrator shall deny the application. Before denying any application, the Administrator shall issue an order to show cause pursuant to § 1301.37 and, if requested by the applicant, shall hold a hearing on the application pursuant to § 1301.41.

(b) If in response to a show cause order a hearing is requested by an applicant for registration or reregistration to manufacture in bulk a basic class of controlled substance listed in Schedule I or II, notice that a hearing has been requested shall be published in the FEDERAL REGISTER and shall be mailed simultaneously to the applicant and to all persons to whom notice of the application was mailed. Any person entitled to file comments or objections to the issuance of the proposed registration pursuant to § 1301.33(a) may participate in the hearing by filing notice of appearance in accordance with § 1301.43. Such persons shall have 30 days to file a notice of appearance after the date of publication of the notice of a request for a hearing in the FEDERAL REGISTER.

(c) The Certificate of Registration (DEA Form 223) shall contain the name, address, and registration number of the registrant, the activity authorized by the registration, the schedules and/or Administration Controlled Substances Code Number (as set forth in part 1308 of this chapter) of the controlled substances which the registrant is authorized to handle, the amount of fee paid (or exemption), and the expiration date of the registration. The registrant shall maintain the certificate of registration at the registered location in a readily retrievable manner and shall permit inspection of the certificate by any official, agent or employee of the Administration or of any Federal, State, or local agency engaged in enforcement of laws relating to controlled substances.

[62 FR 13954, Mar. 24, 1997]

§ 1301.36 Suspension or revocation of registration; suspension of registration pending final order; extension of registration pending final order.

(a) For any registration issued under section 303 of the Act (21 U.S.C. 823), the Administrator may:

(1) Suspend the registration pursuant to section 304(a) of the Act (21 U.S.C. 824(a)) for any period of time.

(2) Revoke the registration pursuant to section 304(a) of the Act (21 U.S.C. 824(a)).

(b) For any registration issued under section 1008 of the Act (21 U.S.C. 958), the Administrator may:

(1) Suspend the registration pursuant to section 1008(d) of the Act (21 U.S.C. 958(d)) for any period of time.

(2) Revoke the registration pursuant to section 1008(d) of the Act (21 U.S.C. 958(d)) if he/she determines that such registration is inconsistent with the public interest as defined in section 1008 or with the United States obligations under international treaties, conventions, or protocols in effect on October 12, 1984.

(c) The Administrator may limit the revocation or suspension of a registration to the particular controlled substance, or substances, with respect to which grounds for revocation or suspension exist.

(d) Before revoking or suspending any registration, the Administrator shall issue an order to show cause pursuant to § 1301.37 and, if requested by the registrant, shall hold a hearing pursuant to § 1301.41.

(e) The Administrator may suspend any registration simultaneously with or at any time subsequent to the service upon the registrant of an order to show cause why such registration should not be revoked or suspended, in any case where he/she finds that there is an imminent danger to the public health or safety. If the Administrator so suspends, he/she shall serve with the order to show cause pursuant to § 1301.37 an order of immediate suspension which shall contain a statement of his findings regarding the danger to public health or safety.

(f) Upon service of the order of the Administrator suspending or revoking registration, the registrant shall immediately deliver his/her Certificate of Registration, any order forms, and any import or export permits in his/her possession to the nearest office of the Administration. The suspension or revocation of a registration shall suspend or revoke any individual manufacturing or procurement quota fixed for the registrant pursuant to part 1303 of this chapter and any import or export permits issued to the registrant pursuant to part 1312 of this chapter. Also, upon service of the order of the Administrator revoking or suspending registration, the registrant shall, as instructed by the Administrator:

(1) Deliver all controlled substances in his/her possession to the nearest office of the Administration or to authorized agents of the Administration; or

(2) Place all controlled substances in his/her possession under seal as described in sections 304(f) or 1008(d)(6) of the Act (21 U.S.C. 824(f) or 958(d)(6)).

(g) In the event that revocation or suspension is limited to a particular controlled substance or substances, the registrant shall be given a new Certificate of Registration for all substances not affected by such revocation or suspension; no fee shall be required to be paid for the new Certificate of Registration. The registrant shall deliver the old Certificate of Registration and, if appropriate, any order forms in his/her possession to the nearest office of

the Administration. The suspension or revocation of a registration, when limited to a particular basic class or classes of controlled substances, shall suspend or revoke any individual manufacturing or procurement quota fixed for the registrant for such class or classes pursuant to part 1303 of this chapter and any import or export permits issued to the registrant for such class or classes pursuant to part 1312 of this chapter. Also, upon service of the order of the Administrator revoking or suspending registration, the registrant shall, as instructed by the Administrator:

(1) Deliver to the nearest office of the Administration or to authorized agents of the Administration all of the particular controlled substance or substances affected by the revocation or suspension which are in his/her possession; or

(2) Place all of such substances under seal as described in sections 304(f) or 958(d)(6) of the Act (21 U.S.C. 824(f) or 958(d)(6)).

(h) Any suspension shall continue in effect until the conclusion of all proceedings upon the revocation or suspension, including any judicial review thereof, unless sooner withdrawn by the Administrator or dissolved by a court of competent jurisdiction. Any registrant whose registration is suspended under paragraph (e) of this section may request a hearing on the revocation or suspension of his/her registration at a time earlier than specified in the order to show cause pursuant to § 1301.37. This request shall be granted by the Administrator, who shall fix a date for such hearing as early as reasonably possible.

(i) In the event that an applicant for reregistration (who is doing business under a registration previously granted and not revoked or suspended) has applied for reregistration at least 45 days before the date on which the existing registration is due to expire, and the Administrator has issued no order on the application on the date on which the existing registration is due to expire, the existing registration of the applicant shall automatically be extended and continue in effect until the date on which the Administrator so issues his/her order. The Administrator may extend any other existing registration under the circumstances contemplated in this section even though the registrant failed to apply for reregistration at least 45 days before expiration of the existing registration, with or without request by the registrant, if the Administrator finds that such extension is not inconsistent with the public health and safety.

[62 FR 13955, Mar. 24, 1997]

§1301.37 Order to show cause.

(a) If, upon examination of the application for registration from any applicant and other information gathered by the Administration regarding the applicant, the Administrator is unable to make the determinations required by the applicable provisions of section 303 and/or section 1008 of the Act (21 U.S.C. 823 and 958) to register the applicant, the Administrator shall serve upon the applicant an order to show cause why the registration should not be denied.

(b) If, upon information gathered by the Administration regarding any registrant, the Administrator determines that the registration of such registrant is subject to suspension or revocation pursuant to section 304 or section 1008 of the Act (21 U.S.C. 824 and 958), the Administrator shall serve upon the registrant an order to show cause why the registration should not be revoked or suspended.

(c) The order to show cause shall call upon the applicant or registrant to appear before the Administrator at a time and place stated in the order, which shall not be less than 30 days after the date of receipt of the order. The order to show cause shall also contain a statement of the legal basis for such hearing and for the denial, revocation, or suspension of registration and a summary of the matters of fact and law asserted.

(d) Upon receipt of an order to show cause, the applicant or registrant must, if he/she desires a hearing, file a request for a hearing pursuant to §1301.43. If a hearing is requested, the Administrator shall hold a hearing at the time and place stated in the order, pursuant to §1301.41.

(e) When authorized by the Administrator, any agent of the Administra-

tion may serve the order to show cause.

[62 FR 13955, Mar. 24, 1997]

HEARINGS

§1301.41 Hearings generally.

(a) In any case where the Administrator shall hold a hearing on any registration or application therefor, the procedures for such hearing shall be governed generally by the adjudication procedures set forth in the Administrative Procedure Act (5 U.S.C. 551–559) and specifically by sections 303, 304, and 1008 of the Act (21 U.S.C. 823–824 and 958), by §§1301.42–1301.46 of this part, and by the procedures for administrative hearings under the Act set forth in §§1316.41–1316.67 of this chapter.

(b) Any hearing under this part shall be independent of, and not in lieu of, criminal prosecutions or other proceedings under the Act or any other law of the United States.

[62 FR 13956, Mar. 24, 1997]

§1301.42 Purpose of hearing.

If requested by a person entitled to a hearing, the Administrator shall hold a hearing for the purpose of receiving factual evidence regarding the issues involved in the denial, revocation, or suspension of any registration, and the granting of any application for registration to import or to manufacture in bulk a basic class of controlled substance listed in Schedule I or II. Extensive argument should not be offered into evidence but rather presented in opening or closing statements of counsel or in memoranda or proposed findings of fact and conclusions of law.

[62 FR 13956, Mar. 24, 1997]

§1301.43 Request for hearing or appearance; waiver.

(a) Any person entitled to a hearing pursuant to §1301.32 or §§1301.34–1301.36 and desiring a hearing shall, within 30 days after the date of receipt of the order to show cause (or the date of publication of notice of the application for registration in the FEDERAL REGISTER in the case of §1301.34), file with the Administrator a written request for a hearing in the form prescribed in § 1316.47 of this chapter.

(b) Any person entitled to participate in a hearing pursuant to § 1301.34 or § 1301.35(b) and desiring to do so shall, within 30 days of the date of publication of notice of the request for a hearing in the FEDERAL REGISTER, file with the Administrator a written notice of intent to participate in such hearing in the form prescribed in § 1316.48 of this chapter. Any person filing a request for a hearing need not also file a notice of appearance.

(c) Any person entitled to a hearing or to participate in a hearing pursuant to § 1301.32 or §§ 1301.34–1301.36 may, within the period permitted for filing a request for a hearing or a notice of appearance, file with the Administrator a waiver of an opportunity for a hearing or to participate in a hearing, together with a written statement regarding such person's position on the matters of fact and law involved in such hearing. Such statement, if admissible, shall be made a part of the record and shall be considered in light of the lack of opportunity for cross-examination in determining the weight to be attached to matters of fact asserted therein.

(d) If any person entitled to a hearing or to participate in a hearing pursuant to § 1301.32 or §§ 1301.34–1301.36 fails to file a request for a hearing or a notice of appearance, or if such person so files and fails to appear at the hearing, such person shall be deemed to have waived the opportunity for a hearing or to participate in the hearing, unless such person shows good cause for such failure.

(e) If all persons entitled to a hearing or to participate in a hearing waive or are deemed to waive their opportunity for the hearing or to participate in the hearing, the Administrator may cancel the hearing, if scheduled, and issue his/her final order pursuant to § 1301.46 without a hearing.

[62 FR 13956, Mar. 24, 1997]

§ 1301.44 Burden of proof.

(a) At any hearing on an application to manufacture any controlled substance listed in Schedule I or II, the applicant shall have the burden of proving that the requirements for such registration pursuant to section 303(a) of the Act (21 U.S.C. 823(a)) are satisfied. Any other person participating in the hearing pursuant to § 1301.35(b) shall have the burden of proving any propositions of fact or law asserted by such person in the hearing.

(b) At any hearing on the granting or denial of an applicant to be registered to conduct a narcotic treatment program or as a compounder, the applicant shall have the burden of proving that the requirements for each registration pursuant to section 303(g) of the Act (21 U.S.C. 823(g)) are satisfied.

(c) At any hearing on the granting or denial of an application to be registered to import or export any controlled substance listed in Schedule I or II, the applicant shall have the burden of proving that the requirements for such registration pursuant to sections 1008(a) and (d) of the Act (21 U.S.C. 958 (a) and (d)) are satisfied. Any other person participating in the hearing pursuant to § 1301.34 shall have the burden of proving any propositions of fact or law asserted by him/her in the hearings.

(d) At any other hearing for the denial of a registration, the Administration shall have the burden of proving that the requirements for such registration pursuant to section 303 or section 1008(c) and (d) of the Act (21 U.S.C. 823 or 958(c) and (d)) are not satisfied.

(e) At any hearing for the revocation or suspension of a registration, the Administration shall have the burden of proving that the requirements for such revocation or suspension pursuant to section 304(a) or section 1008(d) of the Act (21 U.S.C. 824(a) or 958(d)) are satisfied.

[62 FR 13956, Mar. 24, 1997]

§ 1301.45 Time and place of hearing.

The hearing will commence at the place and time designated in the order to show cause or notice of hearing published in the FEDERAL REGISTER (unless expedited pursuant to § 1301.36(h)) but thereafter it may be moved to a different place and may be continued from day to day or recessed to a later day without notice other than announcement thereof by the presiding officer at the hearing.

[62 FR 13956, Mar. 24, 1997]

§ 1301.46 Final order.

As soon as practicable after the presiding officer has certified the record to the Administrator, the Administrator shall issue his/her order on the granting, denial, revocation, or suspension of registration. In the event that an application for registration to import or to manufacture in bulk a basic class of any controlled substance listed in Schedule I or II is granted, or any application for registration is denied, or any registration is revoked or suspended, the order shall include the findings of fact and conclusions of law upon which the order is based. The order shall specify the date on which it shall take effect. The Administrator shall serve one copy of his/her order upon each party in the hearing.

[62 FR 13956, Mar. 24, 1997]

MODIFICATION, TRANSFER AND
TERMINATION OF REGISTRATION

§ 1301.51 Modification in registration.

Any registrant may apply to modify his/her registration to authorize the handling of additional controlled substances or to change his/her name or address, by submitting a letter of request to the Registration Unit, Drug Enforcement Administration, Department of Justice, Post Office Box 28083, Central Station, Washington, DC 20005. The letter shall contain the registrant's name, address, and registration number as printed on the certificate of registration, and the substances and/or schedules to be added to his/her registration or the new name or address and shall be signed in accordance with § 1301.13(j). If the registrant is seeking to handle additional controlled substances listed in Schedule I for the purpose of research or instructional activities, he/she shall attach three copies of a research protocol describing each research project involving the additional substances, or two copies of a statement describing the nature, extent, and duration of such instructional activities, as appropriate. No fee shall be required to be paid for the modification. The request for modification shall be handled in the same manner as an application for registration. If the modification in registration is approved, the Administrator shall issue a new certificate of registration (DEA Form 223) to the registrant, who shall maintain it with the old certificate of registration until expiration.

[62 FR 13956, Mar. 24, 1997]

§ 1301.52 Termination of registration; transfer of registration; distribution upon discontinuance of business.

(a) Except as provided in paragraph (b) of this section, the registration of any person shall terminate if and when such person dies, ceases legal existence, or discontinues business or professional practice. Any registrant who ceases legal existence or discontinues business or professional practice shall notify the Administrator promptly of such fact.

(b) No registration or any authority conferred thereby shall be assigned or otherwise transferred except upon such conditions as the Administration may specifically designate and then only pursuant to written consent. Any person seeking authority to transfer a registration shall submit a written request, providing full details regarding the proposed transfer of registration, to the Deputy Assistant Administrator, Office of Diversion Control, Drug Enforcement Administration, Department of Justice, Washington, DC 20537.

(c) Any registrant desiring to discontinue business activities altogether or with respect to controlled substances (without transferring such business activities to another person) shall return for cancellation his/her certificate of registration, and any unexecuted order forms in his/her possession, to the Registration Unit, Drug Enforcement Administration, Department of Justice, Post Office Box 28083, Central Station, Washington, DC 20005. Any controlled substances in his/her possession may be disposed of in accordance with § 1307.21 of this chapter.

(d) Any registrant desiring to discontinue business activities altogether or with respect to controlled substance (by transferring such business activities to another person) shall submit in person or by registered or certified mail, return receipt requested, to the Special Agent in Charge in his/her area, at least 14 days in advance of the date of the proposed transfer (unless the Special Agent in Charge waives this time limitation in individual instances), the following information:

(1) The name, address, registration number, and authorized business activity of the registrant discontinuing the business (registrant-transferor);

(2) The name, address, registration number, and authorized business activity of the person acquiring the business (registrant-transferee);

(3) Whether the business activities will be continued at the location registered by the person discontinuing business, or moved to another location (if the latter, the address of the new location should be listed);

(4) Whether the registrant-transferor has a quota to manufacture or procure any controlled substance listed in Schedule I or II (if so, the basic class or class of the substance should be indicated); and

(5) The date on which the transfer of controlled substances will occur.

(e) Unless the registrant-transferor is informed by the Special Agent in Charge, before the date on which the transfer was stated to occur, that the transfer may not occur, the registrant-transferor may distribute (without being registered to distribute) controlled substances in his/her possession to the registrant-transferee in accordance with the following:

(1) On the date of transfer of the controlled substances, a complete inventory of all controlled substances being transferred shall be taken in accordance with § 1304.11 of this chapter. This inventory shall serve as the final inventory of the registrant-transferor and the initial inventory of the registrant-transferee, and a copy of the inventory shall be included in the records of each person. It shall not be necessary to file a copy of the inventory with the Administration unless requested by the Special Agent in Charge. Transfers of any substances listed in Schedule I or II shall require the use of order forms in accordance with part 1305 of this chapter.

(2) On the date of transfer of the controlled substances, all records required to be kept by the registrant-transferor with reference to the controlled substances being transferred, under part 1304 of this chapter, shall be transferred to the registrant-transferee. Responsibility for the accuracy of records prior to the date of transfer remains with the transferor, but responsibility for custody and maintenance shall be upon the transferee.

(3) In the case of registrants required to make reports pursuant to part 1304 of this chapter, a report marked "Final" will be prepared and submitted by the registrant-transferor showing the disposition of all the controlled substances for which a report is required; no additional report will be required from him, if no further transactions involving controlled substances are consummated by him. The initial report of the registrant-transferee shall account for transactions beginning with the day next succeeding the date of discontinuance or transfer of business by the transferor-registrant and the substances transferred to him shall be reported as receipts in his/her initial report.

[62 FR 13957, Mar. 24, 1997]

SECURITY REQUIREMENTS

§ 1301.71 Security requirements generally.

(a) All applicants and registrants shall provide effective controls and procedures to guard against theft and diversion of controlled substances. In order to determine whether a registrant has provided effective controls against diversion, the Administrator shall use the security requirements set forth in §§ 1301.72–1301.76 as standards for the physical security controls and operating procedures necessary to prevent diversion. Materials and construction which will provide a structural equivalent to the physical security controls set forth in §§ 1301.72, 1301.73 and 1301.75 may be used in lieu of the materials and construction described in those sections.

(b) Substantial compliance with the standards set forth in §§ 1301.72–1301.76 may be deemed sufficient by the Administrator after evaluation of the overall security system and needs of the applicant or registrant. In evaluating the overall security system of a registrant or applicant, the Administrator may consider any of the following factors as he may deem relevant to the need for strict compliance with security requirements:

(1) The type of activity conducted (e.g., processing of bulk chemicals, preparing dosage forms, packaging, labeling, cooperative buying, etc.);

(2) The type and form of controlled substances handled (e.g., bulk liquids or dosage units, usable powders or nonusable powders);

(3) The quantity of controlled substances handled;

(4) The location of the premises and the relationship such location bears on security needs;

(5) The type of building construction comprising the facility and the general characteristics of the building or buildings;

(6) The type of vault, safe, and secure enclosures or other storage system (e.g., automatic storage and retrieval system) used;

(7) The type of closures on vaults, safes, and secure enclosures;

(8) The adequacy of key control systems and/or combination lock control systems;

(9) The adequacy of electric detection and alarm systems, if any including use of supervised transmittal lines and standby power sources;

(10) The extent of unsupervised public access to the facility, including the presence and characteristics of perimeter fencing, if any;

(11) The adequacy of supervision over employees having access to manufacturing and storage areas;

(12) The procedures for handling business guests, visitors, maintenance personnel, and nonemployee service personnel;

(13) The availability of local police protection or of the registrant's or applicant's security personnel;

(14) The adequacy of the registrant's or applicant's system for monitoring the receipt, manufacture, distribution, and disposition of controlled substances in its operations; and

(15) The applicability of the security requirements contained in all Federal, State, and local laws and regulations governing the management of waste.

(c) When physical security controls become inadequate as a result of a controlled substance being transferred to a different schedule, or as a result of a noncontrolled substance being listed on any schedule, or as a result of a significant increase in the quantity of controlled substances in the possession of the registrant during normal business operations, the physical security controls shall be expanded and extended accordingly. A registrant may adjust physical security controls within the requirements set forth in §§ 1301.72–1301.76 when the need for such controls decreases as a result of a controlled substance being transferred to a different schedule, or a result of a controlled substance being removed from control, or as a result of a significant decrease in the quantity of controlled substances in the possession of the registrant during normal business operations.

(d) Any registrant or applicant desiring to determine whether a proposed security system substantially complies with, or is the structural equivalent of, the requirements set forth in §§ 1301.72–1301.76 may submit any plans, blueprints, sketches or other materials regarding the proposed security system either to the Special Agent in Charge in the region in which the system will be used, or to the Diversion Operations Section, Drug Enforcement Administration, Department of Justice, Washington, DC 20537.

(e) Physical security controls of locations registered under the Harrison Narcotic Act or the Narcotics Manufacturing Act of 1960 on April 30, 1971, shall be deemed to comply substantially with the standards set forth in §§ 1301.72, 1301.73 and 1301.75. Any new facilities or work or storage areas constructed or utilized for controlled substances, which facilities or work or storage areas have not been previously approved by the Administration, shall not necessarily be deemed to comply substantially with the standards set forth in §§ 1301.72, 1301.73 and 1301.75, notwithstanding that such facilities or work or storage areas have physical security controls similar to those previously approved by the Administration.

[36 FR 18729, Sept. 21, 1971. Redesignated at 38 FR 26609, Sept. 24, 1973, and amended at 46 FR 28841, May 29, 1981; 47 FR 41735, Sept. 22, 1982; 51 FR 5319, Feb. 13, 1986; 68 FR 41228, July 11, 2003]

§ 1301.72 Physical security controls for non-practitioners; narcotic treatment programs and compounders for narcotic treatment programs; storage areas.

(a) *Schedules I and II.* Raw material, bulk materials awaiting further processing, and finished products which are controlled substances listed in Schedule I or II (except GHB that is manufactured or distributed in accordance with an exemption under section 505(i) of the FFDCA which shall be subject to the requirements of paragraph (b) of this section) shall be stored in one of the following secured areas:

(1) Where small quantities permit, a safe or steel cabinet;

(i) Which safe or steel cabinet shall have the following specifications or the equivalent: 30 man-minutes against surreptitious entry, 10 man-minutes against forced entry, 20 man-hours against lock manipulation, and 20 man-hours against radiological techniques;

(ii) Which safe or steel cabinet, if it weighs less than 750 pounds, is bolted or cemented to the floor or wall in such a way that it cannot be readily removed; and

(iii) Which safe or steel cabinet, if necessary, depending upon the quantities and type of controlled substances stored, is equipped with an alarm system which, upon attempted unauthorized entry, shall transmit a signal directly to a central protection company or a local or State police agency which has a legal duty to respond, or a 24-hour control station operated by the registrant, or such other protection as the Administrator may approve.

(2) A vault constructed before, or under construction on, September 1, 1971, which is of substantial construction with a steel door, combination or key lock, and an alarm system; or

(3) A vault constructed after September 1, 1971:

(i) The walls, floors, and ceilings of which vault are constructed of at least 8 inches of reinforced concrete or other substantial masonry, reinforced vertically and horizontally with ½-inch steel rods tied 6 inches on center, or the structural equivalent to such reinforced walls, floors, and ceilings;

(ii) The door and frame unit of which vault shall conform to the following

specifications or the equivalent: 30 man-minutes against surreptitious entry, 10 man-minutes against forced entry, 20 man-hours against lock manipulation, and 20 man-hours against radiological techniques;

(iii) Which vault, if operations require it to remain open for frequent access, is equipped with a "day-gate" which is self-closing and self-locking, or the equivalent, for use during the hours of operation in which the vault door is open;

(iv) The walls or perimeter of which vault are equipped with an alarm, which upon unauthorized entry shall transmit a signal directly to a central station protection company, or a local or State police agency which has a legal duty to respond, or a 24-hour control station operated by the registrant, or such other protection as the Administrator may approve, and, if necessary, holdup buttons at strategic points of entry to the perimeter area of the vault;

(v) The door of which vault is equipped with contact switches; and

(vi) Which vault has one of the following: Complete electrical lacing of the walls, floor and ceilings; sensitive ultrasonic equipment within the vault; a sensitive sound accumulator system; or such other device designed to detect illegal entry as may be approved by the Administration.

(b) *Schedules III, IV and V.* Raw material, bulk materials awaiting further processing, and finished products which are controlled substances listed in Schedules III, IV, and V, and GHB when it is manufactured or distributed in accordance with an exemption under section 505(i) of the FFDCA, shall be stored in the following secure storage areas:

(1) A safe or steel cabinet as described in paragraph (a)(1) of this section;

(2) A vault as described in paragraph (a)(2) or (3) of this section equipped with an alarm system as described in paragraph (b)(4)(v) of this section;

(3) A building used for storage of Schedules III through V controlled substances with perimeter security which limits access during working hours and provides security after working hours and meets the following specifications:

(i) Has an electronic alarm system as described in paragraph (b)(4)(v) of this section,

(ii) Is equipped with self-closing, self-locking doors constructed of substantial material commensurate with the type of building construction, provided, however, a door which is kept closed and locked at all times when not in use and when in use is kept under direct observation of a responsible employee or agent of the registrant is permitted in lieu of a self-closing, self-locking door. Doors may be sliding or hinged. Regarding hinged doors, where hinges are mounted on the outside, such hinges shall be sealed, welded or otherwise constructed to inhibit removal. Locking devices for such doors shall be either of the multiple-position combination or key lock type and:

(*a*) In the case of key locks, shall require key control which limits access to a limited number of employees, or;

(*b*) In the case of combination locks, the combination shall be limited to a minimum number of employees and can be changed upon termination of employment of an employee having knowledge of the combination;

(4) A cage, located within a building on the premises, meeting the following specifications:

(i) Having walls constructed of not less than No. 10 gauge steel fabric mounted on steel posts, which posts are:

(*a*) At least one inch in diameter;

(*b*) Set in concrete or installed with lag bolts that are pinned or brazed; and

(*c*) Which are placed no more than ten feet apart with horizontal one and one-half inch reinforcements every sixty inches;

(ii) Having a mesh construction with openings of not more than two and one-half inches across the square,

(iii) Having a ceiling constructed of the same material, or in the alternative, a cage shall be erected which reaches and is securely attached to the structural ceiling of the building. A lighter gauge mesh may be used for the ceilings of large enclosed areas if walls are at least 14 feet in height,

(iv) Is equipped with a door constructed of No. 10 gauge steel fabric on a metal door frame in a metal door flange, and in all other respects conforms to all the requirements of 21 CFR 1301.72(b)(3)(ii), and

(v) Is equipped with an alarm system which upon unauthorized entry shall transmit a signal directly to a central station protection agency or a local or state police agency, each having a legal duty to respond, or to a 24-hour control station operated by the registrant, or to such other source of protection as the Administrator may approve;

(5) An enclosure of masonry or other material, approved in writing by the Administrator as providing security comparable to a cage;

(6) A building or enclosure within a building which has been inspected and approved by DEA or its predecessor agency, BND, and continues to provide adequate security against the diversion of Schedule III through V controlled substances, of which fact written acknowledgment has been made by the Special Agent in Charge of DEA for the area in which such building or enclosure is situated;

(7) Such other secure storage areas as may be approved by the Administrator after considering the factors listed in §1301.71(b);

(8)(i) Schedule III through V controlled substances may be stored with Schedules I and II controlled substances under security measures provided by 21 CFR 1301.72(a);

(ii) Non-controlled drugs, substances and other materials may be stored with Schedule III through V controlled substances in any of the secure storage areas required by 21 CFR 1301.72(b), provided that permission for such storage of non-controlled items is obtained in advance, in writing, from the Special Agent in Charge of DEA for the area in which such storage area is situated. Any such permission tendered must be upon the Special Agent in Charge's written determination that such non-segregated storage does not diminish security effectiveness for Schedules III through V controlled substances.

(c) *Multiple storage areas.* Where several types or classes of controlled substances are handled separately by the registrant or applicant for different purposes (e.g., returned goods, or goods in process), the controlled substances may be stored separately, provided that each storage area complies with the requirements set forth in this section.

(d) *Accessibility to storage areas.* The controlled substances storage areas shall be accessible only to an absolute minimum number of specifically authorized employees. When it is necessary for employee maintenance personnel, nonemployee maintenance personnel, business guests, or visitors to be present in or pass through controlled substances storage areas, the registrant shall provide for adequate observation of the area by an employee specifically authorized in writing.

[36 FR 18730, Sept. 21, 1971, as amended at 37 FR 15919, Aug. 8, 1972. Redesignated at 38 FR 26609, Sept. 24, 1973]

EDITORIAL NOTE: For FEDERAL REGISTER citations affecting § 1301.72, see the List of CFR Sections Affected, which appears in the Finding Aids section of the printed volume and on GPO Access.

§ 1301.73 Physical security controls for non-practitioners; compounders for narcotic treatment programs; manufacturing and compounding areas.

All manufacturing activities (including processing, packaging and labeling) involving controlled substances listed in any schedule and all activities of compounders shall be conducted in accordance with the following:

(a) All in-process substances shall be returned to the controlled substances storage area at the termination of the process. If the process is not terminated at the end of a workday (except where a continuous process or other normal manufacturing operation should not be interrupted), the processing area or tanks, vessels, bins or bulk containers containing such substances shall be securely locked, with adequate security for the area or building. If such security requires an alarm, such alarm, upon unauthorized entry, shall transmit a signal directly to a central station protection company, or local or state police agency which has a legal duty to respond, or a 24-hour control station operated by the registrant.

(b) Manufacturing activities with controlled substances shall be conducted in an area or areas of clearly defined limited access which is under surveillance by an employee or employees designated in writing as responsible for the area. "Limited access" may be provided, in the absence of physical dividers such as walls or partitions, by traffic control lines or restricted space designation. The employee designated as responsible for the area may be engaged in the particular manufacturing operation being conducted: *Provided,* That he is able to provide continuous surveillance of the area in order that unauthorized persons may not enter or leave the area without his knowledge.

(c) During the production of controlled substances, the manufacturing areas shall be accessible to only those employees required for efficient operation. When it is necessary for employee maintenance personnel, nonemployee maintenance personnel, business guests, or visitors to be present in or pass through manufacturing areas during production of controlled substances, the registrant shall provide for adequate observation of the area by an employee specifically authorized in writing.

[36 FR 18731, Sept. 21, 1971. Redesignated at 38 FR 26609, Sept. 24, 1973 and amended at 39 FR 37984, Oct. 25, 1974]

§ 1301.74 Other security controls for non-practitioners; narcotic treatment programs and compounders for narcotic treatment programs.

(a) Before distributing a controlled substance to any person who the registrant does not know to be registered to possess the controlled substance, the registrant shall make a good faith inquiry either with the Administration or with the appropriate State controlled substances registration agency, if any, to determine that the person is registered to possess the controlled substance.

(b) The registrant shall design and operate a system to disclose to the registrant suspicious orders of controlled substances. The registrant shall inform the Field Division Office of the Administration in his area of suspicious orders when discovered by the registrant. Suspicious orders include orders of unusual size, orders deviating substantially from a normal pattern, and orders of unusual frequency.

(c) The registrant shall notify the Field Division Office of the Administration in his area, in writing, of any theft or significant loss of any controlled substances within one business day of discovery of the theft or loss. The supplier is responsible for reporting all in-transit losses of controlled substances by the common or contract carrier selected pursuant to paragraph (e) of this section, within one business day of discovery of such theft or loss. The registrant shall also complete, and submit to the Field Division Office in his area, DEA Form 106 regarding the theft or loss. Thefts and significant losses must be reported whether or not the controlled substances are subsequently recovered or the responsible parties are identified and action taken against them. When determining whether a loss is significant, a registrant should consider, among others, the following factors:

(1) The actual quantity of controlled substances lost in relation to the type of business;

(2) The specific controlled substances lost;

(3) Whether the loss of the controlled substances can be associated with access to those controlled substances by specific individuals, or whether the loss can be attributed to unique activities that may take place involving the controlled substances;

(4) A pattern of losses over a specific time period, whether the losses appear to be random, and the results of efforts taken to resolve the losses; and, if known,

(5) Whether the specific controlled substances are likely candidates for diversion;

(6) Local trends and other indicators of the diversion potential of the missing controlled substance.

(d) The registrant shall not distribute any controlled substance listed in Schedules II through V as a complimentary sample to any potential or current customer (1) without the prior written request of the customer, (2) to be used only for satisfying the legitimate medical needs of patients of the customer, and (3) only in reasonable quantities. Such request must contain the name, address, and registration number of the customer and the name

and quantity of the specific controlled substance desired. The request shall be preserved by the registrant with other records of distribution of controlled substances. In addition, the requirements of part 1305 of the chapter shall be complied with for any distribution of a controlled substance listed in Schedule II. For purposes of this paragraph, the term "customer" includes a person to whom a complimentary sample of a substance is given in order to encourage the prescribing or recommending of the substance by the person.

(e) When shipping controlled substances, a registrant is responsible for selecting common or contract carriers which provide adequate security to guard against in-transit losses. When storing controlled substances in a public warehouse, a registrant is responsible for selecting a warehouseman which will provide adequate security to guard against storage losses; wherever possible, the registrant shall store controlled substances in a public warehouse which complies with the requirements set forth in §1301.72. In addition, the registrant shall employ precautions (e.g., assuring that shipping containers do not indicate that contents are controlled substances) to guard against storage or in-transit losses.

(f) When distributing controlled substances through agents (e.g., detailmen), a registrant is responsible for providing and requiring adequate security to guard against theft and diversion while the substances are being stored or handled by the agent or agents.

(g) Before the initial distribution of carfentanil etorphine hydrochloride and/or diprenorphine to any person, the registrant must verify that the person is authorized to handle the substances(s) by contacting the Drug Enforcement Administration.

(h) The acceptance of delivery of narcotic substances by a narcotic treatment program shall be made only by a licensed practitioner employed at the facility or other authorized individuals designated in writing. At the time of delivery, the licensed practitioner or other authorized individual designated in writing (excluding persons currently or previously dependent on narcotic drugs), shall sign for the narcotics and place his specific title (if any) on any invoice. Copies of these signed invoices shall be kept by the distributor.

(i) Narcotics dispensed or administered at a narcotic treatment program will be dispensed or administered directly to the patient by either (1) the licensed practitioner, (2) a registered nurse under the direction of the licensed practitioner, (3) a licensed practical nurse under the direction of the licensed practitioner, or (4) a pharmacist under the direction of the licensed practitioner.

(j) Persons enrolled in a narcotic treatment program will be required to wait in an area physically separated from the narcotic storage and dispensing area. This requirement will be enforced by the program physician and employees.

(k) All narcotic treatment programs must comply with standards established by the Secretary of Health and Human Services (after consultation with the Administration) respecting the quantities of narcotic drugs which may be provided to persons enrolled in a narcotic treatment program for unsupervised use.

(l) DEA may exercise discretion regarding the degree of security required in narcotic treatment programs based on such factors as the location of a program, the number of patients enrolled in a program and the number of physicians, staff members and security guards. Similarly, such factors will be taken into consideration when evaluating existing security or requiring new security at a narcotic treatment program.

[36 FR 7778, Apr. 24, 1971; 36 FR 13386, July 21, 1971, as amended at 36 FR 18731, Sept. 21, 1971. Redesignated at 38 FR 26609, Sept. 24, 1973]

EDITORIAL NOTE: For FEDERAL REGISTER citations affecting § 1301.74, see the List of CFR Sections Affected, which appears in the Finding Aids section of the printed volume and on GPO Access.

§ 1301.75 Physical security controls for practitioners.

(a) Controlled substances listed in Schedule I shall be stored in a securely locked, substantially constructed cabinet.

(b) Controlled substances listed in Schedules II, III, IV, and V shall be stored in a securely locked, substantially constructed cabinet. However, pharmacies and institutional practitioners may disperse such substances throughout the stock of noncontrolled substances in such a manner as to obstruct the theft or diversion of the controlled substances.

(c) This section shall also apply to nonpractitioners authorized to conduct research or chemical analysis under another registration.

(d) Carfentanil etorphine hydrochloride and diprenorphine shall be stored in a safe or steel cabinet equivalent to a U.S. Government Class V security container.

[39 FR 3674, Jan. 29, 1974, as amended at 39 FR 17838, May 21, 1974; 54 FR 33674, Aug. 16, 1989; 62 FR 13957, Mar. 24, 1997]

§ 1301.76 Other security controls for practitioners.

(a) The registrant shall not employ, as an agent or employee who has access to controlled substances, any person who has been convicted of a felony offense relating to controlled substances or who, at any time, had an application for registration with the DEA denied, had a DEA registration revoked or has surrendered a DEA registration for cause. For purposes of this subsection, the term "for cause" means a surrender in lieu of, or as a consequence of, any federal or state administrative, civil or criminal action resulting from an investigation of the individual's handling of controlled substances.

(b) The registrant shall notify the Field Division Office of the Administration in his area, in writing, of the theft or significant loss of any controlled substances within one business day of discovery of such loss or theft. The registrant shall also complete, and submit to the Field Division Office in his area, DEA Form 106 regarding the loss or theft. When determining whether a loss is significant, a registrant should consider, among others, the following factors:

(1) The actual quantity of controlled substances lost in relation to the type of business;

(2) The specific controlled substances lost;

(3) Whether the loss of the controlled substances can be associated with access to those controlled substances by specific individuals, or whether the loss can be attributed to unique activities that may take place involving the controlled substances;

(4) A pattern of losses over a specific time period, whether the losses appear to be random, and the results of efforts taken to resolve the losses; and, if known,

(5) Whether the specific controlled substances are likely candidates for diversion;

(6) Local trends and other indicators of the diversion potential of the missing controlled substance.

(c) Whenever the registrant distributes a controlled substance (without being registered as a distributor, as permitted in § 1301.13(e)(1) and/or §§ 1307.11–1307.12) he/she shall comply with the requirements imposed on non-practitioners in § 1301.74 (a), (b), and (e).

(d) Central fill pharmacies must comply with § 1301.74(e) when selecting private, common or contract carriers to transport filled prescriptions to a retail pharmacy for delivery to the ultimate user. When central fill pharmacies contract with private, common or contract carriers to transport filled prescriptions to a retail pharmacy, the central fill pharmacy is responsible for reporting in-transit losses upon discovery of such loss by use of a DEA Form 106. Retail pharmacies must comply with § 1301.74(e) when selecting private, common or contract carriers to retrieve filled prescriptions from a central fill pharmacy. When retail pharmacies contract with private, common or contract carriers to retrieve filled prescriptions from a central fill pharmacy, the retail pharmacy is responsible for reporting in-transit losses upon discovery of such loss by use of a DEA Form 106.

[36 FR 7778, Apr. 24, 1971, as amended at 36 FR 18731, Sept. 21, 1971; 37 FR 15919, Aug. 8, 1972. Redesignated at 38 FR 26609, Sept. 24, 1973; 47 FR 41735, Sept. 22, 1982; 56 FR 36728, Aug. 1, 1991; 62 FR 13957, Mar. 24, 1997; 68 FR 37409, June 24, 2003; 70 FR 47097, Aug. 12, 2005]

§ 1301.77 Security controls for freight forwarding facilities.

(a) All Schedule II–V controlled substances that will be temporarily stored at the freight forwarding facility must be either:

(1) stored in a segregated area under constant observation by designated responsible individual(s); or

(2) stored in a secured area that meets the requirements of Section 1301.72(b) of this Part. For purposes of this requirement, a facility that may be locked down (*i.e.*, secured against physical entry in a manner consistent with requirements of Section 1301.72(b)(3)(ii) of this part) and has a monitored alarm system or is subject to continuous monitoring by security personnel will be deemed to meet the requirements of Section 1301.72(b)(3) of this Part.

(b) Access to controlled substances must be kept to an absolute minimum number of specifically authorized individuals. Non-authorized individuals may not be present in or pass through controlled substances storage areas without adequate observation provided by an individual authorized in writing by the registrant.

(c) Controlled substances being transferred through a freight forwarding facility must be packed in sealed, unmarked shipping containers.

[65 FR 44678, July 19, 2000; 65 FR 45829, July 25, 2000]

EMPLOYEE SCREENING—NON-
PRACTITIONERS

§ 1301.90 Employee screening procedures.

It is the position of DEA that the obtaining of certain information by non-practitioners is vital to fairly assess the likelihood of an employee committing a drug security breach. The need to know this information is a matter of business necessity, essential to overall controlled substances security. In this regard, it is believed that conviction of crimes and unauthorized use of controlled substances are activities that are proper subjects for inquiry. It is, therefore, assumed that the following questions will become a part of an employer's comprehensive employee screening program:

Question. Within the past five years, have you been convicted of a felony, or within the past two years, of any misdemeanor or are you presently formally charged with committing a criminal offense? (Do not include any traffic violations, juvenile offenses or military convictions, except by general court-martial.) If the answer is yes, furnish details of conviction, offense, location, date and sentence.

Question. In the past three years, have you ever knowingly used any narcotics, amphetamines or barbiturates, other than those prescribed to you by a physician? If the answer is yes, furnish details.

Advice. An authorization, in writing, that allows inquiries to be made of courts and law enforcement agencies for possible pending charges or convictions must be executed by a person who is allowed to work in an area where access to controlled substances clearly exists. A person must be advised that any false information or omission of information will jeopardize his or her position with respect to employment. The application for employment should inform a person that information furnished or recovered as a result of any inquiry will not necessarily preclude employment, but will be considered as part of an overall evaluation of the person's qualifications. The maintaining of fair employment practices, the protection of the person's right of privacy, and the assurance that the results of such inquiries will be treated by the employer in confidence will be explained to the employee.

[40 FR 17143, Apr. 17, 1975]

§ 1301.91 Employee responsibility to report drug diversion.

Reports of drug diversion by fellow employees is not only a necessary part of an overall employee security program but also serves the public interest at large. It is, therefore, the position of DEA that an employee who has knowledge of drug diversion from his employer by a fellow employee has an obligation to report such information to a responsible security official of the employer. The employer shall treat such information as confidential and shall take all reasonable steps to protect the confidentiality of the information and the identity of the employee furnishing information. A failure to report information of drug diversion will be considered in determining the feasibility of continuing to allow an employee to work in a drug security area.

The employer shall inform all employees concerning this policy.

[40 FR 17143, Apr. 17, 1975]

§ 1301.92 Illicit activities by employees.

It is the position of DEA that employees who possess, sell, use or divert controlled substances will subject themselves not only to State or Federal prosecution for any illicit activity, but shall also immediately become the subject of independent action regarding their continued employment. The employer will assess the seriousness of the employee's violation, the position of responsibility held by the employee, past record of employment, etc., in determining whether to suspend, transfer, terminate or take other action against the employee.

[40 FR 17143, Apr. 17, 1975]

§ 1301.93 Sources of information for employee checks.

DEA recommends that inquiries concerning employees' criminal records be made as follows:

Local inquiries. Inquiries should be made by name, date and place of birth, and other identifying information, to local courts and law enforcement agencies for records of pending charges and convictions. Local practice may require such inquiries to be made in person, rather than by mail, and a copy of an authorization from the employee may be required by certain law enforcement agencies.

DEA inquiries. Inquiries supplying identifying information should also be furnished to DEA Field Division Offices along with written consent from the concerned individual for a check of DEA files for records of convictions. The Regional check will result in a national check being made by the Field Division Office.

[40 FR 17143, Apr. 17, 1975, as amended at 47 FR 41735, Sept. 22, 1982]

PART 1302—LABELING AND PACKAGING REQUIREMENTS FOR CONTROLLED SUBSTANCES

1302.06 Sealing of controlled substances.
1302.07 Labeling and packaging requirements for imported and exported substances.

AUTHORITY: 21 U.S.C. 821, 825, 871(b), 958(e).

SOURCE: 36 FR 7785, Apr. 24, 1971, unless otherwise noted. Redesignated at 38 FR 26609, Sept. 24, 1973.

§1302.01 Scope of part 1302.

Requirements governing the labeling and packaging of controlled substances pursuant to sections 1305 and 1008(d) of the Act (21 U.S.C. 825 and 958(d)) are set forth generally by those sections and specifically by the sections of this part.

[36 FR 13386, July 21, 1971. Redesignated at 38 FR 26609, Sept. 24, 1973]

§1302.02 Definitions.

Any term contained in this part shall have the definition set forth in section 102 of the Act (21 U.S.C. 802) or part 1300 of this chapter.

[62 FR 13958, Mar. 24, 1997]

§1302.03 Symbol required; exceptions.

(a) Each commercial container of a controlled substance (except for a controlled substance excepted by the Administrator pursuant to §1308.31 of this chapter) shall have printed on the label the symbol designating the schedule in which such controlled substance is listed. Each such commercial container, if it otherwise has no label, must bear a label complying with the requirement of this part.

(b) Each manufacturer shall print upon the labeling of each controlled substance distributed by him the symbol designating the schedule in which such controlled substance is listed.

(c) The following symbols shall designate the schedule corresponding thereto:

Schedule	
Schedule I	CI or C–I.
Schedule II	CII or C–II.
Schedule III	CIII or C–III.
Schedule IV	CIV or C–IV.
Schedule V	CV or C–V.

The word "schedule" need not be used. No distinction need be made between narcotic and nonnarcotic substances.

(d) The symbol is not required on a carton or wrapper in which a commercial container is held if the symbol is easily legible through such carton or wrapper.

(e) The symbol is not required on a commercial container too small or otherwise unable to accommodate a label, if the symbol is printed on the box or package from which the commercial container is removed upon dispensing to an ultimate user.

(f) The symbol is not required on a commercial container containing, or on the labeling of, a controlled substance being utilized in clinical research involving blind and double blind studies.

[36 FR 7785, Apr. 24, 1971, as amended at 36 FR 18731, Sept. 21, 1971. Redesignated at 38 FR 26609, Sept. 24, 1973]

§1302.04 Location and size of symbol on label and labeling.

The symbol shall be prominently located on the label or the labeling of the commercial container and/or the panel of the commercial container normally displayed to dispensers of any controlled substance. The symbol on labels shall be clear and large enough to afford easy identification of the schedule of the controlled substance upon inspection without removal from the dispenser's shelf. The symbol on all other labeling shall be clear and large enough to afford prompt identification of the controlled substance upon inspection of the labeling.

[62 FR 13958, Mar. 24, 1997]

§1302.05 Effective dates of labeling requirements.

All labels on commercial containers of, and all labeling of, a controlled substance which either is transferred to another schedule or is added to any schedule shall comply with the requirements of §1302.03, on or before the effective date established in the final order for the transfer or addition.

[62 FR 13958, Mar. 24, 1997]

§1302.06 Sealing of controlled substances.

On each bottle, multiple dose vial, or other commercial container of any controlled substance, there shall be securely affixed to the stopper, cap, lid, covering, or wrapper or such container a seal to disclose upon inspection any tampering or opening of the container.

[62 FR 13958, Mar. 24, 1997]

§ 1302.07 Labeling and packaging requirements for imported and exported substances.

(a) The symbol requirements of §§ 1302.03–1302.05 apply to every commercial container containing, and to all labeling of, controlled substances imported into the jurisdiction of and/or the customs territory of the United States.

(b) The symbol requirements of §§ 1302.03–1302.05 do not apply to any commercial containers containing, or any labeling of, a controlled substance intended for export from the jurisdiction of the United States.

(c) The sealing requirements of § 1302.06 apply to every bottle, multiple dose vial, or other commercial container of any controlled substance listed in schedule I or II, or any narcotic controlled substance listed in schedule III or IV, imported into, exported from, or intended for export from, the jurisdiction of and/or the customs territory of the United States.

[62 FR 13958, Mar. 24, 1997]

PART 1303—QUOTAS

GENERAL INFORMATION

AUTHORITY: 21 U.S.C. 821, 826, 871(b).

GENERAL INFORMATION

§ 1303.01 Scope of part 1303.

Procedures governing the establishment of production and manufacturing quotas on basic classes of controlled substances listed in schedules I and II pursuant to section 306 of the Act (21 U.S.C. 826) are governed generally by that section and specifically by the sections of this part.

[36 FR 7786, Apr. 24, 1971. Redesignated at 38 FR 26609, Sept. 24, 1973]

§ 1303.02 Definitions.

Any term contained in this part shall have the definition set forth in section 102 of the Act (21 U.S.C. 802) or part 1300 of this chapter.

[62 FR 13958, Mar. 24, 1997]

AGGREGATE PRODUCTION AND PROCUREMENT QUOTAS

§ 1303.11 Aggregate production quotas.

(a) The Administrator shall determine the total quantity of each basic class of controlled substance listed in Schedule I or II necessary to be manufactured during the following calendar year to provide for the estimated medical, scientific, research and industrial needs of the United States, for lawful export requirements, and for the establishment and maintenance of reserve stocks.

(b) In making his determinations, the Administrator shall consider the following factors:

(1) Total net disposal of the class by all manufacturers during the current and 2 preceding years;

(2) Trends in the national rate of net disposal of the class;

(3) Total actual (or estimated) inventories of the class and of all substances manufactured from the class, and trends in inventory accumulation;

(4) Projected demand for such class as indicated by procurement quotas requested pursuant to §1303.12; and

(5) Other factors affecting medical, scientific, research, and industrial needs in the United States and lawful export requirements, as the Administrator finds relevant, including changes in the currently accepted medical use in treatment with the class or the substances which are manufactured from it, the economic and physical availability of raw materials for use in manufacturing and for inventory purposes, yield and stability problems, potential disruptions to production (including possible labor strikes), and recent unforeseen emergencies such as floods and fires.

(c) The Administrator shall, on or before May 1 of each year, publish in the FEDERAL REGISTER, general notice of an aggregate production quota for any basic class determined by him under this section. A copy of said notice shall be mailed simultaneously to each person registered as a bulk manufacturer of the basic class. The Administrator shall permit any interested person to file written comments on or objections to the proposal and shall designate in the notice the time during which such filings may be made. The Administrator may, but shall not be required to, hold a public hearing on one or more issues raised by the comments and objections filed with him. In the event the Administrator decides to hold such a hearing, he shall publish notice of the hearing in the FEDERAL REGISTER, which notice shall summarize the issues to be heard and shall set the time for the hearing which shall nnt be less than 30 days after the date of publication of the notice. After consideration of any comments or objections, or after a hearing if one is ordered by the Administrator, the Administrator shall issue and publish in the FEDERAL REGISTER his final order determining the aggregate production quota for the basic class of controlled substance. The order shall include the findings of fact and conclusions of law upon which the order is based. The order shall specify the date on which it shall take effect. A copy of said order shall be mailed simultaneously to each

person registered as a bulk manufacturer of the basic class.

[36 FR 7786, Apr. 24, 1971, as amended at 37 FR 15919, Aug. 8, 1972. Redesignated at 38 FR 26609, Sept. 24, 1973]

§1303.12 Procurement quotas.

(a) In order to determine the estimated needs for, and to insure an adequate and uninterrupted supply of, basic classes of controlled substances listed in Schedules I and II (except raw opium being imported by the registrant pursuant to an import permit) the Administrator shall issue procurement quotas authorizing persons to procure and use quantities of each basic class of such substances for the purpose of manufacturing such class into dosage forms or into other substances.

(b) Any person who is registered to manufacture controlled substances listed in any schedule and who desires to use during the next calendar year any basic class of controlled substances listed in Schedule I or II (except raw opium being imported by the registrant pursuant to an import permit) for purposes of manufacturing, shall apply on DEA Form 250 for a procurement quota for such basic class. A separate application must be made for each basic class desired to be procured or used. The applicant shall state whether he intends to manufacture the basic class himself or purchase it from another manufacturer. The applicant shall state separately each purpose for which the basic class is desired, the quantity desired for that purpose during the next calendar year, and the quantities used and estimated to be used, if any, for that purpose during the current and preceding 2 calendar years. If the purpose is to manufacture the basic class into dosage form, the applicant shall state the official name, common or usual name, chemical name, or brand name of that form. If the purpose is to manufacture another substance, the applicant shall state the official name, common or usual name, chemical name, or brand name of the substance, and, if a controlled substance listed in any schedule, the schedule number and Administration Controlled Substances Code Number, as set forth in part 1308 of this chapter, of the substance. If the purpose is to manufacture another basic class of controlled substance listed in Schedule I or II, the applicant shall also state the quantity of the other basic class which the applicant has applied to manufacture pursuant to § 1303.22 and the quantity of the first basic class necessary to manufacture a specified unit of the second basic class. DEA Form 250 shall be filed on or before April 1 of the year preceding the calendar year for which the procurement quota is being applied. Copies of DEA Form 250 may be obtained from, and shall be filed with, the Drug & Chemical Evaluation Section, Drug Enforcement Administration, Department of Justice, Washington, DC 20537.

(c) The Administrator shall, on or before July 1 of the year preceding the calendar year during which the quota shall be effective, issue to each qualified applicant a procurement quota authorizing him to procure and use:

(1) All quantities of such class necessary to manufacture all quantities of other basic classes of controlled substances listed in Schedules I and II which the applicant is authorized to manufacture pursuant to § 1303.23; and

(2) Such other quantities of such class as the applicant has applied to procure and use and are consistent with his past use, his estimated needs, and the total quantity of such class that will be produced.

(d) Any person to whom a procurement quota has been issued may at any time request an adjustment in the quota by applying to the Administrator with a statement showing the need for the adjustment. Such application shall be filed with the Drug & Chemical Evaluation Section, Drug Enforcement Administration, Department of Justice, Washington, DC 20537. The Administrator shall increase or decrease the procurement quota of such person if and to the extent that he finds, after considering the factors enumerated in paragraph (c) of this section and any occurrences since the issuance of the procurement quota, that the need justifies an adjustment.

(e) The following persons need not obtain a procurement quota:

(1) Any person who is registered to manufacture a basic class of controlled substance listed in Schedule I or II and who uses all of the quantity he manufactures in the manufacture of a substance not controlled under the Act;

(2) Any person who is registered or authorized to conduct chemical analysis with controlled substances (for controlled substances to be used in such analysis only); and

(3) Any person who is registered to conduct research with a basic class of controlled substance listed in Schedule I or II and who is authorized to manufacture a quantity of such class pursuant to § 1301.13 of this chapter.

(f) Any person to whom a procurement quota has been issued, authorizing that person to procure and use a quantity of a basic class of controlled substances listed in Schedules I or II during the current calendar year, shall, at or before the time of giving an order to another manufacturer requiring the distribution of a quantity of such basic class, certify in writing to such other manufacturer that the quantity of such basic class ordered does not exceed the person's unused and available procurement quota of such basic class for the current calendar year. The written certification shall be executed by the same individual who signed the DEA Form 222 transmitting the order. Manufacturers shall not fill an order from persons required to apply for a procurement quota under paragraph (b) of this section unless the order is accompanied by a certification as required under this section. The certification required by this section shall contain the following: The date of the certification; the name and address of the bulk manufacturer to whom the certification is directed; a reference to the number of the DEA Form 222 to which the certification applies; the name of the person giving the order to which the certification applies; the name of the basic class specified in the DEA Form 222 to which the certification applies; the appropriate schedule within which is listed the basic class specified in the DEA Form 222 to which the certification applies; a statement that the quantity (expressed in grams) of the basic class specified in the DEA Form 222 to which the certification applies does not exceed the unused and available procurement quota of such basic class, issued to the person giving the order, for the current calendar year; and the signature of the individual who signed the DEA Form 222 to which the certification applies.

[36 FR 7786, Apr. 24, 1971, as amended at 36 FR 13386, July 21, 1971; 36 FR 18731, Sept. 21, 1971; 37 FR 15919, Aug. 8, 1972. Redesignated at 38 FR 26609, Sept. 24, 1973]

EDITORIAL NOTE: For FEDERAL REGISTER citations affecting § 1303.12, see the List of CFR Sections Affected, which appears in the Finding Aids section of the printed volume and on GPO Access.

§ 1303.13 Adjustments of aggregate production quotas.

(a) The Administrator may at any time increase or reduce the aggregate production quota for a basic class of controlled substance listed in Schedule I or II which he has previously fixed pursuant to § 1303.11.

(b) In determining to adjust the aggregate production quota, the Administrator shall consider the following factors:

(1) Changes in the demand for that class, changes in the national rate of net disposal of the class, and changes in the rate of net disposal of the class by registrants holding individual manufacturing quotas for that class;

(2) Whether any increased demand for that class, the national and/or individual rates of net disposal of that class are temporary, short term, or long term;

(3) Whether any increased demand for that class can be met through existing inventories, increased individual manufacturing quotas, or increased importation, without increasing the aggregate production quota, taking into account production delays and the probability that other individual manufacturing quotas may be suspended pursuant to § 1303.24(b);

(4) Whether any decreased demand for that class will result in excessive inventory accumulation by all persons registered to handle that class (including manufacturers, distributors, practitioners, importers, and exporters), notwithstanding the possibility that individual manufacturing quotas may be suspended pursuant to § 1303.24(b) or abandoned pursuant to § 1303.27;

(5) Other factors affecting medical, scientific, research, and industrial needs in the United States and lawful export requirements, as the Administrator finds relevant, including changes in the currently accepted medical use in treatment with the class or the substances which are manufactured from it, the economic and physical availability of raw materials for use in manufacturing and for inventory purposes, yield and stability problems, potential disruptions to production (including possible labor strikes), and recent unforeseen emergencies such as floods and fires.

(c) The Administrator in the event he determines to increase or reduce the aggregate production quota for a basic class of controlled substance, shall publish in the FEDERAL REGISTER general notice of an adjustment in the aggregate production quota for that class determined by him under this section. A copy of said notice shall be mailed simultaneously to each person registered as a bulk manufacturer of the basic class. The Administrator shall permit any interested person to file written comments on or objections to the proposal and shall designate in the notice the time during which such filings may be made. The Administrator may, but shall not be required to, hold a public hearing on one or more issues raised by the comments and objections filed with him. In the event the Administrator decides to hold such a hearing, he shall publish notice of the hearing in the FEDERAL REGISTER, which notice shall summarize the issues to be heard and shall set the time for the hearing, which shall not be less than 10 days after the date of publication of the notice. After consideration of any comments or objections, or after a hearing if one is ordered by the Administrator, the Administrator shall issue and publish in the FEDERAL REGISTER his final order determining the aggregate production for the basic class of controlled substance. The order shall include the findings of fact and conclusions of law upon which the order is based. The order shall specify the date on which it shall take effect. A copy of said order shall be mailed simultaneously to each person registered as a bulk manufacturer of the basic class.

[37 FR 15919, Aug. 8, 1972. Redesignated at 38 FR 26609, Sept. 24, 1973]

INDIVIDUAL MANUFACTURING QUOTAS

§ 1303.21 Individual manufacturing quotas.

(a) The Administrator shall, on or before July 1 of each year, fix for and issue to each person who is registered to manufacture a basic class of controlled substance listed in Schedule I or II, and who applies for a manufacturing quota, an individual manufacturing quota authorizing that person to manufacture during the next calendar year a quantity of that basic class. Any manufacturing quota fixed and issued by the Administrator shall be subject to his authority to reduce or limit it at a later date pursuant to § 1303.26 and to his authority to revoke or suspend it at any time pursuant to §§ 1301.36 of this chapter.

(b) No individual manufacturing quota shall be required for registrants listed in § 1303.12(e).

[36 FR 7786, Apr. 24, 1971. Redesignated at 38 FR 26609, Sept. 24, 1973, as amended at 62 FR 13958, Mar. 24, 1997]

§ 1303.22 Procedure for applying for individual manufacturing quotas.

Any person who is registered to manufacture any basic class of controlled substance listed in Schedule I or II and who desires to manufacture a quantity of such class shall apply on DEA Form 189 for a manufacturing quota for such quantity of such class. Copies of DEA Form 189 may be obtained from, and shall be filed (on or before May 1 of the year preceding the calendar year for which the manufacturing quota is being applied) with, the Drug & Chemical Evaluation Section, Drug Enforcement Administration, Department of Justice, Washington, D.C. 20537. A separate application must be made for each basic class desired to be manufactured. The applicant shall state:

(a) The name and Administration Controlled Substances Code Number, as set forth in part 1308 of this chapter, of the basic class.

(b) For the basic class in each of the current and preceding 2 calendar years,

(1) The authorized individual manufacturing quota, if any;

(2) The actual or estimated quantity manufactured;

(3) The actual or estimated net disposal;

(4) The actual or estimated inventory allowance pursuant to § 1303.24; and

(5) The actual or estimated inventory as of December 31;

(c) For the basic class in the next calendar year,

(1) The desired individual manufacturing quota; and

(2) Any additional factors which the applicant finds relevant to the fixing of his individual manufacturing quota, including the trend of (and recent changes in) his and the national rates of net disposal, his production cycle and current inventory position, the econolic and physical availability of raw materials for use in manufacturing and for inventory purposes, yield and stability problems, potential disruptions to production (including possible labor strikes) and recent unforeseen emergencies such as floods and fires.

[36 FR 7786, Apr. 24, 1971, as amended at 36 FR 13386, July 21, 1971; 37 FR 15920, Aug. 8, 1972. Redesignated at 38 FR 26609, Sept. 24, 1973, and amended at 46 FR 28841, May 29, 1981; 51 FR 5319, Feb. 13, 1986; 62 FR 13958, Mar. 24, 1997]

§ 1303.23 Procedure for fixing individual manufacturing quotas.

(a) In fixing individual manufacturing quotas for a basic class of controlled substance listed in Schedule I or II, the Administrator shall allocate to each applicant who is currently manufacturing such class a quota equal to 100 percent of the estimated net disposal of that applicant for the next calendar year, adjusted—

(1) By the amount necessary to increase or reduce the estimated inventory of the applicant on December 31 of the current year to his estimated inventory allowance for the next calendar year, pursuant to § 1303.24, and

(2) By any other factors which the Administrator deems relevant to the fixing of the individual manufacturing quota of the applicant, including the trend of (and recent changes in) his and the national rates of net disposal, his production cycle and current inventory position, the economic and physical availability of raw materials for use in

manufacturing and for inventory purposes, yield and stability problems, potential disruptions to production (including possible labor strikes), and recent unforeseen emergencies such as floods and fires.

(b) In fixing individual manufacturing quotas for a basic class of controlled substance listed in Schedule I or II, the Administrator shall allocate to each applicant who is not currently manufacturing such class a quota equal to 100 percent of the reasonably estimated net disposal of that applicant for the next calendar year, as determined by the Administrator, adjusted—

(1) By the amount necessary to provide the applicant his estimated inventory allowance for the next calendar year, pursuant to §1303.24, and

(2) By any other factors which the Administrator deems relevant to the fixing of the individual manufacturing quota of the applicant, including the trend of (and recent changes in) the national rate of net disposal, his production cycle and current inventory position, the economic and physical availability of raw materials for use in manufacturing and for inventory purposes, yield and stability problems, potential disruptions to production (including possible labor strikes), and recent unforeseen emergencies such as floods and fires.

(c) The Administrator shall, on or before March 1 of each year, adjust the individual manufacturing quota allocated for that year to each applicant in paragraph (a) of this section by the amount necessary to increase or reduce the actual inventory of the applicant to December 31 of the preceding year to his estimated inventory allowance for the current calendar year, pursuant to §1303.24.

[36 FR 7786, Apr. 24, 1971, as amended at 37 FR 15920, Aug. 8, 1972. Redesignated at 38 FR 26609, Sept. 24, 1973]

§1303.24 Inventory allowance.

(a) For the purpose of determining individual manufacturing quotas pursuant to §1303.23, each registered manufacturer shall be allowed as a part of such quota an amount sufficient to maintain an inventory equal to,

(1) For current manufacturers, 50 percent of his average estimated net disposal for the current calendar year and the last preceding calendar year; or

(2) For new manufacturers, 50 percent of his reasonably estimated net disposal for the next calendar year as determined by the Administrator.

(b) During each calendar year each registered manufacturer shall be allowed to maintain an inventory of a basic class not exceeding 65 percent of his estimated net disposal of that class for that year, as determined at the time his quota for that year was determined. At any time the inventory of a basic class held by a manufacturer exceeds 65 percent of his estimated net disposal, his quota for that class is automatically suspended and shall remain suspended until his inventory is less than 60 percent of his estimated net disposal. The Administrator may, upon application and for good cause shown, permit a manufacturer whose quota is, or is likely to be, suspended pursuant to this paragraph to continue manufacturing and to accumulate an inventory in excess of 65 percent of his estimated net disposal, upon such conditions and within such limitations as the Administrator may find necessary or desirable.

(c) If, during a calendar year, a registrant has manufactured the entire quantity of a basic class allocated to him under an individual manufacturing quota, and his inventory of that class is less than 40 percent of his estimated net disposal of that class for that year, the Administrator may, upon application pursuant to §1303.25, increase the quota of such registrant sufficiently to allow restoration of the inventory to 50 percent of the estimated net disposal for that year.

[36 FR 7786, Apr. 24, 1971, as amended at 36 FR 13386, July 21, 1971. Redesignated at 38 FR 26609, Sept. 24, 1973]

§1303.25 Increase in individual manufacturing quotas.

(a) Any registrant who holds an individual manufacturing quota for a basic class of controlled substance listed in Schedule I or II may file with the Administrator an application on Administration Form 189 for an increase in such quota in order for him to meet his estimated net disposal, inventory and other requirements during the remainder of such calendar year.

(b) The Administrator, in passing upon a registrant's application for an increase in his individual manufacturing quota, shall take into consideration any occurrences since the filing of such registrant's initial quota application that may require an increased manufacturing rate by such registrant during the balance of the calendar year. In passing upon such application the Administrator may also take into consideration the amount, if any, by which his determination of the total quantity for the basic class of controlled substance to be manufactured under § 1303.11 exceeds the aggregate of all the individual manufacturing quotas for the basic class of controlled substance, and the equitable distribution of such excess among other registrants.

[36 FR 7786, Apr. 24, 1971, as amended at 36 FR 13386, July 21, 1971. Redesignated at 38 FR 26609, Sept. 24, 1973]

§ 1303.26 Reduction in individual manufacturing quotas.

The Administrator may at any time reduce an individual manufacturing quota for a basic class of controlled substance listed in Schedule I or II which he has previously fixed in order to prevent the aggregate of the individual manufacturing quotas and import permits outstanding or to be granted from exceeding the aggregate production quota which has been established for that class pursuant to § 1303.11, as adjusted pursuant to § 1303.13. If a quota assigned to a new manufacturer pursuant to § 1303.23(b), or if a quota assigned to any manufacturer is increased pursuant to § 1303.24(c), or if an import permit issued to an importer pursuant to part 1312 of this chapter, causes the total quantity of a basic class to be manufactured and imported during the year to exceed the aggregate production quota which has been established for that class pursuant to § 1303.11, as adjusted pursuant to § 1303.13, the Administrator may proportionately reduce the individual manufacturing quotas and import permits of all other registrants to keep the aggregate produc-

tion quota within the limits originally established, or, alternatively, the Administrator may reduce the individual manufacturing quota of any registrant whose quota is suspended pursuant to § 1303.24(b) or § 1301.36 of this chapter, or is abandoned pursuant to § 1303.27.

[36 FR 7786, Apr. 24, 1971, as amended at 37 FR 15920, Aug. 8, 1972. Redesignated at 38 FR 26609, Sept. 24, 1973, as amended at 62 FR 13958, Mar. 24, 1997]

§ 1303.27 Abandonment of quota.

Any manufacturer assigned an individual manufacturing quota for any basic class pursuant to § 1303.23 may at any time abandon his right to manufacture all or any part of such quota by filing with the Drug & Chemical Evaluation Section a written notice of such abandonment, stating the name and Administration Controlled Substances Code Number, as set forth in part 1308 of this chapter, of the substance and the amount which he has chosen not to manufacture. The Administrator may, in his discretion, allocate such amount among the other manufacturers in proportion to their respective quotas.

[36 FR 7786, Apr. 24, 1971, as amended at 36 FR 13386, July 21, 1971. Redesignated at 38 FR 26609, Sept. 24, 1973, and amended at 46 FR 28841, May 29, 1981; 51 FR 5319, Feb. 13, 1986; 62 FR 13958, Mar. 24, 1997]

HEARINGS

§ 1303.31 Hearings generally.

(a) In any case where the Administrator shall hold a hearing regarding the determination of an aggregate production quota pursuant to § 1303.11(c), or regarding the adjustment of an aggregate production quota pursuant to § 1303.13(c), the procedures for such hearing shall be governed generally by the rule making procedures set forth in the Administrative Procedure Act (5 U.S.C. 551-559) and specifically by section 306 of the Act (21 U.S.C. 826), by §§ 1303.32-1303.37, and by the procedures for administrative hearings under the Act set forth in §§ 1316.41-1316.67 of this chapter.

(b) In any case where the Administrator shall hold a hearing regarding the issuance, adjustment, suspension, or denial of a procurement quota pursuant to §1303.12, or the issuance, adjustment, suspension, or denial of an individual manufacturing quota pursuant to §§1303.21–1303.27, the procedures for such hearing shall be governed generally by the adjudication procedures set forth in the Administrative Procedures Act (5 U.S.C. 551–559) and specifically by section 306 of the Act (21 U.S.C. 826), by §§1303.32–1303.37, and by the procedures for administrative hearings under the Act set forth in §§1316.41–1316.67 of this chapter.

[36 FR 7786, Apr. 24, 1971, as amended at 37 FR 15920, Aug. 8, 1972. Redesignated at 38 FR 26609, Sept. 24, 1973]

§1303.32 Purpose of hearing.

(a) The Administrator may, in his sole discretion, hold a hearing for the purpose of receiving factual evidence regarding any one or more issues (to be specified by him) involved in the determination or adjustment of any aggregate production quota.

(b) If requested by a person applying for or holding a procurement quota or an individual manufacturing quota, the Administrator shall hold a hearing for the purpose of receiving factual evidence regarding the issues involved in the issuance, adjustment, suspension, or denial of such quota to such person, but the Administrator need not hold a hearing on the suspension of a quota pursuant to §1301.36 of this chapter separate from a hearing on the suspension of registration pursuant to those sections.

(c) Extensive argument should not be offered into evidence but rather presented in opening or closing statements of counsel or in memoranda or proposed findings of fact and conclusions of law.

[36 FR 7786, Apr. 24, 1971, as amended at 37 FR 15920, Aug. 8, 1972. Redesignated at 38 FR 26609, Sept. 24, 1973, as amended at 62 FR 13958, Mar. 24, 1997]

§1303.33 Waiver or modification of rules.

The Administrator or the presiding officer (with respect to matters pending before him) may modify or waive any rule in this part by notice in advance of the hearing, if he determines that no party in the hearing will be unduly prejudiced and the ends of justice will thereby be served. Such notice of modification or waiver shall be made a part of the record of the hearing.

[36 FR 7786, Apr. 24, 1971. Redesignated at 38 FR 26609, Sept. 24, 1973]

§1303.34 Request for hearing or appearance; waiver.

(a) Any applicant or registrant who desires a hearing on the issuance, adjustment, suspension, or denial of his procurement and/or individual manufacturing quota shall, within 30 days after the date of receipt of the issuance, adjustment, suspension, or denial of such quota, file with the Administrator a written request for a hearing in the form prescribed in §1316.47 of this chapter. Any interested person who desires a hearing on the determination of an aggregate production quota shall, within the time prescribed in §1303.11(c), file with the Administrator a written request for a hearing in the form prescribed in §1316.47 of this chapter, including in the request a statement of the grounds for a hearing.

(b) Any interested person who desires to participate in a hearing on the determination or adjustment of an aggregate production quota, which hearing is ordered by the Administrator pursuant to §1303.11(c) or §1303.13(c) may do so by filing with the Administrator, within 30 days of the date of publication of notice of the hearing in the FEDERAL REGISTER, a written notice of his intention to participate in such hearing in the form prescribed in §1316.48 of this chapter.

(c) Any person entitled to a hearing or to participate in a hearing pursuant to paragraph (b) of this section, may, within the period permitted for filing a request for a hearing of notice of appearance, file with the Administrator a waiver of an opportunity for a hearing or to participate in a hearing, together with a written statement regarding his position on the matters of fact and law involved in such hearing. Such statement, if admissible, shall be made a part of the record and shall be considered in light of the lack of opportunity for cross-examination in determining the weight to be attached to matters of fact asserted therein.

(d) If any person entitled to a hearing or to participate in a hearing pursuant to paragraph (b) of this section, fails to file a request for a hearing or notice of appearance, or if he so files and fails to appear at the hearing, he shall be deemed to have waived his opportunity for the hearing or to participate in the hearing, unless he shows good cause for such failure.

(e) If all persons entitled to a hearing or to participate in a hearing waive or are deemed to waive their opportunity for the hearing or to participate in the hearing, the Administrator may cancel the hearing, if scheduled, and issue his final order pursuant to § 1303.37 without a hearing.

[36 FR 7786, Apr. 24, 1971, as amended at 36 FR 18731, Sept. 21, 1971; 37 FR 15920, Aug. 8, 1972. Redesignated at 38 FR 26609, Sept. 24, 1973]

§ 1303.35   Burden of proof.

(a) At any hearing regarding the determination or adjustment of an aggregate production quota, each interested person participating in the hearing shall have the burden of proving any propositions of fact or law asserted by him in the hearing.

(b) At any hearing regarding the issuance, adjustment, suspension, or denial of a procurement or individual manufacturing quota, the Administration shall have the burden of proving that the requirements of this part for such issuance, adjustment, suspension, or denial are satisfied.

[36 FR 7786, Apr. 24, 1971, as amended at 37 FR 15920, Aug. 8, 1972. Redesignated at 38 FR 26609, Sept. 24, 1973, as amended at 62 FR 13958, Mar. 24, 1997]

§ 1303.36   Time and place of hearing.

(a) If any applicant or registrant requests a hearing on the issuance, adjustment, suspension, or denial of his procurement and/or individual manufacturing quota pursuant to § 1303.34, the Administrator shall hold such hearing. Notice of the hearing shall be given to the applicant or registrant of the time and place at least 30 days prior to the hearing, unless the applicant or registrant waives such notice and requests the hearing be held at an earlier time, in which case the Admin-

istrator shall fix a date for such hearing as early as reasonably possible.

(b) The hearing will commence at the place and time designated in the notice given pursuant to paragraph (a) of this section or in the notice of hearing published in the FEDERAL REGISTER pursuant to § 1303.11(c) or § 1303.13 (c), but thereafter it may be moved to a different place and may be continued from day to day or recessed to a later day without notice other than announcement thereof by the presiding officer at the hearing.

[36 FR 7786, Apr. 24, 1971, as amended at 37 FR 15920, Aug. 8, 1972. Redesignated at 38 FR 26609, Sept. 24, 1973]

§ 1303.37   Final order.

As soon as practicable after the presiding officer has certified the record to the Administrator, the Administrator shall issue his order on the determination or adjustment of the aggregate production quota or on the issuance, adjustment, suspension, or denial of the procurement quota or individual manufacturing quota, as case may be. The order shall include the findings of fact and conclusions of law upon which the order is based. The order shall specify the date on which it shall take effect. The Administrator shall serve one copy of his order upon each party in the hearing.

[36 FR 7786, Apr. 24, 1971, as amended at 37 FR 15920, Aug. 8, 1972. Redesignated at 38 FR 26609, Sept. 24, 1973]

PART 1304—RECORDS AND REPORTS OF REGISTRANTS

GENERAL INFORMATION

1304.22 Records for manufacturers, distributors, dispensers, researchers, importers, and exporters.
1304.23 Records for chemical analysts.
1304.24 Records for maintenance treatment programs and detoxification treatment programs.
1304.25 Records for treatment programs which compound narcotics for treatment programs and other locations.
1304.26 Additional recordkeeping requirements applicable to drug products containing gamma-hydroxybutyric acid.

REPORTS

1304.31 Reports from manufacturers importing narcotic raw material.
1304.32 Reports of manufacturers importing coca leaves.
1304.33 Reports to ARCOS.

AUTHORITY: 21 U.S.C. 821, 827, 871(b), 958(e), 965, unless otherwise noted.

GENERAL INFORMATION

§ 1304.01   Scope of part 1304.

Inventory and other records and reports required under section 307 or section 1008(d) of the Act (21 U.S.C. 827 and 958(d)) shall be in accordance with, and contain the information required by, those sections and by the sections of this part.

[36 FR 7789, Apr. 24, 1971. Redesignated at 38 FR 26609, Sept. 24, 1973]

§ 1304.02   Definitions.

Any term contained in this part shall have the definition set forth in section 102 of the Act (21 U.S.C. 802) or part 1300 of this chapter.

[62 FR 13958, Mar. 24, 1997]

§ 1304.03   Persons required to keep records and file reports.

(a) Each registrant shall maintain the records and inventories and shall file the reports required by this part, except as exempted by this section. Any registrant who is authorized to conduct other activities without being registered to conduct those activities, either pursuant to § 1301.22(b) of this chapter or pursuant to §§ 1307.11–1307.15 of this chapter, shall maintain the records and inventories and shall file the reports required by this part for persons registered to conduct such activities. This latter requirement should not be construed as requiring stocks of controlled substances being used in various activities under one registration to be stored separately, nor that separate records are required for each activity. The intent of the Administration is to permit the registrant to keep one set of records which are adapted by the registrant to account for controlled substances used in any activity. Also, the Administration does not wish to acquire separate stocks of the same substance to be purchased and stored for separate activities. Otherwise, there is no advantage gained by permitting several activities under one registration. Thus, when a researcher manufactures a controlled item, he must keep a record of the quantity manufactured; when he distributes a quantity of the item, he must use and keep invoices or order forms to document the transfer; when he imports a substance, he keeps as part of his records the documentation required of an importer; and when substances are used in chemical analysis, he need not keep a record of this because such a record would not be required of him under a registration to do chemical analysis. All of these records may be maintained in one consolidated record system. Similarly, the researcher may store all of his controlled items in one place, and every two years take inventory of all items on hand, regardless of whether the substances were manufactured by him, imported by him, or purchased domestically by him, of whether the substances will be administered to subjects, distributed to other researchers, or destroyed during chemical analysis.

(b) A registered individual practitioner is required to keep records, as described in § 1304.04, of controlled substances in Schedules II, III, IV, and V which are dispensed, other than by prescribing or administering in the lawful course of professional practice.

(c) A registered individual practitioner is not required to keep records of controlled substances in Schedules II, III, IV, and V which are prescribed in the lawful course of professional practice, unless such substances are prescribed in the course of maintenance or detoxification treatment of an individual.

(d) A registered individual practitioner is not required to keep records of controlled substances listed in Schedules II, III, IV and V which are administered in the lawful course of professional practice unless the practitioner regularly engages in the dispensing or administering of controlled substances and charges patients, either separately or together with charges for other professional services, for substances so dispensed or administered. Records are required to be kept for controlled substances administered in the course of maintenance or detoxification treatment of an individual.

(e) Each registered mid-level practitioner shall maintain in a readily retrievable manner those documents required by the state in which he/she practices which describe the conditions and extent of his/her authorization to dispense controlled substances and shall make such documents available for inspection and copying by authorized employees of the Administration. Examples of such documentation include protocols, practice guidelines or practice agreements.

(f) Registered persons using any controlled substances while conducting preclinical research, in teaching at a registered establishment which maintains records with respect to such substances or conducting research in conformity with an exemption granted under section 505(i) or 512(j) of the Federal Food, Drug, and Cosmetic Act (21 U.S.C. 355(i) or 360b(j)) at a registered establishment which maintains records in accordance with either of those sections, are not required to keep records if he/she notifies the Administration of the name, address, and registration number of the establishment maintaining such records. This notification shall be given at the time the person applies for registration or reregistration and shall be made in the form of an attachment to the application, which shall be filed with the application.

(g) A distributing registrant who utilizes a freight forwarding facility shall maintain records to reflect transfer of controlled substances through the facility. These records must contain the date, time of transfer, number of cartons, crates, drums or other packages in which commercial containers of controlled substances are shipped and authorized signatures for each transfer. A distributing registrant may, as part of the initial request to operate a freight forwarding facility, request permission to store records at a central location. Approval of the request to maintain central records would be implicit in the approval of the request to operate the facility. Otherwise, a request to maintain records at a central location must be submitted in accordance with § 1304.04 of this part. These records must be maintained for a period of two years.

[36 FR 7790, Apr. 24, 1971, as amended at 36 FR 18731, Sept. 21, 1971; 37 FR 15920, Aug. 8, 1972. Redesignated at 38 FR 26609, Sept. 24, 1973, and amended at 50 FR 40523, Oct. 4, 1985; 51 FR 5320, Feb. 13, 1986; 51 FR 26154, July 21, 1986; 58 FR 31175, June 1, 1993; 62 FR 13958, Mar. 24, 1997; 65 FR 44679, July 19, 2000]

§ 1304.04 Maintenance of records and inventories.

(a) Except as provided in paragraphs (a)(1) and (a)(2) of this section, every inventory and other records required to be kept under this part must be kept by the registrant and be available, for at least 2 years from the date of such inventory or records, for inspection and copying by authorized employees of the Administration.

(1) Financial and shipping records (such as invoices and packing slips but not executed order forms subject to §§ 1305.17 and 1305.27 of this chapter) may be kept at a central location, rather than at the registered location, if the registrant has notified the Administration of his intention to keep central records. Written notification must be submitted by registered or certified mail, return receipt requested, in triplicate, to the Special Agent in Charge of the Administration in the area in which the registrant is located. Unless the registrant is informed by the Special Agent in Charge that permission to keep central records is denied, the registrant may maintain central records commencing 14 days after receipt of his notification by the Special Agent in Charge. All notifications must include the following:

(i) The nature of the records to be kept centrally.

(ii) The exact location where the records will be kept.

(iii) The name, address, DEA registration number and type of DEA registration of the registrant whose records are being maintained centrally.

(iv) Whether central records will be maintained in a manual, or computer readable, form.

(2) A registered retail pharmacy that possesses additional registrations for automated dispensing systems at long term care facilities may keep all records required by this part for those additional registered sites at the retail pharmacy or other approved central location.

(b) All registrants that are authorized to maintain a central recordkeeping system shall be subject to the following conditions:

(1) The records to be maintained at the central record location shall not include executed order forms, prescriptions and/or inventories which shall be maintained at each registered location.

(2) If the records are kept on microfilm, computer media or in any form requiring special equipment to render the records easily readable, the registrant shall provide access to such equipment with the records. If any code system is used (other than pricing information), a key to the code shall be provided to make the records understandable.

(3) The registrant agrees to deliver all or any part of such records to the registered location within two business days upon receipt of a written request from the Administration for such records, and if the Administration chooses to do so in lieu of requiring delivery of such records to the registered location, to allow authorized employees of the Administration to inspect such records at the central location upon request by such employees without a warrant of any kind.

(4) In the event that a registrant fails to comply with these conditions, the Special Agent in Charge may cancel such central recordkeeping authorization, and all other central recordkeeping authorizations held by the registrant without a hearing or other procedures. In the event of a cancellation of central recordkeeping authorizations under this paragraph the reg-

istrant shall, within the time specified by the Special Agent in Charge, comply with the requirements of this section that all records be kept at the registered location.

(c) Registrants need not notify the Special Agent in Charge or obtain central recordkeeping approval in order to maintain records on an in-house computer system.

(d) ARCOS participants who desire authorization to report from other than their registered locations must obtain a separate central reporting identifier. Request for central reporting identifiers will be submitted to: ARCOS Unit, P.O. Box 28293, Central Station, Washington, DC 20005.

(e) All central recordkeeping permits previously issued by the Administration expired September 30, 1980.

(f) Each registered manufacturer, distributor, importer, exporter, narcotic treatment program and compounder for narcotic treatment program shall maintain inventories and records of controlled substances as follows:

(1) Inventories and records of controlled substances listed in Schedules I and II shall be maintained separately from all of the records of the registrant; and

(2) Inventories and records of controlled substances listed in Schedules III, IV, and V shall be maintained either separately from all other records of the registrant or in such form that the information required is readily retrievable from the ordinary business records of the registrant.

(g) Each registered individual practitioner required to keep records and institutional practitioner shall maintain inventories and records of controlled substances in the manner prescribed in paragraph (f) of this section.

(h) Each registered pharmacy shall maintain the inventories and records of controlled substances as follows:

(1) Inventories and records of all controlled substances listed in Schedules I and II shall be maintained separately from all other records of the pharmacy, and prescriptions for such substances shall be maintained in a separate prescription file; and

(2) Inventories and records of controlled substances listed in Schedules

III, IV, and V shall be maintained either separately from all other records of the pharmacy or in such form that the information required is readily retrievable from ordinary business records of the pharmacy, and prescriptions for such substances shall be maintained either in a separate prescription file for controlled substances listed in Schedules III, IV, and V only or in such form that they are readily retrievable from the other prescription records of the pharmacy. Prescriptions will be deemed readily retrievable if, at the time they are initially filed, the face of the prescription is stamped in red ink in the lower right corner with the letter "C" no less than 1 inch high and filed either in the prescription file for controlled substances listed in Schedules I and II or in the usual consecutively numbered prescription file for non-controlled substances. However, if a pharmacy employs an ADP system or other electronic record-keeping system for prescriptions which permits identification by prescription number and retrieval of original documents by prescriber's name, patient's name, drug dispensed, and date filled, then the requirement to mark the hard copy prescription with a red "C" is waived.

(Authority: 21 U.S.C. 821 and 871(b); 28 CFR 0.100)

[36 FR 7790, Apr. 24, 1971, as amended at 36 FR 13386, July 21, 1971. Redesignated at 38 FR 26609, Sept. 24, 1973, and amended at 39 FR 37985, Oct. 25, 1974; 45 FR 44266, July 1, 1980; 47 FR 41735, Sept. 22, 1982; 51 FR 5320, Feb. 13, 1986; 62 FR 13959, Mar. 24, 1997; 70 FR 25466, May 13, 2005]

§ 1304.05 Records of authorized central fill pharmacies and retail pharmacies.

(a) Every retail pharmacy that utilizes the services of a central fill pharmacy must keep a record of all central fill pharmacies, including name, address and DEA number, that are authorized to fill prescriptions on its behalf. The retail pharmacy must also verify the registration for each central fill pharmacy authorized to fill prescriptions on its behalf. These records must be made available upon request for inspection by DEA.

(b) Every central fill pharmacy must keep a record of all retail pharmacies, including name, address and DEA number, for which it is authorized to fill prescriptions. The central fill pharmacy must also verify the registration for all retail pharmacies for which it is authorized to fill prescriptions. These records must be made available upon request for inspection by DEA.

[68 FR 37410, June 24, 2003]

INVENTORY REQUIREMENTS

§ 1304.11 Inventory requirements.

(a) *General requirements.* Each inventory shall contain a complete and accurate record of all controlled substances on hand on the date the inventory is taken, and shall be maintained in written, typewritten, or printed form at the registered location. An inventory taken by use of an oral recording device must be promptly transcribed. Controlled substances shall be deemed to be "on hand" if they are in the possession of or under the control of the registrant, including substances returned by a customer, ordered by a customer but not yet invoiced, stored in a warehouse on behalf of the registrant, and substances in the possession of employees of the registrant and intended for distribution as complimentary samples. A separate inventory shall be made for each registered location and each independent activity registered, except as provided in paragraph (e)(4) of this section. In the event controlled substances in the possession or under the control of the registrant are stored at a location for which he/she is not registered, the substances shall be included in the inventory of the registered location to which they are subject to control or to which the person possessing the substance is responsible. The inventory may be taken either as of opening of business or as of the close of business on the inventory date and it shall be indicated on the inventory.

(b) *Initial inventory date.* Every person required to keep records shall take an inventory of all stocks of controlled substances on hand on the date he/she first engages in the manufacture, distribution, or dispensing of controlled substances, in accordance with paragraph (e) of this section as applicable.

In the event a person commences business with no controlled substances on hand, he/she shall record this fact as the initial inventory.

(c) *Biennial inventory date.* After the initial inventory is taken, the registrant shall take a new inventory of all stocks of controlled substances on hand at least every two years. The biennial inventory may be taken on any date which is within two years of the previous biennial inventory date.

(d) *Inventory date for newly controlled substances.* On the effective date of a rule by the Administrator pursuant to §§ 1308.45, 1308.46, or 1308.47 of this chapter adding a substance to any schedule of controlled substances, which substance was, immediately prior to that date, not listed on any such schedule, every registrant required to keep records who possesses that substance shall take an inventory of all stocks of the substance on hand. Thereafter, such substance shall be included in each inventory made by the registrant pursuant to paragraph (c) of this section.

(e) *Inventories of manufacturers, distributors, dispensers, researchers, importers, exporters and chemical analysts.* Each person registered or authorized (by § 1301.13 or §§ 1307.11–1307.13 of this chapter) to manufacture, distribute, dispense, import, export, conduct research or chemical analysis with controlled substances and required to keep records pursuant to § 1304.03 shall include in the inventory the information listed below.

(1) *Inventories of manufacturers.* Each person registered or authorized to manufacture controlled substances shall include the following information in the inventory:

(i) For each controlled substance in bulk form to be used in (or capable of use in) the manufacture of the same or other controlled or non-controlled substances in finished form, the inventory shall include:

(A) The name of the substance and

(B) The total quantity of the substance to the nearest metric unit weight consistent with unit size.

(ii) For each controlled substance in the process of manufacture on the inventory date, the inventory shall include:

(A) The name of the substance;

(B) The quantity of the substance in each batch and/or stage of manufacture, identified by the batch number or other appropriate identifying number; and

(C) The physical form which the substance is to take upon completion of the manufacturing process (e.g., granulations, tablets, capsules, or solutions), identified by the batch number or other appropriate identifying number, and if possible the finished form of the substance (e.g., 10-milligram tablet or 10-milligram concentration per fluid ounce or milliliter) and the number or volume thereof.

(iii) For each controlled substance in finished form the inventory shall include:

(A) The name of the substance;

(B) Each finished form of the substance (e.g., 10-milligram tablet or 10-milligram concentration per fluid ounce or milliliter);

(C) The number of units or volume of each finished form in each commercial container (e.g., 100-tablet bottle or 3-milliliter vial); and

(D) The number of commercial containers of each such finished form (e.g. four 100-tablet bottles or six 3-milliliter vials).

(iv) For each controlled substance not included in paragraphs (e)(1) (i), (ii) or (iii) of this section (e.g., damaged, defective or impure substances awaiting disposal, substances held for quality control purposes, or substances maintained for extemporaneous compoundings) the inventories shall include:

(A) The name of the substance;

(B) The total quantity of the substance to the nearest metric unit weight or the total number of units of finished form; and

(C) The reason for the substance being maintained by the registrant and whether such substance is capable of use in the manufacture of any controlled substance in finished form.

(2) *Inventories of distributors.* Except for reverse distributors covered by paragraph (e)(3) of this section, each

person registered or authorized to distribute controlled substances shall include in the inventory the same information required of manufacturers pursuant to paragraphs (e)(1)(iii) and (iv) of this section.

(3) *Inventories of dispensers, researchers, and reverse distributors.* Each person registered or authorized to dispense, conduct research, or act as a reverse distributor with controlled substances shall include in the inventory the same information required of manufacturers pursuant to paragraphs (e)(1)(iii) and (iv) of this section. In determining the number of units of each finished form of a controlled substance in a commercial container which has been opened, the dispenser, researcher, or reverse distributor shall do as follows:

(i) If the substance is listed in Schedule I or II, make an exact count or measure of the contents, or

(ii) If the substance is listed in Schedule III, IV or V, make an estimated count or measure of the contents, unless the container holds more than 1,000 tablets or capsules in which case he/she must make an exact count of the contents.

(4) *Inventories of importers and exporters.* Each person registered or authorized to import or export controlled substances shall include in the inventory the same information required of manufacturers pursuant to paragraphs (e)(1) (iii) and (iv) of this section. Each such person who is also registered as a manufacturer or as a distributor shall include in his/her inventory as an importer or exporter only those stocks of controlled substances that are actually separated from his stocks as a manufacturer or as a distributor (e.g., in transit or in storage for shipment).

(5) *Inventories of chemical analysts.* Each person registered or authorized to conduct chemical analysis with controlled substances shall include in his inventory the same information required of manufacturers pursuant to paragraphs (e)(1) (iii) and (iv) of this section as to substances which have been manufactured, imported, or received by such person. If less than 1 kilogram of any controlled substance (other than a hallucinogenic controlled substance listed in Schedule I), or less than 20 grams of a hallucinogenic sub-

stance listed in Schedule I (other than lysergic acid diethylamide), or less than 0.5 gram of lysergic acid diethylamide, is on hand at the time of inventory, that substance need not be included in the inventory. Laboratories of the Administration may possess up to 150 grams of any hallucinogenic substance in Schedule I without regard to a need for an inventory of those substances. No inventory is required of known or suspected controlled substances received as evidentiary materials for analysis.

[62 FR 13959, Mar. 24, 1997, as amended at 68 FR 41228, July 11, 2003]

CONTINUING RECORDS

§ 1304.21 General requirements for continuing records.

(a) Every registrant required to keep records pursuant to § 1304.03 shall maintain on a current basis a complete and accurate record of each such substance manufactured, imported, received, sold, delivered, exported, or otherwise disposed of by him/her, except that no registrant shall be required to maintain a perpetual inventory.

(b) Separate records shall be maintained by a registrant for each registered location except as provided in § 1304.04 (a). In the event controlled substances are in the possession or under the control of a registrant at a location for which he is not registered, the substances shall be included in the records of the registered location to which they are subject to control or to which the person possessing the substance is responsible.

(c) Separate records shall be maintained by a registrant for each independent activity for which he/she is registered, except as provided in § 1304.22(d).

(d) In recording dates of receipt, importation, distribution, exportation, or other transfers, the date on which the controlled substances are actually received, imported, distributed, exported, or otherwise transferred shall be used as the date of receipt or distribution of any documents of transfer (e.g., invoices or packing slips).

[36 FR 7792, Apr. 24, 1971, as amended at 36 FR 13386, July 21, 1971. Redesignated at 38 FR 26609, Sept. 24, 1973, as amended at 62 FR 13960, Mar. 24, 1997]

§1304.22 Records for manufacturers, distributors, dispensers, researchers, importers and exporters.

Each person registered or authorized (by §1301.13(e) or §§1307.11–1307.13 of this chapter) to manufacture, distribute, dispense, import, export or conduct research with controlled substances shall maintain records with the information listed below.

(a) *Records for manufacturers.* Each person registered or authorized to manufacture controlled substances shall maintain records with the following information:

(1) For each controlled substance in bulk form to be used in, or capable of use in, or being used in, the manufacture of the same or other controlled or noncontrolled substances in finished form,

(i) The name of the substance;

(ii) The quantity manufactured in bulk form by the registrant, including the date, quantity and batch or other identifying number of each batch manufactured;

(iii) The quantity received from other persons, including the date and quantity of each receipt and the name, address, and registration number of the other person from whom the substance was received;

(iv) The quantity imported directly by the registrant (under a registration as an importer) for use in manufacture by him/her, including the date, quantity, and import permit or declaration number for each importation;

(v) The quantity used to manufacture the same substance in finished form, including:

(A) The date and batch or other identifying number of each manufacture;

(B) The quantity used in the manufacture;

(C) The finished form (e.g., 10-milligram tablets or 10-milligram concentration per fluid ounce or milliliter);

(D) The number of units of finished form manufactured;

(E) The quantity used in quality control;

(F) The quantity lost during manufacturing and the causes therefore, if known;

(G) The total quantity of the substance contained in the finished form;

(H) The theoretical and actual yields; and

(I) Such other information as is necessary to account for all controlled substances used in the manufacturing process;

(vi) The quantity used to manufacture other controlled and noncontrolled substances, including the name of each substance manufactured and the information required in paragraph (a)(1)(v) of this section;

(vii) The quantity distributed in bulk form to other persons, including the date and quantity of each distribution and the name, address, and registration number of each person to whom a distribution was made;

(viii) The quantity exported directly by the registrant (under a registration as an exporter), including the date, quantity, and export permit or declaration number of each exportation;

(ix) The quantity distributed or disposed of in any other manner by the registrant (e.g., by distribution of complimentary samples or by destruction), including the date and manner of distribution or disposal, the name, address, and registration number of the person to whom distributed, and the quantity distributed or disposed; and

(x) The originals of all written certifications of available procurement quotas submitted by other persons (as required by §1303.12(f) of this chapter) relating to each order requiring the distribution of a basic class of controlled substance listed in Schedule I or II.

(2) For each controlled substance in finished form,

(i) The name of the substance;

(ii) Each finished form (e.g., 10-milligram tablet or 10-milligram concentration per fluid ounce or milliliter) and the number of units or volume of finished form in each commercial container (e.g., 100-tablet bottle or 3-milliliter vial);

(iii) The number of containers of each such commercial finished form manufactured from bulk form by the registrant, including the information required pursuant to paragraph (a)(1)(v) of this section;

(iv) The number of units of finished forms and/or commercial containers acquired from other persons, including the date of and number of units and/or commercial containers in each acquisition to inventory and the name, address, and registration number of the person from whom the units were acquired;

(v) The number of units of finished forms and/or commercial containers imported directly by the person (under a registration or authorization to import), including the date of, the number of units and/or commercial containers in, and the import permit or declaration number for, each importation;

(vi) The number of units and/or commercial containers manufactured by the registrant from units in finished form received from others or imported, including:

(A) The date and batch or other identifying number of each manufacture;

(B) The operation performed (e.g., repackaging or relabeling);

(C) The number of units of finished form used in the manufacture, the number manufactured and the number lost during manufacture, with the causes for such losses, if known; and

(D) Such other information as is necessary to account for all controlled substances used in the manufacturing process;

(vii) The number of commercial containers distributed to other persons, including the date of and number of containers in each reduction from inventory, and the name, address, and registration number of the person to whom the containers were distributed;

(viii) The number of commercial containers exported directly by the registrant (under a registration as an exporter), including the date, number of containers and export permit or declaration number for each exportation; and

(ix) The number of units of finished forms and/or commercial containers distributed or disposed of in any other manner by the registrant (e.g., by distribution of complimentary samples or by destruction), including the date and manner of distribution or disposal, the name, address, and registration number of the person to whom distributed, and the quantity in finished form distributed or disposed.

(b) *Records for distributors.* Except as provided in paragraph (e) of this section, each person registered or authorized to distribute controlled substances shall maintain records with the same information required of manufacturers pursuant to paragraphs (a)(2)(i), (ii), (iv), (v), (vii), (viii) and (ix) of this section.

(c) *Records for dispensers and researchers.* Each person registered or authorized to dispense or conduct research with controlled substances shall maintain records with the same information required of manufacturers pursuant to paragraph (a)(2)(i), (ii), (iv), (vii), and (ix) of this section. In addition, records shall be maintained of the number of units or volume of such finished form dispensed, including the name and address of the person to whom it was dispensed, the date of dispensing, the number of units or volume dispensed, and the written or typewritten name or initials of the individual who dispensed or administered the substance on behalf of the dispenser. In addition to the requirements of this paragraph, practitioners dispensing gamma-hydroxybutyric acid under a prescription must also comply with § 1304.26.

(d) *Records for importers and exporters.* Each person registered or authorized to import or export controlled substances shall maintain records with the same information required of manufacturers pursuant to paragraphs (a)(2) (i), (iv), (v) and (vii) of this section. In addition, the quantity disposed of in any other manner by the registrant (except quantities used in manufacturing by an importer under a registration as a manufacturer), which quantities are to be recorded pursuant to paragraphs (a)(1) (iv) and (v) of this section; and the quantity (or number of units or volume in finished form) exported, including the date, quantity (or number of units or volume), and the export permit or declaration number for each exportation, but excluding all quantities (and number of units and volumes) manufactured by an exporter under a registration as a manufacturer, which quantities (and numbers of units and volumes) are to be recorded pursuant to paragraphs (a)(1)(xiii) or (a)(2)(xiii) of this section.

(e) *Records for reverse distributors.* Each person registered to distribute controlled substances as a reverse distributor shall maintain records with the following information for each controlled substance:

(1) For each controlled substance in bulk form the following:

(i) The name of the controlled substance.

(ii) The total quantity of the controlled substance to the nearest metric unit weight consistent with unit size.

(iii) The quantity received from other persons, including the date and quantity of each receipt and the name, address, and registration number of the other person from whom the controlled substance was received.

(iv) The quantity returned to the original manufacturer of the controlled substance or the manufacturer's agent, including the date of and quantity of each distribution and the name, address and registration number of the manufacturer or manufacturer's agent to whom the controlled substance was distributed.

(v) The quantity disposed of including the date and manner of disposal and the signatures of two responsible employees of the registrant who witnessed the disposal.

(2) For each controlled substance in finished form the following:

(i) The name of the substance.

(ii) Each finished form (*e.g.*, 10-milligram tablet or 10-milligram concentration per fluid ounce or milliliter) and the number of units or volume of finished form in each commercial container (*e.g.*, 100-tablet bottle or 3-milliliter vial).

(iii) The number of commercial containers of each such finished form received from other persons, including the date of and number of containers in each receipt and the name, address, and registration number of the person from whom the containers were received.

(iv) The number of commercial containers of each such finished form distributed back to the original manufacturer of the substance or the manufacturer's agent, including the date of and number of containers in each distribution and the name, address, and registration number of the manufacturer or manufacturer's agent to whom the containers were distributed.

(v) The number of units or volume of finished forms and/or commercial containers disposed of including the date and manner of disposal, the quantity of the substance in finished form disposed, and the signatures of two responsible employees of the registrant who witnessed the disposal.

[62 FR 13960, Mar. 24, 1997, as amended at 68 FR 41229, July 11, 2003; 70 FR 293, Jan. 4, 2005]

§1304.23 Records for chemical analysts.

(a) Each person registered or authorized (by §1301.22(b) of this chapter) to conduct chemical analysis with controlled substances shall maintain records with the following information (to the extent known and reasonably ascertainable by him) for each controlled substance:

(1) The name of the substance;

(2) The form or forms in which the substance is received, imported, or manufactured by the registrant (e.g., powder, granulation, tablet, capsule, or solution) and the concentration of the substance in such form (e.g., C.P., U.S.P., N.F., 10-milligram tablet or 10-milligram concentration per milliliter);

(3) The total number of the forms received, imported or manufactured (e.g., 100 tablets, thirty 1-milliliter vials, or 10 grams of powder), including the date and quantity of each receipt, importation, or manufacture and the name, address, and registration number, if any, of the person from whom the substance was received;

(4) The quantity distributed, exported, or destroyed in any manner by the registrant (except quantities used in chemical analysis or other laboratory work), including the date and manner of distribution, exportation, or destruction, and the name, address, and registration number, if any, of each person to whom the substance was distributed or exported.

(b) Records of controlled substances used in chemical analysis or other laboratory work are not required.

(c) Records relating to known or suspected controlled substances received as evidentiary material for analysis are not required under paragraph (a) of this section.

[36 FR 7793, Apr. 24, 1971, as amended at 36 FR 13386, July 21, 1971; 36 FR 18732, Sept. 21, 1971. Redesignated at 38 FR 26609, Sept. 24, 1973, and further redesignated at 62 FR 13961, Mar. 24, 1997]

§ 1304.24 Records for maintenance treatment programs and detoxification treatment programs.

(a) Each person registered or authorized (by § 1301.22 of this chapter) to maintain and/or detoxify controlled substance users in a narcotic treatment program shall maintain records with the following information for each narcotic controlled substance:

(1) Name of substance;

(2) Strength of substance;

(3) Dosage form;

(4) Date dispensed;

(5) Adequate identification of patient (consumer);

(6) Amount consumed;

(7) Amount and dosage form taken home by patient; and

(8) Dispenser's initials.

(b) The records required by paragraph (a) of this section will be maintained in a dispensing log at the narcotic treatment program site and will be maintained in compliance with § 1304.22 without reference to § 1304.03.

(c) All sites which compound a bulk narcotic solution from bulk narcotic powder to liquid for on-site use must keep a separate batch record of the compounding.

(d) Records of identity, diagnosis, prognosis, or treatment of any patients which are maintained in connection with the performance of a narcotic treatment program shall be confidential, except that such records may be disclosed for purposes and under the circumstances authorized by part 310 and 42 CFR part 2.

[39 FR 37985, Oct. 25, 1974. Redesignated and amended at 62 FR 13961, Mar. 24, 1997]

§ 1304.25 Records for treatment programs which compound narcotics for treatment programs and other locations.

Each person registered or authorized by § 1301.22 of this chapter to compound narcotic drugs for off-site use in a narcotic treatment program shall maintain records which include the following information for each narcotic drug:

(a) For each narcotic controlled substance in bulk form to be used in, or capable of use in, or being used in, the compounding of the same or other noncontrolled substances in finished form:

(1) The name of the substance;

(2) The quantity compounded in bulk form by the registrant, including the date, quantity and batch or other identifying number of each batch compounded;

(3) The quantity received from other persons, including the date and quantity of each receipt and the name, address and registration number of the other person from whom the substance was received;

(4) The quantity imported directly by the registrant (under a registration as an importer) for use in compounding by him, including the date, quantity and import permit or declaration number of each importation;

(5) The quantity used to compound the same substance in finished form, including:

(i) The date and batch or other identifying number of each compounding;

(ii) The quantity used in the compound;

(iii) The finished form (e.g., 10-milligram tablets or 10-milligram concentration per fluid ounce or milliliter;

(iv) The number of units of finished form compounded;

(v) The quantity used in quality control;

(vi) The quantity lost during compounding and the causes therefore, if known;

(vii) The total quantity of the substance contained in the finished form;

(viii) The theoretical and actual yields; and

(ix) Such other information as is necessary to account for all controlled substances used in the compounding process;

(6) The quantity used to manufacture other controlled and non-controlled substances; including the name of each substance manufactured and the information required in paragraph (a)(5) of this section;

(7) The quantity distributed in bulk form to other programs, including the date and quantity of each distribution and the name, address and registration number of each program to whom a distribution was made;

(8) The quantity exported directly by the registrant (under a registration as an exporter), including the date, quantity, and export permit or declaration number of each exploration; and

(9) The quantity disposed of by destruction, including the reason, date and manner of destruction. All other destruction of narcotic controlled substances will comply with §1307.22.

(b) For each narcotic controlled substance in finished form:

(1) The name of the substance;

(2) Each finished form (e.g., 10-milligram tablet or 10 milligram concentration per fluid ounce or milliliter) and the number of units or volume or finished form in each commercial container (e.g., 100-tablet bottle or 3-milliliter vial);

(3) The number of containers of each such commercial finished form compounded from bulk form by the registrant, including the information required pursuant to paragraph (a)(5) of this section;

(4) The number of units of finished forms and/or commercial containers received from other persons, including the date of and number of units and/or commercial containers in each receipt and the name, address and registration number of the person from whom the units were received;

(5) The number of units of finished forms and/or commercial containers imported directly by the person (under a registration or authorization to import), including the date of, the number of units and/or commercial containers in, and the import permit or declaration number for, each importation;

(6) The number of units and/or commercial containers compounded by the registrant from units in finished form

received from others or imported, including:

(i) The date and batch or other identifying number of each compounding;

(ii) The operation performed (e.g., repackaging or relabeling);

(iii) The number of units of finished form used in the compound, the number compounded and the number lost during compounding, with the causes for such losses, if known; and

(iv) Such other information as is necessary to account for all controlled substances used in the compounding process;

(7) The number of containers distributed to other programs, including the date, the number of containers in each distribution, and the name, address and registration number of the program to whom the containers were distributed;

(8) The number of commercial containers exported directly by the registrant (under a registration as an exporter), including the date, number of containers and export permit or declaration number for each exportation; and

(9) The number of units of finished forms and/or commercial containers destroyed in any manner by the registrant, including the reason, the date and manner of destruction. All other destruction of narcotic controlled substances will comply with §1307.22.

[39 FR 37985, Oct. 25, 1974. Redesignated at 62 FR 13961, Mar. 24, 1997]

§1304.26 Additional recordkeeping requirements applicable to drug products containing gamma-hydroxy-butyric acid.

In addition to the recordkeeping requirements for dispensers and researchers provided in §1304.22, practitioners dispensing gamma-hydroxybutyric acid that is manufactured or distributed in accordance with an application under section 505 of the Federal Food, Drug, and Cosmetic Act must maintain and make available for inspection and copying by the Attorney General, all of the following information for each prescription:

(a) Name of the prescribing practitioner.

(b) Prescribing practitioner's Federal and State registration numbers, with the expiration dates of these registrations.

(c) Verification that the prescribing practitioner possesses the appropriate registration to prescribe this controlled substance.

(d) Patient's name and address.

(e) Patient's insurance provider, if available.

[70 FR 293, Jan. 4, 2005]

REPORTS

§ 1304.31 Reports from manufacturers importing narcotic raw material.

(a) Every manufacturer which imports or manufactures from narcotic raw material (opium, poppy straw, and concentrate of poppy straw) shall submit information which accounts for the importation and for all manufacturing operations performed between importation and the production in bulk or finished marketable products, standardized in accordance with the U.S. Pharmacopeia, National Formulary or other recognized medical standards. Reports shall be signed by the authorized official and submitted quarterly on company letterhead to the Drug Enforcement Administration, Drug and Chemical Evaluation Section, Washington, D.C. 20537, on or before the 15th day of the month immediately following the period for which it is submitted.

(b) The following information shall be submitted for each type of narcotic raw material (quantities are expressed as grams of anhydrous morphine alkaloid):

(1) Beginning inventory;

(2) Gains on reweighing;

(3) Imports;

(4) Other receipts;

(5) Quantity put into process;

(6) Losses on reweighing;

(7) Other dispositions and

(8) Ending inventory.

(c) The following information shall be submitted for each narcotic raw material derivative including morphine, codeine, thebaine, oxycodone, hydrocodone, medicinal opium, manufacturing opium, crude alkaloids and other derivatives (quantities are expressed as grams of anhydrous base or anhydrous morphine alkaloid for manufacturing opium and medicinal opium):

(1) Beginning inventory;

(2) Gains on reweighing;

(3) Quantity extracted from narcotic raw material;

(4) Quantity produced/manufactured/synthesized;

(5) Quantity sold;

(6) Quantity returned to conversion processes for reworking;

(7) Quantity used for conversion;

(8) Quantity placed in process;

(9) Other dispositions;

(10) Losses on reweighing and

(11) Ending inventory.

(d) The following information shall be submitted for importation of each narcotic raw material:

(1) Import permit number;

(2) Date shipment arrived at the United States port of entry;

(3) Actual quantity shipped;

(4) Assay (percent) of morphine, codeine and thebaine and

(5) Quantity shipped, expressed as anhydrous morphine alkaloid.

(e) Upon importation of crude opium, samples will be selected and assays made by the importing manufacturer in the manner and according to the method specified in the U.S. Pharmacopoeia. Where final assay data is not determined at the time of rendering report, the report shall be made on the basis of the best data available, subject to adjustment, and the necessary adjusting entries shall be made on the next report.

(f) Where factory procedure is such that partial withdrawals of opium are made from individual containers, there shall be attached to each container a stock record card on which shall be kept a complete record of all withdrawals therefrom.

(g) All in-process inventories should be expressed in terms of end-products and not precursors. Once precursor material has been changed or placed into process for the manufacture of a specified end-product, it must no longer be accounted for as precursor stocks available for conversion or use, but rather as end-product in-process inventories.

[62 FR 13961, Mar. 24, 1997]

§1304.32 Reports of manufacturers importing coca leaves.

(a) Every manufacturer importing or manufacturing from raw coca leaves shall submit information accounting for the importation and for all manufacturing operations performed between the importation and the manufacture of bulk or finished products standardized in accordance with U.S. Pharmacopoeia, National Formulary, or other recognized standards. The reports shall be submitted quarterly on company letterhead to the Drug Enforcement Administration, Drug and Chemical Evaluation Section, Washington, DC 20537, on or before the 15th day of the month immediately following the period for which it is submitted.

(b) The following information shall be submitted for raw coca leaf, ecgonine, ecgonine for conversion or further manufacture, benzoylecgonine, manufacturing coca extracts (list for tinctures and extracts; and others separately), other crude alkaloids and other derivatives (quantities should be reported as grams of actual quantity involved and the cocaine alkaloid content or equivalency):

(1) Beginning inventory;
(2) Imports;
(3) Gains on reweighing;
(4) Quantity purchased;
(5) Quantity produced;
(6) Other receipts;
(7) Quantity returned to processes for reworking;
(8) Material used in purification for sale;
(9) Material used for manufacture or production;
(10) Losses on reweighing;
(11) Material used for conversion;
(12) Other dispositions and
(13) Ending inventory.

(c) The following information shall be submitted for importation of coca leaves:

(1) Import permit number;
(2) Date the shipment arrived at the United States port of entry;
(3) Actual quantity shipped;
(4) Assay (percent) of cocaine alkaloid and
(5) Total cocaine alkaloid content.

(d) Upon importation of coca leaves, samples will be selected and assays made by the importing manufacturer in accordance with recognized chemical procedures. These assays shall form the basis of accounting for such coca leaves, which shall be accounted for in terms of their cocaine alkaloid content or equivalency or their total anhydrous coca alkaloid content. Where final assay data is not determined at the time of submission, the report shall be made on the basis of the best data available, subject to adjustment, and the necessary adjusting entries shall be made on the next report.

(e) Where factory procedure is such that partial withdrawals of medicinal coca leaves are made from individual containers, there shall be attached to the container a stock record card on which shall be kept a complete record of withdrawals therefrom.

(f) All in-process inventories should be expressed in terms of end-products and not precursors. Once precursor material has been changed or placed into process for the manufacture of a specified end-product, it must no longer be accounted for as precursor stocks available for conversion or use, but rather as end-product in-process inventories.

[62 FR 13962, Mar. 24, 1997]

§1304.33 Reports to ARCOS.

(a) *Reports generally.* All reports required by this section shall be filed with the ARCOS Unit, PO 28293, Central Station, Washington, DC 20005 on DEA Form 333, or on media which contains the data required by DEA Form 333 and which is acceptable to the ARCOS Unit.

(b) *Frequency of reports.* Acquisition/Distribution transaction reports shall be filed every quarter not later than the 15th day of the month succeeding the quarter for which it is submitted; except that a registrant may be given permission to file more frequently (but not more frequently than monthly), depending on the number of transactions being reported each time by that registrant. Inventories shall provide data on the stocks of each reported controlled substance on hand as of the close of business on December 31 of each year, indicating whether the substance is in storage or in process of manufacturing. These reports shall be filed not later than January 15 of the following year. Manufacturing transaction reports shall be filed annually for each calendar year not later than January 15 of the following year, except that a registrant may be given permission to file more frequently (but not more frequently than quarterly).

(c) *Persons reporting.* For controlled substances in Schedules I, II, narcotic controlled substances in Schedule III, and gamma-hydroxybutyric acid drug product controlled substances in Schedule III, each person who is registered to manufacture in bulk or dosage form, or to package, repackage, label or relabel, and each person who is registered to distribute, including each person who is registered to reverse distribute, shall report acquisition/distribution transactions. In addition to reporting acquisition/distribution transactions, each person who is registered to manufacture controlled substances in bulk or dosage form shall report manufacturing transactions on controlled substances in Schedules I and II, each narcotic controlled substance listed in Schedules III, IV, and V, gamma-hydroxybutyric acid drug product controlled substances in Schedule III, and on each psychotropic controlled substance listed in Schedules III and IV as identified in paragraph (d) of this section.

(d) *Substances covered.* (1) Manufacturing and acquisition/distribution transaction reports shall include data on each controlled substance listed in Schedules I and II, on each narcotic controlled substance listed in Schedule III (but not on any material, compound, mixture or preparation containing a quantity of a substance having a stimulant effect on the central nervous system, which material, compound, mixture or preparation is listed in Schedule III or on any narcotic controlled substance listed in Schedule V), and on gamma-hydroxybutyric acid drug products listed in Schedule III. Additionally, reports on manufacturing transactions shall include the following psychotropic controlled substances listed in Schedules III and IV:

(i) Schedule III

(A) Benzphetamine;

(B) Cyclobarbital;

(C) Methyprylon; and

(D) Phendimetrazine.

(ii) Schedule IV

(A) Barbital;

(B) Diethylpropion (Amfepramone);

(C) Ethchlorvynol;

(D) Ethinamate;

(E) Lefetamine (SPA);

(F) Mazindol;

(G) Meprobamate;

(H) Methylphenobarbital;

(I) Phenobarbital;

(J) Phentermine; and

(K) Pipradrol.

(2) Data shall be presented in such a manner as to identify the particular form, strength, and trade name, if any, of the product containing the controlled substance for which the report is being made. For this purpose, persons filing reports shall utilize the National Drug Code Number assigned to the product under the National Drug Code System of the Food and Drug Administration.

(e) *Transactions reported.* Acquisition/distribution transaction reports shall provide data on each acquisition to inventory (identifying whether it is, e.g., by purchase or transfer, return from a customer, or supply by the Federal Government) and each reduction from inventory (identifying whether it is, e.g., by sale or transfer, theft, destruction or seizure by Government agencies). Manufacturing reports shall provide data on material manufactured, manufacture from other material, use in manufacturing other material and use in producing dosage forms.

(f) *Exceptions.* A registered institutional practitioner who repackages or relabels exclusively for distribution or who distributes exclusively to (for dispensing by) agents, employees, or affiliated institutional practitioners of the registrant may be exempted from filing reports under this section by applying to the ARCOS Unit of the Administration.

(Approved by the Office of Management and Budget under control number 1117–0003)

[62 FR 13962, Mar. 24, 1997, as amended at 68 FR 41229, July 11, 2003; 70 FR 294, Jan. 4, 2005]

PART 1305—ORDERS FOR SCHEDULE I AND II CONTROLLED SUBSTANCES

Subpart A—General Requirements

AUTHORITY: 21 U.S.C. 821, 828, 871(b), unless otherwise noted.

SOURCE: 70 FR 16911, Apr. 1, 2005, unless otherwise noted.

Subpart A—General Requirements

§ 1305.01 Scope of part 1305.

Procedures governing the issuance, use, and preservation of orders for Schedule I and II controlled substances are set forth generally by section 308 of the Act (21 U.S.C. 828) and specifically by the sections of this part.

§ 1305.02 Definitions.

Any term contained in this part shall have the definition set forth in the Act or part 1300 of this chapter.

§ 1305.03 Distributions requiring a Form 222 or a digitally signed electronic order.

Either a DEA Form 222 or its electronic equivalent as set forth in subpart C of this part and Part 1311 of this chapter is required for each distribution of a Schedule I or II controlled substance except for the following:

(a) Distributions to persons exempted from registration under Part 1301 of this chapter.

(b) Exports from the United States that conform with the requirements of the Act.

(c) Deliveries to a registered analytical laboratory or its agent approved by DEA.

(d) Delivery from a central fill pharmacy, as defined in § 1300.01(b)(44) of this chapter, to a retail pharmacy.

§ 1305.04 Persons entitled to order Schedule I and II controlled substances.

(a) Only persons who are registered with DEA under section 303 of the Act (21 U.S.C. 823) to handle Schedule I or II controlled substances, and persons who are registered with DEA under section 1008 of the Act (21 U.S.C. 958) to export these substances may obtain and use DEA Form 222 (order forms) or issue electronic orders for these substances. Persons not registered to handle Schedule I or II controlled substances and persons registered only to import controlled substances are not entitled to obtain Form 222 or issue electronic orders for these substances.

(b) An order for Schedule I or II controlled substances may be executed only on behalf of the registrant named on the order and only if his or her registration for the substances being purchased has not expired or been revoked or suspended.

§ 1305.05 Power of attorney.

(a) A registrant may authorize one or more individuals, whether or not located at his or her registered location, to issue orders for Schedule I and II

71

controlled substances on the registrant's behalf by executing a power of attorney for each such individual, if the power of attorney is retained in the files, with executed Forms 222 where applicable, for the same period as any order bearing the signature of the attorney. The power of attorney must be available for inspection together with other order records.

(b) A registrant may revoke any power of attorney at any time by executing a notice of revocation.

(c) The power of attorney and notice of revocation must be similar to the following format:

Power of Attorney for DEA Forms 222 and Electronic Orders

_____
(Name of registrant)

_____
(Address of registrant)

_____
(DEA registration number)

I, _____ (name of person granting power), the undersigned, who am authorized to sign the current application for registration of the above-named registrant under the Controlled Substances Act or Controlled Substances Import and Export Act, have made, constituted, and appointed, and by these presents, do make, constitute, and appoint _____ (name of attorney-in-fact), my true and lawful attorney for me in my name, place, and stead, to execute applications for Forms 222 and to sign orders for Schedule I and II controlled substances, whether these orders be on Form 222 or electronic, in accordance with 21 U.S.C. 828 and Part 1305 of Title 21 of the Code of Federal Regulations. I hereby ratify and confirm all that said attorney must lawfully do or cause to be done by virtue hereof.

_____
(Signature of person granting power)

I, _____ (name of attorney-in-fact), hereby affirm that I am the person named herein as attorney-in-fact and that the signature affixed hereto is my signature.

(signature of attorney-in-fact)

Witnesses:

1. _____

2. _____

Signed and dated on the _____ day of _____, (year), at _____ .

Notice of Revocation

The foregoing power of attorney is hereby revoked by the undersigned, who is authorized to sign the current application for registration of the above-named registrant under the Controlled Substances Act or the Controlled Substances Import and Export Act. Written notice of this revocation has been given to the attorney-in-fact _____ this same day.

_____
(Signature of person revoking power)

Witnesses:

1. _____

2. _____

Signed and dated on the _____ day of _____ , (year), at _____ .

(d) A power of attorney must be executed by the person who signed the most recent application for DEA registration or reregistration; the person to whom the power of attorney is being granted; and two witnesses.

(e) A power of attorney must be revoked by the person who signed the most recent application for DEA registration or reregistration, and two witnesses.

§ 1305.06 Persons entitled to fill orders for Schedule I and II controlled substances.

An order for Schedule I and II controlled substances, whether on a DEA Form 222 or an electronic order, may be filled only by a person registered with DEA as a manufacturer or distributor of controlled substances listed in Schedule I or II pursuant to section 303 of the Act (21 U.S.C. 823) or as an importer of such substances pursuant to section 1008 of the Act (21 U.S.C. 958), except for the following:

(a) A person registered with DEA to dispense the substances, or to export the substances, if he/she is discontinuing business or if his/her registration is expiring without reregistration, may dispose of any Schedule I or II controlled substances in his/her possession with a DEA Form 222 or an electronic order in accordance with § 1301.52 of this chapter.

(b) A purchaser who has obtained any Schedule I or II controlled substance by either a DEA Form 222 or an electronic order may return the substance to the supplier of the substance with either a DEA Form 222 or an electronic order from the supplier.

(c) A person registered to dispense Schedule II substances may distribute the substances to another dispenser with either a DEA Form 222 or an electronic order only in the circumstances described in § 1307.11 of this chapter.

(d) A person registered or authorized to conduct chemical analysis or research with controlled substances may distribute a Schedule I or II controlled substance to another person registered or authorized to conduct chemical analysis, instructional activities, or research with the substances with either a DEA Form 222 or an electronic order, if the distribution is for the purpose of furthering the chemical analysis, instructional activities, or research.

(e) A person registered as a compounder of narcotic substances for use at off-site locations in conjunction with a narcotic treatment program at the compounding location, who is authorized to handle Schedule II narcotics, is authorized to fill either a DEA Form 222 or an electronic order for distribution of narcotic drugs to off-site narcotic treatment programs only.

§ 1305.07 Special procedure for filling certain orders.

A supplier of carfentanil, etorphine hydrochloride, or diprenorphine, if he or she determines that the purchaser is a veterinarian engaged in zoo and exotic animal practice, wildlife management programs, or research, and is authorized by the Administrator to handle these substances, may fill the order in accordance with the procedures set forth in § 1305.17 except that:

(a) A DEA Form 222 or an electronic order for carfentanil, etorphine hydrochloride, and diprenorphine must contain only these substances in reasonable quantities.

(b) The substances must be shipped, under secure conditions using substantial packaging material with no markings on the outside that would indicate

the content, only to the purchaser's registered location.

Subpart B—DEA Form 222

§ 1305.11 Procedure for obtaining DEA Forms 222.

(a) DEA Forms 222 are issued in mailing envelopes containing either seven or fourteen forms, each form containing an original, duplicate, and triplicate copy (respectively, Copy 1, Copy 2, and Copy 3). A limit, which is based on the business activity of the registrant, will be imposed on the number of DEA Forms 222, which will be furnished on any requisition unless additional forms are specifically requested and a reasonable need for such additional forms is shown.

(b) Any person applying for a registration that would entitle him or her to obtain a DEA Form 222 may requisition the forms by so indicating on the application form; a DEA Form 222 will be supplied upon the registration of the applicant. Any person holding a registration entitling him or her to obtain a DEA Form 222 may requisition the forms for the first time by contacting any Division Office or the Registration Section of the Administration. Any person already holding a DEA Form 222 may requisition additional forms on DEA Form 222a, which is mailed to a registrant approximately 30 days after each shipment of DEA Forms 222 to that registrant, or by contacting any Division Office or the Registration Section of the Administration. All requisition forms (DEA Form 222a) must be submitted to the DEA Registration Section.

(c) Each requisition must show the name, address, and registration number of the registrant and the number of books of DEA Forms 222 desired. Each requisition must be signed and dated by the same person who signed the most recent application for registration or for reregistration, or by any person authorized to obtain and execute DEA Forms 222 by a power of attorney under § 1305.05.

(d) DEA Forms 222 will be serially numbered and issued with the name, address, and registration number of the registrant, the authorized activity, and schedules of the registrant. This information cannot be altered or changed by the registrant; any errors must be corrected by the Registration Section of the Administration by returning the forms with notification of the error.

§ 1305.12 Procedure for executing DEA Forms 222.

(a) A purchaser must prepare and execute a DEA Form 222 simultaneously in triplicate by means of interleaved carbon sheets that are part of the DEA Form 222. DEA Form 222 must be prepared by use of a typewriter, pen, or indelible pencil.

(b) Only one item may be entered on each numbered line. An item must consist of one or more commercial or bulk containers of the same finished or bulk form and quantity of the same substance. The number of lines completed must be noted on that form at the bottom of the form, in the space provided. DEA Forms 222 for carfentanil, etorphine hydrochloride, and diprenorphine must contain only these substances.

(c) The name and address of the supplier from whom the controlled substances are being ordered must be entered on the form. Only one supplier may be listed on any form.

(d) Each DEA Form 222 must be signed and dated by a person authorized to sign an application for registration or a person granted power of attorney to sign a Form 222 under § 1305.05. The name of the purchaser, if different from the individual signing the DEA Form 222, must also be inserted in the signature space.

(e) Unexecuted DEA Forms 222 may be kept and may be executed at a location other than the registered location printed on the form, provided that all unexecuted forms are delivered promptly to the registered location upon an inspection of the location by any officer authorized to make inspections, or to enforce, any Federal, State, or local law regarding controlled substances.

§ 1305.13 Procedure for filling DEA Forms 222.

(a) A purchaser must submit Copy 1 and Copy 2 of the DEA Form 222 to the supplier and retain Copy 3 in the purchaser's files.

(b) A supplier may fill the order, if possible and if the supplier desires to do so, and must record on Copies 1 and 2 the number of commercial or bulk containers furnished on each item and the date on which the containers are shipped to the purchaser. If an order cannot be filled in its entirety, it may be filled in part and the balance supplied by additional shipments within 60 days following the date of the DEA Form 222. No DEA Form 222 is valid more than 60 days after its execution by the purchaser, except as specified in paragraph (f) of this section.

(c) The controlled substances must be shipped only to the purchaser and the location printed by the Administration on the DEA Form 222, except as specified in paragraph (f) of this section.

(d) The supplier must retain Copy 1 of the DEA Form 222 for his or her files and forward Copy 2 to the Special Agent in Charge of the Drug Enforcement Administration in the area in which the supplier is located. Copy 2 must be forwarded at the close of the month during which the order is filled. If an order is filled by partial shipments, Copy 2 must be forwarded at the close of the month during which the final shipment is made or the 60-day validity period expires.

(e) The purchaser must record on Copy 3 of the DEA Form 222 the number of commercial or bulk containers furnished on each item and the dates on which the containers are received by the purchaser.

(f) DEA Forms 222 submitted by registered procurement officers of the Defense Supply Center of the Defense Logistics Agency for delivery to armed services establishments within the United States may be shipped to locations other than the location printed on the DEA Form 222, and in partial shipments at different times not to exceed six months from the date of the order, as designated by the procurement officer when submitting the order.

§ 1305.14 Procedure for endorsing DEA Forms 222.

(a) A DEA Form 222, made out to any supplier who cannot fill all or a part of the order within the time limitation set forth in § 1305.13, may be endorsed to another supplier for filling. The endorsement must be made only by the supplier to whom the DEA Form 222 was first made, must state (in the spaces provided on the reverse sides of Copies 1 and 2 of the DEA Form 222) the name and address of the second supplier, and must be signed by a person authorized to obtain and execute DEA Forms 222 on behalf of the first supplier. The first supplier may not fill any part of an order on an endorsed form. The second supplier may fill the order, if possible and if the supplier desires to do so, in accordance with § 1305.13(b), (c), and (d), including shipping all substances directly to the purchaser.

(b) Distributions made on endorsed DEA Forms 222 must be reported by the second supplier in the same manner as all other distributions except that where the name of the supplier is requested on the reporting form, the second supplier must record the name, address, and registration number of the first supplier.

§ 1305.15 Unaccepted and defective DEA Forms 222.

(a) A DEA Form 222 must not be filled if either of the following apply:

(1) The order is not complete, legible, or properly prepared, executed, or endorsed.

(2) The order shows any alteration, erasure, or change of any description.

(b) If a DEA Form 222 cannot be filled for any reason under this section, the supplier must return Copies 1 and 2 to the purchaser with a statement as to the reason (e.g., illegible or altered).

(c) A supplier may for any reason refuse to accept any order and if a supplier refuses to accept the order, a statement that the order is not accepted is sufficient for purposes of this paragraph.

(d) When a purchaser receives an unaccepted order, Copies 1 and 2 of the DEA Form 222 and the statement must be attached to Copy 3 and retained in the files of the purchaser in accordance with § 1305.17. A defective DEA Form 222 may not be corrected; it must be replaced by a new DEA Form 222 for the order to be filled.

§ 1305.16 Lost and stolen DEA Forms 222.

(a) If a purchaser ascertains that an unfilled DEA Form 222 has been lost, he or she must execute another in triplicate and attach a statement containing the serial number and date of the lost form, and stating that the goods covered by the first DEA Form 222 were not received through loss of that DEA Form 222. Copy 3 of the second form and a copy of the statement must be retained with Copy 3 of the DEA Form 222 first executed. A copy of the statement must be attached to Copies 1 and 2 of the second DEA Form 222 sent to the supplier. If the first DEA Form 222 is subsequently received by the supplier to whom it was directed, the supplier must mark upon the face "Not accepted" and return Copies 1 and 2 to the purchaser, who must attach it to Copy 3 and the statement.

(b) Whenever any used or unused DEA Forms 222 are stolen or lost (other than in the course of transmission) by any purchaser or supplier, the purchaser or supplier must immediately upon discovery of the theft or loss, report the theft or loss to the Special Agent in Charge of the Drug Enforcement Administration in the Divisional Office responsible for the area in which the registrant is located, stating the serial number of each form stolen or lost.

(c) If the theft or loss includes any original DEA Forms 222 received from purchasers and the supplier is unable to state the serial numbers of the DEA Forms 222, the supplier must report the date or approximate date of receipt and the names and addresses of the purchasers.

(d) If an entire book of DEA Forms 222 is lost or stolen, and the purchaser is unable to state the serial numbers of the DEA Forms 222 in the book, the purchaser must report, in lieu of the numbers of the forms contained in the book, the date or approximate date of issuance.

(e) If any unused DEA Form 222 reported stolen or lost is subsequently recovered or found, the Special Agent in Charge of the Drug Enforcement Administration in the Divisional Office responsible for the area in which the registrant is located must immediately be notified.

§ 1305.17 Preservation of DEA Forms 222.

(a) The purchaser must retain Copy 3 of each executed DEA Form 222 and all copies of unaccepted or defective forms with each statement attached.

(b) The supplier must retain Copy 1 of each DEA Form 222 that it has filled.

(c) DEA Forms 222 must be maintained separately from all other records of the registrant. DEA Forms 222 are required to be kept available for inspection for a period of two years. If a purchaser has several registered locations, the purchaser must retain Copy 3 of the executed DEA Form 222 and any attached statements or other related documents (not including unexecuted DEA Forms 222, which may be kept elsewhere under § 1305.12(e)), at the registered location printed on the DEA Form 222.

(d) The supplier of carfentanil, etorphine hydrochloride, and diprenorphine must maintain DEA Forms 222 for these substances separately from all other DEA Forms 222 and records required to be maintained by the registrant.

§ 1305.18 Return of unused DEA Forms 222.

If the registration of any purchaser terminates (because the purchaser dies, ceases legal existence, discontinues business or professional practice, or changes the name or address as shown on the purchaser's registration) or is suspended or revoked under § 1301.36 of this chapter for all Schedule I and II controlled substances for which the purchaser is registered, the purchaser must return all unused DEA Forms 222 to the nearest office of the Administration.

§ 1305.19 Cancellation and voiding of DEA Forms 222.

(a) A purchaser may cancel part or all of an order on a DEA Form 222 by notifying the supplier in writing of the cancellation. The supplier must indicate the cancellation on Copies 1 and 2 of the DEA Form 222 by drawing a line through the canceled items and printing "canceled" in the space provided for number of items shipped.

(b) A supplier may void part or all of an order on a DEA Form 222 by notifying the purchaser in writing of the voiding. The supplier must indicate the voiding in the manner prescribed for cancellation in paragraph (a) of this section.

Subpart C—Electronic Orders

§ 1305.21 Requirements for electronic orders.

(a) To be valid, the purchaser must sign an electronic order for a Schedule I or II controlled substance with a digital signature issued to the purchaser, or the purchaser's agent, by DEA as provided in part 1311 of this chapter.

(b) The following data fields must be included on an electronic order for Schedule I and II controlled substances:

(1) A unique number the purchaser assigns to track the order. The number must be in the following 9-character format: the last two digits of the year, X, and six characters as selected by the purchaser.

(2) The purchaser's DEA registration number.

(3) The name of the supplier.

(4) The complete address of the supplier (may be completed by either the purchaser or the supplier).

(5) The supplier's DEA registration number (may be completed by either the purchaser or the supplier).

(6) The date the order is signed.

(7) The name (including strength where appropriate) of the controlled substance product or the National Drug Code (NDC) number (the NDC number may be completed by either the purchaser or the supplier).

(8) The quantity in a single package or container.

(9) The number of packages or containers of each item ordered.

(c) An electronic order may include controlled substances that are not in schedules I and II and non-controlled substances.

§1305.22 Procedure for filling electronic orders.

(a) A purchaser must submit the order to a specific supplier. The supplier may initially process the order (e.g., entry of the order into the computer system, billing functions, inventory identification, etc.) centrally at any location, regardless of the location's registration with DEA. Following centralized processing, the supplier may distribute the order to one or more registered locations maintained by the supplier for filling. The registrant must maintain control of the processing of the order at all times.

(b) A supplier may fill the order for a Schedule I or II controlled substance, if possible and if the supplier desires to do so and is authorized to do so under §1305.06.

(c) A supplier must do the following before filling the order:

(1) Verify the integrity of the signature and the order by using software that complies with Part 1311 of this chapter to validate the order.

(2) Verify that the digital certificate has not expired.

(3) Check the validity of the certificate holder's certificate by checking the Certificate Revocation List. The supplier may cache the Certificate Revocation List until it expires.

(4) Verify the registrant's eligibility to order the controlled substances by checking the certificate extension data.

(d) The supplier must retain an electronic record of every order, and, linked to each order, a record of the number of commercial or bulk containers furnished on each item and the date on which the supplier shipped the containers to the purchaser. The linked record must also include any data on the original order that the supplier completes. Software used to handle digitally signed orders must comply with part 1311 of this chapter.

(e) If an order cannot be filled in its entirety, a supplier may fill it in part and supply the balance by additional shipments within 60 days following the date of the order. No order is valid more than 60 days after its execution by the purchaser, except as specified in paragraph (h) of this section.

(f) A supplier must ship the controlled substances to the registered location associated with the digital certificate used to sign the order, except as specified in paragraph (h) of this section.

(g) When a purchaser receives a shipment, the purchaser must create a record of the quantity of each item received and the date received. The record must be electronically linked to the original order and archived.

(h) Registered procurement officers of the Defense Supply Center of the Defense Logistics Agency may order controlled substances for delivery to armed services establishments within the United States. These orders may be shipped to locations other than the registered location, and in partial shipments at different times not to exceed six months from the date of the order, as designated by the procurement officer when submitting the order.

§1305.23 Endorsing electronic orders.

A supplier may not endorse an electronic order to another supplier to fill.

§1305.24 Central processing of orders.

(a) A supplier that has one or more registered locations and maintains a central processing computer system in which orders are stored may have one or more of the supplier's registered locations fill an electronic order if the supplier does the following:

(1) Assigns each item on the order to a specific registered location for filling.

(2) Creates a record linked to the central file noting both which items a location filled and the location identity.

(3) Ensures that no item is filled by more than one location.

(4) Maintains the original order with all linked records on the central computer system.

(b) A company that has central processing of orders must assign responsibility for filling parts of orders only to registered locations that the company owns and operates.

§1305.25 Unaccepted and defective electronic orders.

(a) No electronic order may be filled if:

(1) The required data fields have not been completed.

(2) The order is not signed using a digital certificate issued by DEA.

(3) The digital certificate used had expired or had been revoked prior to signature.

(4) The purchaser's public key will not validate the digital signature.

(5) The validation of the order shows that the order is invalid for any reason.

(b) If an order cannot be filled for any reason under this section, the supplier must notify the purchaser and provide a statement as to the reason (*e.g.*, improperly prepared or altered). A supplier may, for any reason, refuse to accept any order, and if a supplier refuses to accept the order, a statement that the order is not accepted is sufficient for purposes of this paragraph.

(c) When a purchaser receives an unaccepted electronic order from the supplier, the purchaser must electronically link the statement of nonacceptance to the original order. The original order and the statement must be retained in accordance with § 1305.27.

(d) Neither a purchaser nor a supplier may correct a defective order; the purchaser must issue a new order for the order to be filled.

§ 1305.26 Lost electronic orders.

(a) If a purchaser determines that an unfilled electronic order has been lost before or after receipt, the purchaser must provide, to the supplier, a signed statement containing the unique tracking number and date of the lost order and stating that the goods covered by the first order were not received through loss of that order.

(b) If the purchaser executes an order to replace the lost order, the purchaser must electronically link an electronic record of the second order and a copy of the statement with the record of the first order and retain them.

(c) If the supplier to whom the order was directed subsequently receives the first order, the supplier must indicate that it is "Not Accepted" and return it to the purchaser. The purchaser must link the returned order to the record of that order and the statement.

§ 1305.27 Preservation of electronic orders.

(a) A purchaser must, for each order filled, retain the original signed order and all linked records for that order for two years. The purchaser must also retain all copies of each unaccepted or defective order and each linked statement.

(b) A supplier must retain each original order filled and the linked records for two years.

(c) If electronic order records are maintained on a central server, the records must be readily retrievable at the registered location.

§ 1305.28 Canceling and voiding electronic orders.

(a) A supplier may void all or part of an electronic order by notifying the purchaser of the voiding. If the entire order is voided, the supplier must make an electronic copy of the order, indicate on the copy "Void," and return it to the purchaser. The supplier is not required to retain a record of orders that are not filled.

(b) The purchaser must retain an electronic copy of the voided order.

(c) To partially void an order, the supplier must indicate in the linked record that nothing was shipped for each item voided.

§ 1305.29 Reporting to DEA.

A supplier must, for each electronic order filled, forward either a copy of the electronic order or an electronic report of the order in a format that DEA specifies to DEA within two business days.

PART 1306—PRESCRIPTIONS

GENERAL INFORMATION

AUTHORITY: 21 U.S.C. 821, 829, 871(b), unless otherwise noted.

SOURCE: 36 FR 7799, Apr. 24, 1971; 36 FR 13386, July 21, 1971, unless otherwise noted. Redesignated at 38 FR 26609, Sept. 24, 1973.

GENERAL INFORMATION

§ 1306.01 Scope of part 1306.

Rules governing the issuance, filling and filing of prescriptions pursuant to section 309 of the Act (21 U.S.C. 829) are set forth generally in that section and specifically by the sections of this part.

§ 1306.02 Definitions.

Any term contained in this part shall have the definition set forth in section 102 of the Act (21 U.S.C. 802) or part 1300 of this chapter.

[62 FR 13964, Mar. 24, 1997]

§ 1306.03 Persons entitled to issue prescriptions.

(a) A prescription for a controlled substance may be issued only by an individual practitioner who is:
(1) Authorized to prescribe controlled substances by the jurisdiction in which he is licensed to practice his profession and
(2) Either registered or exempted from registration pursuant to §§ 1301.22(c) and 1301.23 of this chapter.

(b) A prescription issued by an individual practitioner may be communicated to a pharmacist by an employee or agent of the individual practitioner.

[36 FR 7799, Apr. 24, 1971, as amended at 36 FR 18732, Sept. 21, 1971. Redesignated at 38 FR 26609, Sept. 24, 1973, as amended at 62 FR 13966, Mar. 24, 1997]

§ 1306.04 Purpose of issue of prescription.

(a) A prescription for a controlled substance to be effective must be issued for a legitimate medical purpose by an individual practitioner acting in the usual course of his professional practice. The responsibility for the proper prescribing and dispensing of controlled substances is upon the prescribing practitioner, but a corresponding responsibility rests with the pharmacist who fills the prescription. An order purporting to be a prescription issued not in the usual course of professional treatment or in legitimate and authorized research is not a prescription within the meaning and intent of section 309 of the Act (21 U.S.C. 829) and the person knowingly filling such a purported prescription, as well as the person issuing it, shall be subject to the penalties provided for violations of the provisions of law relating to controlled substances.

(b) A prescription may not be issued in order for an individual practitioner to obtain controlled substances for supplying the individual practitioner for the purpose of general dispensing to patients.

(c) A prescription may not be issued for "detoxification treatment" or "maintenance treatment," unless the prescription is for a Schedule III, IV, or V narcotic drug approved by the Food and Drug Administration specifically for use in maintenance or detoxification treatment and the practitioner is in compliance with requirements in § 1301.28 of this chapter.

[36 FR 7799, Apr. 24, 1971. Redesignated at 38 FR 26609, Sept. 24, 1973, and amended at 39 FR 37986, Oct. 25, 1974; 70 FR 36343, June 23, 2005]

§ 1306.05 Manner of issuance of prescriptions.

(a) All prescriptions for controlled substances shall be dated as of, and signed on, the day when issued and shall bear the full name and address of the patient, the drug name, strength, dosage form, quantity prescribed, directions for use and the name, address and registration number of the practitioner. In addition, a prescription for a Schedule III, IV, or V narcotic drug approved by FDA specifically for "detoxification treatment" or "maintenance treatment" must include the identification number issued by the Administrator under § 1301.28(d) of this chapter or a written notice stating that the practitioner is acting under the good faith exception of § 1301.28(e). Where a prescription is for gamma-hydroxybutyric acid, the practitioner shall note on the face of the prescription the medical need of the patient for the prescription. A practitioner may sign a prescription in the same manner as he would sign a check or legal document (*e.g.*, J.H. Smith or John H. Smith). Where an oral order is not permitted, prescriptions shall be written with ink or indelible pencil or typewriter and shall be manually signed by the practitioner. The prescriptions may be prepared by the secretary or agent for the signature of a practitioner, but the prescribing practitioner is responsible in case the prescription does not conform in all essential respects to the law and regulations. A corresponding liability rests upon the pharmacist, including a pharmacist employed by a central fill pharmacy, who fills a prescription not prepared in the form prescribed by DEA regulations.

(b) An individual practitioner exempted from registration under § 1301.22(c) of this chapter shall include on all prescriptions issued by him or her the registration number of the hospital or other institution and the special internal code number assigned to him or her by the hospital or other institution as provided in § 1301.22(c) of this chapter, in lieu of the registration number of the practitioner required by this section. Each written prescription shall have the name of the physician stamped, typed, or handprinted on it, as well as the signature of the physician.

(c) An official exempted from registration under § 1301.22(c) shall include on all prescriptions issued by him his branch of service or agency (e.g., "U.S. Army" or "Public Health Service") and his service identification number, in lieu of the registration number of the practitioner required by this section. The service identification number for a Public Health Service employee is his Social Security identification number. Each prescription shall have the name of the officer stamped, typed, or handprinted on it, as well as the signature of the officer.

[36 FR 7799, Apr. 24, 1971, as amended at 36 FR 18733, Sept. 21, 1971. Redesignated at 38 FR 26609, Sept. 24, 1973; and amended at 56 FR 25026, June 3, 1991; 60 FR 36641, July 18, 1995; 62 FR 13966, Mar. 24, 1997; 68 FR 37410, June 24, 2003; 70 FR 294, Jan. 4, 2005; 70 FR 36343, June, 23, 2005]

§ 1306.06 Persons entitled to fill prescriptions.

A prescription for a controlled substance may only be filled by a pharmacist, acting in the usual course of his professional practice and either registered individually or employed in a registered pharmacy, a registered central fill pharmacy, or registered institutional practitioner.

[68 FR 37410, June 24, 2003, as amended at 70 FR 36343, June 23, 2005]

§ 1306.07 Administering or dispensing of narcotic drugs.

(a) A practitioner may administer or dispense directly (but not prescribe) a narcotic drug listed in any schedule to a narcotic dependant person for the purpose of maintenance or detoxification treatment if the practitioner meets both of the following conditions:

(1) The practitioner is separately registered with DEA as a narcotic treatment program.

(2) The practitioner is in compliance with DEA regulations regarding treatment qualifications, security, records, and unsupervised use of the drugs pursuant to the Act.

(b) Nothing in this section shall prohibit a physician who is not specifically registered to conduct a narcotic treatment program from administering (but not prescribing) narcotic drugs to a person for the purpose of relieving acute withdrawal symptoms when necessary while arrangements are being made for referral for treatment. Not more than one day's medication may be administered to the person or for the person's use at one time. Such emergency treatment may be carried out for not more than three days and may not be renewed or extended.

(c) This section is not intended to impose any limitations on a physician or authorized hospital staff to administer or dispense narcotic drugs in a hospital to maintain or detoxify a person as an incidental adjunct to medical or surgical treatment of conditions other than addiction, or to administer or dispense narcotic drugs to persons with intractable pain in which no relief or cure is possible or none has been found after reasonable efforts.

(d) A practitioner may administer or dispense (including prescribe) any Schedule III, IV, or V narcotic drug approved by the Food and Drug Administration specifically for use in maintenance or detoxification treatment to a narcotic dependent person if the practitioner complies with the requirements of §1301.28 of this chapter.

[39 FR 37986, Oct. 25, 1974, as amended at 70 FR 36344, June 23, 2005]

CONTROLLED SUBSTANCES LISTED IN SCHEDULE II

§1306.11 Requirement of prescription.

(a) A pharmacist may dispense directly a controlled substance listed in Schedule II, which is a prescription drug as determined under the Federal Food, Drug, and Cosmetic Act, only pursuant to a written prescription signed by the practitioner, except as provided in paragraph (d) of this section. A prescription for a Schedule II controlled substance may be transmitted by the practitioner or the practitioner's agent to a pharmacy via facsimile equipment, provided that the original written, signed prescription is presented to the pharmacist for review prior to the actual dispensing of the controlled substance, except as noted in paragraph (e), (f), or (g) of this section. The original prescription shall be maintained in accordance with §1304.04(h) of this chapter.

(b) An individual practitioner may administer or dispense directly a controlled substance listed in Schedule II in the course of his professional practice without a prescription, subject to §1306.07.

(c) An institutional practitioner may administer or dispense directly (but not prescribe) a controlled substance listed in Schedule II only pursuant to a written prescription signed by the prescribing individual practitioner or to an order for medication made by an individual practitioner which is dispensed for immediate administration to the ultimate user.

(d) In the case of an emergency situation, as defined by the Secretary in §290.10 of this title, a pharmacist may dispense a controlled substance listed in Schedule II upon receiving oral authorization of a prescribing individual practitioner, provided that:

(1) The quantity prescribed and dispensed is limited to the amount adequate to treat the patient during the emergency period (dispensing beyond the emergency period must be pursuant to a written prescription signed by the prescribing individual practitioner);

(2) The prescription shall be immediately reduced to writing by the pharmacist and shall contain all information required in §1306.05, except for the signature of the prescribing individual practitioner;

(3) If the prescribing individual practitioner is not known to the pharmacist, he must make a reasonable effort to determine that the oral authorization came from a registered individual practitioner, which may include a callback to the prescribing individual practitioner using his phone number as listed in the telephone directory and/or other good faith efforts to insure his identity; and

(4) Within 7 days after authorizing an emergency oral prescription, the prescribing individual practitioner shall cause a written prescription for the emergency quantity prescribed to be delivered to the dispensing pharmacist. In addition to conforming to the requirements of §1306.05, the prescription shall have written on its face "Authorization for Emergency Dispensing,"

81

and the date of the oral order. The written prescription may be delivered to the pharmacist in person or by mail, but if delivered by mail it must be postmarked within the 7 day period. Upon receipt, the dispensing pharmacist shall attach this prescription to the oral emergency prescription which had earlier been reduced to writing. The pharmacist shall notify the nearest office of the Administration if the prescribing individual practitioner fails to deliver a written prescription to him; failure of the pharmacist to do so shall void the authority conferred by this paragraph to dispense without a written prescription of a prescribing individual practitioner.

(5) Central fill pharmacies shall not be authorized under this paragraph to prepare prescriptions for a controlled substance listed in Schedule II upon receiving an oral authorization from a retail pharmacist or an individual practitioner.

(e) A prescription prepared in accordance with § 1306.05 written for a Schedule II narcotic substance to be compounded for the direct administration to a patient by parenteral, intravenous, intramuscular, subcutaneous or intraspinal infusion may be transmitted by the practitioner or the practitioner's agent to the pharmacy by facsimile. The facsimile serves as the original written prescription for purposes of this paragraph (e) and it shall be maintained in accordance with § 1304.04(h) of this chapter.

(f) A prescription prepared in accordance with § 1306.05 written for Schedule II substance for a resident of a Long Term Care Facility may be transmitted by the practitioner or the practitioner's agent to the dispensing pharmacy by facsimile. The facsimile serves as the original written prescription for purposes of this paragraph (f) and it shall be maintained in accordance with § 1304.04(h).

(g) A prescription prepared in accordance with § 1306.05 written for a Schedule II narcotic substance for a patient enrolled in a hospice care program certified and/or paid for by Medicare under Title XVIII or a hospice program which is licensed by the state may be transmitted by the practitioner or the practitioner's agent to the dispensing phar-

macy by facsimile. The practitioner or the practitioner's agent will note on the prescription that the patient is a hospice patient. The facsimile serves as the original written prescription for purposes of this paragraph (g) and it shall be maintained in accordance with § 1304.04(h).

[36 FR 7799, Apr. 24, 1971, as amended at 36 FR 18733, Sept. 21, 1971. Redesignated at 38 FR 26609, Sept. 24, 1973 and amended at 53 FR 4964, Feb. 19, 1988; 59 FR 26111, May 19, 1994; 59 FR 30832, June 15, 1994; 62 FR 13964, Mar. 24, 1997; 65 FR 45713, July 25, 2000; 68 FR 37410, June 24, 2003]

§ 1306.12 Refilling prescriptions; issuance of multiple prescriptions.

(a) The refilling of a prescription for a controlled substance listed in Schedule II is prohibited.

(b)(1) An individual practitioner may issue multiple prescriptions authorizing the patient to receive a total of up to a 90-day supply of a Schedule II controlled substance provided the following conditions are met:

(i) Each separate prescription is issued for a legitimate medical purpose by an individual practitioner acting in the usual course of professional practice;

(ii) The individual practitioner provides written instructions on each prescription (other than the first prescription, if the prescribing practitioner intends for that prescription to be filled immediately) indicating the earliest date on which a pharmacy may fill each prescription;

(iii) The individual practitioner concludes that providing the patient with multiple prescriptions in this manner does not create an undue risk of diversion or abuse;

(iv) The issuance of multiple prescriptions as described in this section is permissible under the applicable state laws; and

(v) The individual practitioner complies fully with all other applicable requirements under the Act and these regulations as well as any additional requirements under state law.

(2) Nothing in this paragraph (b) shall be construed as mandating or encouraging individual practitioners to issue multiple prescriptions or to see their patients only once every 90 day

when prescribing Schedule II controlled substances. Rather, individual practitioners must determine on their own, based on sound medical judgment, and in accordance with established medical standards, whether it is appropriate to issue multiple prescriptions and how often to see their patients when doing so.

[72 FR 64929, Nov. 19, 2007]

§ 1306.13 Partial filling of prescriptions.

(a) The partial filling of a prescription for a controlled substance listed in Schedule II is permissible, if the pharmacist is unable to supply the full quantity called for in a written or emergency oral prescription and he makes a notation of the quantity supplied on the face of the written prescription (or written record of the emergency oral prescription). The remaining portion of the prescription may be filled within 72 hours of the first partial filling; however, if the remaining portion is not or cannot be filled within the 72-hour period, the pharmacist shall so notify the prescribing individual practitioner. No further quantity may be supplied beyond 72 hours without a new prescription.

(b) A prescription for a Schedule II controlled substance written for a patient in a Long Term Care Facility (LTCF) or for a patient with a medical diagnosis documenting a terminal illness may be filled in partial quantities to include individual dosage units. If there is any question whether a patient may be classified as having a terminal illness, the pharmacist must contact the practitioner prior to partially filling the prescription. Both the pharmacist and the prescribing practitioner have a corresponding responsibility to assure that the controlled substance is for a terminally ill patient. The pharmacist must record on the prescription whether the patient is "terminally ill" or an "LTCF patient." A prescription that is partially filled and does not contain the notation "terminally ill" or "LTCF patient" shall be deemed to have been filled in violation of the Act. For each partial filling, the dispensing pharmacist shall record on the back of the prescription (or on another appro-

priate record, uniformly maintained, and readily retrievable) the date of the partial filling, quantity dispensed, remaining quantity authorized to be dispensed, and the identification of the dispensing pharmacist. The total quantity of Schedule II controlled substances dispensed in all partial fillings must not exceed the total quantity prescribed. Schedule II prescriptions for patients in a LTCF or patients with a medical diagnosis documenting a terminal illness shall be valid for a period not to exceed 60 days from the issue date unless sooner terminated by the discontinuance of medication.

(c) Information pertaining to current Schedule II prescriptions for patients in a LTCF or for patients with a medical diagnosis documenting a terminal illness may be maintained in a computerized system if this system has the capability to permit:

(1) Output (display or printout) of the original prescription number, date of issue, identification of prescribing individual practitioner, identification of patient, address of the LTCF or address of the hospital or residence of the patient, identification of medication authorized (to include dosage, form, strength and quantity), listing of the partial fillings that have been dispensed under each prescription and the information required in § 1306.13(b).

(2) Immediate (real time) updating of the prescription record each time a partial filling of the prescription is conducted.

(3) Retrieval of partially filled Schedule II prescription information is the same as required by § 1306.22(b) (4) and (5) for Schedule III and IV prescription refill information.

(Authority: 21 U.S.C. 801, *et seq.*)

[36 FR 7799, Apr. 24, 1971. Redesignated at 38 FR 26609, Sept. 24, 1973, and amended at 45 FR 54330, July 15, 1980; 56 FR 25027, June 3, 1991; 62 FR 13965, Mar. 24, 1997]

§ 1306.14 Labeling of substances and filling of prescriptions.

(a) The pharmacist filling a written or emergency oral prescription for a controlled substance listed in Schedule II shall affix to the package a label showing date of filling, the pharmacy name and address, the serial number of the prescription, the name of the patient, the name of the prescribing practitioner, and directions for use and cautionary statements, if any, contained in such prescription or required by law.

(b) If the prescription is filled at a central fill pharmacy, the central fill pharmacy shall affix to the package a label showing the retail pharmacy name and address and a unique identifier, (*i.e.* the central fill pharmacy's DEA registration number) indicating that the prescription was filled at the central fill pharmacy, in addition to the information required under paragraph (a) of this section.

(c) The requirements of paragraph (a) of this section do not apply when a controlled substance listed in Schedule II is prescribed for administration to an ultimate user who is institutionalized: *Provided,* That:

(1) Not more than 7-day supply of the controlled substance listed in Schedule II is dispensed at one time;

(2) The controlled substance listed in Schedule II is not in the possession of the ultimate user prior to the administration;

(3) The institution maintains appropriate safeguards and records regarding the proper administration, control, dispensing, and storage of the controlled substance listed in Schedule II; and

(4) The system employed by the pharmacist in filling a prescription is adequate to identify the supplier, the product, and the patient, and to set forth the directions for use and cautionary statements, if any, contained in the prescription or required by law.

(d) All written prescriptions and written records of emergency oral prescriptions shall be kept in accordance with requirements of § 1304.04(h) of this chapter.

(e) Where a prescription that has been prepared in accordance with section 1306.12(b) contains instructions from the prescribing practitioner indicating that the prescription shall not be filled until a certain date, no pharmacist may fill the prescription before that date.

[36 FR 13368, July 21, 1971, as amended at 37 FR 15921, Aug. 8, 1972. Redesignated at 38 FR 26609, Sept. 24, 1973, as amended at 62 FR 13965, Mar. 24, 1997; 68 FR 37410, June 24, 2003; 72 FR 64930, Nov. 19, 2007]

§ 1306.15 Provision of prescription information between retail pharmacies and central fill pharmacies for prescriptions of Schedule II controlled substances.

Prescription information may be provided to an authorized central fill pharmacy by a retail pharmacy for dispensing purposes. The following requirements shall also apply:

(a) Prescriptions for controlled substances listed in Schedule II may be transmitted electronically from a retail pharmacy to a central fill pharmacy including via facsimile. The retail pharmacy transmitting the prescription information must:

(1) Write the word "CENTRAL FILL" on the face of the original prescription and record the name, address, and DEA registration number of the central fill pharmacy to which the prescription has been transmitted and, the name of the retail pharmacy pharmacist transmitting the prescription, and the date of transmittal;

(2) Ensure that all information required to be on a prescription pursuant to Section 1306.05 of this part is transmitted to the central fill pharmacy (either on the face of the prescription or in the electronic transmission of information);

(3) Maintain the original prescription for a period of two years from the date the prescription was filled;

(4) Keep a record of receipt of the filled prescription, including the date of receipt, the method of delivery (private, common or contract carrier) and the name of the retail pharmacy employee accepting delivery.

(b) The central fill pharmacy receiving the transmitted prescription must

(1) Keep a copy of the prescription (i sent via facsimile) or an electronic record of all the information transmitted by the retail pharmacy, including the name, address, and DEA registration number of the retail pharmacy transmitting the prescription;

(2) Keep a record of the date of receipt of the transmitted prescription, the name of the pharmacist filling the prescription, and the date of filling of the prescription;

(3) Keep a record of the date the filled prescription was delivered to the retail pharmacy and the method of delivery (*i.e.* private, common or contract carrier).

[68 FR 37410, June 24, 2003]

CONTROLLED SUBSTANCES LISTED IN
SCHEDULES III, IV, AND V

§1306.21 Requirement of prescription.

(a) A pharmacist may dispense directly a controlled substance listed in Schedule III, IV, or V which is a prescription drug as determined under the Federal Food, Drug, and Cosmetic Act, only pursuant to either a written prescription signed by a practitioner or a facsimile of a written, signed prescription transmitted by the practitioner or the practitioner's agent to the pharmacy or pursuant to an oral prescription made by an individual practitioner and promptly reduced to writing by the pharmacist containing all information required in §1306.05, except for the signature of the practitioner.

(b) An individual practitioner may administer or dispense directly a controlled substance listed in Schedule III, IV, or V in the course of his/her professional practice without a prescription, subject to §1306.07.

(c) An institutional practitioner may administer or dispense directly (but not prescribe) a controlled substance listed in Schedule III, IV, or V only pursuant to a written prescription signed by an individual practitioner, or pursuant to a facsimile of a written prescription or order for medication transmitted by the practitioner or the practitioner's agent to the institutional practitioner-pharmacist, or pursuant to an oral prescription made by an individual practitioner and promptly reduced to writing by the pharmacist (containing all information required in Section 1306.05 except for the signature of the individual practitioner), or pursuant to an order for medication made by an individual practitioner which is dispensed for immediate administration to the ultimate user, subject to §1306.07.

[62 FR 13965, Mar. 24, 1997]

§1306.22 Refilling of prescriptions.

(a) No prescription for a controlled substance listed in Schedule III or IV shall be filled or refilled more than six months after the date on which such prescription was issued and no such prescription authorized to be refilled may be refilled more than five times. Each refilling of a prescription shall be entered on the back of the prescription or on another appropriate document. If entered on another document, such as a medication record, the document must be uniformly maintained and readily retrievable. The following information must be retrievable by the prescription number consisting of the name and dosage form of the controlled substance, the date filled or refilled, the quantity dispensed, initials of the dispensing pharmacist for each refill, and the total number of refills for that prescription. If the pharmacist merely initials and dates the back of the prescription it shall be deemed that the full face amount of the prescription has been dispensed. The prescribing practitioner may authorize additional refills of Schedule III or IV controlled substances on the original prescription through an oral refill authorization transmitted to the pharmacist provided the following conditions are met:

(1) The total quantity authorized, including the amount of the original prescription, does not exceed five refills nor extend beyond six months from the date of issue of the original prescription.

(2) The pharmacist obtaining the oral authorization records on the reverse of the original prescription the date, quantity of refill, number of additional refills authorized, and initials the prescription showing who received the authorization from the prescribing practitioner who issued the original prescription.

(3) The quantity of each additional refill authorized is equal to or less than the quantity authorized for the initial filling of the original prescription.

(4) The prescribing practitioner must execute a new and separate prescription for any additional quantities beyond the five refill, six-month limitation.

(b) As an alternative to the procedures provided by subsection (a), an automated data processing system may be used for the storage and retrieval of refill information for prescription orders for controlled substances in Schedule III and IV, subject to the following conditions:

(1) Any such proposed computerized system must provide on-line retrieval (via CRT display or hard-copy printout) of original prescription order information for those prescription orders which are currently authorized for refilling. This shall include, but is not limited to, data such as the original prescription number, date of issuance of the original prescription order by the practitioner, full name and address of the patient, name, address, and DEA registration number of the practitioner, and the name, strength, dosage form, quantity of the controlled substance prescribed (and quantity dispensed if different from the quantity prescribed), and the total number of refills authorized by the prescribing practitioner.

(2) Any such proposed computerized system must also provide on-line retrieval (via CRT display or hard-copy printout) of the current refill history for Schedule III or IV controlled substance prescription orders (those authorized for refill during the past six months.) This refill history shall include, but is not limited to, the name of the controlled substance, the date of refill, the quantity dispensed, the identification code, or name or initials of the dispensing pharmacist for each refill and the total number of refills dispensed to date for that prescription order.

(3) Documentation of the fact that the refill information entered into the computer each time a pharmacist refills an original prescription order for a Schedule III or IV controlled substance is correct must be provided by the individual pharmacist who makes use of such a system. If such a system provides a hard-copy printout of each day's controlled substance prescription order refill data, that printout shall be verified, dated, and signed by the individual pharmacist who refilled such a prescription order. The individual pharmacist must verify that the data indicated is correct and then sign this document in the same manner as he would sign a check or legal document (e.g., J. H. Smith, or John H. Smith). This document shall be maintained in a separate file at that pharmacy for a period of two years from the dispensing date. This printout of the day's controlled substance prescription order refill data must be provided to each pharmacy using such a computerized system within 72 hours of the date on which the refill was dispensed. It must be verified and signed by each pharmacist who is involved with such dispensing. In lieu of such a printout, the pharmacy shall maintain a bound log book, or separate file, in which each individual pharmacist involved in such dispensing shall sign a statement (in the manner previously described) each day, attesting to the fact that the refill information entered into the computer that day has been reviewed by him and is correct as shown. Such a book or file must be maintained at the pharmacy employing such a system for a period of two years after the date of dispensing the appropriately authorized refill.

(4) Any such computerized system shall have the capability of producing a printout of any refill data which the user pharmacy is responsible for maintaining under the Act and its implementing regulations. For example, this would include a refill-by-refill audit trail for any specified strength and dosage form of any controlled substance (by either brand or generic name or both). Such a printout must include name of the prescribing practitioner, name and address of the patient, quantity dispensed on each refill, date of dispensing for each refill, name or identification code of the dispensing pharmacist, and the number of the original prescription order. In any computerized system employed by a user pharmacy the central record keeping location must be capable of sending the printout to the pharmacy within 48 hours, and if a DEA Special

Agent or Diversion Investigator requests a copy of such printout from the user pharmacy, it must, if requested to do so by the Agent or Investigator, verify the printout transmittal capability of its system by documentation (e.g., postmark).

(5) In the event that a pharmacy which employs such a computerized system experiences system down-time, the pharmacy must have an auxiliary procedure which will be used for documentation of refills os Schedule III and IV controlled substance prescription orders. This auxiliary procedure must insure that refills are authorized by the original prescription order, that the maximum number of refills has not been exceeded, and that all of the appropriate data is retained for on-line data entry as soon as the computer system is available for use again.

(c) When filing refill information for original prescription orders for Schedule III or IV controlled substances, a pharmacy may use only one of the two systems described in paragraphs (a) or (b) of this section.

[36 FR 7799, Apr. 24, 1971; 36 FR 13386, July 21, 1971. Redesignated at 38 FR 26609, Sept. 24, 1973, and amended at 42 FR 28878, June 6, 1977; 45 FR 44266, July 1, 1980; 52 FR 3605, Feb. 5, 1987; 62 FR 13966, Mar. 24, 1997]

§1306.23 Partial filling of prescriptions.

The partial filling of a prescription for a controlled substance listed in Schedule III, IV, or V is permissible, provided that:

(a) Each partial filling is recorded in the same manner as a refilling,

(b) The total quantity dispensed in all partial fillings does not exceed the total quantity prescribed, and

(c) No dispensing occurs after 6 months after the date on which the prescription was issued.

[36 FR 18733, Sept. 21, 1971. Redesignated at 38 FR 26609, Sept. 24, 1973, and amended at 51 FR 5320, Feb. 13, 1986; 62 FR 13965, Mar. 24, 1997]

§1306.24 Labeling of substances and filing of prescriptions.

(a) The pharmacist filling a prescription for a controlled substance listed in Schedule III, IV, or V shall affix to the package a label showing the pharmacy name and address, the serial number and date of initial filling, the name of the patient, the name of the practitioner issuing the prescription, and directions for use and cautionary statements, if any, contained in such prescription as required by law.

(b) If the prescription is filled at a central fill pharmacy, the central fill pharmacy shall affix to the package a label showing the retail pharmacy name and address and a unique identifier, (i.e. the central fill pharmacy's DEA registration number) indicating that the prescription was filled at the central fill pharmacy, in addition to the information required under paragraph (a) of this section.

(c) The requirements of paragraph (a) of this section do not apply when a controlled substance listed in Schedule III, IV, or V is prescribed for administration to an ultimate user who is institutionalized: Provided, That:

(1) Not more than a 34-day supply or 100 dosage units, whichever is less, of the controlled substance listed in Schedule III, IV, or V is dispensed at one time;

(2) The controlled substance listed in Schedule III, IV, or V is not in the possession of the ultimate user prior to administration;

(3) The institution maintains appropriate safeguards and records the proper administration, control, dispensing, and storage of the controlled substance listed in Schedule III, IV, or V; and

(4) The system employed by the pharmacist in filling a prescription is adequate to identify the supplier, the product and the patient, and to set forth the directions for use and cautionary statements, if any, contained in the prescription or required by law.

(d) All prescriptions for controlled substances listed in Schedules III, IV, and V shall be kept in accordance with §1304.04(h) of this chapter.

[62 FR 13965, Mar. 24, 1997, as amended at 68 FR 37411, June 24, 2003]

§1306.25 Transfer between pharmacies of prescription information for Schedules III, IV, and V controlled substances for refill purposes.

(a) The transfer of original prescription information for a controlled substance listed in Schedules III, IV or V for the purpose of refill dispensing is permissible between pharmacies on a one time basis only. However, pharmacies electronically sharing a real-time, on-line database may transfer up to the maximum refills permitted by law and the prescriber's authorization. Transfers are subject to the following requirements:

(1) The transfer is communicated directly between two licensed pharmacists and the transferring pharmacist records the following information:

(i) Write the word "VOID" on the face of the invalidated prescription.

(ii) Record on the reverse of the invalidated prescription the name, address and DEA registration number of the pharmacy to which it was transferred and the name of the pharmacist receiving the prescription information.

(iii) Record the date of the transfer and the name of the pharmacist transferring the information.

(b) The pharmacist receiving the transferred prescription information shall reduce to writing the following:

(1) Write the word "transfer" on the face of the transferred prescription.

(2) Provide all information required to be on a prescription pursuant to 21 CFR 1306.05 and include:

(i) Date of issuance of original prescription;

(ii) Original number of refills authorized on original prescription;

(iii) Date of original dispensing;

(iv) Number of valid refills remaining and date(s) and locations of previous refill(s);

(v) Pharmacy's name, address, DEA registration number and prescription number from which the prescription information was transferred;

(vi) Name of pharmacist who transferred the prescription.

(vii) Pharmacy's name, address, DEA registration number and prescription number from which the prescription was originally filled;

(3) The original and transferred prescription(s) must be maintained for a period of two years from the date of last refill.

(c) Pharmacies electronically accessing the same prescription record must satisfy all information requirements of a manual mode for prescription transferral.

(d) The procedure allowing the transfer of prescription information for refill purposes is permissible only if allowable under existing state or other applicable law.

[46 FR 48919, Oct. 5, 1981. Redesignated and amended at 62 FR 13966, Mar. 24, 1997]

§ 1306.26 Dispensing without prescription.

A controlled substance listed in Schedules II, III, IV, or V which is not a prescription drug as determined under the Federal Food, Drug, and Cosmetic Act, may be dispensed by a pharmacist without a prescription to a purchaser at retail, provided that:

(a) Such dispensing is made only by a pharmacist (as defined in part 1300 of this chapter), and not by a nonpharmacist employee even if under the supervision of a pharmacist (although after the pharmacist has fulfilled his professional and legal responsibilities set forth in this section, the actual cash, credit transaction, or delivery, may be completed by a nonpharmacist);

(b) Not more than 240 cc. (8 ounces) of any such controlled substance containing opium, nor more than 120 cc. (4 ounces) of any other such controlled substance nor more than 48 dosage units of any such controlled substance containing opium, nor more than 24 dosage units of any other such controlled substance may be dispensed at retail to the same purchaser in any given 48-hour period;

(c) The purchaser is at least 18 years of age;

(d) The pharmacist requires every purchaser of a controlled substance under this section not known to him to furnish suitable identification (including proof of age where appropriate);

(e) A bound record book for dispensing of controlled substances under this section is maintained by the pharmacist, which book shall contain the name and address of the purchaser, the name and quantity of controlled substance purchased, the date of each purchase, and the name or initials of the pharmacist who dispensed the substance to the purchaser (the book shall be maintained in accordance with the recordkeeping requirement of §1304.04 of this chapter); and

(f) A prescription is not required for distribution or dispensing of the substance pursuant to any other Federal, State or local law.

(g) Central fill pharmacies may not dispense controlled substances to a purchaser at retail pursuant to this section.

[36 FR 7799, Apr. 24, 1971, as amended at 36 FR 18733, Sept. 21, 1971. Redesignated at 38 FR 26609, Sept. 24, 1973, and further redesigated and amended at 62 FR 13966, Mar. 24, 1997; 68 FR 37411, June 24, 2003]

§ 1306.27 Provision of prescription information between retail pharmacies and central fill pharmacies for initial and refill prescriptions of Schedule III, IV, or V controlled substances.

Prescription information may be provided to an authorized central fill pharmacy by a retail pharmacy for dispensing purposes. The following requirements shall also apply:

(a) Prescriptions for controlled substances listed in Schedule III, IV or V may be transmitted electronically from a retail pharmacy to a central fill pharmacy including via facsimile. The retail pharmacy transmitting the prescription information must:

(1) Write the word "CENTRAL FILL" on the face of the original prescription and record the name, address, and DEA registration number of the central fill pharmacy to which the prescription has been transmitted and the name of the retail pharmacy pharmacist transmitting the prescription, and the date of transmittal;

(2) Ensure that all information required to be on a prescription pursuant to §1306.05 of this part is transmitted to the central fill pharmacy (either on the face of the prescription or in the electronic transmission of information);

(3) Indicate in the information transmitted the number of refills already dispensed and the number of refills remaining;

(4) Maintain the original prescription for a period of two years from the date the prescription was last refilled;

(5) Keep a record of receipt of the filled prescription, including the date of receipt, the method of delivery (pri-

vate, common or contract carrier) and the name of the retail pharmacy employee accepting delivery.

(b) The central fill pharmacy receiving the transmitted prescription must:

(1) Keep a copy of the prescription (if sent via facsimile) or an electronic record of all the information transmitted by the retail pharmacy, including the name, address, and DEA registration number of the retail pharmacy transmitting the prescription;

(2) Keep a record of the date of receipt of the transmitted prescription, the name of the licensed pharmacist filling the prescription, and dates of filling or refilling of the prescription;

(3) Keep a record of the date the filled prescription was delivered to the retail pharmacy and the method of delivery (*i.e.* private, common or contract carrier).

[68 FR 37411, June 24, 2003]

PART 1307—MISCELLANEOUS

AUTHORITY: 21 U.S.C. 821, 822(d), 871(b), unless otherwise noted.

SOURCE: 36 FR 7801, Apr. 24, 1971, unless otherwise noted. Redesignated at 38 FR 26609, Sept. 24, 1973.

GENERAL INFORMATION

§ 1307.01 Definitions.

Any term contained in this part shall have the definition set forth in section 102 of the Act (21 U.S.C. 802) or part 1300 of this chapter.

[62 FR 13966, Mar. 24, 1997]

§ 1307.02 Application of State law and other Federal law.

Nothing in this chapter shall be construed as authorizing or permitting any person to do any act which such person is not authorized or permitted to do under other Federal laws or obligations under international treaties, conventions or protocols, or under the law of the State in which he/she desires to do such act nor shall compliance with such parts be construed as compliance with other Federal or State laws unless expressly provided in such other laws.

[62 FR 13966, Mar. 24, 1997]

§ 1307.03 Exceptions to regulations.

Any person may apply for an exception to the application of any provision of this chapter by filing a written request stating the reasons for such exception. Requests shall be filed with the Administrator, Drug Enforcement Administration, Department of Justice, Washington, DC 20537. The Administrator may grant an exception in his discretion, but in no case shall he/she be required to grant an exception to any person which is otherwise required by law or the regulations cited in this section.

[62 FR 13966, Mar. 24, 1997]

SPECIAL EXCEPTIONS FOR MANUFACTURE AND DISTRIBUTION OF CONTROLLED SUBSTANCES

§ 1307.11 Distribution by dispenser to another practitioner or reverse distributor.

(a) A practitioner who is registered to dispense a controlled substance may distribute (without being registered to distribute) a quantity of such substance to—

(1) Another practitioner for the purpose of general dispensing by the practitioner to patients, provided that—

(i) The practitioner to whom the controlled substance is to be distributed is registered under the Act to dispense that controlled substance;

(ii) The distribution is recorded by the distributing practitioner in accordance with § 1304.22(c) of this chapter and by the receiving practitioner in accordance with § 1304.22(c) of this chapter;

(iii) If the substance is listed in Schedule I or II, an order form is used as required in part 1305 of this chapter; and

(iv) The total number of dosage units of all controlled substances distributed by the practitioner pursuant to this section and § 1301.25 of this chapter during each calendar year in which the practitioner is registered to dispense does not exceed 5 percent of the total number of dosage units of all controlled substances distributed and dispensed by the practitioner during the same calendar year.

(2) A reverse distributor who is registered to receive such controlled substances.

(b) If, during any calendar year in which the practitioner is registered to dispense, the practitioner has reason to believe that the total number of dosage units of all controlled substances which will be distributed by him pursuant to paragraph (a)(1) of this section and § 1301.25 of this chapter will exceed 5 percent of this total number of dosage units of all controlled substances distributed and dispensed by him during that calendar year, the practitioner shall obtain a registration to distribute controlled substances.

(c) The distributions that a registered retail pharmacy makes to automated dispensing systems at long term care facilities for which the retail pharmacy also holds registrations do not count toward the 5 percent limit in paragraphs (a)(1)(iv) and (b) of this section.

[68 FR 41229, July 11, 2003, as amended at 70 FR 25466, May 13, 2005]

§ 1307.12 Distribution to supplier or manufacturer.

(a) Any person lawfully in possession of a controlled substance listed in any schedule may distribute (without being registered to distribute) that substance to the person from whom he/she obtained it or to the manufacturer of the substance, or, if designated, to the manufacturer's registered agent for accepting returns, provided that a written record is maintained which indicates the date of the transaction, the name, form and quantity of the substance, the name, address, and registration number, if any, of the person making the distribution, and the name, address, and registration number, if known, of the supplier or manufacturer. In the case of returning a controlled substance in Schedule I or II, an order form shall be used in the manner prescribed in part 1305 of this chapter and be maintained as the written record of the transaction. Any person not required to register pursuant to sections 302(c) or 1007(b)(1) of the Act (21 U.S.C. 822(c) or 957(b)(1)) shall be exempt from maintaining the records required by this section.

(b) Distributions referred to in paragraph (a) may be made through a freight forwarding facility operated by the person to whom the controlled substance is being returned provided that prior arrangement has been made for the return and the person making the distribution delivers the controlled substance directly to an agent or employee of the person to whom the controlled substance is being returned.

[65 FR 44679, July 19, 2000; 65 FR 45829, July 25, 2000, as amended at 68 FR 41229, July 11, 2003]

§1307.13 Incidental manufacture of controlled substances.

Any registered manufacturer who, incidentally but necessarily, manufactures a controlled substance as a result of the manufacture of a controlled substance or basic class of controlled substance for which he is registered and has been issued an individual manufacturing quota pursuant to part 1303 of this chapter (if such substance or class is listed in Schedule I or II) shall be exempt from the requirement of registration pursuant to part 1301 of this chapter and, if such incidentally manufactured substance is listed in Schedule I or II, shall be exempt from the requirement of an individual manufacturing quota pursuant to part 1303 of this

chapter, if such substances are disposed of in accordance with §1307.21.

[36 FR 7801, Apr. 24, 1971. Redesignated at 38 FR 26609, Sept. 24, 1973, and further redesignated at 62 FR 13967, Mar. 24, 1997]

DISPOSAL OF CONTROLLED SUBSTANCES

§1307.21 Procedure for disposing of controlled substances.

(a) Any person in possession of any controlled substance and desiring or required to dispose of such substance may request assistance from the Special Agent in Charge of the Administration in the area in which the person is located for authority and instructions to dispose of such substance. The request should be made as follows:

(1) If the person is a registrant, he/she shall list the controlled substance or substances which he/she desires to dispose of on DEA Form 41, and submit three copies of that form to the Special Agent in Charge in his/her area; or

(2) If the person is not a registrant, he/she shall submit to the Special Agent in Charge a letter stating:

(i) The name and address of the person;

(ii) The name and quantity of each controlled substance to be disposed of;

(iii) How the applicant obtained the substance, if known; and

(iv) The name, address, and registration number, if known, of the person who possessed the controlled substances prior to the applicant, if known.

(b) The Special Agent in Charge shall authorize and instruct the applicant to dispose of the controlled substance in one of the following manners:

(1) By transfer to person registered under the Act and authorized to possess the substance;

(2) By delivery to an agent of the Administration or to the nearest office of the Administration;

(3) By destruction in the presence of an agent of the Administration or other authorized person; or

(4) By such other means as the Special Agent in Charge may determine to assure that the substance does not become available to unauthorized persons.

(c) In the event that a registrant is required regularly to dispose of controlled substances, the Special Agent in Charge may authorize the registrant to dispose of such substances, in accordance with paragraph (b) of this section, without prior approval of the Administration in each instance, on the condition that the registrant keep records of such disposals and file periodic reports with the Special Agent in Charge summarizing the disposals made by the registrant. In granting such authority, the Special Agent in Charge may place such conditions as he deems proper on the disposal of controlled substances, including the method of disposal and the frequency and detail of reports.

(d) This section shall not be construed as affecting or altering in any way the disposal of controlled substances through procedures provided in laws and regulations adopted by any State.

[36 FR 7801, Apr. 24, 1971, as amended at 37 FR 15922, Aug. 8, 1972. Redesignated at 38 FR 26609, Sept. 24, 1973, and amended at 47 FR 41735, Sept. 22, 1982; 62 FR 13967, Mar. 24, 1997]

§ 1307.22 Disposal of controlled substances by the Administration.

Any controlled substance delivered to the Administration under § 1307.21 or forfeited pursuant to section 511 of the Act (21 U.S.C. 881) may be delivered to any department, bureau, or other agency of the United States or of any State upon proper application addressed to the Administrator, Drug Enforcement Administration, Department of Justice, Washington, DC 20537 The application shall show the name, address, and official title of the person or agency to whom the controlled drugs are to be delivered, including the name and quantity of the substances desired and the purpose for which intended. The delivery of such controlled drugs shall be ordered by the Administrator, if, in his opinion, there exists a medical or scientific need therefor.

[38 FR 7801, Apr. 24, 1971. Redesignated at 38 FR 26609, Sept. 24, 1973, as amended at 62 FR 13967, Mar. 24, 1997]

SPECIAL EXEMPT PERSONS

§ 1307.31 Native American Church.

The listing of peyote as a controlled substance in Schedule I does not apply to the nondrug use of peyote in bona fide religious ceremonies of the Native American Church, and members of the Native American Church so using peyote are exempt from registration. Any person who manufactures peyote for or distributes peyote to the Native American Church, however, is required to obtain registration annually and to comply with all other requirements of law.

PART 1308—SCHEDULES OF CONTROLLED SUBSTANCES

GENERAL INFORMATION

EXEMPT CANNABIS PLANT MATERIAL, AND PRODUCTS MADE THEREFROM, THAT CONTAIN TETRAHYDROCANNABINOLS

1308.35 Exemption of certain cannabis plant material, and products made therefrom, that contain tetrahydrocannabinols.

HEARINGS

1308.41 Hearings generally.
1308.42 Purpose of hearing.
1308.43 Initiation of proceedings for rule-making.
1308.44 Request for hearing or appearance; waiver.
1308.45 Final order.
1308.46 Control required under international treaty.
1308.47 Control of immediate precursors.
1308.49 Emergency scheduling.

AUTHORITY: 21 U.S.C. 811, 812, 871(b), unless otherwise noted.

SOURCE: 38 FR 8254, Mar. 30, 1973, unless otherwise noted. Redesignated at 38 FR 26609, Sept. 24, 1973.

GENERAL INFORMATION

§ 1308.01 Scope of part 1308.

Schedules of controlled substances established by section 202 of the Act (21 U.S.C. 812), as they are changed, updated, and republished from time to time, are set forth in this part.

§ 1308.02 Definitions.

Any term contained in this part shall have the definition set forth in section 102 of the Act (21 U.S.C. 802) or part 1300 of this chapter.

[62 FR 13967, Mar. 24, 1997]

§ 1308.03 Administration Controlled Substances Code Number.

(a) Each controlled substance, or basic class thereof, has been assigned an "Administration Controlled Substances Code Number" for purposes of identification of the substances or class on certain Certificates of Registration issued by the Administration pursuant to §§ 1301.35 of this chapter and on certain order forms issued by the Administration pursuant to § 1305.05(d) of this chapter. Applicants for procurement and/or individual manufacturing quotas must include the appropriate code number on the application as required in §§ 1303.12(b) and 1303.22(a) of this chapter. Applicants for import and export permits must in-clude the appropriate code number on the application as required in §§ 1312.12(a) and 1312.22(a) of this chapter. Authorized registrants who desire to import or export a controlled substance for which an import or export permit is not required must include the appropriate Administration Controlled Substances Code Number beneath or beside the name of each controlled substance listed on the DEA Form 236 (Controlled Substance Import/Export Declaration) which is executed for such importation or exportation as required in §§ 1312.18(c) and 1312.27(b) of this chapter.

(b) Except as stated in paragraph (a) of this section, no applicant or registrant is required to use the Administration Controlled Substances Code Number for any purpose.

[38 FR 8254, Mar. 30, 1973. Redesignated at 38 FR 26609, Sept. 24, 1973 and amended at 51 FR 15318, Apr. 23, 1986; 62 FR 13968, Mar. 24, 1997]

SCHEDULES

§ 1308.11 Schedule I.

(a) Schedule I shall consist of the drugs and other substances, by whatever official name, common or usual name, chemical name, or brand name designated, listed in this section. Each drug or substance has been assigned the DEA Controlled Substances Code Number set forth opposite it.

(b) *Opiates.* Unless specifically excepted or unless listed in another schedule, any of the following opiates, including their isomers, esters, ethers, salts, and salts of isomers, esters and ethers, whenever the existence of such isomers, esters, ethers and salts is possible within the specific chemical designation (for purposes of paragraph (b)(34) only, the term isomer includes the optical and geometric isomers):

(1) Acetyl-alpha-methylfentanyl (N-[1-(1-methyl-2-phenethyl)-4-piperidinyl]-N-phenylacetamide)	9815
(2) Acetylmethadol	9601
(3) Allylprodine	9602
(4) Alphacetylmethadol (except levo-alphacetylmethadol also known as levo-alpha-acetylmethadol, levomethadyl acetate, or LAAM)	9603
(5) Alphameprodine	9604
(6) Alphamethadol	9605
(7) Alpha-methylfentanyl (N-[1-(alpha-methyl-beta-phenyl)ethyl-4-piperidyl] propionanilide; 1-(1-methyl-2-phenylethyl)-4-(N-propanilido) piperidine)	9814
(8) Alpha-methylthiofentanyl (N-[1-methyl-2-(2-thienyl)ethyl-4-piperidinyl]-N-phenylpropanamide)	9832
(9) Benzethidine	9606
(10) Betacetylmethadol	9607

(11) Beta-hydroxyfentanyl (*N*-[1-(2-hydroxy-2-phenethyl)-4-piperidinyl]-*N*-phenylpropanamide) 9830
(12) Beta-hydroxy-3-methylfentanyl (other name: N-[1-(2-hydroxy-2-phenethyl)-3-methyl-4-piperidinyl]-N-phenylpropanamide 9831
(13) Betameprodine 9608
(14) Betamethadol 9609
(15) Betaprodine 9611
(16) Clonitazene 9612
(17) Dextromoramide 9613
(18) Diampromide 9615
(19) Diethylthiambutene 9616
(20) Difenoxin 9168
(21) Dimenoxadol 9617
(22) Dimepheptanol 9618
(23) Dimethylthiambutene 9619
(24) Dioxaphetyl butyrate 9621
(25) Dipipanone 9622
(26) Ethylmethylthiambutene 9623
(27) Etonitazene 9624
(28) Etoxeridine 9625
(29) Furethidine 9626
(30) Hydroxypethidine 9627
(31) Ketobemidone 9628
(32) Levomoramide 9629
(33) Levophenacylmorphan 9631
(34) 3-Methylfentanyl (*N*-[3-methyl-1-(2-phenylethyl)-4-piperidyl]-*N*-phenylpropanamide) 9813
(35) 3-methylthiofentanyl (*N*-[(3-methyl-1-(2-thienyl)ethyl-4-piperidinyl]-*N*-phenylpropanamide) 9833
(36) Morpheridine 9632
(37) MPPP (1-methyl-4-phenyl-4-propionoxypiperidine) 9661
(38) Noracymethadol 9633
(39) Norlevorphanol 9634
(40) Normethadone 9635
(41) Norpipanone 9636
(42) Para-fluorofentanyl (*N*-(4-fluorophenyl)-*N*-[1-(2-phenethyl)-4-piperidinyl] propanamide 9812
(43) PEPAP (1-(-2-phenethyl)-4-phenyl-4-acetoxypiperidine 9663
(44) Phenadoxone 9637
(45) Phenampromide 9638
(46) Phenomorphan 9647
(47) Phenoperidine 9641
(48) Piritramide 9642
(49) Proheptazine 9643
(50) Properidine 9644
(51) Propiram 9649
(52) Racemoramide 9645
(53) Thiofentanyl (*N*-phenyl-*N*-[1-(2-thienyl)ethyl-4-piperidinyl]-propanamide 9835
(54) Tilidine 9750
(55) Trimeperidine 9646

(c) *Opium derivatives.* Unless specifically excepted or unless listed in another schedule, any of the following opium derivatives, its salts, isomers, and salts of isomers whenever the existence of such salts, isomers, and salts of isomers is possible within the specific chemical designation:

(1) Acetorphine 9319
(2) Acetyldihydrocodeine 9051
(3) Benzylmorphine 9052
(4) Codeine methylbromide 9070
(5) Codeine-N-Oxide 9053
(6) Cyprenorphine 9054
(7) Desomorphine 9055
(8) Dihydromorphine 9145
(9) Drotebanol 9335
(10) Etorphine (except hydrochloride salt) 9056
(11) Heroin 9200
(12) Hydromorphinol 9301

(13) Methyldesorphine 9302
(14) Methyldihydromorphine 9304
(15) Morphine methylbromide 9305
(16) Morphine methylsulfonate 9306
(17) Morphine-N-Oxide 9307
(18) Myrophine 9308
(19) Nicocodeine 9309
(20) Nicomorphine 9312
(21) Normorphine 9313
(22) Pholcodine 9314
(23) Thebacon 9315

(d) *Hallucinogenic substances.* Unless specifically excepted or unless listed in another schedule, any material, compound, mixture, or preparation, which contains any quantity of the following hallucinogenic substances, or which contains any of its salts, isomers, and salts of isomers whenever the existence of such salts, isomers, and salts of isomers is possible within the specific chemical designation (for purposes of this paragraph only, the term "isomer" includes the optical, position and geometric isomers):

(1) Alpha-ethyltryptamine 7249
  Some trade or other names: etryptamine; Monase; α-ethyl-1H-indole-3-ethanamine; 3-(2-aminobutyl) indole; α-ET; and AET.
(2) 4-bromo-2,5-dimethoxy-amphetamine 7391
  Some trade or other names: 4-bromo-2,5-dimethoxy-α-methylphenethylamine; 4-bromo-2,5-DMA
(3) 4-Bromo-2,5-dimethoxyphenethylamine 7392
  Some trade or other names: 2-(4-bromo-2,5-dimethoxyphenyl)-1-aminoethane; alpha-desmethyl DOB; 2C-B, Nexus.
(4) 2,5-dimethoxyamphetamine 7396
  Some trade or other names: 2,5-dimethoxy-α-methylphenethylamine; 2,5-DMA
(5) 2,5-dimethoxy-4-ethylamphet-amine 7399
  Some trade or other names: DOET
(6) 2,5-dimethoxy-4-(n)-propylthiophenethylamine (other name: 2C–T–7) 7348
(7) 4-methoxyamphetamine 7411
  Some trade or other names: 4-methoxy-α-methylphenethylamine; paramethoxyamphetamine, PMA
(8) 5-methoxy-3,4-mdthylenedioxy-amphetamine 7401
(9) 4-methyl-2,5-dimethoxy-amphetamine 7395
  Some trade and other names: 4-methyl-2,5-dimethoxy-α-methylphenethylamine; "DOM" and "STP"
(10) 3,4-methylenedioxy amphetamine 7400
(11) 3,4-methylenedioxymethamphetamine (MDMA) 7405
(12) 3,4-methylenedioxy-N-ethylamphetamine (also known as N-ethyl-alpha-methyl-3,4(methylenedioxy)phenethylamine, N-ethyl MDA, MDE, MDEA 7404
(13) N-hydroxy-3,4-methylenedioxyamphetamine (also known as N-hydroxy-alpha-methyl-3,4(methylenedioxy)phenethylamine, and N-hydroxy MDA 7402
(14) 3,4,5-trimethoxy amphetamine 7390
(15) Alpha-methyltryptamine (other name: AMT) 7432

(16) Bufotenine 7433
   Some trade and other names: 3-(β-Dimethylaminoethyl)-5-hydroxyindole; 3-(2-dimethylaminoethyl)-5-indolol; N, N-dimethylserotonin; 5-hydroxy-N,N-dimethyltryptamine; mappine

(17) Diethyltryptamine 7434
   Some trade and other names: N,N-Diethyltryptamine; DET

(18) Dimethyltryptamine 7435
   Some trade or other names: DMT

(19) 5-methoxy-N,N-diisopropyltryptamine (other name: 5-MeO-DIPT) .... 7439.

(20) Ibogaine 7260
   Some trade and other names: 7-Ethyl-6,6β,7,8,9,10,12,13-octahydro-2-methoxy-6,9-methano-5H-pyrido [1′, 2′:1,2] azepino [5,4-b] indole; Tabernanthe iboga

(21) Lysergic acid diethylamide 7315
(22) Marihuana 7360
(23) Mescaline 7381
(24) Parahexyl—7374; some trade or other names: 3-Hexyl-1-hydroxy-7,8,9,10-tetrahydro-6,6,9-trimethyl-6H-dibenzo[b,d]pyran; Synhexyl.

(25) Peyote 7415
   Meaning all parts of the plant presently classified botanically as *Lophophora williamsii Lemaire*, whether growing or not, the seeds thereof, any extract from any part of such plant, and every compound, manufacture, salts, derivative, mixture, or preparation of such plant, its seeds or extracts (Interprets 21 USC 812(c), Schedule I(c) (12))

(26) N-ethyl-3-piperidyl benzilate 7482
(27) N-methyl-3-piperidyl benzilate 7484
(28) Psilocybin 7437
(29) Psilocyn 7438
(30) Tetrahydrocannabinols 7370
   Meaning tetrahydrocannabinols naturally contained in a plant of the genus Cannabis (cannabis plant), as well as synthetic equivalents of the substances contained in the cannabis plant, or in the resinous extractives of such plant, and/or synthetic substances, derivatives, and their isomers with similar chemical structure and pharmacological activity to those substances contained in the plant, such as the following:
   1 cis or trans tetrahydrocannabinol, and their optical isomers
   6 cis or trans tetrahydrocannabinol, and their optical isomers
   3, 4 cis or trans tetrahydrocannabinol, and its optical isomers
   (Since nomenclature of these substances is not internationally standardized, compounds of these structures, regardless of numerical designation of atomic positions covered.)

(31) Ethylamine analog of phencyclidine 7455
   Some trade or other names: N-ethyl-1-phenylcyclohexylamine, (1-phenylcyclohexyl)ethylamine, N-(1-phenylcyclohexyl)ethylamine, cyclohexamine, PCE

(32) Pyrrolidine analog of phencyclidine 7458
   Some trade or other names: 1-(1-phenylcyclohexyl)-pyrrolidine, PCPy, PHP

(33) Thiophene analog of phencyclidine 7470

Some trade or other names: 1-[1-(2-thienyl)-cyclohexyl]-piperidine, 2-thienylanalog of phencyclidine, TPCP, TCP

(34) 1-[1-(2-thienyl)cyclohexyl]pyrrolidine 7473
   Some other names: TCPy

(e) *Depressants.* Unless specifically excepted or unless listed in another schedule, any material, compound, mixture, or preparation which contains any quantity of the following substances having a depressant effect on the central nervous system, including its salts, isomers, and salts of isomers whenever the existence of such salts, isomers, and salts of isomers is possible within the specific chemical designation:

(1) gamma-hydroxybutyric acid (some other names include GHB; gamma-hydroxybutyrate; 4-hydroxybutyrate; 4-hydroxybutanoic acid; sodium oxybate; sodium oxybutyrate) 2010
(2) Mecloqualone 2572
(3) Methaqualone 2565

(f) *Stimulants.* Unless specifically excepted or unless listed in another schedule, any material, compound, mixture, or preparation which contains any quantity of the following substances having a stimulant effect on the central nervous system, including its salts, isomers, and salts of isomers:

(1) Aminorex (Some other names: aminoxaphen; 2-amino-5-phenyl-2-oxazoline; or 4,5-dihydro-5-phenly-2-oxazolamine) 1585
(2) N-Benzylpiperazine (some other names: BZP, 1-benzylpiperazine) 7493
(3) Cathinone 1235
   Some trade or other names: 2-amino-1-phenyl-1-propanone, alpha-aminopropiophenone, 2-aminopropiophenone, and norephedrone
(4) Fenethylline 1503
(5) Methcathinone (Some other names: 2-(methylamino)-propiophenone; alpha-(methylamino)propiophenone; 2-(methylamino)-1-phenylpropan-1-one; alpha-N-methylaminopropiophenone; monomethylpropion; ephedrone; N-methylcathinone; methylcathinone; AL–464; AL–422; AL–463 and UR1432), its salts, optical isomers and salts of optical isomers 1237
(6) (±)cis-4-methylaminorex ((±)cis-4,5-dihydro-4-meth-yl-5-phenyl-2-oxazolamine) 1590
(7) N-ethylamphetamine 1475
(8) N,N-dimethylamphetamine (also known as N,N-alpha-trimethyl-benzeneethanamine; N,N-alpha-trimethylphenethylamine) 1480

(g) *Temporary listing of substances subject to emergency scheduling.* Any material, compound, mixture or preparation which contains any quantity of the following substances:

(1) N-[1-benzyl-4-piperidyl]-N-phenylpropanamide (benzylfentanyl), its optical isomers, salts and salts of isomers 9818
(2) N-[1-(2-thienyl)methyl-4-piperidyl]-N-phenylpropanamide (thenylfentanyl), its optical isolers, salts and salts of isomers 9834

[39 FR 22141, June 20, 1974]

EDITORIAL NOTE: For FEDERAL REGISTER citations affecting § 1308.11, see the List of CFR Sections Affected, which appears in the Finding Aids section of the printed volume and on GPO Access.

§ 1308.12   Schedule II.

(a) Schedule II shall consist of the drugs and other substances, by whatever official name, common or usual name, chemical name, or brand name designated, listed in this section. Each drug or substance has been assigned the Controlled Substances Code Number set forth opposite it.

(b) *Substances, vegetable origin or chemical synthesis.* Unless specifically excepted or unless listed in another schedule, any of the following substances whether produced directly or indirectly by extraction from substances of vegetable origin, or independently by means of chemical synthesis, or by a combination of extraction and chemical synthesis:

(1) Opium and opiate, and any salt, compound, derivative, or preparation of opium or opiate excluding apomorphine, thebaine-derived butorphanol, dextrorphan, nalbuphine, nalmefene, naloxone, and naltrexone, and their respective salts, but including the following:

(i) Codeine	9050
(ii) Dihydroetorphine	9334
(iii) Ethylmorphine	9190
(iv) Etorphine hydrochloride	9059
(v) Granulated opium	9640
(vi) Hydrocodone	9193
(vii) Hydromorphone	9150
(viii) Metopon	9260
(ix) Morphine	9300
(x) Opium extracts	9610
(xi) Opium fluid	9620
(xii) Oripavine	9330
(xiii) Oxycodone	9143
(xiv) Oxymorphone	9652
(xv) Powdered opium	9639
(xvi) Raw opium	9600
(xvii) Thebaine	9333
(xviii) Tincture of opium	9630

(2) Any salt, compound, derivative, or preparation thereof which is chemically equivalent or identical with any of the substances referred to in paragraph (b) (1) of this section, except that these substances shall not include the isoquinoline alkaloids of opium.

(3) Opium poppy and poppy straw.

(4) Coca leaves (9040) and any salt, compound, derivative or preparation of coca leaves (including cocaine (9041) and ecgonine (9180) and their salts, isomers, derivatives and salts of isomers and derivatives), and any salt, compound, derivative, or preparation thereof which is chemically equivalent or identical with any of these substances, except that the substances shall not include decocainized coca leaves or extraction of coca leaves, whhch extractions do not contain cocaine or ecgonine.

(5) Concentrate of poppy straw (the crude extract of poppy straw in either liquid, solid or powder form which contains the phenanthrene alkaloids of the opium poppy), 9670.

(c) *Opiates.* Unless specifically excepted or unless in another schedule any of the following opiates, including its isomers, esters, ethers, salts and salts of isomers, esters and ethers whenever the existence of such isomers, esters, ethers, and salts is possible within the specific chemical designation, dextrorphan and levopropoxyphene excepted:

(1) Alfentanil	9737
(2) Alphaprodine	9010
(3) Anileridine	9020
(4) Bezitramide	9800
(5) Bulk dextropropoxyphene (non-dosage forms)	9273
(6) Carfentanil	9743
(7) Dihydrocodeine	9120
(8) Diphenoxylate	9170
(9) Fentanyl	9801
(10) Isomethadone	9226
(11) Levo-alphacetylmethadol	9648
[Some other names: levo-alpha-acetylmethadol, levomethadyl acetate, LAAM]	
(12) Levomethorphan	9210
(13) Levorphanol	9220
(14) Metazocine	9240
(15) Methadone	9250
(16) Methadone-Intermediate, 4-cyano-2-dimethylamino-4,4-diphenyl butane	9254
(17) Moramide-Intermediate, 2-methyl-3-morpholino-1,1-diphenylpropane-carboxylic acid	9802
(18) Pethidine (meperidine)	9230
(19) Pethidine-Intermediate-A, 4-cyano-1-methyl-4-phenylpiperidine	9232
(20) Pethidine-Intermediate-B, ethyl-4-phenylpiperidine-4-carboxylate	9233
(21) Pethidine-Intermediate-C, 1-methyl-4-phenylpiperidine-4-carboxylic acid	9234
(22) Phenazocine	9715
(23) Piminodine	9730
(24) Racemethorphan	9732
(25) Racemorphan	9733
(26) Remifentanil	9739
(27) Sufentanil	9740

(d) *Stimulants.* Unless specifically excepted or unless listed in another schedule, any material, compound, mixture, or preparation which contains any quantity of the following substances having a stimulant effect on the central nervous system:

(1) Amphetamine, its salts, optical isomers, and salts of its optical isomers	1100
(2) Methamphetamine, its salts, isomers, and salts of its isomers	1105
(3) Phenmetrazine and its salts	1631
(4) Methylphenidate	1724
(5) Lisdexamfetamine, its salts, isomers, and salts of its isomers	1205.

(e) *Depressants.* Unless specifically excepted or unless listed in another schedule, any material, compound, mixture, or preparation which contains any quantity of the following substances having a depressant effect on the central nervous system, including its salts, isomers, and salts of isomers whenever the existence of such salts, isomers, and salts of isomers is possible within the specific chemical designation:

(1) Amobarbital	2125
(2) Glutethimide	2550
(3) Pentobarbital	2270
(4) Phencyclidine	7471
(5) Secobarbital	2315

(f) *Hallucinogenic substances.*

(1) Nabilone	7379
[Another name for nabilone: (±)-*trans*-3-(1,1-dimethylheptyl)-6,6a,7,8,10,10a-hexahydro-1-hydroxy-6,6-dimethyl-9H-dibenzo[b,d]pyran-9-one]	

(g) *Immediate precursors.* Unless specifically excepted or unless listed in another schedule, any material, compound, mixture, or preparation which contains any quantity of the following substances:

(1) Immediate precursor to amphetamine and methamphetamine:

(i) Phenylacetone	8501
Some trade or other names: phenyl-2-propanone; P2P; benzyl methyl ketone; methyl benzyl ketone;	

(2) Immediate precursors to phencyclidine (PCP):

(i) 1-phenylcyclohexylamine	7460
(ii) 1-piperidinocyclohexanecarbonitrile (PCC)	8603

[39 FR 22142, June 20, 1974]

EDITORIAL NOTE: For FEDERAL REGISTER citations affecting §1308.12, see the List of CFR Sections Affected, which appears in the Finding Aids section of the printed volume and on GPO Access.

§1308.13 Schedule III.

(a) Schedule III shall consist of the drugs and other substances, by what-

ever official name, common or usual name, chemical name, or brand name designated, listed in this section. Each drug or substance has been assigned the DEA Controlled Substances Code Number set forth opposite it.

(b) *Stimulants.* Unless specifically excepted or unless listed in another schedule, any material, compound, mixture, or preparation which contains any quantity of the following substances having a stimulant effect on the central nervous sxstem, including its salts, isomers (whether optical, position, or geometric), and salts of such isomers whenever the existence of such salts, isomers, and salts of isomers is possible within the specific chemical designation:

(1) Those compounds, mixtures, or preparations in dosage unit form containing any stimulant substances listed in schedule II which compounds, mixtures, or preparations were listed on August 25, 1971, as excepted compounds under §1308.32, and any other drug of the quantitative composition shown in that list for those drugs or which is the same except that it contains a lesser quantity of controlled substances	1405
(2) Benzphetamine	1228
(3) Chlorphentermine	1645
(4) Clortermine	1647
(5) Phendimetrazine	1615

(c) *Depressants.* Unless specifically excepted or unless listed in another schedule, any material, compound, mixture, or preparation which contains any quantity of the following substances having a depressant effect on the central nervous system:

(1) Any compound, mixture or preparation containing:	
(i) Amobarbital	2126
(ii) Secobarbital	2316
(iii) Pentobarbital	2271
or any salt thereof and one or more other active medicinal ingredients which are not listed in any schedule.	
(2) Any suppository dosage form containing:	
(i) Amobarbital	2126
(ii) Secobarbital	2316
(iii) Pentobarbital	2271
or any salt of any of these drugs and approved by the Food and Drug Administration for marketing only as a suppository.	
(3) Any substance which contains any quantity of a derivative of barbituric acid or any salt thereof	2100
(4) Chlorhexadol	2510
(5) Embutramide	2020
(6) Any drug product containing gamma hydroxybutyric acid, including its salts, isomers, and salts of isomers, for which an application is approved under section 505 of the Federal Food, Drug, and Cosmetic Act	2012
(7) Ketamine, its salts, isomers, and salts of isomers	7285
[Some other names for ketamine: (±)-2-(2-chlorophenyl)-2-(methylamino)-cyclohexanone]	
(8) Lysergic acid	7300
(9) Lysergic acid amide	7310
(10) Methyprylon	2575

(11) Sulfondiethylmethane 2600
(12) Sulfonethylmethane 2605
(13) Sulfonmethane 2610
(14) Tiletamine and zolazepam or any salt thereof 7295
    Some trade or other names for a tiletamine-zolazepam combination product:
      Telazol..
    Some trade or other names for tiletamine:
      2-(ethylamino)-2-(2-thienyl)-cyclohexanone..
    Some trade or other names for zolazepam:
      4-(2-fluorophenyl)-6,8-dihydro-1,3,8-trimethylpyrazolo-[3,4-*e*]   [1,4]-diazepin-7(1*H*)-one, flupyrazapon..

(d) Nalorphine 9400.

(e) *Narcotic drugs.* Unless specifically excepted or unless listed in another schedule:

(1) Any material, compound, mixture, or preparation containing any of the following narcotic drugs, or their salts calculated as the free anhydrous base or alkaloid, in limited quantities as set forth below:
    (i) Not more than 1.8 grams of codeine per 100 milliliters or not more than 90 milligrams per dosage unit, with an equal or greater quantity of an isoquinoline alkaloid of opium 9803
    (ii) Not more than 1.8 grams of codeine per 100 milliliters or not more than 90 milligrams per dosage unit, with one or more active, nonnarcotic ingredients in recognized therapeutic amounts 9804
    (iii) Not more than 300 milligrams of dihydrocodeinone (hydrocodone) per 100 milliliters or not more than 15 milligrams per dosage unit, with a fourfold or greater quantity of an isoquinoline alkaloid of opium 9805
    (iv) Not more than 300 milligrams of dihydrocodeinone (hydrocodone) per 100 milliliters or not more than 15 milligrams per dosage unit, with one or more active nonnarcotic ingredients in recognized therapeutic amounts 9806
    (v) Not more than 1.8 grams of dihydrocodeine per 100 milliliters or not more than 90 milligrams per dosage unit, with one or more active nonnarcotic ingredients in recognized therapeutic amounts ... 9807
    (vi) Not more than 300 milligrams of ethylmorphine per 100 milliliters or not more than 15 milligrams per dosage unit, with one or more active, nonnarcotic ingredients in recognized therapeutic amounts ... 9808
    (vii) Not more than 500 milligrams of opium per 100 milliliters or per 100 grams or not more than 25 milligrams per dosage unit, with one or more active, nonnarcotic ingredients in recognized therapeutic amounts ... 9809
    (viii) Not more than 50 milligrams of morphine per 100 milliliters or per 100 grams, with one or more active, nonnarcotic ingredients in recognized therapeutic amounts 9810
(2) Any material, compound, mixture, or preparation containing any of the following narcotic drugs or their salts, as set forth below:
    (i) Buprenorphine 9064
    (ii) [Reserved].

(f) *Anabolic Steroids.* Unless specifically excepted or unless listed in another schedule, any material, compound, mixture or preparation containing any quantity of the following

substances, including its salts, esters and ethers:

(1) Anabolic steroids (see § 1300.01 of this chapter)—4000

(2) [Reserved]

(g) *Hallucinogenic substances.* (1) Dronabinol (synthetic) in sesame oil and encapsulated in a soft gelatin capsule in a U.S. Food and Drug Administration approved product—7369.

[Some other names for dronabinol: (6a*R-trans*)-6a,7,8,10a-tetrahydro-6,6,9-trimethyl-3-pentyl-6*H*-dibenzo [*b,d*]pyran-1-ol] or (-)-delta-9-(*trans*)-tetrahydrocannabinol]

(2) [Reserved]

[39 FR 22142, June 20, 1974, as amended at 41 FR 43401, Oct. 1, 1976; 43 FR 3359, Jan. 25, 1978; 44 FR 40888, July 13, 1979; 46 FR 52334, Oct. 27, 1981; 51 FR 5320, Feb. 13, 1986; 52 FR 2222, Jan. 21, 1987; 52 FR 5952, Feb. 27, 1987; 56 FR 5754, Feb. 13, 1991; 56 FR 11932, Mar. 21, 1991; 62 FR 13968, Mar. 24, 1997; 64 FR 35930, July 2, 1999; 64 FR 37675, July 13, 1999; 65 FR 13238, Mar. 13, 2000; 65 FR 17440, Apr. 3, 2000; 67 FR 62370, Oct. 7, 2002; 70 FR 74657, Dec. 16, 2005; 71 FR 51116, Aug. 29, 2006]

§ 1308.14 Schedule IV.

(a) Schedule IV shall consist of the drugs and other substances, by whatever official name, common or usual name, chemical name, or brand name designated, listed in this section. Each drug or substance has been assigned the DEA Controlled Substances Code Number set forth opposite it.

(b) *Narcotic drugs.* Unless specifically excepted or unless listed in another schedule, any material, compound, mixture, or preparation containing any of the following narcotic drugs, or their salts calculated as the free anhydrous base or alkaloid, in limited quantities as set forth below:

(1) Not more than 1 milligram of difenoxin and not less than 25 micrograms of atropine sulfate per dosage unit 9167
(2) Dextropropoxyphene (alpha-(+)-4-dimethylamino-1,2-diphenyl-3-methyl-2-propionoxybutane) 9278

(c) *Depressants.* Unless specifically excepted or unless listed in another schedule, any material, compound, mixture, or preparation which contains any quantity of the following substances, including its salts, isomers, and salts of isomers whenever the existence of such salts, isomers, and salts of isomers is possible within the specific chemical designation:

98

(1)	Alprazolam	2882
(2)	Barbital	2145
(3)	Bromazepam	2748
(4)	Camazepam	2749
(5)	Chloral betaine	2460
(6)	Chloral hydrate	2465
(7)	Chlordiazepoxide	2744
(8)	Clobazam	2751
(9)	Clonazepam	2737
(10)	Clorazepate	2768
(11)	Clotiazepam	2752
(12)	Cloxazolam	2753
(13)	Delorazepam	2754
(14)	Diazepam	2765
(15)	Dichloralphenazone	2467
(16)	Estazolam	2756
(17)	Ethchlorvynol	2540
(18)	Ethinamate	2545
(19)	Ethyl loflazepate	2758
(20)	Fludiazepam	2759
(21)	Flunitrazepam	2763
(22)	Flurazepam	2767
(23)	Halazepam	2762
(24)	Haloxazolam	2771
(25)	Ketazolam	2772
(26)	Loprazolam	2773
(27)	Lorazepam	2885
(28)	Lormetazepam	2774
(29)	Mebutamate	2800
(30)	Medazepam	2836
(31)	Meprobamate	2820
(32)	Methohexital	2264
(33)	Methylphenobarbital (mephobarbital)	2250
(34)	Midazolam	2884
(35)	Nimetazepam	2837
(36)	Nitrazepam	2834
(37)	Nordiazepam	2838
(38)	Oxazepam	2835
(39)	Oxazolam	2839
(40)	Paraldehyde	2585
(41)	Petrichloral	2591
(42)	Phenobarbital	2285
(43)	Pinazepam	2883
(44)	Prazepam	2764
(45)	Quazepam	2881
(46)	Temazepam	2925
(47)	Tetrazepam	2886
(48)	Triazolam	2887
(49)	Zaleplon	2781
(50)	Zolpidem	2783
(51)	Zopiclone	2784

(d) *Fenfluramine.* Any material, compound, mixture, or preparation which contains any quantity of the following substances, including its salts, isomers (whether optical, position, or geometric), and salts of such isomers, whenever the existence of such salts, isomers, and salts of isomers is possible:

(1) Fenfluramine	1670

(e) *Stimulants.* Unless specifically excepted or unless listed in another schedule, any material, compound, mixture, or preparation which contains any quantity of the following substances having a stimulant effect on the central nervous system, including its salts, isomers and salts of isomers:

(1) Cathine ((+)-norpseudoephedrine)	1230

(2) Diethylpropion	1610
(3) Fencamfamin	1760
(4) Fenproporex	1575
(5) Mazindol	1605
(6) Mefenorex	1580
(7) Modafinil	1680
(8) Pemoline (including organometallic complexes and chelates thereof)	1530
(9) Phentermine	1640
(10) Pipradrol	1750
(11) Sibutramine	1675
(12) SPA ((-)-1-dimethylamino- 1,2-diphenylethane)	1635

(f) *Other substances.* Unless specifically excepted or unless listed in another schedule, any material, compound, mixture or preparation which contains any quantity of the following substances, including its salts:

(1) Pentazocine	9709
(2) Butorphanol (including its optical isomers)	9720

[39 FR 22143, June 20, 1974]

EDITORIAL NOTE: For FEDERAL REGISTER citations affecting § 1308.14, see the List of CFR Sections Affected, which appears in the Finding Aids section of the printed volume and on GPO Access.

§ 1308.15   Schedule V.

(a) Schedule V shall consist of the drugs and other substances, by whatever official name, common or usual name, chemical name, or brand name designated, listed in this section.

(b) *Narcotic drugs.* Unless specifically excepted or unless listed in another schedule, any material, compound, mixture, or preparation containing any of the following narcotic drugs and their salts, as set forth below:

(1) [Reserved]

(c) *Narcotic drugs containing non-narcotic active medicinal ingredients.* Any compound, mixture, or preparation containing any of the following narcotic drugs, or their salts calculated as the free anhydrous base or alkaloid, in limited quantities as set forth below, which shall include one or more non-narcotic active medicinal ingredients in sufficient proportion to confer upon the compound, mixture, or preparation valuable medicinal qualities other than those possessed by narcotic drugs alone:

(1) Not more than 200 milligrams of codeine per 100 milliliters or per 100 grams.

(2) Not more than 100 milligrams of dihydrocodeine per 100 milliliters or per 100 grams.

(3) Not more than 100 milligrams of ethylmorphine per 100 milliliters or per 100 grams.

(4) Not more than 2.5 milligrams of diphenoxylate and not less than 25 micrograms of atropine sulfate per dosage unit.

(5) Not more than 100 milligrams of opium per 100 milliliters or per 100 grams.

(6) Not more than 0.5 milligram of difenoxin and not less than 25 micrograms of atropine sulfate per dosage unit.

(d) *Stimulants.* Unless specifically exempted or excluded or unless listed in another schedule, any material, compound, mixture, or preparation which contains any quantity of the following substances having a stimulant effect on the central nervous system, including its salts, isomers and salts of isomers:

(1) Pyrovalerone ....1485.
(2) [Reserved]

(e) *Depressants.* Unless specifically exempted or excluded or unless listed in another schedule, any material, compound, mixture, or preparation which contains any quantity of the following substances having a depressant effect on the central nervous system, including its salts:

(1) Pregabalin [(S)-3-(aminomethyl)-5-methylhexanoic acid] 2782
(2) [Reserved]

[39 FR 22143, June 20, 1974, as amended at 43 FR 38383, Aug. 28, 1978; 44 FR 40888, July 13, 1979; 47 FR 49841, Nov. 3, 1982; 50 FR 8108, Feb. 28, 1985; 52 FR 5952, Feb. 27, 1987; 53 FR 10870, Apr. 4, 1988; 56 FR 61372, Dec. 3, 1991; 67 FR 62370, Oct. 7, 2002; 70 FR 43635, July 28, 2005]

EXCLUDED NONNARCOTIC SUBSTANCES

§ 1308.21 Application for exclusion of a nonnarcotic substance.

(a) Any person seeking to have any nonnarcotic drug that may, under the Federal Food, Drug, and Cosmetic Act (21 U.S.C. 301), be lawfully sold over the counter without a prescription, excluded from any schedule, pursuant to section 201(g)(1) of the Act (21 U.S.C. 811(g)(1)), may apply to the Administrator, Drug Enforcement Administration, Department of Justice, Washington, DC 20537.

(b) An application for an exclusion under this section shall contain the following information:

(1) The name and address of the applicant;

(2) The name of the substance for which exclusion is sought; and

(3) The complete quantitative composition of the substance.

(c) Within a reasonable period of time after the receipt of an application for an exclusion under this section, the Administrator shall notify the applicant of his acceptance or nonacceptance of his application, and if not accepted, the reason therefore. The Administrator need not accept an application for filing if any of the requirements prescribed in paragraph (b) of this section is lacking or is not set forth as to be readily understood. If the applicant desires, he may amend the application to meet the requirements of paragraph (b) of this section. If the application is accepted for filing, the Administrator shall issue and publish in the FEDERAL REGISTER his order on the application, which shall include a reference to the legal authority under which the order is issued and the findings of fact and conclusions of law upon which the order is based. This order shall specify the date on which it shall take effect. The Administrator shall permit any interested person to file written comments on or objections to the order within 60 days of the date of publication of his order in the FEDERAL REGISTER. If any such comments or objections raise significant issues regarding any finding of fact or conclusion of law upon which the order is based, the Administrator shall immediately suspend the effectiveness of the order until he may reconsider the application in light of the comments and objections filed. Thereafter, the Administrator shall reinstate, revoke, or amend his original order as he determines appropriate.

(d) The Administrator may at any time revoke any exclusion granted pursuant to section 201(g) of the Act (21 U.S.C. 811(g)) by following the procedures set forth in paragraph (c) of this section for handling an application for an exclusion which has been accepted for filing.

[38 FR 8254, Mar. 30, 1973, as amended at 70 FR 74657, Dec. 16, 2005]

§ 1308.22 Excluded substances.

The following nonnarcotic substances which may, under the Federal Food, Drug, and Cosmetic Act (21 U.S.C. 301), be lawfully sold over the counter without a prescription, are excluded from all schedules pursuant to section 201(g) (1) of the Act (21 U.S.C. 811(g) (1)):

EXCLUDED NONNARCOTIC PRODUCTS

Company	Trade name	NDC code	Form	Controlled substance	(mg or mg/ml)
Bioline Laboratories	Theophed	00719–1945	TB	Phenobarbital	8.00
Goldline Laboratories	Guiaphed Elixir	00182–1377	EL	Phenobarbital	4.00
Goldline Laboratories	Tedrigen Tablets	00182–0134	TB	Phenobarbital	8.00
Hawthorne Products Inc	Choate's Leg Freeze		LQ	Chloral hydrate	246.67
Parke-Davis & Co	Tedral	00071–0230	TB	Phenobarbital	8.00
Parke-Davis & Co	Tedral Elixir	00071–0242	EX	Phenobarbital	40.00
Parke-Davis & Co	Tedral S.A.	00071–0231	TB	Phenobarbital	8.00
Parke-Davis & Co	Tedral Suspension	00071–0237	SU	Phenobarbital	80.00
Parmed Pharmacy	Asma-Ese	00349–2018	TB	Phenobarbital	8.10
Rondex Labs	Azma-Aids	00367–3153	TB	Phenobarbital	8.00
Smith Kline Consumer	Benzedrex	49692–0928	IN	Propylhexedrine	250.00
Sterling Drug, Inc	Bronkolixir	00057–1004	EL	Phenobarbital	0.80
Sterling Drug, Inc	Bronkotabs	00057–1005	TB	Phenobarbital	8.00
Vicks Chemical Co	Vicks Inhaler	23900–0010	IN	l-Desoxyephedrine	113.00
White Hall Labs	Primatene (P-tablets)	00573–2940	TB	Phenobarbital	8.00

[38 FR 8255, Mar. 30, 1973. Redesignated at 38 FR 26609, Sept. 24, 1973, and amended at 41 FR 16553, Apr. 20, 1976; 41 FR 53477, Dec. 7, 1976; 46 FR 51603, Oct. 21, 1981; 47 FR 45867, Oct. 14, 1982; 54 FR 2100, Jan. 19, 1989; 55 FR 12162, Mar. 30, 1990; 62 FR 13968, Mar. 24, 1997]

EXEMPT CHEMICAL PREPARATIONS

§ 1308.23 Exemption of certain chemical preparations; application.

(a) The Administrator may, by regulation, exempt from the application of all or any part of the Act any chemical preparation or mixture containing one or more controlled substances listed in any schedule, which preparation or mixture is intended for laboratory, industrial, educational, or special research purposes and not for general administration to a human being or other animal, if the preparation or mixture either:

(1) Contains no narcotic controlled substance and is packaged in such a form or concentration that the packaged quantity does not present any significant potential for abuse (the type of packaging and the history of abuse of the same or similar preparations may be considered in determining the potential for abuse of the preparation or mixture); or

(2) Contains either a narcotic or nonnarcotic controlled substance and one or more adulterating or denaturing agents in such a manner, combination, quantity, proportion, or concentration, that the preparation or mixture does not present any potential for abuse. If the preparation or mixture contains a narcotic controlled substance, the preparation or mixture must be formulated in such a manner that it incorporates methods of denaturing or other means so that the preparation or mixture is not liable to be abused or have ill effects, if abused, and so that the narcotic substance cannot in practice be removed.

(b) Any person seeking to have any preparation or mixture containing a controlled substance and one or more noncontrolled substances exempted from the application of all or any part of the Act, pursuant to paragraph (a) of this section, may apply to the Administrator, Drug Enforcement Administration, Department of Justice, Washington, DC 20537.

(c) An application for an exemption under this section shall contain the following information:

101

(1) The name, address, and registration number, if any, of the applicant;

(2) The name, address, and registration number, if any, of the manufacturer or importer of the preparation or mixture, if not the applicant;

(3) The exact trade name or other designation of the preparation or mixture;

(4) The complete qualitative and quantitative composition of the preparation or mixture (including all active and inactive ingredients and all controlled and noncontrolled substances);

(5) The form of the immediate container in which the preparation or mixture will be distributed with sufficient descriptive detail to identify the preparation or mixture (e.g., bottle, packet, vial, soft plastic pillow, agar gel plate, etc.);

(6) The dimensions or capacity of the immediate container of the preparation or mixture;

(7) The label and labeling, as defined in part 1300 of this chapter, of the immediate container and the commercial containers, if any, of the preparation or mixture;

(8) A brief statement of the facts which the applicant believes justify the granting of an exemption under this paragraph, including information on the use to which the preparation or mixture will be put;

(9) The date of the application; and

(10) Which of the information submitted on the application, if any, is deemed by the applicant to be a trade secret or otherwise confidential and entitled to protection under subsection 402(a)(8) of the Act (21 U.S.C. 842(a) (8)) or any other law restricting public disclosure of information.

(d) The Administrator may require the applicant to submit such documents or written statements of fact relevant to the application as he deems necessary to determine whether the application should be granted.

(e) Within a reasonable period of time after the receipt of an application for an exemption under this section, the Administrator shall notify the applicant of his acceptance or nonacceptance of his application, and if not accepted, the reason therefor. The Administrator need not accept an application for filing if any of the requirements prescribed in paragraph (c) or requested pursuant to paragraph (d) is lacking or is not set forth as to be readily understood. If the applicant desires, he may amend the application to meet the requirements of paragraphs (c) and (d) of this section. If the application is accepted for filing, the Administrator shall issue and publish in the FEDERAL REGISTER his order on the application, which shall include a reference to the legal authority under which the order is based. This order shall specify the date on which it shall take effect. The Administrator shall permit any interested person to file written comments on or objections to the order within 60 days of the date of publication of his order in the FEDERAL REGISTER. If any such comments or objections raise significant issues regarding any finding of fact or conclusion of law upon which the order is based, the Administrator shall immediately suspend the effectiveness of the order until he may reconsider the application in light of the comments and objections filed. Thereafter, the Administrator shall reinstate, revoke, or amend his original order as he determines appropriate.

(f) The Administrator may at any time revoke or modify any exemption granted pursuant to this section by following the procedures set forth in paragraph (e) of this section for handling an application for an exemption which has been accepted for filing. The Administrator may also modify or revoke the criteria by which exemptions are granted (and thereby modify or revoke all preparations and mixtures granted under the old criteria) and modify the scope of exemptions at any time.

[38 FR 8254, Mar. 30, 1973. Redesignated at 38 FR 26609, Sept. 24, 1973, and amended at 46 FR 28841, May 29, 1981; 62 FR 13968, Mar. 24, 1997]

§ 1308.24 Exempt chemical preparations.

(a) The chemical preparations and mixtures approved pursuant to § 1308.23 are exempt from application of sections 302, 303, 305, 306, 307, 308, 309, 1002, 1003 and 1004 of the Act (21 U.S.C. 822–823, 825–829, 952–954) and § 1301.74 of this chapter, to the extent described in paragraphs (b) to (h) of this section.

Substances set forth in paragraph (j) of this section shall be exempt from the application of sections 305, 306, 307, 308, 309, 1002, 1003 and 1004 of the Act (21 U.S.C. 825–829, 952–954) and §§ 1301.71–1301.73 and 1301.74 (a), (b), (d), (e) and (f) of this chapter to the extent as hereinafter may be provided.

(b) Registration and security: Any person who manufactures an exempt chemical preparation or mixture must be registered under the Act and comply with all relevant security requirements regarding controlled substances being used in the manufacturing process until the preparation or mixture is in the form described in paragraph (i) of this section. Any other person who handles an exempt chemical preparation after it is in the form described in paragraph (i) of this section is not required to be registered under the Act to handle that preparation, and the preparation is not required to be stored in accordance with security requirements regarding controlled substances.

(c) Labeling: In lieu of the requirements set forth in part 1302 of this chapter, the label and the labeling of an exempt chemical preparation must be prominently marked with its full trade name or other description and the name of the manufacturer or supplier as set forth in paragraph (i) of this section, in such a way that the product can be readily identified as an exempt chemical preparation. The label and labeling must also include in a prominent manner the statement "For industrial use only" or "For chemical use only" or "For in vitro use only—not for human or animal use" or "Diagnostic reagent—for professional use only" or a comparable statement warning the person reading it that human or animal use is not intended. The symbol designating the schedule of the controlled substance is not required on either the label or the labeling of the exempt chemical preparation, nor is it necessary to list all ingredients of the preparation.

(d) Records and reports: Any person who manufactures an exempt chemical preparation or mixture must keep complete and accurate records and file all reports required under part 1304 of this chapter regarding all controlled substances being used in the manufac-

turing process until the preparation or mixture is in the form described in paragraph (i) of this section. In lieu of records and reports required under part 1304 of this chapter regarding exempt chemical preparations, the manufacturer need only record the name, address, and registration number, if any, of each person to whom the manufacturer distributes any exempt chemical preparation. Each importer or exporter of an exempt narcotic chemical preparation must submit a semiannual report of the total quantity of each substance imported or exported in each calendar half-year within 30 days of the close of the period to the Drug and Chemical Evaluation Section, Drug Enforcement Administration, Department of Justice, Washington, DC 20537. Any other person who handles an exempt chemical preparation after it is in the form described in paragraph (i) of this section is not required to maintain records or file reports.

(e) Quotas, order forms, prescriptions, import, export, and transshipment requirements: Once an exempt chemical preparation is in the form described in paragraph (i) of this section, the requirements regarding quotas, order forms, prescriptions, import permits and declarations, export permit and declarations, and transshipment and intransit permits and declarations do not apply. These requirements do apply, however, to any controlled substances used in manufacturing the exempt chemical preparation before it is in the form described in paragraph (i) of this section.

(f) Criminal penalties: No exemption granted pursuant to § 1308.23 affects the criminal liability for illegal manufacture, distribution, or possession of controlled substances contained in the exempt chemical preparation. Distribution, possession, and use of an exempt chemical preparation are lawful for registrants and nonregistrants only as long as such distribution, possession, or use is intended for laboratory, industrial, or educational purposes and not for immediate or subsequent administration to a human being or other animal.

(g) Bulk materials: For materials exempted in bulk quantities, the Administrator may prescribe requirements other than those set forth in paragraphs (b) through (e) of this section on a case-by-case basis.

(h) Changes in chemical preparations: Any change in the quantitative or qualitative composition of the preparation or mixture after the date of application, or change in the trade name or other designation of the preparation or mixture, set forth in paragraph (i) of this section, requires a new application for exemption.

(i) A listing of exempt chemical preparations may be obtained by submitting a written request to the Drug and Chemical Evaluation Section, Drug Enforcement Administration, Washington, DC 20537.

(j) The following substances are designated as exempt chemical preparations for the purposes set forth in this section.

(1) *Chloral.* When packaged in a sealed, oxygen-free environment, under nitrogen pressure, safeguarded against exposure to the air.

(2) *Emit^R Phenobarbital Enzyme Reagent B.* In one liter quantities each with a 5 ml. retention sample for repackaging as an exempt chemical preparation only.

[38 FR 8255, Mar. 30, 1973]

EDITORIAL NOTE: For FEDERAL REGISTER citations affecting § 1308.24, see the List of CFR Sections Affected, which appears in the Finding Aids section of the printed volume and on GPO Access.

EXCLUDED VETERINARY ANABOLIC STEROID IMPLANT PRODUCTS

§ 1308.25 Exclusion of a veterinary anabolic steroid implant product; application.

(a) Any person seeking to have any anabolic steroid product, which is expressly intended for administration through implants to cattle or other nonhuman species and which has been approved by the Secretary of Health and Human Services for such administration, identified as being excluded from any schedule, pursuant to section 102(41)(B)(i) of the Act (21 U.S.C. 802(41)(B)(i)), may apply to the Administrator, Drug Enforcement Administration, Department of Justice, Washington, DC 20537.

(b) An application for any exclusion under this section shall be submitted in triplicate and contain the following information:

(1) The name and address of the applicant;

(2) The name of the product;

(3) The chemical structural formula or description for any anabolic steroid contained in the product;

(4) A complete description of dosage and quantitative composition of the dosage form;.

(5) The conditions of use including whether or not Federal law restricts this product to use by or on the order of a licensed veterinarian;

(6) A description of the delivery system in which the dosage form will be distributed with sufficient detail to identify the product (e.g. 20 cartridge brown plastic belt);

(7) The label and labeling of the immediate container and the commercial containers, if any, of the product;.

(8) The name and address of the manufacturer of the dosage form if different from that of the applicant; and

(9) Evidence that the product has been approved by the Secretary of Health and Human Services for administration through implant to cattle or other nonhuman species.

(c) Within a reasonable period of time after the receipt of an application for an exclusion under this section, the Administrator shall notify the applicant of his acceptance or nonacceptance of the application, and if not accepted, the reason therefore. The Administrator need not accept an application for filing if any of the requirements prescribed in paragraph (b) of this section is lacking or is not set forth as to be readily understood. The applicant may amend the application to meet the requirements of paragraph (b) of this section. If the application is accepted for filing, the Administrator shall issue and have published in the FEDERAL REGISTER his order on the application, which shall include a reference to the legal authority under which the order is issued and the findings of fact and conclusions of law upon which the order is based. This order shall specify the date on which it will take effect. The Administrator shall permit any interested person to file written comments on or objections to the order within 60 days of the date of publication in the FEDERAL REGISTER. If any such comments or objections raise significant issues regarding any finding of fact or conclusion of law upon which the order is based, the Administrator shall immediately suspend the effectiveness of the order until he may reconsider the application in light of the comments and objections filed. Thereafter, the Administrator shall reinstate, revoke, or amend his original order as he determines appropriate.

(d) The Administrator may at any time revoke or modify any designation of excluded status granted pursuant to this section by following the procedures set forth in paragraph (c) of this section for handling an application for an exclusion which has been accepted for filing.

[56 FR 42936, Aug. 30, 1991]

§1308.26 Excluded veterinary anabolic steroid implant products.

(a) Products containing an anabolic steroid, that are expressly intended for administration through implants to cattle or other nonhuman species and which have been approved by the Secretary of Health and Human Services for such administration are excluded from all schedules pursuant to section 102(41)(B)(I) of the Act (21 U.S.C. 802(41)(B)(I)). A listing of the excluded products may be obtained by submitting a written request to the Drug and Chemical Evaluation Section, Drug Enforcement Administration, Washington DC 20537.

(b) In accordance with section 102(41)(B)(ii) of the Act (21 U.S.C. 802(41)(B)(ii)) if any person prescribes, dispenses, or distributes a product listed in paragraph (a) of this section for human use, such person shall be considered to have prescribed, dispensed, or distributed an anabolic steroid within the meaning of section 102(41)(A) of the Act (21 U.S.C. 802(41)(A)).

[56 FR 42936, Aug. 30, 1991, as amended at 57 FR 19534, May 7, 1992; 58 FR 15088, Mar. 19, 1993; 62 FR 13967, Mar. 24, 1997]

EXEMPTED PRESCRIPTION PRODUCTS

§1308.31 Application for exemption of a nonnarcotic prescription product.

(a) Any person seeking to have any compound, mixture, or preparation containing any nonnarcotic controlled substance listed in §1308.12(e), or in §1308.13 (b) or (c), or in §1308.14, or in §1308.15, exempted from application of all or any part of the Act pursuant to section 201(g)(3)(A), of the Act (21 U.S.C. 811(g)(3)(A). may apply to the Administrator, Drug Enforcement Administration, Washington, DC 20537, for such exemption.

(b) An application for an exemption under this section shall contain the following information:

(1) The complete quantitative composition of the dosage form.

(2) Description of the unit dosage form together with complete labeling.

(3) A summary of the pharmacology of the product including animal investigations and clinical evaluations and studies, with emphasis on the psychic and/or physiological dependence liability (this must be done for each of the active ingredients separately and for the combination product).

(4) Details of synergisms and antagonisms among ingredients.

(5) Deterrent effects of the noncontrolled ingredients.

(6) Complete copies of all literature in support of claims.

(7) Reported instances of abuse.

(8) Reported and anticipated adverse effects.

(9) Number of dosage units produced for the past 2 years.

(c) Within a reasonable period of time after the receipt of an application for an exemption under this section, the Administrator shall notify the applicant of his acceptance or non-acceptance of the application, and if not accepted, the reason therefor. The Administrator need not accept an application for filing if any of the requirements prescribed in paragraph (b) of this section is lacking or is not set forth so as to be readily understood. If the applicant desires, he may amend the application to meet the requirements of paragraph (b) of this section. If accepted for filing, the Administrator shall publish in the FEDERAL

REGISTER general notice of this proposed rulemaking in granting or denying the application. Such notice shall include a reference to the legal authority under which the rule is proposed, a statement of the proposed rule granting or denying an exemption, and, in the discretion of the Administrator, a summary of the subjects and issues involved. The Administrator shall permit any interested person to file written comments on or objections to the proposal and shall designate in the notice of proposed rule making the time during which such filings may be made. After consideration of the application and any comments on or objections to his proposed rulemaking, the Administrator shall issue and publish in the FEDERAL REGISTER his final order on the application, which shall set forth the findings of fact and conclusions of law upon which the order is based. This order shall specify the date on which it shall take effect, which shall not be less than 30 days from the date of publication in the FEDERAL REGISTER unless the Administrator finds that conditions of public health or safety necessitate an earlier effective date, in which event the Administrator shall specify in the order his findings as to such conditions.

(d) The Administrator may revoke any exemption granted pursuant to section 201(g)(3)(A) of the Act (21 U.S.C. 811(g)(3)(A)) by following the procedures set forth in paragraph (c) of this section for handling an application for an exemption which has been accepted for filing.

[38 FR 8254, Mar. 30, 1973. Redesignated at 38 FR 26609, Sept. 24, 1973, as amended at 44 FR 18968, Mar. 30, 1979; 52 FR 9803, Mar. 27, 1987]

§ 1308.32 Exempted prescription products.

The compounds, mixtures, or preparations that contain a nonnarcotic controlled substance listed in § 1308.12(e) or in § 1308.13 (b) or (c) or in § 1308.14 or in § 1308.15 listed in the Table of Exempted Prescription Products have been exempted by the Administrator from the application of sections 302 through 305, 307 through 309, 1002 through 1004 of the Act (21 U.S.C. 822–825, 827–829, and 952–954) and §§ 1301.13, 1301.22, and §§ 1301.71 through

1301.76 of this chapter for administrative purposes only. An exception to the above is that those products containing butalbital shall not be exempt from the requirement of 21 U.S.C. 952–954 concerning importation, exportation, transshipment and in-transit shipment of controlled substances. Any deviation from the quantitative composition of any of the listed drugs shall require a petition of exemption in order for the product to be exempted. A listing of the Exempted Prescription Products may be obtained by submitting a written request to the Drug and Chemical Evaluation Section, Drug Enforcement Administration, Washington, DC 20537.

[62 FR 13967, Mar. 24, 1997]

EXEMPT ANABOLIC STEROID PRODUCTS

§ 1308.33 Exemption of certain anabolic steroid products; application.

(a) The Administrator, upon the recommendation of Secretary of Health and Human Services, may, by regulation, exempt from the application of all or any part of the Act any compound, mixture, or preparation containing an anabolic steroid as defined in part 1300 of this chapter, which is intended for administration to a human being or animal, if, because of its concentration, preparation, formulation, or delivery system, it has no significant potential for abuse.

(b) Any person seeking to have any compound, mixture, or preparation containing an anabolic steroid as defined in part 1300 of this chapter exempted from the application of all or any part of the Act, pursuant to paragraph (a) of this section, may apply to the Administrator, Drug Enforcement Administration, Department of Justice, Washington, DC 20537.

(c) An application for an exemption under this section shall be submitted in triplicate and contain the following information:

(1) The name and address of the applicant;

(2) The name of the product;

(3) The chemical structural formula or description for any anabolic steroid contained in the product;

(4) The complete description of dosage and quantitative composition of the dosage form;

(5) A description of the delivery system, if applicable;

(6) The indications and conditions for use in which species, including whether or not this product is a prescription drug;

(7) Information to facilitate identification of the dosage form, such as shape, color, coating, and scoring;

(8) The label and labeling of the immediate container and the commercial containers, if any, of the product;

(9) The units in which the dosage form is ordinarily available; and

(10) The facts which the applicant believes justify:

(i) A determination that the product has no significant potential for abuse and

(ii) a granting of an exemption under this section.

(d) Within a reasonable period of time after the receipt of the application for an exemption under this section, the Administrator shall notify the applicant of his acceptance or nonacceptance of the application, and if not accepted, the reason therefor. The Administrator need not accept an application for filing if any of the requirements prescribed in paragraph (c) of this section is lacking or is not set forth so as to be readily understood. The applicant may amend the application to meet the requirements of paragraph (c) of this section. If accepted for filing, the Administrator will request from the Secretary for Health and Human Services his recommendation, as to whether such product which contains an anabolic steroid should be considered for exemption from certain portions of the Controlled Substances Act. On receipt of the recommendation of the Secretary, the Administrator shall make a determination as to whether the evidence submitted or otherwise available sufficiently establishes that the product possesses no significant potential for abuse. The Administrator shall issue and publish in the FEDERAL REGISTER his order on the application, which shall include a reference to the legal authority under which the order is issued, and the findings of fact and conclusions of law upon which the order is based. This order shall specify the date on which it will take effect. The Administrator shall permit any interested person to file written comments on or objections to the order within 60 days of the date of publication of his order in the FEDERAL REGISTER. If any such comments or objections raise significant issues regarding any finding of fact or conclusion of law upon which the order is based, the Administrator shall immediately suspend the effectiveness of the order until he may reconsider the application in light of the comments and objections filed. Thereafter, the Administrator shall reinstate, revoke, or amend his original order as he determines appropriate.

(e) The Administrator may revoke any exemption granted pursuant to section 1903(a) of Public Law 101–647 by following the procedures set forth in paragraph (d) of this section for handling an application for an exemption which has been accepted for filing.

[56 FR 42936, Aug. 30, 1991; 57 FR 10815, Mar. 31, 1992, as amended at 62 FR 13968, Mar. 24, 1997; 70 FR 74657, Dec. 16, 2005]

§1308.34 Exempt anabolic steroid products.

The list of compounds, mixtures, or preparations that contain an anabolic steroid that have been exempted by the Administrator from application of sections 302 through 309 and 1002 through 1004 of the Act (21 U.S.C. 822–829 and 952–954) and §§1301.13, 1301.22, and 1301.71 through 1301.76 of this chapter for administrative purposes only may be obtained by submitting a written request to the Drug and Chemical Evaluation Section, Drug Enforcement Administration, Washington, DC 20537.

[62 FR 13967, Mar. 24, 1997]

EXEMPT CANNABIS PLANT MATERIAL, AND PRODUCTS MADE THEREFROM, THAT CONTAIN TETRAHYDROCANNABINOLS

§1308.35 Exemption of certain cannabis plant material, and products made therefrom, that contain tetrahydrocannabinols.

(a) Any processed plant material or animal feed mixture containing any amount of tetrahydrocannabinols (THC) that is both:

(1) Made from any portion of a plant of the genus Cannabis excluded from the definition of marijuana under the

Act [i.e., the mature stalks of such plant, fiber produced from such stalks, oil or cake made from the seeds of such plant, any other compound, manufacture, salt, derivative, mixture, or preparation of such mature stalks (except the resin extracted therefrom), fiber, oil, or cake, or the sterilized seed of such plant which is incapable of germination] and

(2) Not used, or intended for use, for human consumption, has been exempted by the Administrator from the application of the Act and this chapter.

(b) As used in this section, the following terms shall have the meanings specified:

(1) The term *processed plant material* means cannabis plant material that has been subject to industrial processes, or mixed with other ingredients, such that it cannot readily be converted into any form that can be used for human consumption.

(2) The term *animal feed mixture* means sterilized cannabis seeds mixed with other ingredients (not derived from the cannabis plant) in a formulation that is designed, marketed, and distributed for animal consumption (and not for human consumption).

(3) The term *used for human consumption* means either:

(i) Ingested orally or

(ii) Applied by any means such that THC enters the human body.

(4) The term *intended for use for human consumption* means any of the following:

(i) Designed by the manufacturer for human consumption;

(ii) Marketed for human consumption; or

(iii) Distributed, exported, or imported, with the intent that it be used for human consumption.

(c) In any proceeding arising under the Act or this chapter, the burden of going forward with the evidence that a material, compound, mixture, or preparation containing THC is exempt from control pursuant to this section shall be upon the person claiming such exemption, as set forth in section 515(a)(1) of the Act (21 U.S.C. 885(a)(1)). In order to meet this burden with respect to a product or plant material that has not been expressly exempted from control by the Administrator pursuant to § 1308.23, the person claiming the exemption must present rigorous scientific evidence, including well-documented scientific studies by experts trained and qualified to evaluate the effects of drugs on humans.

[66 FR 51544, Oct. 9, 2001]

HEARINGS

§ 1308.41   Hearings generally.

In any case where the Administrator shall hold a hearing on the issuance, amendment, or repeal of rules pursuant to section 201 of the Act, the procedures for such hearing and accompanying proceedings shall be governed generally by the rulemaking procedures set forth in the Administrative Procedure Act (5 U.S.C. 551–559) and specifically by section 201 of the Act (21 U.S.C. 811), by §§ 1308.42–1308.51, and by §§ 1316.41–1316.67 of this chapter.

§ 1308.42   Purpose of hearing.

If requested by any interested person after proceedings are initiated pursuant to § 1308.43, the Administrator shall hold a hearing for the purpose of receiving factual evidence and expert opinion regarding the issues involved in the issuance, amendment or repeal of a rule issuable pursuant to section 201(a) of the Act (21 U.S.C. 811(a)). Extensive argument should not be offered into evidence but rather presented in opening or closing statements of counsel or in memoranda or proposed findings of fact and conclusions of law. Additional information relating to hearings to include waivers or modification of rules, request for hearing, burden of proof, time and place, and final order are set forth in part 1316 of this chapter.

[62 FR 13968, Mar. 24, 1997]

§ 1308.43   Initiation of proceedings for rulemaking.

(a) Any interested person may submit a petition to initiate proceedings for the issuance, amendment, or repeal of any rule or regulation issuable pursuant to the provisions of section 201 of the Act.

(b) Petitions shall be submitted in quintuplicate to the Administrator in the following form:

(Date)

ADMINISTRATOR, DRUG ENFORCEMENT
ADMINISTRATION
Department of Justice,
Washington, DC 20537.

DEAR SIR: The undersigned
hereby petitions the Administrator to initiate proceedings for the issuance (amendment or repeal) of a rule or regulation pursuant to section 201 of the Controlled Substances Act.

Attached hereto and constituting a part of this petition are the following:

(A) The proposed rule in the form proposed by the petitioner. (If the petitioner seeks the amendment or repeal of an existing rule, the existing rule, together with a reference to the section in the Code of Federal Regulations where it appears, should be included.)

(B) A statement of the grounds which the petitioner relies for the issuance (amendment or repeal) of the rule. (Such grounds shall include a reasonably concise statement of the facts relied upon by the petitioner, including a summary of any relevant medical or scientific evidence known to the petitioner.)

All notices to be sent regarding this petition should be addressed to:

_____
(Name)

_____
(Street Address)

_____
(City and State)

Respectfully yours,

_____
(Signature of petitioner)

(c) Within a reasonable period of time after the receipt of a petition, the Administrator shall notify the petitioner of his acceptance or nonacceptance of the petition, and if not accepted, the reason therefor. The Administrator need not accept a petition for filing if any of the requirements prescribed in paragraph (b) of this section is lacking or is not set forth so as to be readily understood. If the petitioner desires, he may amend the petition to meet the requirements of paragraph (b) of this section. If accepted for filing, a petition may be denied by the Administrator within a reasonable period of time thereafter if he finds the grounds upon which the petitioner relies are not sufficient to justify the initiation of proceedings.

(d) The Administrator shall, before initiating proceedings for the issuance, amendment, or repeal of any rule either to control a drug or other substance, or to transfer a drug or other substance from one schedule to another, or to remove a drug or other substance entirely from the schedules, and after gathering the necessary data, request from the Secretary a scientific and medical evaluation and the Secretary's recommendations as to whether such drug or other substance should be so controlled, transferred, or removed as a controlled substance. The recommendations of the Secretary to the Administrator shall be binding on the Administrator as to such scientific and medical matters, and if the Secretary recommends that a drug or other substance not be controlled, the Administrator shall not control that drug or other substance.

(e) If the Administrator determines that the scientific and medical evaluation and recommendations of the Secretary and all other relevant data constitute substantial evidence of potential for abuse such as to warrant control or additional control over the drug or other substance, or substantial evidence that the drug or other substances should be subjected to lesser control or removed entirely from the schedules, he shall initiate proceedings for control, transfer, or removal as the case may be.

(f) If and when the Administrator determines to initiate proceedings, he shall publish in the FEDERAL REGISTER general notice of any proposed rule making to issue, amend, or repeal any rule pursuant to section 201 of the Act. Such published notice shall include a statement of the time, place, and nature of any hearings on the proposal in the event a hearing is requested pursuant to § 1308.44. Such hearings may not be commenced until after the expiration of at least 30 days from the date the general notice is published in the FEDERAL REGISTER. Such published notice shall also include a reference to the legal authority under which the rule is proposed, a statement of the proposed rule, and, in the discretion of the Administrator, a summary of the subjects and issues involved.

(g) The Administrator may permit any interested persons to file written comments on or objections to the proposal and shall designate in the notice of proposed rule making the time during which such filings may be made.

[38 FR 8254, Mar. 30, 1973. Redesignated at 38 FR 26609, Sept. 24, 1973, and further redesignated and amended at 62 FR 13968, Mar. 24, 1997]

§ 1308.44 Request for hearing or appearance; waiver.

(a) Any interested person desiring a hearing on a proposed rulemaking, shall, within 30 days after the date of publication of notice of the proposed rulemaking in the FEDERAL REGISTER, file with the Administrator a written request for a hearing in the form prescribed in § 1316.47 of this chapter.

(b) Any interested person desiring to participate in a hearing pursuant to § 1308.41 shall, within 30 days after the date of publication of the notice of hearing in the FEDERAL REGISTER, file with the Administrator a written notice of his intention to participate in such hearing in the form prescribed in § 1316.48 of this chapter. Any person filing a request for a hearing need not also file a notice of appearance; the request for a hearing shall be deemed to be a notice of appearance.

(c) Any interested person may, within the period permitted for filing a request for a hearing, file with the Administrator a waiver of an opportunity for a hearing or to participate in a hearing, together with a written statement regarding his position on the matters of fact and law involved in such hearing. Such statement, if admissible, shall be made a part of the record and shall be considered in light of the lack of opportunity for cross-examination in determining the weight to be attached to matters of fact asserted therein.

(d) If any interested person fails to file a request for a hearing; or if he so files and fails to appear at the hearing, he shall be deemed to have waived his opportunity for the hearing or to participate in the hearing, unless he shows good cause for such failure.

(e) If all interested persons waive or are deemed to waive their opportunity for the hearing or to participate in the hearing, the Administrator may cancel the hearing, if scheduled, and issue his final order pursuant to § 1308.45 without a hearing.

[38 FR 8254, Mar. 30, 1973. Redesignated at 38 FR 26609, Sept. 24, 1973, and further redesignated and amended at 62 FR 13968, Mar. 24, 1997]

§ 1308.45 Final order.

As soon as practicable after the presiding officer has certified the record to the Administrator, the Administrator shall cause to be published in the FEDERAL REGISTER his order in the proceeding, which shall set forth the final rule and the findings of fact and conclusions of law upon which the rule is based. This order shall specify the date on which it shall take effect, which shall not be less than 30 days from the date of publication in the FEDERAL REGISTER unless the Administrator finds that conditions of public health or safety necessitate an earlier effective date, in which event the Administrator shall specify in the order his findings as to such conditions.

[38 FR 8254, Mar. 30, 1973. Redesignated at 38 FR 26609, Sept. 24, 1973, and further redesignated at 62 FR 13968, Mar. 24, 1997]

§ 1308.46 Control required under international treaty.

Pursuant to section 201(d) of the Act (21 U.S.C. 811(d)), where control of a substance is required by U.S. obligations under international treaties, conventions, or protocols in effect on May 1, 1971, the Administrator shall issue and publish in the FEDERAL REGISTER an order controlling such substance under the schedule he deems most appropriate to carry out obligations. Issuance of such an order shall be without regard to the findings required by subsections 201(a) or 202(b) of the Act (21 U.S.C. 811(a) or 812(b)) and without regard to the procedures prescribed by § 1308.41 or subsections 201 (a) and (b) of the Act (21 U.S.C. 811 (a) and (b)). An order controlling a substance shall become effective 30 days from the date of publication in the FEDERAL REGISTER, unless the Administrator finds that conditions of public health or safety necessitate an earlier effective date, in which event the Administrator shall specify in the order his findings as to such conditions.

[38 FR 8254, Mar. 30, 1973. Redesignated at 38 FR 26609, Sept. 24, 1973, and further redesignated at 62 FR 13968, Mar. 24, 1997]

§ 1308.47 Control of immediate precursors.

Pursuant to section 201(e) of the Act (21 U.S.C. 811(e)), the Administrator may, without regard to the findings required by subsection 201(a) or 202 (b) of the Act (21 U.S.C. 811(a) or 812(b)) and without regard to the procedures prescribed by § 1308.41 or subsections 201 (a) and (b) of the Act (21 U.S.C. 811(a) and (b)), issue and publish in the FEDERAL REGISTER an order controlling an immediate precursor. The order shall designate the schedule in which the immediate precursor is to be placed, which shall be the same schedule in which the controlled substance of which it is an immediate precursor is placed or any other schedule with a higher numerical designation. An order controlling an immediate precursor shall become effective 30 days from the date of publication in the FEDERAL REGISTER, unless the Administrator finds that conditions of public health or safety necessitate an earlier effective date, in which event the Administrator shall specify in the order his findings as to such conditions.

[38 FR 8254, Mar. 30, 1973. Redesignated at 38 FR 26609, Sept. 24, 1973, and further redesignated at 62 FR 13968, Mar. 24, 1997]

§ 1308.49 Emergency scheduling.

Pursuant to 21 U.S.C. 811(h) and without regard to the requirements of 21 U.S.C. 811(b) relating to the scientific and medical evaluation of the Secretary of Health and Human Services, the Administrator may place a substance into Schedule I on a temporary basis, if he determines that such action is necessary to avoid an imminent hazard to the public safety. An order issued under this section may not be effective before the expiration of 30 days from:

(a) The date of publication by the Administrator of a notice in the FEDERAL REGISTER of his intention to issue such

order and the grounds upon which such order is to be issued, and

(b) The date the Administrator has transmitted notification to the Secretary of Health and Human Services of his intention to issue such order. An order issued under this section shall be vacated upon the conclusion of a subsequent rulemaking proceeding initiated under section 201(a) (21 U.S.C. 811(a)) with respect to such substance or at the end of one year from the effective date of the order scheduling the substance, except that during the pendency of proceedings under section 201(a) (21 U.S.C. 811(a)) with respect to the substance, the Administrator may extend the temporary scheduling for up to six months.

[51 FR 15318, Apr. 23, 1986. Redesignated and amended at 62 FR 13968, Mar. 24, 1997]

PART 1309—REGISTRATION OF MANUFACTURERS, DISTRIBUTORS, IMPORTERS AND EXPORTERS OF LIST I CHEMICALS

AUTHORITY: 21 U.S.C. 821, 822, 823, 824, 830, 871(b), 875, 877, 886a, 958.

SOURCE: 60 FR 32454, June 22, 1995, unless otherwise noted.

GENERAL INFORMATION

§ 1309.01 Scope of part 1309.

Procedures governing the registration of manufacturers, distributors, importers and exporters of List I chemicals pursuant to Sections 102, 302, 303, 1007 and 1008 of the Act (21 U.S.C. 802, 822, 823, 957 and 958) are set forth generally by those sections and specifically by the sections of this part.

§ 1309.02 Definitions.

Any term used in this part shall have the definition set forth in section 102 of the Act (21 U.S.C. 802) or part 1300 of this chapter.

[62 FR 13968, Mar. 24, 1997]

§ 1309.03 Information; special instructions.

Information regarding procedures under these rules and instructions supplementing these rules will be furnished upon request by writing to the Drug Enforcement Administration, Chemical Operations Section, Office of Diversion Control, Washington, D.C. 20537.

FEES FOR REGISTRATION AND REREGISTRATION

§ 1309.11 Fee amounts.

(a) For each application for registration or reregistration to manufacture for distribution the applicant shall pay an annual fee of $2,293.

(b) For each application for registration or reregistration to distribute (either retail distribution or non-retail distribution), import, or export a List I chemical, the applicant shall pay an annual fee of $1,147.

[71 FR 51114, Aug. 29, 2006]

§ 1309.12 Time and method of payment; refund.

(a) For each application for registration or reregistration to manufacture for distribution, distribute (either retail distribution or non-retail distribution), import, or export a List I chemical, the applicant shall pay the fee when the application for registration or reregistration is submitted for filing.

(b) Payment should be made in the form of a personal, certified, or cashier's check or money order made payable to "Drug Enforcement Administration." Payments made in the form of stamps, foreign currency, or third party endorsed checks will not be accepted. These application fees are not refundable.

[71 FR 51114, Aug. 29, 2006]

REQUIREMENTS FOR REGISTRATION

§ 1309.21 Persons required to register.

(a) Every person who distributes, imports, or exports any List I chemical other than those List I chemicals contained in a product exempted under § 1300.02(b)(28)(i)(D) of this chapter (irrespective of the threshold provision under §1300.02(b)(28)(i)(D)(2) of this chapter), or who proposes to engage in the distribution, importation, or exportation of any List I chemical, shall obtain annually a registration specific to the List I chemicals to be handled, unless exempted by law or pursuant to §§1309.24 through 1309.26 of this part. Only persons actually engaged in such activities are required to obtain a registration; related or affiliated persons who are not engaged in such activities are not required to be registered. (For example, a stockholder or parent corporation of a corporation distributing List I chemicals is not required to obtain a registration.)

(b) Every person who distributes or exports a List I chemical they have manufactured, other than a List I chemical contained in a product exempted under §1300.02(b)(28)(i)(D) of this chapter, or proposes to distribute or export a List I chemical they have manufactured, shall obtain annually a registration specific to the List I chemicals to be handled, unless exempted by law or pursuant to §§1309.24 through 1309.26 of this part.

[67 FR 14860, Mar. 28, 2002]

§1309.22 Separate registration for independent activities.

(a) The following groups of activities are deemed to be independent of each other:

(1) Retail distributing of List I chemicals;

(2) Non-Retail distributing of List I chemicals;

(3) Importing List I chemicals; and

(4) Exporting List I chemicals.

(b) Every person who engages in more than one group of independent activities shall obtain a separate registration for each group of activities, unless otherwise exempted by the Act or §1309.24 through 1309.26, except that a person registered to import any List I chemical shall be authorized to distribute that List I chemical after importation, but no other chemical that the person is not registered to import.

[60 FR 32454, June 22, 1995, as amended at 61 FR 32926, June 26, 1996; 67 FR 14860, Mar. 28, 2002]

§1309.23 Separate registration for separate locations.

(a) A separate registration is required for each principal place of business at one general physical location where List I chemicals are distributed, imported, or exported by a person.

(b) The following locations shall be deemed to be places not subject to the registration requirement:

(1) A warehouse where List I chemicals are stored by or on behalf of a registered person, unless such chemicals are distributed directly from such warehouse to locations other than the registered location from which the chemicals were originally delivered; and

(2) An office used by agents of a registrant where sales of List I chemicals are solicited, made, or supervised but which neither contains such chemicals (other than chemicals for display purposes) nor serves as a distribution point for filling sales orders.

§1309.24 Waiver of registration requirement for certain activities.

(a) The requirement of registration is waived for any agent or employee of a person who is registered to engage in any group of independent activities, if such agent or employee is acting in the usual course of his or her business or employment.

(b) The requirement of registration is waived for any person who distributes a product containing a List I chemical that is regulated pursuant to §1300.02(b)(28)(i)(D), if that person is registered with the Administration to manufacture, distribute or dispense a controlled substance.

(c) The requirement of registration is waived for any person who imports or exports a product containing a List I chemical that is regulated pursuant to §1300.02(b)(28)(i)(D), if that person is registered with the Administration to engage in the same activity with a controlled substance.

(d) The requirement of registration is waived for any person who distributes a prescription drug product containing a List I chemical that is regulated pursuant to §1300.02(b)(28)(i)(D) of this chapter.

(e) The requirement of registration is waived for any retail distributor whose

113

activities with respect to List I chemicals are limited to the distribution of below-threshold quantities of a pseudoephedrine, phenylpropanolamine, or combination ephedrine product that is regulated pursuant to § 1300.02(b)(28)(i)(D) of this chapter, in a single transaction to an individual for legitimate medical use, irrespective of whether the form of packaging of the product meets the definition of "ordinary over-the-counter pseudoephedrine or phenylpropanolamine product" under § 1300.02(b)(31) of this chapter.

(f) The requirement of registration is waived for any person whose activities with respect to List I chemicals are limited to the distribution of red phosphorus, white phosphorus, or hypophosphorous acid (and its salts) to: another location operated by the same firm solely for internal end-use; or an EPA or State licensed waste treatment or disposal firm for the purpose of waste disposal.

(g) The requirement of registration is waived for any person whose distribution of red phosphorus or white phosphorus is limited solely to residual quantities of chemical returned to the producer, in reusable rail cars and intermodal tank containers which conform to International Standards Organization specifications (with capacities greater than or equal to 2,500 gallons in a single container).

(h) The requirement of registration is waived for any person whose activities with respect to List I chemicals are limited solely to the distribution of Lugol's Solution (consisting of 5 percent iodine and 10 percent potassium iodide in an aqueous solution) in original manufacturer's packaging of one fluid ounce (30 ml) or less.

(i) The requirement of registration is waived for any manufacturer of a List I chemical, if that chemical is produced solely for internal consumption by the manufacturer and there is no subsequent distribution or exportation of the List I chemical.

(j) If any person exempted under paragraph (b), (c), (d), (e), (f) or (g) of this section also engages in the distribution, importation or exportation of a List I chemical, other than as described in such paragraph, the person shall obtain a registration for such ac-

tivities, as required by § 1309.21 of this part.

(k) The Administrator may, upon finding that continuation of the waiver would not be in the public interest, suspend or revoke a waiver granted under paragraph (b), (c), (d), (e), (f) or (g) of this section pursuant to the procedures set forth in §§ 1309.43 through 1309.46 and 1309.51 through 1309.55 of this part. In considering the revocation or suspension of a person's waiver granted pursuant to paragraph (b) or (c) of this section, the Administrator shall also consider whether action to revoke or suspend the person's controlled substance registration pursuant to 21 U.S.C. 824 is warranted.

(l) Any person exempted from the registration requirement under this section shall comply with the security requirements set forth in §§ 1309.71–1309.73 of this part and the record-keeping and reporting requirements set forth under parts 1310 and 1313 of this chapter.

[67 FR 14860, Mar. 28, 2002, as amended at 68 FR 37414, June 24, 2003; 68 FR 57803, Oct. 7, 2003; 72 FR 35930, July 2, 2007]

§ 1309.25 Temporary exemption from registration for chemical registration applicants.

(a) Each person required by section 302 of the Act (21 U.S.C. 822) to obtain a registration to distribute, import, or export a combination ephedrine product is temporarily exempted from the registration requirement, provided that the person submits a proper application for registration on or before July 12, 1997. The exemption will remain in effect for each person who has made such application until the Administration has approved or denied that application. This exemption applies only to registration; all other chemical control requirements set forth in this part 1309 and parts 1310 and 1313 of this chapter remain in full force and effect.

(b) Each person required by section 302 of the Act (21 U.S.C. 822) to obtain a registration to distribute, import, or export a pseudoephedrine or phenylpropanolamine drug product is temporarily exempted from the registration requirement, provided that the person submits a proper application for registration on or before October 3, 1997. The exemption will remain in effect for each person who has made such application until the Administration has approved or denied that application. This exemption applies only to registration; all other chemical control requirements set forth in this part 1309 and parts 1310 and 1313 of this chapter remain in full force and effect.

[67 FR 14860, Mar. 28, 2002]

§1309.26 Exemption of law enforcement officials.

(a) The requirement of registration is waived for the following persons in the circumstances described in this section:

(1) Any officer or employee of the Administration, any officer of the U.S. Customs Service, any officer or employee of the United States Food and Drug Administration, any other Federal officer who is lawfully engaged in the enforcement of any Federal law relating to listed chemicals, controlled substances, drugs or customs, and is duly authorized to possess and distribute List I chemicals in the course of official duties; and

(2) Any officer or employee of any State, or any political subdivision or agency thereof, who is engaged in the enforcement of any State or local law relating to listed chemicals and controlled substances and is duly authorized to possess and distribute List I chemicals in the course of his official duties.

(b) Any official exempted by this section may, when acting in the course of official duties, possess any List I chemical and distribute any such chemical to any other official who is also exempted by this section and acting in the course of official duties.

APPLICATION FOR REGISTRATION

1309.31 Time for application for registration; expiration date.

(a) Any person who is required to be registered and who is not so registered may apply for registration at any time. No person required to be registered shall engage in any activity for which registration is required until the application for registration is approved and a Certificate of Registration is issued by the Administrator to such person.

(b) Any person who is registered may apply to be reregistered not more than 60 days before the expiration date of his registration.

(c) At the time a person is first registered, that person shall be assigned to one of twelve groups, which shall correspond to the months of the year. The expiration date of the registrations of all registrants within any group will be the last day of the month designated for that group. In assigning any of the above persons to a group, the Administration may select a group the expiration date of which is less than one year from the date such business activity was registered. If the person is assigned to a group which has an expiration date less than eleven months from the date of which the person is registered, the registration shall not expire until one year from that expiration date; in all other cases, the registration shall expire on the expiration date following the date on which the person is registered.

§1309.32 Application forms; contents; signature.

(a) Any person who is required to be registered pursuant to §1309.21 and is not so registered, shall apply on DEA Form 510.

(b) Any person who is registered pursuant to Section 1309.21, shall apply for reregistration on DEA Form 510a.

(c) DEA Form 510 may be obtained at any divisional office of the Administration or by writing to the Registration Unit, Drug Enforcement Administration, Department of Justice, Post Office Box 28083, Central Station, Washington, DC 20005. DEA Form 510a will be mailed to each List I chemical registrant approximately 60 days before the expiration date of his or her registration; if any registered person does not receive such forms within 45 days before the expiration date of the registration, notice must be promptly given of such fact and DEA Form 510a must be requested by writing to the Registration Unit of the Administration at the foregoing address.

(d) Each application for registration shall include the Administration Chemical Code Number, as set forth in

115

§ 1310.02 of this chapter, for each List I chemical to be distributed, imported, or exported.

(e) Registration shall not entitle a person to engage in any activity with any List I chemical not specified in his or her application.

(f) Each application shall include all information called for in the form, unless the item is not applicable, in which case this fact shall be indicated.

(g) Each application, attachment, or other document filed as part of an application, shall be signed by the applicant, if an individual; by a partner of the applicant, if a partnership; or by an officer of the applicant, if a corporation, corporate division, association, trust or other entity. An applicant may authorize one or more individuals, who would not otherwise be authorized to do so, to sign applications for the applicant by filing with the application or other document a power of attorney for each such individual. The power of attorney shall be signed by a person who is authorized to sign applications under this paragraph and shall contain the signature of the individual being authorized to sign the application or other document. The power of attorney shall be valid until revoked by the applicant.

§ 1309.33 Filing of application; joint filings.

(a) All applications for registration shall be submitted for filing to the Registration Unit, Drug Enforcement Administration, Chemical Registration/ODC, Post Office Box 2427, Arlington, Virginia 22202–2427. The appropriate registration fee and any required attachments must accompany the application.

(b) Any person required to obtain more than one registration may submit all applications in one package. Each application must be complete and must not refer to any accompanying application for required information.

§ 1309.34 Acceptance for filing; defective applications.

(a) Applications submitted for filing are dated upon receipt. If found to be complete, the application will be accepted for filing. Applications failing to comply with the requirements of this part will not generally be accepted for filing. In the case of minor defects as to completeness, the Administrator may accept the application for filing with a request to the applicant for additional information. A defective application will be returned to the applicant within 10 days of receipt with a statement of the reason for not accepting the application for filing. A defective application may be corrected and resubmitted for filing at any time.

(b) Accepting an application for filing does not preclude any subsequent request for additional information pursuant to § 1309.35 and has no bearing on whether the application will be granted.

§ 1309.35 Additional information.

The Administrator may require an applicant to submit such documents or written statements of fact relevant to the application as he deems necessary to determine whether the application should be granted. The failure of the applicant to provide such documents or statements within a reasonable time after being requested to do so shall be deemed to be a waiver by the applicant of an opportunity to present such documents or facts for consideration by the Administrator in granting or denying the application.

§ 1309.36 Amendments to and withdrawals of applications.

(a) An application may be amended or withdrawn without permission of the Administration at any time before the date on which the applicant receives an order to show cause pursuant to § 1309.46. An application may be amended or withdrawn with permission of the Administrator at any time where good cause is shown by the applicant or where the amendment or withdrawal is in the public interest.

(b) After an application has been accepted for filing, the request by the applicant that it be returned or the failure of the applicant to respond to official correspondence regarding the application, including a request that the applicant submit the required fee when sent by registered or certified mail, return receipt requested, shall be deemed to be a withdrawal of the application.

ACTION ON APPLICATIONS FOR REGISTRATION: REVOCATION OR SUSPENSION OF REGISTRATION

§ 1309.41 Administrative review generally.

The Administrator may inspect, or cause to be inspected, the establishment of an applicant or registrant, pursuant to subpart A of part 1316 of this chapter. The Administrator shall review the application for registration and other information gathered by the Administrator regarding an applicant in order to determine whether the applicable standards of Section 303 of the Act (21 U.S.C. 823) have been met by the applicant.

§ 1309.42 Certificate of registration; denial of registration.

(a) The Administrator shall issue a Certificate of Registration (DEA Form 511) to an applicant if the issuance of registration or reregistration is required under the applicable provisions of section 303 of the Act (21 U.S.C. 823). In the event that the issuance of registration or reregistration is not required, the Administrator shall deny the application. Before denying any application, the Administrator shall issue an order to show cause pursuant to Section 1309.46 and, if requested by the applicant, shall hold a hearing on the application pursuant to § 1309.51.

(b) The Certificate of Registration (DEA Form 511) shall contain the name, address, and registration number of the registrant, the activity authorized by the registration, the amount of fee paid, and the expiration date of the registration. The registrant shall maintain the certificate of registration at the registered location in a readily retrievable manner and shall permit inspection of the certificate by any official, agent or employee of the Administration or of any Federal, State, or local agency engaged in enforcement of laws relating to List I chemicals or controlled substances.

1309.43 Suspension or revocation of registration.

(a) The Administrator may suspend any registration pursuant to section 304(a) of the Act (21 U.S.C. 824(a)) for any period of time he determines.

(b) The Administrator may revoke any registration pursuant to section 304(a) of the Act (21 U.S.C. 824(a)).

(c) Before revoking or suspending any registration, the Administrator shall issue an order to show cause pursuant to Section 1309.46 and, if requested by the registrant, shall hold a hearing pursuant to Section 1309.51. Notwithstanding the requirements of this Section, however, the Administrator may suspend any registration pending a final order pursuant to § 1309.44.

(d) Upon service of the order of the Administrator suspending or revoking registration, the registrant shall immediately deliver his or her Certificate of Registration to the nearest office of the Administration. Also, upon service of the order of the Administrator revoking or suspending registration, the registrant shall, as instructed by the Administrator:

(1) Deliver all List I chemicals in his or her possession that were obtained under the authority of a registration or an exemption from registration granted by the Administrator by regulation, to the nearest office of the Administration or to authorized agents of the Administration; or

(2) Place all such List I chemicals in his or her possession under seal as described in section 304(f) of the Act (21 U.S.C. 824(f)).

(e) In the event that revocation or suspension is limited to a particular chemical or chemicals, the registrant shall be given a new Certificate of Registration for all substances not affected by such revocation or suspension; no fee shall be required for the new Certificate of Registration. The registrant shall deliver the old Certificate of Registration to the nearest office of the Administration. Also, upon service of the order of the Administrator revoking or suspending registration with respect to a particular chemical or chemicals, the registrant shall, as instructed by the Administrator:

(1) Deliver to the nearest office of the Administration or to authorized agents of the Administration all of the particular chemical or chemicals in his or her possession that were obtained under the authority of a registration or an exemption from registration granted by the Administrator by regulation,

which are affected by the revocation or suspension; or

(2) Place all of such chemicals under seal as described in section 304(f) of the Act (21 U.S.C. 824(f)).

[60 FR 32454, June 22, 1995, as amended at 62 FR 5916, Feb. 10, 1997]

§ 1309.44 Suspension of registration pending final order.

(a) The Administrator may suspend any registration simultaneously with or at any time subsequent to the service upon the registrant of an order to show cause why such registration should not be revoked or suspended, in any case where he finds that there is an imminent danger to the public health or safety. If the Administrator so suspends, he shall serve with the order to show cause pursuant to § 1309.46 an order of immediate suspension that shall contain a statement of his findings regarding the danger to public health or safety.

(b) Upon service of the order of immediate suspension, the registrant shall promptly return his Certificate of Registration to the nearest office of the Administration. Also, upon service of the order of immediate suspension, the registrant shall, as instructed by the Administrator:

(1) Deliver to the nearest office of the Administration or to authorized agents of the Administration all of the particular chemical or chemicals that were obtained under the authority of a registration or an exemption from registration granted by the Administrator by regulation, which are affected by the revocation or suspension; or

(2) Place all of such chemicals under seal as described in section 304(f) of the Act (21 U.S.C. 824(f)).

(c) Any suspension shall continue in effect until the conclusion of all proceedings upon the revocation or suspension, including any judicial review thereof, unless sooner withdrawn by the Administrator or dissolved by a court of competent jurisdiction. Any registrant whose registration is suspended under this section may request a hearing on the revocation or suspension of his registration at a time earlier than specified in the order to show cause pursuant to Section 1309.46,

which request shall be granted by the Administrator, who shall fix a date for such hearing as early as reasonably possible.

[60 FR 32454, June 22, 1995, as amended at 62 FR 5916, Feb. 10, 1997]

§ 1309.45 Extension of registration pending final order.

In the event that an applicant for re-registration (who is doing business under a registration previously granted and not revoked or suspended) has applied for reregistration at least 45 days before the date on which the existing registration is due to expire, and the Administrator has issued no order on the application on the date on which the existing registration is due to expire, the existing registration of the applicant shall automatically be extended and continue in effect until the date on which the Administrator so issues his order. The Administrator may extend any other existing registration under the circumstances contemplated in this section even though the registrant failed to apply for reregistration at least 45 days before expiration of the existing registration, with or without request by the registrant, if the Administrator finds that such extension is not inconsistent with the public health and safety.

§ 1309.46 Order to show cause.

(a) If, upon examination of the application for registration from any applicant and other information gathered by the Administration regarding the applicant, the Administrator is unable to make the determinations required by the applicable provisions of section 303 of the Act (21 U.S.C. 823) to register the applicant, the Administrator shall serve upon the applicant an order to show cause why the application for registration should not be denied.

(b) If, upon information gathered by the Administration regarding any registrant, the Administrator determines that the registration of such registrant is subject to suspension or revocation pursuant to section 304 of the Act (21 U.S.C. 824), the Administrator shall serve upon the registrant an order to show cause why the registration should not be revoked or suspended.

(c) The order to show cause shall call upon the applicant or registrant to appear before the Administrator at a time and place stated in the order, which shall not be less than 30 days after the date of receipt of the order. The order to show cause shall also contain a statement of the legal basis for such hearing and for the denial, revocation, or suspension of registration and a summary of the matters of fact and law asserted.

(d) Upon Receipt of an order to show cause, the applicant or registrant must, if he desires a hearing, file a request for a hearing pursuant to § 1309.54. If a hearing is requested, the Administrator shall hold a hearing at the time and place stated in the order, pursuant to § 1309.51.

(e) When authorized by the Administrator, any agent of the Administration may serve the order to show cause.

HEARINGS

§ 1309.51 Hearings generally.

(a) In any case where the Administrator shall hold a hearing on any registration or application therefore, the procedures for such hearing shall be governed generally by the adjudication procedures set forth in the Administrative Procedure Act (5 U.S.C. 551–559) and specifically by sections 303 and 304 of the Act (21 U.S.C. 823–824), by §§ 1309.52 through 1309.57, and by the procedures for administrative hearings under the Act set forth in §§ 1316.41 through 1316.67 of this chapter.

(b) Any hearing under this part shall be independent of, and not in lieu of, criminal prosecutions or other proceedings under the Act or any other law of the United States.

§ 1309.52 Purpose of hearing.

If requested by a person entitled to a hearing, the Administrator shall hold a hearing for the purpose of receiving factual evidence regarding the issues involved in the denial, revocation, or suspension of any registration. Extensive argument should not be offered into evidence but rather presented in opening or closing statements of counsel or in memoranda or proposed findings of fact and conclusions of law.

§ 1309.53 Request for hearing or appearance; waiver.

(a) Any person entitled to a hearing pursuant to §§ 1309.42 and 1309.43 and desiring a hearing shall, within 30 days after the date of receipt of the order to show cause, file with the Administrator a written request for a hearing in the form prescribed in § 1316.47 of this chapter.

(b) Any person entitled to a hearing pursuant to §§ 1309.42 and 1309.43 may, within the period permitted for filing a request for a hearing, file with the Administrator a waiver of an opportunity for a hearing, together with a written statement regarding his position on the matters of fact and law involved in such hearing. Such statement, if admissible, shall be made a part of the record and shall be considered in light of the lack of opportunity for cross-examination in determining the weight to be attached to matters of fact asserted therein.

(c) If any person entitled to a hearing pursuant to §§ 1309.42 and 1309.43 fails to file a request for a hearing, or if he so files and fails to appear at the hearing, he shall be deemed to have waived his opportunity for the hearing, unless he shows good cause for such failure.

(d) If any person entitled to a hearing waives or is deemed to waive his or her opportunity for the hearing, the Administrator may cancel the hearing, if scheduled, and issue his final order pursuant to § 1309.57 without a hearing.

[60 FR 32454, June 22, 1995. Redesignated at 62 FR 13968, Mar. 24, 1997]

§ 1309.54 Burden of proof.

(a) At any hearing for the denial of a registration, the Administration shall have the burden of proving that the requirements for such registration pursuant to section 303 of the Act (21 U.S.C. 823) are not satisfied.

(b) At any hearing for the revocation or suspension of a registration, the Administration shall have the burden of proving that the requirements for such revocation or suspension pursuant to section 304(a) of the Act (21 U.S.C. 824(a)) are satisfied.

[60 FR 32454, June 22, 1995. Redesignated at 62 FR 13968, Mar. 24, 1997]

119

§ 1309.55 Time and place of hearing.

The hearing will commence at the place and time designated in the order to show cause or notice of hearing published in the FEDERAL REGISTER (unless expedited pursuant to Section 1309.44(c)) but thereafter it may be moved to a different place and may be continued from day to day or recessed to a later day without notice other than announcement thereof by the presiding officer at the hearing.

[60 FR 32454, June 22, 1995. Redesignated at 62 FR 13968, Mar. 24, 1997]

MODIFICATION, TRANSFER AND TERMINATION OF REGISTRATION

§ 1309.61 Modification in registration.

Any registrant may apply to modify his or her registration to authorize the handling of additional List I chemicals or to change his or her name or address, by submitting a letter of request to the Drug Enforcement Administration, Chemical Registration/ODC, Post Office Box 2427, Arlington, Virginia 22202–2427. The letter shall contain the registrant's name, address, and registration number as printed on the certificate of registration, and the List I chemicals to be added to his registration or the new name or address and shall be signed in accordance with § 1309.32(g). No fee shall be required to be paid for the modification. The request for modification shall be handled in the same manner as an application for registration. If the modification in registration is approved, the Administrator shall issue a new certificate of registration (DEA Form 511) to the registrant, who shall maintain it with the old certificate of registration until expiration.

§ 1309.62 Termination of registration.

(a) The registration of any person shall terminate if and when such person dies, ceases legal existence, or discontinues business or professional practice. Any registrant who cases legal existence or discontinues business or professional practice shall promptly notify the Special Agent in Charge of the Administration in the area in which the person is located of such fact and seek authority and in-

structions to dispose of any List I chemicals obtained under the authority of that registration.

(b) The Special Agent in Charge shall authorize and instruct the person to dispose of the List I chemical in one of the following manners:

(1) By transfer to person registered under the Act and authorized to possess the substances;

(2) By delivery to an agent of the Administration or to the nearest office of the Administration;

(3) By such other means as the Special Agent in Charge may determine to assure that the substance does not become available to unauthorized persons.

[60 FR 32454, June 22, 1995, as amended at 62 FR 5916, Feb. 10, 1997]

§ 1309.63 Transfer of registration.

No registration or any authority conferred thereby shall be assigned or otherwise transferred except upon such conditions as the Administrator may specifically designate and then only pursuant to his written consent.

SECURITY REQUIREMENTS

§ 1309.71 General security requirements.

(a) All applicants and registrants must provide effective controls and procedures to guard against theft and diversion of List I chemicals. Chemicals must be stored in containers sealed in such a manner as to indicate any attempts at tampering with the container. Where chemicals cannot be stored in sealed containers, access to the chemicals should be controlled through physical means or through human or electronic monitoring.

(b) In evaluating the effectiveness of security controls and procedures, the Administrator shall consider the following factors:

(1) The type, form, and quantity of List I chemicals handled;

(2) The location of the premises and the relationship such location bears on the security needs;

(3) The type of building construction comprising the facility and the general characteristics of the building or buildings;

(4) The availability of electronic detection and alarm systems;

(5) the extent of unsupervised public access to the facility;

(6) The adequacy of supervision over employees having access to List I chemicals;

(7) The procedures for handling business guests, visitors, maintenance personnel, and nonemployee service personnel in areas where List I chemicals are processed or stored;

(8) The adequacy of the registrant's or applicant's systems for monitoring the receipt, distribution, and disposition of List I chemicals in its operations.

(c) Any registrant or applicant desiring to determine whether a proposed system of security controls and procedures is adequate may submit materials and plans regarding the proposed security controls and procedures either to the Special Agent in Charge in the region in which the security controls and procedures will be used, or to the Chemical Operations Section Office of Diversion Control, Drug Enforcement Administration, Washington, D.C. 20537.

[60 FR 32454, June 22, 1995, as amended at 62 FR 13968, Mar. 24, 1997; 67 FR 14861, Mar. 28, 2002; 71 FR 56023, Sept. 26, 2006]

§ 1309.72 Felony conviction; employer responsibilities.

(a) The registrant shall exercise caution in the consideration of employment of persons who will have access to listed chemicals, who have been convicted of a felony offense relating to controlled substances or listed chemicals, or who have, at any time, had an application for registration with the DEA denied, had a DEA registration revoked, or surrendered a DEA registration for cause. (For purposes of this subsection, the term "for cause" means a surrender in lieu of, or as a consequence of, any Federal or State administrative, civil or criminal action resulting from an investigation of the individual's handling of controlled substances or listed chemicals.) The registrant should be aware of the circumstances regarding the action against the potential employee and the rehabilitative efforts following the action. The registrant shall assess the

risks involved in employing such persons, including the potential for action against the registrant pursuant to § 1309.43, If such person is found to have diverted listed chemicals, and, in the event of employment, shall institute procedures to limit the potential for diversion of List I chemicals.

(b) It is the position of DEA that employees who possess, sell, use or divert listed chemicals or controlled substances will subject themselves not only to State or Federal prosecution for any illicit activity, but shall also immediately become the subject of independent action regarding their continued employment. The employer will assess the seriousness of the employee's violation, the position of responsibility held by the employee, past record of employment, etc., in determining whether to suspend, transfer, terminate or take other action against the employee.

§ 1309.73 Employee responsibility to report diversion.

Reports of listed chemical diversion by fellow employees is not only a necessary part of an overall employee security program but also serves the public interest at large. It is, therefore, the position of DEA that an employee who has knowledge of diversion from his employer by a fellow employee has an obligation to report such information to a responsible security official of the employer. The employer shall treat such information as confidential and shall take all reasonable steps to protect the confidentiality of the information and the identity of the employee furnishing information. A failure to report information of chemical diversion will be considered in determining the feasibility of continuing to allow an employee to work in an area with access to chemicals. The employer shall inform all employees concerning this policy.

PART 1310—RECORDS AND REPORTS OF LISTED CHEMICALS AND CERTAIN MACHINES

Sec.

1310.03 Persons required to keep records and file reports.
1310.04 Maintenance of records.
1310.05 Reports.
1310.06 Content of records and reports.
1310.07 Proof of identity.
1310.08 Excluded transactions.
1310.09 Temporary exemption from registration.
1310.10 Removal of the exemption of drugs distributed under the Food, Drug and Cosmetic Act.
1310.11 Reinstatement of exemption for drug products distributed under the Food, Drug and Cosmetic Act.
1310.12 Exempt chemical mixtures.
1310.13 Exemption of chemical mixtures; application.
1310.14 Exemption of drug products containing ephedrine and therapeutically significant quantities of another active medicinal ingredient.
1310.15 Exempt drug products containing ephedrine and therapeutically significant quantities of another active medicinal ingredient.
1310.21 Sale by Federal departments or agencies of chemicals which could be used to manufacture controlled substances.

AUTHORITY: 21 U.S.C. 802, 827(h), 830, 871(b) 890.

SOURCE: 54 FR 31665, Aug. 1, 1989, unless otherwise noted.

§ 1310.01   Definitions.

Any term used in this part shall have the definition set forth in section 102 of the Act (21 U.S.C. 802) or part 1300 of this chapter.

[62 FR 13968, Mar. 24, 1997]

§ 1310.02   Substances covered.

The following chemicals have been specifically designated by the Administrator of the Drug Enforcement Administration as the listed chemicals subject to the provisions of this part and parts 1309 and 1313 of this chapter. Each chemical has been assigned the DEA Chemical Code Number set forth opposite it.

(a) List I chemicals

(1) Anthranilic acid, its esters, and its salts.............8530
(2) Benzyl cyanide.............8735
(3) Ephedrine, its salts, optical isomers, and salts of optical isomers.............8113
(4) Ergonovine and its salts.............8675
(5) Ergotamine and its salts.............8676
(6) N-Acetylanthranilic acid, its esters, and its salts.............8522
(7) Norpseudoephedrine, its salts, optical isomers, and salts of optical isomers.............8317
(8) Phenylacetic acid, its esters, and its salts.............8791
(9) Phenylpropanolamine, its salts, optical isomers, and salts of optical isomers.............1225
(10) Piperidine and its salts.............2704
(11) Pseudoephedrine, its salts, optical isomers, and salts of optical isomers.............8112
(12) 3,4-Methylenedioxyphenyl-2-propanone.............8502
(13) Methylamine and its salts.............8520
(14) Ethylamine and its salts.............8678
(15) Propionic anhydride.............8328
(16) Isosafrole.............8704
(17) Safrole.............8323
(18) Piperonal.............8750
(19) N-Methylephedrine, its salts, optical isomers, and salts of optical isomers (N-Methylephedrine).............8115
(20) N-Methylpseudoephedrine, its salts, optical isomers, and salts of optical isomers.............8119
(21) Hydriodic Acid.............6695
(22) Benzaldehyde.............8256
(23) Nitroethane.............6724
(24) Gamma-Butyrolactone (Other names include: GBL; Dihydro-2 (3H)-furanone; 1,2-Butanolide; 1,4-Butanolide; 4-Hydroxybutanoic acid lactone; gamma-hydroxybutyric acid lactone).............2011
(25) Red phosphorus.............6795
(26) White phosphorus (Other names: Yellow Phosphorus).............6796
(27) Hypophosphorous acid and its salts (Including ammonium hypophosphite, calcium hypophosphite, iron hypophosphite, potassium hypophosphite, manganese hypophosphite, magnesium hypophosphite and sodium hypophosphite).............6797
(28) N-phenethyl-4-piperidone (NPP).............8332
(29) Iodine.............6699

(b) List II chemicals:

(1) Acetic anhydride.............8519
(2) Acetone.............6532
(3) Benzyl chloride.............8570
(4) Ethyl ether.............6584
(5) Potassium permanganate.............6579
(6) 2-Butanone (or Methyl Ethyl Ketone or MEK).............6714
(7) Toluene.............6594
(8) Hydrochloric acid (including anhydrous hydrogen chloride).............6545
(9) Sulfuric acid.............6552
(10) Methyl Isobutyl Ketone (MIBK).............6715
(11) Sodium Permanganate.............6588

(c) The Administrator may add or delete a substance as a listed chemical by publishing a final rule in the FEDERAL REGISTER following a proposal which shall be published at least 30 days prior to the final rule.

(d) Any person may petition the Administrator to have any substance added or deleted from paragraphs (a) or (b) of this section.

(e) Any petition under this section shall contain the following information:

(1) The name and address of the petitioner;

(2) The name of the chemical to which the petition pertains;

(3) The name and address of the manufacturer(s) of the chemical (if known);

(4) A complete statement of the facts which the petitioner believes justifies the addition or deletion of the substance from paragraphs (a) or (b) of this section;

(5) The date of the petition.

(f) The Administrator may require the petitioner to submit such documents or written statements of fact relevant to the petition as he deems necessary in making a determination.

(g) Within a reasonable period of time after the receipt of the petition, the Administrator shall notify the petitioner of his decision and the reason therefor. The Administrator need not accept a petition if any of the requirements prescribed in paragraph (e) of this section or requested pursuant to paragraph (f) of this section are lacking or are not clearly set forth as to be readily understood. If the petitioner desires, he may amend and resubmit the petition to meet the requirements of paragraphs (e) and (f) of this section.

(h) If a petition is granted or the Administrator, upon his own motion, proposes to add or delete substances as listed chemicals as set forth in paragraph (c) of this section, he shall issue and publish in the FEDERAL REGISTER a proposal to add or delete a substance as a listed chemical. The Administrator shall permit any interested person to file written comments regarding the proposal within 30 days of the date of publication of his order in the FEDERAL REGISTER. The Administrator will consider any comments filed by interested persons and publish a final rule in accordance with his decision in the matter.

[54 FR 31665, Aug. 1, 1989, as amended at 56 FR 48733, Sept. 26, 1991; 57 FR 43615, Sept. 22, 1992; 60 FR 19510, Apr. 19, 1995; 60 FR 32460, June 22, 1995; 62 FR 5917, Feb. 10, 1997; 65 FR 21647, Apr. 24, 2000; 65 FR 47316, Aug. 2, 2000; 66 FR 52675, Oct. 17, 2001; 71 FR 60826, Oct. 17, 2006; 72 FR 20046, Apr. 23, 2007; 72 FR 35391, July 2, 2007; 72 FR 40238, July 24, 2007]

§ 1310.03 Persons required to keep records and file reports.

(a) Each regulated person who engages in a regulated transaction involving a listed chemical, a tableting machine, or an encapsulating machine shall keep a record of the transaction as specified by § 1310.04 and file reports as specified by § 1310.05. However, a non-regulated person who acquires listed chemicals for internal consumption or "end use" and becomes a regulated person by virtue of infrequent or rare distribution of a listed chemical from inventory, shall not be required to maintain receipt records of listed chemicals under this section.

(b) Each regulated person who manufactures a List I or List II chemical shall file reports regarding such manufacture as specified in Section 1310.05.

(c) Each regulated person who engages in a transaction with a nonregulated person or who engages in an export transaction that involves ephedrine, pseudoephedrine, phenylpropanolamine, or gamma-hydroxybutyric acid, including drug products containing these chemicals, and uses or attempts to use the Postal Service or any private or commercial carrier must file monthly reports of each such transaction as specified in § 1310.05 of this part.

[54 FR 31665, Aug. 1, 1989, as amended at 56 FR 8277, Feb. 28, 1991; 61 FR 14023, Mar. 29, 1996; 67 FR 14861, Mar. 28, 2002; 68 FR 57804, Oct. 7, 2003; 70 FR 294, Jan. 4, 2005]

§ 1310.04 Maintenance of records.

(a) Every record required to be kept subject to § 1310.03 for a List I chemical, a tableting machine, or an encapsulating machine shall be kept by the regulated person for 2 years after the date of the transaction.

(b) Every record required to be kept subject to Section 1310.03 for List II chemical shall be kept by the regulated person for two years after the date of the transaction.

(c) A record under this section shall be kept at the regulated person's place of business where the transaction occurred, except that records may be kept at a single, central location of the regulated person if the regulated person has notified the Administration of the intention to do so. Written notification must be submitted by registered or certified mail, return receipt requested, to the Special Agent in Charge of the DEA Divisional Office for the area in which the records are required to be kept.

(d) The records required to be kept under this section shall be readily retrievable and available for inspection and copying by authorized employees of the Administration under the provisions of 21 U.S.C. 880.

(e) The regulated person with more than one place of business where records are required to be kept shall devise a system to detect any party purchasing from several individual locations of the regulated person thereby seeking to avoid the application of the cumulative threshold or evading the requirements of the Act.

(f) For those listed chemicals for which thresholds have been established, the quantitative threshold or the cumulative amount for multiple transactions within a calendar month, to be utilized in determining whether a receipt, sale, importation or exportation is a regulated transaction is as follows:

(1) List I chemicals:

(i) Except as provided in paragraph (f)(1)(ii) of this section, the following thresholds have been established for List I chemicals.

Chemical	Threshold by base weight
(A) Anthranilic acid, its esters, and its salts	30 kilograms.
(B) Benzyl cyanide	1 kilogram.
(C) Ergonovine and its salts	10 grams.
(D) Ergotamine and its salts	20 grams.
(E) N-Acetylanthranilic acid, its esters, and its salts.	40 kilograms.
(F) Norpseudoephedrine, its salts, optical isomers, and salts of optical isomers.	2.5 kilograms.
(G) Phenylacetic acid, its esters, and its salts.	1 kilogram.
(H) Phenylpropanolamine, its salts, optical isomers, and salts of optical isomers.	2.5 kilograms.
(I) Piperidine and its salts	500 grams.
(J) Pseudoephedrine, its salts, optical isomers, and salts of optical isomers.	1 kilogram.
(K) 3,4–Methylenedioxyphenyl-2-propanone	4 kilograms.
(L) Methylamine and its salts	1 kilogram.
(M) Ethylamine and its salts	1 kilogram.
(N) Propionic anhydride	1 gram.
(O) Isosafrole	4 kilograms.
(P) Safrole	4 kilograms.
(Q) Piperonal	4 kilograms.
(R) N-Methylephedrine, its salts, optical isomers, and salts of optical isomers (N-Methylephedrine).	1 kilogram.
(S) N-Methylpseudoephedrine, its salts, optical isomers, and salts of optical isomers.	1 kilogram.
(T) Hydriodic Acid	1.7 kilograms (or 1 liter by volume).
(U) Benzaldehyde	4 kilograms.
(V) Nitroethane	2.5 kilograms.

(ii) For List I chemicals that are scheduled listed chemical products as defined in § 1300.02, the thresholds established in paragraphs (f)(1)(i) and (g) of this section apply only to non-retail distribution, import, and export. Sales of these products at retail are subject to the requirements of part 1314 of this chapter.

(2) List II Chemicals:

(i) Imports and Exports

Chemical	Threshold by volume	Threshold by weight
(A) Acetic anhydride	250 gallons	1,023 kilograms.
(B) Acetone	500 gallons	1,500 kilograms.
(C) Benzyl chloride	N/A	4 kilograms.
(D) Ethyl ether	500 gallons	1,364 kilograms.
(E) Potassium permanganate	N/A	500 kilograms.
(F) 2-Butanone (MEK)	500 gallons	1,455 kilograms.
(G) Toluene	500 gallons	1,591 kilograms.
(H) Sodium permanganate	N/A	500 kilograms

(ii) Domestic Sales

Chemical	Threshold by volume	Threshold by weight
(A) Acetic anhydride	250 gallons	1,023 kilograms.

124

Chemical	Threshold by volume	Threshold by weight
(B) Acetone	50 gallons	150 kilograms.
(C) Benzyl chloride	N/A	1 kilogram.
(D) Ethyl ether	50 gallons	135.8 kilograms.
(E) Potassium permanganate	N/A	55 kilograms.
(F) 2-Butanone (MEK)	50 gallons	145 kilograms.
(G) Toluene	50 gallons	159 kilograms.
(H) Anhydrous Hydrogen chloride	N/A	0.0 kilograms.
(I) Sodium permanganate	N/A	55 kilograms

(iii) The cumulative threshold is not applicable to domestic sales of Acetone, 2-Butanone (MEK), and Toluene.

(iv) Exports, Transshipments and International Transactions to Designated Countries as Set Forth in § 1310.08(b).

Chemical	Threshold by volume	Threshold by weight
(A) Hydrochloric acid (1) Anhydrous Hydrogen chloride.	50 gallons	27 kilograms.
(B) Sulfuric acid	50 gallons	

(v) Export and International Transactions to Designated Countries, and Importations for Transshipment or Transfer to Designated Countries

Chemical	Threshold by volume	Threshold by weight
(A) Methyl Isobutyl Ketone (MIBK). (B) Reserved.	500 gallons	1523 kilograms.

(g) For listed chemicals for which no thresholds have been established, the size of the transaction is not a factor in determining whether the transaction meets the definition of a regulated transaction as set forth in § 1300.02(b)(28) of this chapter. All such transactions, regardless of size, are subject to recordkeeping and reporting requirements as set forth in this part and notification provisions as set forth in part 1313 of this chapter.

(1) Listed chemicals for which no thresholds have been established:

(i) Ephedrine, its salts, optical isomers and salts of optical isomers

(ii) Red phosphorus

(iii) White phosphorus (Other names: Yellow Phosphorus)

(iv) Hypophosphorous acid and its salts

(v) gamma-Butyrolactone (Other names include: GBL; Dihydro-2(3H)-furanone; 1,2-Butanolide; 1,4-Butanolide; 4-Hydroxybutanoic acid lactone; gamma-hydroxybutyric acid lactone)

(vi) N-phenethyl-4-piperidone (NPP)

(vii) Iodine

(2) [Reserved]

(h) The thresholds and conditions in paragraphs (f) and (g) of this section will apply to transactions involving regulated chemical mixtures. For purposes of determining whether the weight or volume of a chemical mixture meets or exceeds the applicable quantitative threshold, the following rules apply:

(1) For chemical mixtures containing List I chemicals or List II chemicals other than those in paragraph (h)(2) of this section, the threshold is determined by the weight of the listed chemical in the chemical mixture.

(2) For the List II chemicals acetone, ethyl ether, 2-butanone, toluene, and methyl isobutyl ketone, the threshold is determined by the weight of the entire chemical mixture.

(3) If two or more listed chemicals are present in a chemical mixture, and the quantity of any of these chemicals equals or exceeds the threshold applicable to that chemical, then the transaction is regulated.

[54 FR 31665, Aug. 1, 1989, as amended at 56 FR 48733, Sept. 26, 1991; 57 FR 43615, Sept. 22, 1992; 59 FR 51367, Oct. 11, 1994; 60 FR 19510, Apr. 19, 1995; 60 FR 32460, June 22, 1995; 60 FR 42436, Aug. 16, 1995; 62 FR 5917, Feb. 10, 1997; 65 FR 47316, Aug. 2, 2000; 66 FR 52675, Oct. 17, 2001; 67 FR 14861, Mar. 28, 2002; 68 FR 11472, Mar. 11, 2003; 68 FR 23203, May 1, 2003; 68 FR 53292, Sept. 10, 2003; 68 FR 57804, Oct. 7, 2003; 69 FR 74970, Dec. 15, 2004; 71 FR 56024, Sept. 26, 2006; 71 FR 60826, Oct. 17, 2006; 72 FR 20046, Apr. 23, 2007; 72 FR 35931, July 2, 2007; 72 FR 40238, July 24, 2007]

§ 1310.05 Reports.

(a) Each regulated person shall report to the Special Agent in Charge of the DEA Divisional Office for the area in which the regulated person making the report is located, as follows:

(1) Any regulated transaction involving an extraordinary quantity of a listed chemical, an uncommon method of payment or delivery, or any other circumstance that the regulated person believes may indicate that the listed chemical will be used in violation of this part.

(2) Any proposed regulated transaction with a person whose description or other identifying characteristic the Administration has previously furnished to the regulated person.

(3) Any unusual or excessive loss or disappearance of a listed chemical under the control of the regulated person. The regulated person responsible for reporting a loss in-transit is the supplier.

(4) Any domestic regulated transaction in a tableting machine or an encapsulating machine.

(b) Each report submitted pursuant to paragraph (a) of this section shall, whenever possible, be made orally to the DEA Divisional Office for the area in which the regulated person making the report is located at the earliest practicable opportunity after the regulated person becomes aware of the circumstances involved and as much in advance of the conclusion of the transaction as possible. Written reports of transactions listed in paragraphs (a)(1), (a)(3) and (a)(4) of this section will subsequently be filed as set forth in § 1310.06 within 15 days after the regulated person becomes aware of the circumstances of the event. A transaction may not be completed with a person whose description or identifying characteristic has previously been furnished to the regulated person by the Administration unless the transaction is approved by the Administration.

(c) Each regulated person who imports or exports a tableting machine, or encapsulation machine, shall file a report (not a 486) of such importation or exportation with the Administration at the following address on or before the date of importation or exportation: Drug Enforcement Administration, P.O. Box 27284, Washington, DC 20038. In order to facilitate the importation or exportation of any tableting machine or encapsulating machine and

implement the purpose of the Act, regulated persons may wish to report to the Administration as far in advance as possible. A copy of the report may be transmitted directly to the Drug Enforcement Administration through electronic facsimile media. Any tableting machine or encapsulating machine may be imported or exported if that machine is needed for medical, commercial, scientific, or other legitimate uses. However, an importation or exportation of a tableting machine or encapsulating machine may not be completed with a person whose description or identifying characteristic has previously been furnished to the regulated person by the Administration unless the transaction is approved by the Administration.

(d) Each regulated bulk manufacturer of a listed chemical shall submit manufacturing, inventory and use data on an annual basis as set forth in § 1310.06(h). This data shall be submitted annually to the Drug and Chemical Evaluation Section, Drug Enforcement Administration (DEA), Washington, D.C. 20537, on or before the 15th day of March of the year immediately following the calendar year for which submitted. A business entity which manufactures a listed chemical may elect to report separately by individual location or report as an aggregate amount for the entire business entity provided that they inform the DEA of which method they will use. This reporting requirement does not apply to drug or other products which are exempted under §§ 1310.01(f)(1)(iv) or 1310.01(f)(1)(v) except as set forth in § 1310.06(h)(5). Bulk manufacturers that produce a listed chemical solely for internal consumption shall not be required to report for that listed chemical. For purposes of these reporting requirements, internal consumption shall consist of any quantity of a listed chemical otherwise not available for further resale or distribution. Internal consumption shall include (but not be limited to) quantities used for quality control testing, quantities consumed in-house or production losses. Internal consumption does not include the quantities of a listed chemical consumed in the production of exempted products. If an existing standard industry report contains the information required in §1310.06(h) and such information is separate or readily retrievable from the report, that report may be submitted in satisfaction of this requirement. Each report shall be submitted to the DEA under company letterhead and signed by an appropriate, responsible official. For purposes of this paragraph only, the term regulated bulk manufacturer of a listed chemical means a person who manufactures a listed chemical by means of chemical synthesis or by extraction from other substances. The term bulk manufacturer does not include persons whose sole activity consists of the repackaging or relabeling of listed chemical products or the manufacture of drug dosage form products which contain a listed chemical.

(e) Each regulated person required to report pursuant to §1310.03(c) of this part shall either:

(1) Submit a written report, containing the information set forth in §1310.06(i) of this part, on or before the 15th day of each month following the month in which the distributions took place. The report shall be submitted under company letterhead, signed by the person authorized to sign the registration application forms on behalf of the registrant, to the Chemical Control Section, Office of Diversion Control, Drug Enforcement Administration, Washington, DC 20537; or

(2) Upon request to and approval by the Administration, submit the report in electronic form, either via computer disk or direct electronic data transmission, in such form as the Administration shall direct. Requests to submit reports in electronic form should be submitted to the Chemical Control Section, Office of Diversion Control, Drug Enforcement Administration, Washington, DC 20537, ATTN: Electronic Reporting.

(f) Except as provided in paragraph (g) of this section, the following distributions to nonregulated persons, and the following export transactions, are not subject to the reporting requirements in §1310.03(c):

(1) Distributions of sample packages of drug products when those packages contain not more than two solid dosage units or the equivalent of two dosage units in liquid form, not to exceed 10 milliliters of liquid per package, and not more than one package is distributed to an individual or residential address in any 30-day period.

(2) Distributions of drug products by retail distributors that may not include face-to-face transactions to the extent that such distributions are consistent with the activities authorized for a retail distributor as specified in §1300.02(b)(29) of this chapter, except that this paragraph does not apply to sales of scheduled listed chemical products at retail.

(3) Distributions of drug products to a resident of a long term care facility or distributions of drug products to a long term care facility for dispensing to or for use by a resident of that facility.

(4) Distributions of drug products in accordance with a valid prescription.

(5) Exports which have been reported to the Administrator under §§1313.31 and 1313.32 of this chapter or which are subject to a waiver granted under §1313.21 of this chapter.

(g) The Administrator may revoke any or all of the exemptions listed in paragraph (f) of this section for an individual regulated person if the Administrator finds that drug products distributed by the regulated person are being used in violation of the regulations in this chapter or the Controlled Substances Act. The Administrator will notify the regulated person of the revocation, as provided in §1313.41(a) of this chapter. The revocation will be effective upon receipt of the notice by the person. The regulated person has the right to an expedited hearing regarding the revocation, as provided in §1313.56(a) of this chapter.

[54 FR 31665, Aug. 1, 1989, as amended at 57 FR 2461, Jan. 22, 1992; 61 FR 14024, Mar. 29, 1996; 61 FR 17958, Apr. 23, 1996; 62 FR 13968, Mar. 24, 1997; 67 FR 14862, Mar. 28, 2002; 67 FR 49569, July 31, 2002; 68 FR 57804, Oct. 7, 2003; 71 FR 56024, Sept. 26, 2006]

§1310.06 **Content of records and reports.**

(a) Each record required by §1310.03 shall include the following:

(1) The name, address, and, if required, DEA registration number of

each party to the regulated transaction.

(2) The date of the regulated transaction.

(3) The name, quantity and form of packaging of the listed chemical or a description of the tableting machine or encapsulating machine (including make, model and serial number).

(4) The method of transfer (company truck, picked up by customer, etc.).

(5) The type of identification used by the purchaser and any unique number on that identification.

(b) For purposes of this section, normal business records shall be considered adequate if they contain the information listed in paragraph (a) of this section and are readily retrievable from other business records of the regulated person. For prescription drug products, prescription and hospital records kept in the normal course of medical treatment shall be considered adequate for satisfying the requirements of paragraph (a) of this section with respect to dispensing to patients, and records required to be maintained pursuant to the Federal Food and Drug Administration regulations relating to the distribution of prescription drugs, as set forth in 21 CFR part 205, shall be considered adequate for satisfying the requirements of paragraph (a) of this section with respect to distributions.

(c) Each report required by Section 1310.05(a) shall include the information as specified by Section 1310.06(a) and, where obtainable, the registration number of the other party, if such party is registered. A report submitted pursuant to § 1310.05(a)(1) or (a)(4) must also include a description of the circumstances leading the regulated person to make the report, such as the reason that the method of payment was uncommon or the loss unusual. If the report is for a loss or disappearance under § 1310.05(a)(4), the circumstances of such loss must be provided (in-transit, theft from premises, etc.)

(d) A suggested format for the reports is provided below:

Supplier:

Registration Number _____
Name _____
Business Address _____
City _____
State _____

Zip _____
Business Phone _____

Purchaser:

Registration Number _____
Name _____
Business Address _____
City _____
State _____
Zip _____
Business Phone _____
Identification _____

Shipping Address (if different than purchaser Address):

Street _____
City _____
State _____
Zip _____
Date of Shipment _____
Name of Listed Chemical(s) _____
Quantity and Form of Packaging _____

Description of Machine:

Make _____
Model _____
Serial # _____
Method of Transfer _____

If Loss or Disappearance:

Date of Loss _____
Type of Loss _____
Description of Circumstances _____

Public reporting burden for this collection of information is estimated to average ten minutes per response, including the time for reviewing instructions, searching existing data sources, gathering and maintaining the data needed, and completing and reviewing the collection of information. Send comments regarding this burden estimate or any other aspect of this collection of information, including suggestions for reducing this burden to the Drug Enforcement Administration, Records Management Section, Washington, D.C. 20537; and to the Office of Management and Budget, Paperwork Reduction Project No. 1117-0024, Washington, D.C. 20503.

(e) Each report of an importation of a tableting machine or an encapsulating machine required by § 1310.05(c) shall include the following information:

(1) The name, address, telephone number, telex number, and, where available, the facsimile number of the regulated person; the name, address, telephone number, telex number, and, where available, the facsimile number

of the import broker or forwarding agent, if any:

(2) The description of each machine (including make, model, and serial number) and the number of machines being received;

(3) The proposed import date, and the first U.S. Customs Port of Entry; and

(4) The name, address, telephone number, telex number, and, where available, the facsimile number of the consignor in the foreign country of exportation.

(f) Each report of an exportation of a tableting machine or an encapsulating machine required by §1310.05(c) shall include the following information:

(1) The name, address, telephone number, telex number, and, where available, the facsimile number of the regulated person; the name, address, telephone number, telex number, and, where available, the facsimile number of the export broker, if any;

(2) The description of each machine (including make, model, and serial number) and the number of machines being shipped;

(3) The proposed export date, the U.S. Customs Port of exportation, and the foreign Port of Entry; and

(4) The name, address, telephone, telex, and, where available, the facsimile number of the consignee in the country where the shipment is destined; the name(s) and address(es) of any intermediate consignee(s).

(g) Declared exports of machines which are refused, rejected, or otherwise deemed undeliverable may be returned to the U.S. exporter of record. A brief written report outlining the circumstances must be sent to the Drug Enforcement Administration, P.O. Box 27284, Washington, DC 20038, following the return within a reasonable time. This provision does not apply to shipments that have cleared foreign customs, been delivered, and accepted by the foreign consignee. Returns to third parties in the United States will be regarded as imports.

(h) Each annual report required by Section 1310.05(d) shall provide the following information for each listed chemical manufactured:

(1) The name, address and chemical registration number (if any) of the

manufacturer and person to contact for information.

(2) The aggregate quantity of each listed chemical that the company manufactured during the preceding calendar year.

(3) The year-end inventory of each listed chemical as of the close of business on the 31st day of December of each year. (For each listed chemical, if the prior period's ending inventory has not previously been reported to DEA, this report should also detail the beginning inventory for the period.) For purposes of this requirement, inventory shall reflect the quantity of listed chemicals, whether in bulk or non-exempt product form, held in storage for later distribution. Inventory does not include waste material for destruction, material stored as an in-process intermediate or other in-process material.

(4) The aggregate quantity of each listed chemical used for internal consumption during the preceding calendar year, unless the chemical is produced solely for internal consumption.

(5) The aggregate quantity of each listed chemical manufactured which becomes a component of a product exempted from Section 1310.01(f)(1)(iv) or 1310.01(f)(1)(v) during the preceding calendar year.

(6) Data shall identify the specific isomer, salt or ester when applicable but quantitative data shall be reported as anhydrous base or acid in kilogram units of measure.

(i) Each monthly report required by §1310.05(e) of this part shall provide the following information for each distribution:

(1) Supplier name and registration number.

(2) Purchaser's name and address.

(3) Name/address shipped to (if different from purchaser's name/address).

(4) Name of the chemical and total amount shipped (i.e. Pseudoephedrine, 250 grams).

(5) Date of shipment.

(6) Product name (if drug product).

(7) Dosage form (if drug product) (i.e., pill, tablet, liquid).

(8) Dosage strength (if drug product) (i.e., 30mg, 60mg, per dose etc.).

(9) Number of dosage units (if drug product) (100 doses per package).

(10) Package type (if drug product) (bottle, blister pack, etc.).

(11) Number of packages (if drug product) (10 bottles).

(12) Lot number (if drug product).

(j) Information provided in reports required by § 1310.05(e) of this part which is exempt from disclosure under section 552(a) of Title 5, by reason of section 552(b)(6) of Title 5, will be provided the same protections from disclosure as are provided in section 310(c) of the Act (21 U.S.C. 830(c)) for confidential business information.

[54 FR 31665, Aug. 1, 1989, as amended at 57 FR 2462, Jan. 22, 1992; 59 FR 51364, Oct. 11, 1994; 60 FR 32461, June 22, 1995; 61 FR 14024, Mar. 29, 1996; 61 FR 32926, June 26, 1996; 67 FR 14862, Mar. 28, 2002; 67 FR 49569, July 31, 2002]

§ 1310.07 Proof of identity.

(a) Each regulated person who engages in a regulated transaction must identify the other party to the transaction. For domestic transaction, this shall be accomplished by having the other party present documents which would verify the identity, or registration status if a registrant, of the other party to the regulated person at the time the order is placed. For export transactions, this shall be accomplished by good faith inquiry through reasonably available research documents or publicly available information which would indicate the existence of the foreign customer. No proof of identity is required for foreign suppliers.

(b) The regulated person must verify the existence and apparent validity of a business entity ordering a listed chemical, tableting machine or encapsulating machine. For domestic transactions, this may be accomplished by such methods as checking the telephone directory, the local credit bureau, the local Chamber of Commerce or the local Better Business Bureau, or, if the business entity is a registrant, by verification of the registration. For export transactions, a good faith inquiry to verify the existence and apparent validity of a foreign business entity may be accomplished by such methods as verifying the business telephone listing through international telephone information, the firm's listing in international or foreign national chemical directories or other commerce directories or trade publications, confirmation through foreign subsidiaries of the U.S. regulated person, verification through the country of destination's embassy Commercial Attache, or official documents provided by the purchaser which confirm the existence and apparent validity of the business entity.

(c) When transacting business with a new representative of a firm, the regulated person must verify the claimed agency status of the representative.

(d) For sales to individuals or cash purchasers, the type of documents and other evidence of proof must consist of at least a signature of the purchaser, a driver's license and one other form of identification. Any exports to individuals or exports paid in cash are suspect and should be handled as such. For such exports, the regulated person shall diligently obtain from the purchaser or independently seek to confirm clear documentation which proves the person is properly identified such as through foreign identity documents, driver's license, passport information and photograph, etc. Any regulated person who fails to adequately prove the identity of the other party to the transaction may be subject to the specific penalties provided for violations of law related to regulated transactions in listed chemicals.

(e) For a new customer who is not an individual or cash customer, the regulated person shall establish the identity of the authorized purchasing agent or agents and have on file that person's signature, electronic password, or other identification. Once the authorized purchasing agent has been established, the agent list may be updated annually rather than on each order. The regulated person must ensure that shipments are not made unless the order is placed by an authorized agent of record.

(f) With respect to electronic orders, the identity of the purchaser shall consist of a computer password, identification number or some other means of identification consistent with electronic orders and with § 1310.07(e).

[54 FR 31665, Aug. 1, 1989, as amended at 60 FR 32461, June 22, 1995]

§ 1310.08 Excluded transactions.

Pursuant to 21 U.S.C. 802(39)(A)(iii), regulation of the following transactions has been determined to be unnecessary for the enforcement of the Chemical Diversion and Trafficking Act and, therefore, they have been excluded from the definitions of regulated transactions:

(a) Domestic and import transactions of hydrochloric and sulfuric acids but not including anhydrous hydrogen chloride.

(b) Exports, transshipments, and international transactions of hydrochloric (including anhydrous hydrogen chloride) and sulfuric acids, except for exports, transshipments and international transactions to the following countries:

(1) Argentina
(2) Bolivia
(3) Brazil
(4) Chile
(5) Colombia
(6) Ecuador
(7) French Guiana
(8) Guyana
(9) Panama
(10) Paraguay
(11) Peru
(12) Suriname
(13) Uruguay
(14) Venezuela

(c) Domestic transactions of Methyl Isobutyl Ketone (MIBK).

(d) Import transactions of Methyl Isobutyl Ketone (MIBK) destined for the United States.

(e) Export transactions, international transactions, and import transactions for transshipment or transfer of Methyl Isobutyl Ketone (MIBK) destined for Canada or any country outside of the Western Hemisphere.

(f) Domestic and international transactions of Lugol's Solution (consisting of 5 percent iodine and 10 percent potassium iodide in an aqueous solution) in original manufacturer's packaging of one-fluid-ounce (30 milliliters) or less, and no greater than one package per transaction.

(g) Import transactions of anhydrous hydrogen chloride.

(h) Domestic distribution of anhydrous hydrogen chloride weighing 12,000 pounds (net weight) or more in a single container.

(i) Domestic distribution of anhydrous hydrogen chloride by pipeline.

(j) Domestic and international return shipments of reusable containers from customer to producer containing residual quantities of red phosphorus or white phosphorus in rail cars and intermodal tank containers which conform to International Standards Organization specifications (with capacities greater than or equal to 2,500 gallons in a single container).

(k) Domestic, import, and export distributions of gamma-butyrolactone weighing 4,000 kilograms (net weight) or more in a single container.

(l) Domestic and import transactions in chemical mixtures that contain acetone, ethyl ether, 2-butanone, and/or toluene, unless regulated because of being formulated with other List I or List II chemical(s) above the concentration limit.

[57 FR 43615, Sept. 22, 1992, as amended at 60 FR 19510, Apr. 19, 1995; 60 FR 32461, June 22, 1995; 62 FR 13968, Mar. 24, 1997; 65 FR 47316, Aug. 2, 2000; 66 FR 52675, Oct. 17, 2001; 68 FR 37414, June 24, 2003; 68 FR 53292, Sept. 10, 2003; 69 FR 74971, Dec. 15, 2004; 72 FR 10928, Mar. 12, 2007; 72 FR 35931, July 2, 2007]

§ 1310.09 Temporary exemption from registration.

(a) Each person required by section 302 of the act (21 U.S.C. 822) to obtain a registration to distribute, import, or export a combination ephedrine product is temporarily exempted from the registration requirement, provided that the person submits a proper application for registration on or before July 12, 1997. The exemption will remain in effect for each person who has made such application until the Administration has approved or denied that application. This exemption applies only to registration; all other chemical control requirements set forth in parts 1309, 1310, and 1313 of this chapter remain in full force and effect.

(b) Each person required by section 302 of the act (21 U.S.C. 822) to obtain a registration to distribute, import, or export a drug product that contains pseudoephedrine or phenylpropanolamine that is regulated pursuant to § 1300.02(b)(28)(1)(D) of this chapter is temporarily exempted from the registration requirement, provided that the person submits a proper application for registration on or before December 3, 1997. The exemption will remain in effect for each person who has made such application until the Administration has approved or denied that application. This exemption applies only to registration; all other chemical control requirements set forth in parts 1309, 1310, and 1313 of this chapter remain in full force and effect.

(c) Each person required by section 302 of the act (21 U.S.C. 822) to obtain a registration to distribute, import, or export GBL is temporarily exempted from the registration requirement, provided that the DEA receives a proper application for registration on or before July 24, 2000. The exemption will remain in effect for each person who has made such application until the Administration has approved or denied that application. This exemption applies only to registration; all other chemical control requirements set forth in parts 1309, 1310, and 1313 of this chapter remain in full force and effect.

(d) Each person required by section 302 of the Act (21 U.S.C. 822) to obtain a registration to distribute, import, or export the List I chemicals red phosphorus, white phosphorus, and hypophosphorous acid (and its salts), is temporarily exempted from the registration requirement, provided that the person submits a proper application for registration on or before December 17, 2001. The exemption will remain in effect for each person who has made such application until the Administration has approved or denied that application. This exemption applies only to registration; all other chemical control requirements set forth in parts 1309, 1310, and 1313 of this chapter remain in full force and effect.

(e) Each person required by section 302 of the Act (21 U.S.C. 822) to obtain a registration to distribute, import, or export regulated chemical mixtures which contain ephedrine, N-methylephedrine, N-methylpseudoephedrine, norpseudoephedrine, phenylpropanolamine, and/or pseudoephedrine, pursuant to §§ 1310.12 and 1310.13, is temporarily exempted from the registration

requirement, provided that DEA receives a proper application for registration or application for exemption on or before June 30, 2003. The exemption will remain in effect for each person who has made such application until the Administration has approved or denied that application. This exemption applies only to registration; all other chemical control requirements set forth in parts 1309, 1310, and 1313 of this chapter remain in full force and effect. Any person who distributes, imports or exports a chemical mixture whose application for exemption is subsequently denied by DEA must obtain a registration with DEA. A temporary exemption from the registration requirement will also be provided for these persons, provided that DEA receives a properly completed application for registration on or before 30 days following the date of official DEA notification that the application for exemption has not been approved. The temporary exemption for such persons will remain in effect until DEA takes final action on their registration application.

(f) Except for chemical mixtures containing the listed chemicals in paragraph (e) of this section, each person required by section 302 of the Act (21 U.S.C. 822) to obtain a registration to distribute, import, or export regulated chemical mixtures, pursuant to §§ 1310.12 and 1310.13, is temporarily exempted from the registration requirement, provided that DEA receives a proper application for registration or application for exemption on or before February 14, 2005. The exemption will remain in effect for each person who has made such. application until the Administration has approved or denied that application. This exemption applies only to registration; all other chemical control requirements set forth in parts 1309, 1310, and 1313 of this chapter remain in full force and effect.

(g) Any person who distributes, imports, or exports a chemical mixture whose application for exemption is subsequently denied by DEA must obtain a registration with DEA. A temporary exemption from the registration requirement will also be provided for these persons, provided that DEA receives a properly completed application for registration on or before 30 days following the date of official DEA notification that the application for exemption has not been approved. The temporary exemption for such persons will remain in effect until DEA takes final action on their registration application.

(h) Each person required under 21 U.S.C. 822 and 21 U.S.C. 957 to obtain a registration to manufacture, distribute, import, or export regulated N-phenethyl-4-piperidone (NPP), including regulated chemical mixtures pursuant to §1310.12, is temporarily exempted from the registration requirement, provided that DEA receives a proper application for registration or application for exemption for a chemical mixture containing NPP pursuant to §1310.13 on or before June 22, 2007. The exemption will remain in effect for each person who has made such application until the Administration has approved or denied that application. This exemption applies only to registration; all other chemical control requirements set forth in the Act and parts 1309, 1310, 1313, and 1316 of this chapter remain in full force and effect. Any person who manufactures, distributes, imports or exports a chemical mixture containing N-phenethyl-4-piperidone (NPP) whose application for exemption is subsequently denied by DEA must obtain a registration with DEA. A temporary exemption from the registration requirement will also be provided for those persons whose application for exemption are denied, provided that DEA receives a properly completed application for registration on or before 30 days following the date of official DEA notification that the application for exemption has been denied. The temporary exemption for such persons will remain in effect until DEA takes final action on their registration application.

(i) Each person required by section 302 of the Act (21 U.S.C. 822) to obtain a registration to manufacture, distribute, import, or export regulated iodine, including regulated iodine chemical mixtures pursuant to §§1310.12 and 1310.13, is temporarily exempted from the registration requirement, provided that the Administration receives a proper application for registration or application for exemption for a chem-

ical mixture containing iodine on or before August 31, 2007. The exemption will remain in effect for each person who has made such application until the Administration has approved or denied that application. This exemption applies only to registration; all other chemical control requirements set forth in the Act and parts 1309, 1310, and 1313 of this chapter remain in full force and effect. Any person who distributes, imports, or exports a chemical mixture containing iodine whose application for exemption is subsequently denied by the Administration must obtain a registration with the Administration. A temporary exemption from the registration requirement will also be provided for these persons, provided that the Administration receives a properly completed application for registration on or before 30 days following the date of official Administration notification that the application for exemption has not been approved. The temporary exemption for such persons will remain in effect until the Administration takes final action on their registration application.

(j) Each person required by section 302 of the Act (21 U.S.C. 822) to obtain a registration to manufacture, distribute, import, or export regulated chemical mixtures which contain ephedrine, and/or pseudoephedrine, pursuant to Sections 1310.12 and 1310.13, is temporarily exempted from the registration requirement, provided that DEA receives a properly completed application for registration or application for exemption on or before August 24, 2007. The exemption will remain in effect for each person who has made such application until the Administration has approved or denied that application. This exemption applies only to registration; all other chemical control requirements set forth in parts 1309, 1310, 1313, and 1315 of this chapter remain in full force and effect. Any person who manufactures, distributes, imports, or exports a chemical mixture whose application for exemption is subsequently denied by DEA must obtain a registration with DEA. A temporary exemption from the registration requirement will also be provided for these persons, provided that DEA receives a properly completed application for registration on or before 30 days following the date of official DEA notification that the application for exemption has not been approved. The temporary exemption for such persons will remain in effect until DEA takes final action on their registration application.

[62 FR 27693, May 21, 1997, as amended at 62 FR 53960, Oct. 17, 1997; 65 FR 21647, Apr. 24, 2000; 66 FR 52675, Oct. 17, 2001; 68 FR 23203, May 1, 2003; 69 FR 74971, Dec. 15, 2004; 72 FR 20046, Apr. 23, 2007; 72 FR 35931, July 2, 2007; 72 FR 40239, July 24, 2007; 72 FR 40744, July 25, 2007]

§ 1310.10 Removal of the exemption of drugs distributed under the Food, Drug and Cosmetic Act.

(a) The Administrator may remove from exemption under § 1310.01(b)(28)(i)(D) any drug or group of drugs that the Administrator finds is being diverted to obtain a listed chemical for use in the illicit production of a controlled substance. In removing a drug or group of drugs from the exemption the Administrator shall consider:

(1) The scope, duration, and significance of the diversion;

(2) Whether the drug or group of drugs is formulated in such a way that it cannot be easily used in the illicit production of a controlled substance; and

(3) Whether the listed chemical can be readily recovered from the drug or group of drugs.

(b) Upon determining that a drug or group of drugs should be removed from the exemption under paragraph (a) of this section, the Administrator shall issue and publish in the FEDERAL REGISTER his proposal to remove the drug or group of drugs from the exemption, which shall include a reference to the legal authority under which the proposal is based. The Administrator shall permit any interested person to file written comments on or objections to the proposal. After considering any comments or objections filed, the Administrator shall publish in the FEDERAL REGISTER his final order.

(c) The Administrator shall limit the removal of a drug or group of drugs from exemption under paragraph (a) of this section to the most identifiable type of the drug or group of drugs for which evidence of diversion exists unless there is evidence, based on the pattern of diversion and other relevant factors, that the diversion will not be limited to that particular drug or group of drugs.

(d) Any manufacturer seeking reinstatement of a particular drug product that has been removed from an exemption may apply to the Administrator for reinstatement of the exemption for that particular drug product on the grounds that the particular drug product is manufactured and distributed in a manner that prevents diversion. In determining whether the exemption should be reinstated the Administrator shall consider:

(1) The package sizes and manner of packaging of the drug product;

(2) The manner of distribution and advertising of the drug product;

(3) Evidence of diversion of the drug product;

(4) Any actions taken by the manufacturer to prevent diversion of the drug product; and

(5) Such other factors as are relevant to and consistent with the public health and safety, including the factors described in paragraph (a) of this section as applied to the drug product.

(e) Within a reasonable period of time after receipt of the application for reinstatement of the exemption, the Administrator shall notify the applicant of his acceptance or non-acceptance of his application, and if not accepted, the reason therefor. If the application is accepted for filing, the Administrator shall issue and publish in the FEDERAL REGISTER his order on the reinstatement of the exemption for the particular drug product, which shall include a reference to the legal authority under which the order is based. This order shall specify the date on which it shall take effect. The Administrator shall permit any interested person to file written comments on or objections to the order. If any such comments raise significant issues regarding any finding of fact or conclusion of law upon which the order is based, the Administrator shall immediately suspend the effectiveness of the order until he may reconsider the application in light of the comments and objections filed. Thereafter, the Administrator shall reinstate, revoke, or amend his original order as he determines appropriate.

(f) Unless the Administrator has evidence that the drug product is being diverted, as determined by applying the factors set forth in paragraph (a) of this section, and the Administrator so notifies the applicant, transactions involving a specific drug product will not be considered regulated transactions during the following periods:

(1) While a bonafide application for reinstatement of exemption under paragraph (d) of this section for the specific drug product is pending resolution, provided that the application for reinstatement is filed not later than 60 days after the publication of the final order removing the exemption; and

(2) For a period of 60 days following the Administrator's denial of an application for reinstatement.

(g) An order published by the Administrator in the FEDERAL REGISTER, pursuant to paragraph (e) of this section, to reinstate an exemption may be modified or revoked with respect to a particular drug product upon a finding that:

(1) Applying the factors set forth in paragraph (a) of this section to the particular drug product, the drug product is being diverted; or

(2) There is a significant change in the data that led to the issuance of the final rule.

[60 FR 32461, June 22, 1995, as amended at 62 FR 13968, Mar. 24, 1997; 67 FR 14862, Mar. 28, 2002]

§ 1310.11 Reinstatement of exemption for drug products distributed under the Food, Drug and Cosmetic Act.

(a) The Administrator has reinstated the exemption for the drug products listed in paragraph (e) of this section from application of sections 302, 303, 310, 1007, and 1008 of the Act (21 U.S.C. 822–823, 830, and 957–958), to the extent described in paragraphs (b), (c), and (d) of this section.

(b) No reinstated exemption granted pursuant to 1310.10 affects the criminal

liability for illegal possession or distribution of listed chemicals contained in the exempt drug product.

(c) Changes in exempt drug product compositions: Any change in the quantitative or qualitative composition, trade name or other designation of an exempt drug product listed in paragraph (d) requires a new application for reinstatement of the exemption.

(d) The following drug products, in the form and quantity listed in the application submitted (indicated as the "date") are designated as reinstated exempt drug products for the purposes set forth in this section:

EXEMPT DRUG PRODUCTS

Supplier	Product name	Form	Date
[Reserved]	....	....	

[60 FR 32462, June 22, 1995]

§ 1310.12 Exempt chemical mixtures.

(a) The chemical mixtures meeting the criteria in paragraphs (c) or (d) of this section are exempted by the Administrator from application of sections 302, 303, 310, 1007, and 1008 of the Act (21 U.S.C. 822, 823, 830, 957 and 958) to the extent described in paragraphs (b) and (c) of this section.

(b) No exemption granted pursuant to this § 1310.12 or § 1310.13 affects the criminal liability for illegal possession, distribution, exportation, or importation of listed chemicals contained in the exempt chemical mixture or the civil liability for unlawful acts related to exempt chemical mixtures, including distribution in violation of 21 U.S.C. 842(a)(11).

(c) Mixtures containing a listed chemical in concentrations equal to or less than those specified in the "Table of Concentration Limits" are designated as exempt chemical mixtures for the purpose set forth in this section. The concentration is determined for liquid-liquid mixtures by using the volume or weight and for mixtures containing solids or gases by using the unit of weight.

TABLE OF CONCENTRATION LIMITS

	DEA chemical code number	Concentration	Special conditions
List I Chemicals			
N-Acetylanthranilic acid, its salts and esters.	8522	20% by Weight	Concentration based on any combination of N-acetylanthranilic acid and its salts and esters.
Anthranilic acid, and its salts and esters.	8530	50% by Weight	Concentration is based on any combination of anthranilic acid and its salts and esters.
Benzaldehyde	8256	50% by Weight or Volume.	
Benzyl cyanide	8570	20% by Weight or Volume.	
Ephedrine, its salts, optical isomers, and salts of optical isomers.	8113	Not exempt at any concentration.	Chemical mixtures containing any amount of ephedrine and/or pseudoephedrine, and their salts, optical isomers and salts of optical isomers are not exempt due to concentration, unless otherwise exempted.
Ergonovine and its salts	8675	Not exempt at any concentration.	Chemical mixtures containing any amount of ergonovine, including its salts, are not exempt.
Ergotamine and its salts	8676	Not exempt at any concentration.	Chemical mixtures containing amount of any ergotamine, including its salts, are not exempt.
Ethylamine and its salts	8678	20% by Weight or Volume	Ethylamine or its salts in an inert carrier solvent is not considered a mixture. Concentration is based on ethylamine in the mixture and not the combination of ethylamine and carrier solvent, if any.
Hydriodic acid	6695	20% by Weight or Volume.	
Iodine	6699	2.2	Calculated as weight/volume (w/v).
Isosafrole	8704	20% by Weight or Volume	Concentration in a mixture cannot exceed 20% if taken alone or in any combination with safrole.
Methylamine and its salts ..	8520	20% by Weight	Methylamine or its salts in an inert carrier solvent is not considered a mixture. Weight is based on methylamine in the mixture and not the combined weight of carrier solvent, if any.
3,4-Methylenedioxyphenyl-2-propanone.	8502	20% by Weight.	
N-Methylephedrine, its salts, optical isomers, and salts of optical isomers.	8115	0.1% by Weight	Concentration based on any combination of salts N-methylephedrine, N-methylpseudoephedrine and their salts, optical isomers and salts of optical isomers.
N-Methylpseudoephedrine, its salts, optical isomers, and salts of optical isomers.	8119	0.1% by Weight	Concentration based on any combination of N-methylpseudoephedrine, N-methylephedrine, and their salts, optical isomers and salts of optical isomers.
Nitroethane	6724	20% by Weight or Volume.	
Norpseudoephedrine, its salts, optical isomers, and salts of optical isomers.	8317	0.6% by Weight	Concentration based on any combination of norpseudoephedrine, phenylpropanolamine and their salts, optical isomers and salts of optical isomers.
N-phenethyl-4-piperidone (NPP).	8332	Not exempt at any concentration.	Chemical mixtures containing any amount of NPP are not exempt.
Phenylacetic acid, and its salts and esters.	8791	40% by Weight	Concentration is based on any combination of phenylacetic acid and its salts and esters.
Phenylpropanolamine, its salts, optical isomers, and salts of optical isomers.	1225	0.6% by Weight	Concentration based on any combination of phenylpropanolamine, norpseudoephedrine and their salts, optical isomers and salts of optical isomers.
Piperidine, and its salts	2704	20% by Weight or Volume	Concentration based on any combination of piperidine and its salts. Concentration based on weight if a solid, weight or volume if a liquid.
Piperonal	8750	20% by Weight or Volume.	
Propionic anhydride	8328	20% by Weight or Volume.	
Pseudoephedrine, its salts, optical isomers, and salts of optical isomers.	8112	Not exempt at any concentration.	Chemical mixtures containing any amount of ephedrine and/or pseudoephedrine, and their salts, optical isomers and salts of optical isomers are not exempt due to concentration, unless otherwise exempted.
Safrole	8323	20% by Volume	Concentration in a mixture cannot exceed 20% if taken alone or in any combination with isosafrole.
List II Chemicals			
Acetic Anhydride	8519	20% by Weight or Volume.	

TABLE OF CONCENTRATION LIMITS—Continued

	DEA chemical code number	Concentration	Special conditions
Acetone	6532	35% by Weight or Volume	Exports only; Limit applies to acetone or any combination of acetone, ethyl ether, 2-butanone, methyl isobutyl ketone, and toluene if present in the mixture by summing the concentrations for each chemical.
Benzyl chloride	8568	20% by Weight or Volume.	
2-butanone	6714	35% by Weight or Volume	Exports only; Limit applies to 2-butanone or any combination of acetone, ethyl ether, 2-butanone, methyl isobutyl ketone, and toluene if present in the mixture by summing the concentrations for each chemical.
Ethyl ether	6584	35% by Weight or Volume	Exports only; Limit applies to ethyl ether or any combination of acetone, ethyl ether, 2-butanone, methyl isobutyl ketone, and toluene if present in the mixture by summing the concentrations for each chemical.
Hydrochloric acid	6545	20% by Weight or Volume	Hydrogen chloride in an inert carrier solvent, such as aqueous or alcoholic solutions, is not considered a mixture. Weight is based on hydrogen chloride in the mixture and not the combined weight of the carrier solvent, if any.
Methyl isobutyl ketone	6715	35% by Weight or Volume	Exports only pursuant to § 1310.08; Limit applies to methyl isobutyl ketone or any combination of acetone, ethyl ether, 2-butanone, methyl isobutyl ketone, and toluene if present in the mixture by summing the concentrations for each chemical.
Potassium permanganate ..	6579	15% by Weight.	
Sodium Permanganate	6588	15% by Weight.	
Sulfuric acid	6552	20% by Weight or Volume	Sulfuric acid in an inert carrier solvent, such as aqueous or alcoholic solutions, is not considered a mixture. Weight is based on sulfuric acid in the mixture and not the combined weight of the carrier solvent, if any.
Toluene	594	35% by Weight or Volume	Exports only; Limit applies to toluene or any combination of acetone, ethyl ether, 2-butanone, methyl isobutyl ketone, and toluene if present in the mixture by summing the concentrations for each chemical.

(d) The following categories of chemical mixtures are automatically exempt from the provisions of the Controlled Substances Act as described in paragraph (a) of this section:

(1) Chemical mixtures that are distributed directly to an incinerator for destruction or directly to an authorized waste recycler or reprocessor where such distributions are documented on United States Environmental Protection Agency Form 8700–22; persons distributing the mixture to the incinerator or recycler must maintain and make available to agents of the Administration, upon request, such documentation for a period of no less than two years.

(2) Completely formulated paints and coatings: Completely formulated paints and coatings are only those formulations that contain all the components of the paint or coating for use in the final application without the need to add any additional substances except a thinner if needed in certain cases. A completely formulated paint or coating is defined as any clear or pigmented liquid, liquefiable or mastic composition designed for application to a substrate in a thin layer that is converted to a clear or opaque solid protective, decorative, or functional adherent film after application. Included in this category are clear coats, topcoats, primers, varnishes, sealers, adhesives, lacquers, stains, shellacs, inks, and temporary protective coatings.

(3) Iodine products classified as iodophors that exist as an iodine complex to include poloxamer-iodine complex, polyvinyl pyrrolidone-iodine complex (i.e., povidone-iodine), undecoylium chloride iodine, nonylphenoxypoly (ethyleneoxy) ethanol-iodine complex, iodine complex

with phosphate ester of alkylaryloxy polyethylene glycol, and iodine complex with ammonium ether sulfate/ polyoxyethylene sorbitan monolaurate.

(4) Iodine products that consist of organically bound iodine (a non-ionic complex) (e.g., iopamidol, iohexol, and amiodarone.)

(e) The Administrator may, at any time, terminate or modify the exemption for any chemical mixture which has been granted an exemption pursuant to the concentration limits as specified in paragraph (c) of this section or pursuant to the category exemption as specified in paragraph (d) of this section. In terminating or modifying an exemption, the Administrator shall issue, and publish in the FEDERAL REGISTER, notification of the removal of an exemption for a product or group of products for which evidence of diversion has been found, as well as the date on which the termination of exemption shall take effect. The Administrator shall permit any interested party to file written comments on or objections to the order within 60 days of the date of publication of the order in the FEDERAL REGISTER. If any such comments or objections raise significant issues regarding any finding of fact or conclusion of law upon which the order is based, the Administrator shall immediately suspend the effectiveness of the order until he may reconsider the order in light of comments and objections filed. Thereafter, the Administrator shall reinstate, terminate, or amend the original order as determined appropriate.

(f) The Administrator may modify any part of the criteria for exemption as specified in paragraphs (c) and (d) of this section upon evidence of diversion or attempted diversion. In doing so, the Administrator shall issue and publish a Notice of Proposed Rulemaking in the FEDERAL REGISTER. The Administrator shall permit any interested persons to file written comments on or objections to the proposal. After considering any comments or objections filed, the Administrator shall publish in the FEDERAL REGISTER a final order.

[68 FR 23204, May 1, 2003, as amended at 69 FR 74971, Dec. 15, 2004; 71 FR 60826, Oct. 17, 2006; 72 FR 20047, Apr. 23, 2007; 72 FR 35931, July 2, 2007; 72 FR 40745, July 25, 2007]

§ 1310.13 Exemption of chemical mixtures; application.

(a) The Administrator may, by publication of a Final Rule in the FEDERAL REGISTER, exempt from the application of all or any part of the Act a chemical mixture consisting of two or more chemical components, at least one of which is not a List I or List II chemical, if:

(1) The mixture is formulated in such a way that it cannot be easily used in the illicit production of a controlled substance; and

(2) The listed chemical or chemicals contained in the chemical mixture cannot be readily recovered.

(b) Any manufacturer seeking an exemption for a chemical mixture, not exempt under § 1310.12, from the application of all or any part of the Act, may apply to the Administrator, Drug Enforcement Administration, Department of Justice, Washington, DC 20537.

(c) An application for exemption under this section shall contain the following information:

(1) The name, address, and registration number, if any, of the applicant;

(2) The date of the application;

(3) The exact trade name(s) of the applicant's chemical mixture and:

(i) If the applicant formulates or manufactures the chemical mixture for other entities, the exact trade names of the chemical mixtures and the names of the entities for which the chemical mixtures were prepared; and

(ii) If a group of mixtures (e.g. formulations having identical function and containing the same listed chemical(s)), the information required in paragraph (c)(3)(i) of this section and a brief narrative of their use.

(4) (i) The complete qualitative and quantitative composition of the chemical mixture (including all listed and all non-listed chemicals); or

(ii) If a group of mixtures, the concentration range for the listed chemical and a listing of all non-listed chemicals with respective concentration ranges.

(5) (i) The chemical and physical properties of the mixture and how they differ from the properties of the listed chemical or chemicals; and

(ii) If a group of mixtures, how the group's properties differ from the properties of the listed chemical.

(6) A statement that the applicant believes justifies an exemption for the chemical mixture or group of mixtures. The statement must explain how the chemical mixture(s) meets the exemption criteria set forth in paragraph (a) of this section.

(7) A statement that the applicant accepts the right of the Administrator to terminate exemption from regulation for the chemical mixture(s) granted exemption under this section.

(8) The identification of any information on the application that is considered by the applicant to be a trade secret or confidential and entitled to protection under U.S. laws restricting the public disclosure of such information.

(d) The Administrator may require the applicant to submit such additional documents or written statements of fact relevant to the application that he deems necessary for determining if the application should be granted.

(e) Within 30 days after the receipt of an application for an exemption under this section, the Administrator will notify the applicant of acceptance or rejection of the application. If the application is not accepted, an explanation will be provided. The Administrator is not required to accept an application if any information required pursuant to paragraph (c) of this section or requested pursuant to paragraph (d) of this section is lacking or not readily understood. The applicant may, however, amend the application to meet the requirements of paragraphs (c) and (d) of this section. If the exemption is granted, the applicant shall be notified in writing and the Administrator shall issue, and publish in the FEDERAL REGISTER, an order on the application. This order shall specify the date on which it shall take effect. The Administrator shall permit any interested person to file written comments on or objections to the order. If any comments or objections raise significant issues regarding any findings of fact or conclusions of law upon which the order is based, the Administrator may suspend the effectiveness of the order until he has reconsidered the application in light of the comments and objections filed.

Thereafter, the Administrator shall reinstate, terminate, or amend the original order as deemed appropriate.

(f) The Administrator may, at any time, terminate or modify an exemption for any product pursuant to paragraph (e) of this section. In terminating or modifying an exemption, the Administrator shall issue, and publish in the FEDERAL REGISTER, notification of the removal of an exempt product or group of exempt products for which evidence of diversion has been found. This order shall specify the date on which the termination of exemption shall take effect. The Administrator shall permit any interested party to file written comments on or objections to the order within 60 days of the date of publication of the order in the FEDERAL REGISTER. If any such comments or objections raise significant issues regarding any finding of fact or conclusion of law upon which the order is based, the Administrator may suspend the effectiveness of the order until he has reconsidered the order in light of comments and objections filed. Thereafter, the Administrator shall reinstate, terminate, or amend the original order as determined appropriate.

(g) A manufacturer of an exempted chemical mixture shall notify DEA in writing, of any change in the quantitative or qualitative composition of a chemical mixture that has been granted an exemption by application. Changes include those greater than the range of concentration given in the application or that remove non-listed chemical(s) given in the application as part of the formulation. A new application will be required only if reformulation results in a new product having a different commercial application or can no longer be defined as part of a group of exempted chemicals. DEA must be notified of reformulation at least 30 days in advance of marketing the reformulated mixture. For a change in name or other designation, code, or any identifier, a written notification is required. DEA must be notified of any changes at least 60 days in advance of the effective date for the change.

(h) Each manufacturer seeking exemption must apply for such an exemption. A formulation granted exemption by publication in the FEDERAL REGISTER will not be exempted for all manufacturers.

(i) The following chemical mixtures, in the form and quantity listed in the application submitted (indicated as the "date") are designated as exempt chemical mixtures for the purposes set forth in this section and are exempted by the Administrator from application of sections 302, 303, 310, 1007, and 1008 of the Act (21 U.S.C. 822, 823, 830, 957 and 958):

EXEMPT CHEMICAL MIXTURES

Manufacturer	Product name [1]	Form	Date
[Reserved]			

[1] Designate product line if a group.

[68 FR 23204, May 1, 2003]

§ 1310.16 Exemptions for certain scheduled listed chemical products.

(a) Upon the application of a manufacturer of a scheduled listed chemical product, the Administrator may by regulation provide that the product is exempt from part 1314 of this chapter if the Administrator determines that the product cannot be used in the illicit manufacture of a controlled substance.

(b) An application for an exemption under this section must contain all of the following information:

(1) The name and address of the applicant.

(2) The exact trade name of the scheduled listed chemical product for which exemption is sought.

(3) The complete quantitative and qualitative composition of the drug product.

(4) A brief statement of the facts that the applicant believes justify the granting of an exemption under this section.

(5) Certification by the applicant that the product may be lawfully marketed or distributed under the Federal, Food, Drug, and Cosmetic Act.

(6) The identification of any information on the application that is considered by the applicant to be a trade secret or confidential and entitled to protection under U.S. laws restricting the public disclosure of such information by government employees.

(c) The Administrator may require the applicant to submit additional documents or written statements of fact relevant to the application that he deems necessary for determining if the application should be granted.

(d) Within a reasonable period of time after the receipt of a completed application for an exemption under this section, the Administrator shall notify the applicant of acceptance or non-acceptance of the application. If the application is not accepted, an explanation will be provided. The Administrator is not required to accept an application if any of the information required in paragraph (b) of this section or requested under paragraph (c) of this section is lacking or not readily understood. The applicant may, however, amend the application to meet the requirements of paragraphs (b) and (c) of this section.

(e) If the application is accepted for filing, the Administrator shall issue and publish in the FEDERAL REGISTER an order on the application, which shall include a reference to the legal authority under which the order is based. This order shall specify the date on which it shall take effect.

(f) The Administrator shall permit any interested person to file written comments on or objections to the order. If any comments or objections raise significant issues regarding any findings of fact or conclusions of law upon which the order is based, the Administrator shall immediately suspend the effectiveness of the order until he may reconsider the application in light of the comments and objections filed. Thereafter, the Administrator shall reinstate, revoke, or amend the original order as deemed appropriate.

[71 FR 56024, Sept. 26, 2006]

§ 1310.21 Sale by Federal departments or agencies of chemicals which could be used to manufacture controlled substances.

(a) A Federal department or agency may not sell from the stocks of the department or agency any chemical which, as determined by the Administrator of the Drug Enforcement Administration, could be used in the manufacture of a controlled substance, unless the Administrator certifies in writing to the head of the department or agency that there is no reasonable cause to believe that the sale of the specific chemical to a specific person would result in the illegal manufacture of a controlled substance. For purposes of this requirement, reasonable cause to believe means that the Administration has knowledge of facts which would cause a reasonable person to reasonably conclude that a chemical would be diverted to the illegal manufacture of a controlled substance.

(b) A Federal department or agency must request certification by submitting a written request to the Administrator, Drug Enforcement Administration, Washington, DC 20537, Attention: Domestic Chemical Control Unit (ODID). A request for certification may be transmitted directly to the Drug Enforcement Administration, Domestic Chemical Control Unit through electronic facsimile media. A request for certification must be submitted no later than fifteen calendar days before the proposed sale is to take place. In order to facilitate the sale of chemicals from Federal departments' or agencies' stocks, Federal departments or agencies may wish to submit requests as far in advance of the fifteen calendar days as possible. The written notification of the proposed sale must include:

(1) The name and amount of the chemical to be sold;

(2) The name and address of the prospective bidder;

(3) The name and address of the prospective end-user, in cases where a sale is being brokered;

(4) Point(s) of contact for the prospective bidder and, where appropriate, prospective end-user; and

(5) The end use of the chemical.

(c) Within fifteen calendar days of receipt of a request for certification, the Administrator will certify in writing to the head of the Federal department or agency that there is, or is not, reasonable cause to believe that the sale of the specific chemical to the specific bidder and end-user would result in the illegal manufacture of a controlled substance. In making this determination, the following factors must be considered:

(1) Past experience of the prospective bidder or end-user in the maintenance of effective controls against diversion of listed chemicals into other than legitimate medical, scientific, and industrial channels;

(2) Compliance of the prospective bidder or end-user with applicable Federal, state and local law;

(3) Prior conviction record of the prospective bidder or end-user relating to listed chemicals or controlled substances under Federal or state laws; and

(4) Such other factors as may be relevant to and consistent with the public health and safety.

(d) If the Administrator certifies to the head of a Federal department or agency that there is no reasonable cause to believe that the sale of a specific chemical to a prospective bidder and end-user will result in the illegal manufacture of a controlled substance, that certification will be effective for one year from the date of issuance with respect to further sales of the same chemical to the same prospective bidder and end-user, unless the Administrator notifies the head of the Federal department or agency in writing that the certification is withdrawn. If the certification is withdrawn, DEA will also provide written notice to the bidder and end-user, which will contain a statement of the legal and factual basis for this determination.

(e) If the Administrator determines there is reasonable cause to believe the sale of the specific chemical to a specific bidder and end-user would result in the illegal manufacture of a controlled substance, DEA will provide written notice to the head of a Federal department or agency refusing to certify the proposed sale under the authority of 21 U.S.C. 890. DEA also will provide, within fifteen calendar days of receiving a request for certification

141

from a Federal department or agency, the same written notice to the prospective bidder and end-user, and this notice also will contain a statement of the legal and factual basis for the refusal of certification. The prospective bidder and end-user may, within thirty calendar days of receipt of notification of the refusal, submit written comments or written objections to the Administrator's refusal. At the same time, the prospective bidder and end-user also may provide supporting documentation to contest the Administrator's refusal. If such written comments or written objections raise issues regarding any finding of fact or conclusion of law upon which the refusal is based, the Administrator will reconsider the refusal of the proposed sale in light of the written comments or written objections filed. Thereafter, within a reasonable time, the Administrator will withdraw or affirm the original refusal of certification as he determines appropriate. The Administrator will provide written reasons for any affirmation of the original refusal. Such affirmation of the original refusal will constitute a final decision for purposes of judicial review under 21 U.S.C. 877.

(f) If the Administrator determines there is reasonable cause to believe that an existing certification should be withdrawn, DEA will provide written notice to the head of a Federal department or agency of such withdrawal under the authority of 21 U.S.C. 890. DEA also will provide, within fifteen calendar days of withdrawal of an existing certification, the same written notice to the bidder and end-user, and this notice also will contain a statement of the legal and factual basis for the withdrawal. The bidder and end-user may, within thirty calendar days of receipt of notification of the withdrawal of the existing certification, submit written comments or written objections to the Administrator's withdrawal. At the same time, the bidder and end-user also may provide supporting documentation to contest the Administrator's withdrawal. If such written comments or written objections raise issues regarding any finding of fact or conclusion of law upon which the withdrawal of the existing certification is based, the Administrator will reconsider the withdrawal of the existing certification in light of the written comments or written objections filed. Thereafter, within a reasonable time, the Administrator will withdraw or affirm the original withdrawal of the existing certification as he determines appropriate. The Administrator will provide written reasons for any affirmation of the original withdrawal of the existing certification. Such affirmation of the original withdrawal of the existing certification will constitute a final decision for purposes of judicial review under 21 U.S.C. 877.

[68 FR 62737, Nov. 6, 2003]

PART 1311—DIGITAL CERTIFICATES

Subpart A—General

Sec.

Subpart B—Obtaining and Using Digital Certificates for Electronic Orders

AUTHORITY: 21 U.S.C. 821, 828, 829, 871(b), 958(e), 965, unless otherwise noted.

SOURCE: 70 FR 16915, Apr. 1, 2005, unless otherwise noted.

Subpart A—General

§ 1311.01   Scope.

This part sets forth the rules governing the use of digital signatures and the protection of private keys by registrants.

§ 1311.02   Definitions.

For the purposes of this chapter:

Biometric authentication means authentication based on measurement of the individual's physical features or repeatable actions where those features or actions are both unique to the individual and measurable.

Cache means to download and store information on a local server or hard drive.

Certificate Policy means a named set of rules that sets forth the applicability of the specific digital certificate to a particular community or class of application with common security requirements.

Certificate Revocation List (CRL) means a list of revoked, but unexpired certificates issued by a Certification Authority.

Certification Authority (CA) means an organization that is responsible for verifying the identity of applicants, authorizing and issuing a digital certificate, maintaining a directory of public keys, and maintaining a Certificate Revocation List.

CSOS means controlled substance ordering system.

Digital certificate means a data record that, at a minimum:

(1) Identifies the certification authority issuing it;

(2) Names or otherwise identifies the certificate holder;

(3) Contains a public key that corresponds to a private key under the sole control of the certificate holder;

(4) Identifies the operational period; and

(5) Contains a serial number and is digitally signed by the Certification Authority issuing it.

Digital signature means a record created when a file is algorithmically transformed into a fixed length digest that is then encrypted using an asymmetric cryptographic private key associated with a digital certificate. The combination of the encryption and algorithm transformation ensure that the signer's identity and the integrity of the file can be confirmed.

Electronic signature means a method of signing an electronic message that identifies a particular person as the source of the message and indicates the person's approval of the information contained in the message.

FIPS means Federal Information Processing Standards. These Federal standards, as incorporated by reference in § 1311.08, prescribe specific performance requirements, practices, formats, communications protocols, etc., for hardware, software, data, etc.

FIPS 140–2, as incorporated by reference in § 1311.08, means a Federal standard for security requirements for cryptographic modules.

FIPS 180–2, as incorporated by reference in § 1311.08, means a Federal secure hash standard.

FIPS 186–2, as incorporated by reference in § 1311.08, means a Federal standard for applications used to generate and rely upon digital signatures.

Key pair means two mathematically related keys having the properties that:

(1) One key can be used to encrypt a message that can only be decrypted using the other key; and

(2) Even knowing one key, it is computationally infeasible to discover the other key.

NIST means the National Institute of Standards and Technology.

Private key means the key of a key pair that is used to create a digital signature.

Public key means the key of a key pair that is used to verify a digital signature. The public key is made available to anyone who will receive digitally signed messages from the holder of the key pair.

Public Key Infrastructure (PKI) means a structure under which a Certification Authority verifies the identity of applicants, issues, renews, and revokes digital certificates, maintains a registry of public keys, and maintains an up-to-date Certificate Revocation List.

§ 1311.05 Standards for technologies for electronic transmission of orders.

(a) A registrant or a person with power of attorney to sign orders for Schedule I and II controlled substances may use any technology to sign and electronically transmit orders if the technology provides all of the following:

(1) *Authentication:* The system must enable a recipient to positively verify the signer without direct communication with the signer and subsequently demonstrate to a third party, if needed, that the sender's identity was properly verified.

(2) *Nonrepudiation:* The system must ensure that strong and substantial evidence is available to the recipient of the sender's identity, sufficient to prevent the sender from successfully denying having sent the data. This criterion includes the ability of a third party to verify the origin of the document.

(3) *Message integrity:* The system must ensure that the recipient, or a third party, can determine whether the contents of the document have been altered during transmission or after receipt.

(b) DEA has identified the following means of electronically signing and transmitting order forms as meeting all of the standards set forth in paragraph (a) of this section.

(1) Digital signatures using Public Key Infrastructure (PKI) technology.

(2) [Reserved]

§ 1311.08 Incorporation by reference.

(a) The following standards are incorporated by reference:

(1) FIPS 140–2, Security Requirements for Cryptographic Modules, May 25, 2001, as amended by Change Notices 2 through 4, December 3, 2002.

(i) Annex A: Approved Security Functions for FIPS PUB 140–2, Security Requirements for Cryptographic Modules, September 23, 2004.

(ii) Annex B: Approved Protection Profiles for FIPS PUB 140–2, Security Requirements for Cryptographic Modules, November 4, 2004.

(iii) Annex C: Approved Random Number Generators for FIPS PUB 140–2, Security Requirements for Cryptographic Modules, January 31, 2005.

(iv) Annex D: Approved Key Establishment Techniques for FIPS PUB 140–2, Security Requirements for Cryptographic Modules, February 23, 2004.

(2) FIPS 180–2, Secure Hash Standard, August 1, 2002, as amended by change notice 1, February 25, 2004.

(3) FIPS 186–2, Digital Signature Standard, January 27, 2000, as amended by Change Notice 1, October 5, 2001.

(b) These standards are available from the National Institute of Standards and Technology, Computer Security Division, Information Technology Laboratory, National Institute of Standards and Technology, 100 Bureau Drive, Gaithersburg, MD 20899–8930 and are available at *http://csrc.nist.gov/.*

(c) These incorporations by reference were approved by the Director of the Federal Register in accordance with 5 U.S.C. 552(a) and 1 CFR part 51. Copies may be inspected at the Drug Enforcement Administration, 600 Army Navy Drive, Arlington, VA 22202 or at the National Archives and Records Administration (NARA). For information on the availability of this material at NARA, call (202) 741–6030, or go to: *http://www.archives.gov/federal_register/code_of_federal_regulations/ibr_locations.html.*

Subpart B—Obtaining and Using Digital Certificates for Electronic Orders

§ 1311.10 Eligibility to obtain a CSOS digital certificate.

The following persons are eligible to obtain a CSOS digital certificate from the DEA Certification Authority to sign electronic orders for controlled substances.

(a) The person who signed the most recent DEA registration application or renewal application and a person authorized to sign a registration application.

(b) A person granted power of attorney by a DEA registrant to sign orders for one or more schedules of controlled substances.

§ 1311.15 Limitations on CSOS digital certificates.

(a) A CSOS digital certificate issued by the DEA Certification Authority will authorize the certificate holder to sign orders for only those schedules of controlled substances covered by the registration under which the certificate is issued.

(b) When a registrant, in a power of attorney letter, limits a certificate applicant to a subset of the registrant's authorized schedules, the registrant is responsible for ensuring that the certificate holder signs orders only for that subset of schedules.

§1311.20 Coordinators for CSOS digital certificate holders.

(a) Each registrant, regardless of number of digital certificates issued, must designate one or more responsible persons to serve as that registrant's CSOS coordinator regarding issues pertaining to issuance of, revocation of, and changes to digital certificates issued under that registrant's DEA registration. While the coordinator will be the main point of contact between one or more DEA registered locations and the CSOS Certification Authority, all digital certificate activities are the responsibility of the registrant with whom the digital certificate is associated. Even when an individual registrant, i.e., an individual practitioner, is applying for a digital certificate to order controlled substances a CSOS Coordinator must be designated; though in such a case, the individual practitioner may also serve as the coordinator.

(b) Once designated, coordinators must identify themselves, on a one-time basis, to the Certification Authority. If a designated coordinator changes, the Certification Authority must be notified of the change and the new responsibilities assumed by each of the registrant's coordinators, if applicable. Coordinators must complete the application that the DEA Certification Authority provides and submit the following:

(1) Two copies of identification, one of which must be a government-issued photographic identification.

(2) A copy of each current DEA Certificate of Registration (DEA form 223) or each registered location for which the coordinator will be responsible or, if the applicant (or their employer) has not been issued a DEA registration, a copy of each application for registra-

tion of the applicant or the applicant's employer.

(3) The applicant must have the completed application notarized and forward the completed application and accompanying documentation to the DEA Certification Authority.

(c) Coordinators will communicate with the Certification Authority regarding digital certificate applications, renewals and revocations. For applicants applying for a digital certificate from the DEA Certification Authority, and for applicants applying for a power of attorney digital certificate for a DEA registrant, the registrant's Coordinator must verify the applicant's identity, review the application package, and submit the completed package to the Certification Authority.

§1311.25 Requirements for obtaining a CSOS digital certificate.

(a) To obtain a certificate to use for signing electronic orders for controlled substances, a registrant or person with power of attorney for a registrant must complete the application that the DEA Certification Authority provides and submit the following:

(1) Two copies of identification, one of which must be a government-issued photographic identification.

(2) A current listing of DEA registrations for which the individual has authority to sign controlled substances orders.

(3) A copy of the power of attorney from the registrant, if applicable.

(4) An acknowledgment that the applicant has read and understands the Subscriber Agreement and agrees to the statement of subscriber obligations that DEA provides.

(b) The applicant must provide the completed application to the registrant's coordinator for CSOS digital certificate holders who will review the application and submit the completed application and accompanying documentation to the DEA Certification Authority.

(c) When the Certification Authority approves the application, it will send the applicant a one-time use reference number and access code, via separate channels, and information on how to use them. Using this information, the applicant must then electronically submit a request for certification of the public digital signature key. After the request is approved, the Certification Authority will provide the applicant with the signed public key certificate.

(d) Once the applicant has generated the key pair, the Certification Authority must prove that the user has possession of the key. For public keys, the corresponding private key must be used to sign the certificate request. Verification of the signature using the public key in the request will serve as proof of possession of the private key.

§ 1311.30 Requirements for storing and using a private key for digitally signing orders.

(a) Only the certificate holder may access or use his or her digital certificate and private key.

(b) The certificate holder must provide FIPS-approved secure storage for the private key, as discussed by FIPS 140-2, 180-2, 186-2, and accompanying change notices and annexes, as incorporated by reference in § 1311.08.

(c) A certificate holder must ensure that no one else uses the private key. While the private key is activated, the certificate holder must prevent unauthorized use of that private key.

(d) A certificate holder must not make back-up copies of the private key.

(e) The certificate holder must report the loss, theft, or compromise of the private key or the password, via a revocation request, to the Certification Authority within 24 hours of substantiation of the loss, theft, or compromise. Upon receipt and verification of a signed revocation request, the Certification Authority will revoke the certificate. The certificate holder must apply for a new certificate under the requirements of § 1311.25.

§ 1311.35 Number of CSOS digital certificates needed.

A purchaser of Schedule I and II controlled substances must obtain a separate CSOS certificate for each registered location for which the purchaser will order these controlled substances.

§ 1311.40 Renewal of CSOS digital certificates.

(a) A CSOS certificate holder must generate a new key pair and obtain a new CSOS digital certificate when the registrant's DEA registration expires or whenever the information on which the certificate is based changes. This information includes the registered name and address, the subscriber's name, and the schedules the registrant is authorized to handle. A CSOS certificate will expire on the date on which the DEA registration on which the certificate is based expires.

(b) The Certification Authority will notify each CSOS certificate holder 45 days in advance of the expiration of the certificate holder's CSOS digital certificate.

(c) If a CSOS certificate holder applies for a renewal before the certificate expires, the certificate holder may renew electronically twice. For every third renewal, the CSOS certificate holder must submit a new application and documentation, as provided in § 1311.25.

(d) If a CSOS certificate expires before the holder applies for a renewal, the certificate holder must submit a new application and documentation, as provided in § 1311.25.

§ 1311.45 Requirements for registrants that allow powers of attorney to obtain CSOS digital certificates under their DEA registration.

(a) A registrant that grants power of attorney must report to the DEA Certification Authority within 6 hours of either of the following (advance notice may be provided, where applicable):

(1) The person with power of attorney has left the employ of the institution.

(2) The person with power of attorney has had his or her privileges revoked.

(b) A registrant must maintain a record that lists each person granted power of attorney to sign controlled substances orders.

§ 1311.50 Requirements for recipients of digitally signed orders.

(a) The recipient of a digitally signed order must do the following before filling the order:

(1) Verify the integrity of the signature and the order by having the system validate the order.

(2) Verify that the certificate holder's CSOS digital certificate has not expired by checking the expiration date against the date the order was signed.

(3) Check the validity of the certificate holder's certificate by checking the Certificate Revocation List.

(4) Check the certificate extension data to determine whether the sender has the authority to order the controlled substance.

(b) A recipient may cache Certificate Revocation Lists for use until they expire.

§1311.55 Requirements for systems used to process digitally signed orders.

(a) A CSOS certificate holder and recipient of an electronic order may use any system to write, track, or maintain orders provided that the system has been enabled to process digitally signed documents and that it meets the requirements of paragraph (b) or (c) of this section.

(b) A system used to digitally sign Schedule I or II orders must meet the following requirements:

(1) The cryptographic module must be FIPS 140–2, Level 1 validated, as incorporated by reference in §1311.08.

(2) The digital signature system and hash function must be compliant with FIPS 186–2 and FIPS 180–2, as incorporated by reference in §1311.08.

(3) The private key must be stored on a FIPS 140–2 Level 1 validated cryptographic module using a FIPS-approved encryption algorithm, as incorporated by reference in §1311.08.

(4) The system must use either a user identification and password combination or biometric authentication to access the private key. Activation data must not be displayed as they are entered.

(5) The system must set a 10-minute inactivity time period after which the certificate holder must reauthenticate the password to access the private key.

(6) For software implementations, when the signing module is deactivated, the system must clear the plain text private key from the system memory to prevent the unauthorized access to, or use of, the private key.

(7) The system must be able to digitally sign and transmit an order.

(8) The system must have a time system that is within five minutes of the official National Institute of Standards and Technology time source.

(9) The system must archive the digitally signed orders and any other records required in part 1305 of this chapter, including any linked data.

(10) The system must create an order that includes all data fields listed under §1305.21(b) of this chapter.

(c) A system used to receive, verify, and create linked records for orders signed with a CSOS digital certificate must meet the following requirements:

(1) The cryptographic module must be FIPS 140–2, Level 1 validated, as incorporated by reference in §1311.08.

(2) The digital signature system and hash function must be compliant with FIPS 186–2 and FIPS 180–2, as incorporated by reference in §1311.08.

(3) The system must determine that an order has not been altered during transmission. The system must invalidate any order that has been altered.

(4) The system must validate the digital signature using the signer's public key. The system must invalidate any order in which the digital signature cannot be validated.

(5) The system must validate that the DEA registration number contained in the body of the order corresponds to the registration number associated with the specific certificate by separately generating the hash value of the registration number and certificate subject distinguished name serial number and comparing that hash value to the hash value contained in the certificate extension for the DEA registration number. If the hash values are not equal the system must invalidate the order.

(6) The system must check the Certificate Revocation List automatically and invalidate any order with a certificate listed on the Certificate Revocation List.

(7) The system must check the validity of the certificate and the Certification Authority certificate and invalidate any order that fails these validity checks.

(8) The system must have a time system that is within five minutes of the official National Institute of Standards and Technology time source.

(9) The system must check the substances ordered against the schedules that the registrant is allowed to order and invalidate any order that includes substances the registrant is not allowed to order.

(10) The system must ensure that an invalid finding cannot be bypassed or ignored and the order filled.

(11) The system must archive the order and associate with it the digital certificate received with the order.

(12) If a registrant sends reports on orders to DEA, the system must create a report in the format DEA specifies, as provided in § 1305.29 of this chapter.

(d) For systems used to process CSOS orders, the system developer or vendor must have an initial independent third-party audit of the system and an additional independent third-party audit whenever the signing or verifying functionality is changed to determine whether it correctly performs the functions listed under paragraphs (b) and (c) of this section. The system developer must retain the most recent audit results and retain the results of any other audits of the software completed within the previous two years.

§ 1311.60   Recordkeeping.

(a) A supplier and purchaser must maintain records of CSOS electronic orders and any linked records for two years. Records may be maintained electronically. Records regarding controlled substances that are maintained electronically must be readily retrievable from all other records.

(b) Electronic records must be easily readable or easily rendered into a format that a person can read. They must be made available to the Administration upon request.

(c) CSOS certificate holders must maintain a copy of the subscriber agreement that the Certification Authority provides for the life of the certificate.

PART 1312—IMPORTATION AND EXPORTATION OF CONTROLLED SUBSTANCES

AUTHORITY: 21 U.S.C. 952, 953, 954, 957, 958.

SOURCE: 36 FR 7815, Apr. 24, 1971, unless otherwise noted. Redesignated at 38 FR 26609, Sept. 24, 1973.

§1312.01 Scope of part 1312.

Procedures governing the importation, exportation, transshipment and intransit shipment of controlled substances pursuant to section 1002, 1003, and 1004 of the Act (21 U.S.C. 952, 953, and 954) are governed generally by those sections and specifically by the sections of this part.

§1312.02 Definitions.

Any term contained in this part shall have the definition set forth in section 102 of the Act (21 U.S.C. 802) or part 1300 of this chapter.

[62 FR 13969, Mar. 24, 1997]

IMPORTATION OF CONTROLLED SUBSTANCES

§1312.11 Requirement of authorization to import.

(a) No person shall import or cause to be imported any controlled substance listed in Schedule I or II or any narcotic controlled substance listed in Schedule III, IV or V or any non-narcotic controlled substance in Schedule III which the Administrator has specifically designated by regulation in §1312.30 of this part or any non-narcotic controlled substance in Schedule IV or V which is also listed in Schedule I or II of the Convention on Psychotropic Substances unless and until such person is properly registered under the Act (or exempt from registration) and the Administrator has issued him a permit to do so pursuant to §1312.13 of this part.

(b) No person shall import or cause to be imported any non-narcotic controlled substance listed in Schedule III, IV or V, excluding those described in paragraph (a) of this section, unless and until such person is properly registered under the Act (or exempt from registration) and has filed an import declaration to do so with the Administrator, pursuant to §1312.18 of this part.

(c) When an import permit or declaration is required, a separate permit or declaration must be obtained for each consignment of controlled substances to be imported.

[36 FR 7815, Apr. 24, 1971, as amended at 37 FR 15923, Aug. 8, 1972. Redesignated at 38 FR 26609, Sept. 24, 1973, and amended at 52 FR 17289, May 7, 1987]

§1312.12 Application for import permit.

(a) An application for a permit to import controlled substances shall be made on DEA Form 357. DEA Form 357 may be obtained from, and shall be filed with, the Drug Enforcement Administration, Drug Operations Section, Washington, DC 20537. Each application shall show the date of execution; the registration number of the importer; a detailed description of each controlled substance to be imported including the drug name, dosage form, National Drug Code (NDC) number, the Administration Controlled Substance Code Number as set forth in part 1308 of this chapter, the number and size of packages or containers, the name and quantity of the controlled substance contained in any finished dosage units, and the net quantity of any controlled substance (expressed in anhydrous acid, base or alkaloid) given in kilograms or parts thereof. The application shall also include the following:

(1) The name, address, and business of the consignor, if known at the time application is submitted, but if unknown at that time, the fact should be indicated and the name and address afterwards furnished to the Administrator as soon as ascertained by the importer;

(2) The foreign port of exportation (i.e., the place where the article will begin its journey of exportation to the United States);

(3) The port of entry into the United States;

(4) The latest date said shipment will leave said foreign port;

(5) The stock on hand of the controlled substance desired to be imported;

(6) The name of the importing carrier or vessel (if known, or if unknown it should be stated whether shipment will be made by express, freight, or otherwise, imports of controlled substances in Schedules I or II and narcotic drugs

in Schedules III, IV, or V by mail being prohibited);

(7) The total tentative allotment to the importer of such controlled substance for the current calendar year;

(8) The total number of kilograms of said allotment for which permits have previously been issued and the total quantity of controlled substance actually imported during the current year to date.

(b) If desired, alternative foreign ports of exportation within the same country may be indicated upon the application (e.g., (1) Calcutta, (2) Bombay). If a formal permit is issued pursuant to such application, it will bear the names of the two ports in the order given in the application and will authorize shipment from either port. Alternate ports in different countries will not be authorized in the same permit.

[36 FR 7815, Apr. 24, 1971, as amended at 36 FR 13387, July 21, 1971. Redesignated at 38 FR 26609, Sept. 24, 1973, and amended at 39 FR 43218, Dec. 11, 1974; 45 FR 74715, Nov. 12, 1980; 51 FR 5319 and 5320, Feb. 13, 1986; 52 FR 17289, May 7, 1987; 62 FR 13969, Mar. 24, 1997]

§ 1312.13 Issuance of import permit.

(a) The Administrator may authorize importation of any controlled substance listed in Schedule I or II or any narcotic drug listed in Schedule III, IV, or V if he finds:

(1) That the substance is crude opium, poppy straw, concentrate of poppy straw, or coca leaves, in such quantity as the Administrator finds necessary to provide for medical, scientific, or other legitimate purposes;

(2) That the substance is necessary to provide for medical and scientific needs or other legitimate needs of the United States during an emergency where domestic supplies of such substance or drug are found to be inadequate, or in any case in which the Administrator finds that competition among domestic manufacturers of the controlled substance is inadequate and will not be rendered adequate by the registration of additional manufacturers under section 303 of the Controlled Substances Act (21 U.S.C. 823); or

(3) That the domestic supply of any controlled substance is inadequate for scientific studies, and that the importation of that substance for scientific

purposes is only for delivery to officials of the United Nations, of the United States, or of any State, or to any person registered or exempted from registration under sections 1007 and 1008 of the Act (21 U.S.C. 957 and 958).

(4) That the importation of the controlled substance is for ballistics or other analytical or scientific purposes, and that the importation of that substance is only for delivery to officials of the United Nations, of the United States, or of any State, or to any person registered or exempted from registration under sections 1007 and 1008 of the Act (21 U.S.C. 957 and 958).

(b) The Administrator may require that such non-narcotic controlled substances in Schedule III as he shall designate by regulation in § 1312.30 of this part be imported only pursuant to the issuance of an import permit. The Administrator may authorize the importation of such substances if he finds that the substance is being imported for medical, scientific or other legitimate uses.

(c) If a non-narcotic substance listed in Schedule IV or V is also listed in Schedule I or II of the Convention on Psychotropic Substances, 1971, it shall be imported only pursuant to the issuance of an import permit. The Administrator may authorize the importation of such substances if it is found that the substance is being imported for medical, scientific or other legitimate uses.

(d) The Administrator may require an applicant to submit such documents or written statements of fact relevant to the application as he deems necessary to determine whether the application should be granted. The failure of the applicant to provide such documents or statements within a reasonable time after being requested to do so shall be deemed to be a waiver by the applicant of an opportunity to present such documents or facts for consideration by the Administrator in granting or denying the application.

(e) Each import permit shall be issued in sextuplet and serially numbered, with all six copies bearing the same serial number and being designated "original" (Copy 1), "duplicate" (Copy 2), etc., respectively. All copies of import permits shall bear the signature of the Director or his delegate, and facsimiles of signatures shall not be used. No permit shall be altered or changed by any person after being signed by the Administrator or his delegate and any change or alteration upon the face of any permit after it shall have been signed by the Administrator or his delegate shall render it void and of no effect. Permits are not transferable. Each copy of the permit shall have printed or stamped thereon the disposition to be made thereof. Each permit shall be dated and shall certify that the importer named therein is thereby permitted as a registrant under the Act, to import, through the port named, one shipment of not to exceed the specified quantity of the named controlled substances, shipment to be made before a specified date. Not more than one shipment shall be made on a single import permit. The permit shall state that the Administrator is satisfied that the consignment proposed to be imported is required for legitimate purposes.

(f) Notwithstanding paragraphs (a)(1) and (a)(2) of this section, the Administrator shall permit, pursuant to section 1002(a)(1) or 1002(a)(2)(A) of the Act (21 U.S.C. 952(a)(1) or (a)(2)(A)), the importation of approved narcotic raw material (opium, poppy straw and concentrate of poppy straw) having as its source:

(1) Turkey,
(2) India,
(3) Spain,
(4) France,
(5) Poland,
(6) Hungary, and
(7) Australia.

(g) At least eighty (80) percent of the narcotic raw material imported into the United States shall have as its original source Turkey and India. Except under conditions of insufficient supplies of narcotic raw materials, not more than twenty (20) percent of the narcotic raw material imported into the United States annually shall have

as its source Spain, France, Poland, Hungary and Australia.

[36 FR 23624, Dec. 11, 1971, as amended at 37 FR 15923, Aug. 8, 1972. Redesignated at 38 FR 26609, Sept. 24, 1973, and amended at 46 FR 41776, Aug. 18, 1981; 52 FR 17289, May 7, 1987; 73 FR 6851, Feb. 6, 2008]

§1312.14 Distribution of copies of import permit.

Copies of the import permit shall be distributed and serve purposes as follows:

(a) The original and quintuplet copies (Copy 1 and Copy 5) shall be transmitted by the Administration to the importer, who shall retain the quintuplet copy (Copy 5) on file as his record of authority for the importation, and shall transmit the original copy (Copy 1) to the foreign exporter. The foreign exporter will submit the original copy (Copy 1) to the proper governmental authority in the exporting country, if required, as a prerequisite to the issuance of an export authorization. This copy of the permit will accompany the shipment. Upon arrival of the imported merchandise, District Director of the U.S. Customs Service at the port of entry will, after appraising the merchandise, forward the original copy (Copy 1) to the Drug Operations Section with a report on the reverse side of such copy, showing the name of the port of importation, date prepared, name and net quantity of each substance, and report of analysis of the merchandise entered.

(b) The duplicate copy (Copy 2) shall be forwarded by the Administration to the proper governmental authorities of the exporting country.

(c) The quadruplet copy (Copy 4) shall be forwarded by the Administration to the District Director of the U.S. Customs Service at the U.S. port of entry, which shall be the customs port of destination in the case of shipments transported under immediate transportation entries, in order that the District Director may compare it with the original copy (Copy 1) and the bill of lading upon arrival of the merchandise. If a discrepancy is noted between corresponding items upon different copies of a permit bearing the same serial number when compared by the District Director, he shall refuse to permit entry of the merchandise until the facts are communicated to the Administration and further instructions are received.

(d) The triplicate copy (Copy 3) and sextuplet copy (Copy 6) shall be retained by the Administration.

[36 FR 7815, Apr. 24, 1971, as amended at 36 FR 13387, July 21, 1971. Redesignated at 38 FR 26609, Sept. 24, 1973, and further amended at 45 FR 74715, Nov. 12, 1980; 51 FR 5319, Feb. 13, 1986; 53 FR 48244, Nov. 30, 1988; 62 FR 13969, Mar. 24, 1997]

§ 1312.15 Shipments in greater or less amount than authorized.

(a) If the shipment made under an import permit is greater than the maximum amount authorized to be imported under the permit, as determined at the weighing by the District Director of the U.S. Customs Service, such difference shall be seized subject to forfeiture, pending an explanation; except that shipments of substances exceeding the maximum authorized amount by less than 1 percent may be released to the importer upon the filing by him of an amended import permit. If the substance is included in Schedule I, it will be summarily forfeited to the Government.

(b) If the shipment made under the permit is less than the maximum amount authorized to be imported under the permit as determined at the weighing by the District Director of the U.S. Customs Service, such difference, when ascertained by the Administration, shall be recredited to the tentative allotment against which the quantity covered by the permit was charged, and the balance of any such tentative allotment with any such recredits will remain available to the importer to whom made (unless previously revoked in whole or in part), for importations pursuant to any permit or permits as are requested and issued during the remainder of the calendar year to which the allotment is applicable. No permit shall be issued for importation of a quantity of controlled substances as a charge against the tentative allotment for a given calendar year, after the close of such calendar year, unless the Director of the

Administration decides to make an exception for good cause shown.

[36 FR 7815, Apr. 24, 1971. Redesignated at 38 FR 26609, Sept. 24, 1973, and amended at 46 FR 28841, May 29, 1981]

§ 1312.16 Cancellation of permit; expiration date.

(a) A permit may be canceled after being issued, at the request of the importer, provided no shipment has been made thereunder. In the event that a permit is lost, the Administrator may, upon the production by the importer of satisfactory proof, by affidavit or otherwise, issue a duplicate permit. Nothing in this part shall affect the right, hereby reserved by the Administrator, to cancel a permit at any time for proper cause.

(b) An import permit shall not be valid after the date specified therein, and in no event shall the date be subsequent to 6 months after the date the permit is issued. Any unused import permit shall be returned for cancellation by the registrant to the Drug Enforcement Administration, Drug Operations Section, Washington, DC 20537.

[36 FR 7815, Apr. 24, 1971. Redesignated at 38 FR 26609, Sept. 24, 1973, and amended at 45 FR 74715, Nov. 12, 1980; 51 FR 5319, Feb. 13, 1986; 53 FR 48244, Nov. 30, 1988; 62 FR 13969, Mar. 24, 1997]

§ 1312.17 Special report from importers.

Whenever requested by the Administrator, importers shall render to him not later than 30 days after receipt of the request therefor a statement under oath of the stocks of controlled substances on hand as of the date specified by the Administrator in his request, and, if desired by the Administrator, an estimate of the probable requirements for legitimate uses of the importer for any subsequent period that may be designated by the Administrator. In lieu of any special statement that may be considered necessary, the Administrator may accept the figures given upon the reports subsequent by said importer under part 1304 of this chapter.

[36 FR 7815, Apr. 24, 1971. Redesignated at 38 FR 26609, Sept. 24, 1973, as amended at 62 FR 13969, Mar. 24, 1997]

§1312.18 Contents of import declaration.

(a) Any non-narcotic controlled substance listed in Schedule III, IV, or V, not subject to the requirement of an import permit pursuant to §1312.13 (b) or (c) of this chapter, may be imported if that substance is needed for medical, scientific or other legitimate uses in the United States, and will be imported pursuant to a controlled substances import declaration.

(b) Any person registered or authorized to import and desiring to import any non-narcotic controlled substance in Schedules III, IV, or V which is not subject to the requirement of an import permit as described in paragraph (a) of this section, must furnish a controlled substances import declaration on DEA Form 236 to the Drug Enforcement Administration, Drug Operations Section, Washington, DC 20537, not later than 15 calendar days prior to the proposed date of importation and distribute four copies of same as hereinafter directed in §1312.19.

(c) DEA Form 236 must be executed in quintuplicate and will include the following information:

(1) The name, address, and registration number of the importer; and the name and address and registration number of the import broker, if any; and

(2) A complete description of the controlled substances to be imported, including drug name, dosage form, National Drug Code (NDC) number, the Administration Controlled Substances Code Number as set forth in part 1308 of this chapter, the number and size of packages or containers, the name and quantity of the controlled substance contained in any finished dosage units, and the net quantity of any controlled substance (expressed in anhydrous acid, base, or alkaloid) given in kilograms or parts thereof; and

(3) The proposed import date, the foreign port of exportation to the United States, the port of entry, and the name, address, and registration number of the recipient in the United States; and

(4) The name and address of the consignor in the foreign country of exportation, and any registration or license numbers if the consignor is required to have such numbers either by the country of exportation or under U.S. law.

(d) Notwithstanding the time limitations included in paragraph (a) of this section, an applicant may obtain a special waiver of these time limitations in emergency or unusual instances, provided that a specific confirmation is received from the Administrator or his delegate advising the registrant to proceed pursuant to the special waiver.

[36 FR 7815, Apr. 24, 1971, as amended at 37 FR 15923, Aug. 8, 1972. Redesignated at 38 FR 26609, Sept. 24, 1973, and amended at 45 FR 74715, Nov. 12, 1980; 51 FR 5319, Feb. 13, 1986; 52 FR 17290, May 7, 1987; 62 FR 13969, Mar. 24, 1997]

§1312.19 Distribution of import declaration.

The required five copies of the controlled substances import declaration will be distributed as follows:

(a) Copy 1, Copy 2, and Copy 3 shall be transmitted to the foreign shipper. The foreign shipper will submit Copy 1 to the proper governmental authority in the foreign country, if required as a prerequisite to export authorization. Copy 1 will then accompany the shipment to its destination, and shall be retained on file by the importer. Copy 2 shall be detached and retained by the appropriate customs official of the foreign country. Copy 3 shall be removed by the District Director of the U.S. Customs Service at the port of entry, who shall sign and date the certification of customs on Copy 3, noting any changes from the entries made by the importer, and shall then forward that copy to the Drug Operations Section of the Administration.

(b) Copy 4 shall be forwarded, within the time limit required in §1312.18, directly to the Drug Enforcement Administration, Drug Operations Section, Washington, DC 20537.

(c) Copy 5 shall be retained by the importer on file as his record of authority for the importation.

[36 FR 7815, Apr. 24, 1971, as amended at 36 FR 13387, July 21, 1971; 37 FR 15923, Aug. 8, 1972. Redesignated at 38 FR 26609, Sept. 24, 1973, and further amended at 45 FR 74715, Nov. 12, 1980; 51 FR 5319, Feb. 13, 1986; 53 FR 48244, Nov. 30, 1988; 62 FR 13969, Mar. 24, 1997]

EXPORTATION OF CONTROLLED
SUBSTANCES

§ 1312.21 Requirement of authorization to export.

(a) No person shall in any manner export or cause to be exported from the United States any controlled substance listed in Schedule I or II, or any narcotic substance listed in Schedule III or IV, or any non-narcotic substance in Schedule III which the Administrator has specifically designated by regulation in § 1312.30 of this part or any non-narcotic substance in Schedule IV or V which is also listed in Schedule I or II of the Convention on Psychotropic Substances unless and until such person is properly registered under the Act (or exempted from registration) and the Administrator has issued a permit pursuant to § 1312.23 of this part.

(b) No person shall in any manner export or cause to be exported from the United States any non-narcotic controlled substance listed in Schedule III, IV, or V, excluding those described in paragraph (a) of this section, or any narcotic controlled substance listed in Schedule V, unless and until such person is properly registered under the Act (or exempted from registration) and has furnished a special controlled substance export invoice as provided by section 1003 of the Act (21 U.S.C. 953(e)) to the Administrator pursuant to § 1312.28 of this part.

(c) A separate authorization repuest is obtained for each consignment of such controlled substances to be exported.

[36 FR 7815, Apr. 24, 1971, as amended at 37 FR 15923, Aug. 8, 1972. Redesignated at 38 FR 26609, Sept. 24, 1973, and amended at 52 FR 17290, May 7, 1987]

§ 1312.22 Application for export permit.

(a) An application for a permit to export controlled substances shall be made on DEA Form 161, and an application for a permit to reexport controlled substances shall be made on DEA Form 161R. Forms may be obtained from, and shall be filed with, the Drug Enforcement Administration, Import/Export Unit, Washington, DC 20537. Each application shall show the exporter's name, address, and registration number; a detailed description of each controlled substance desired to be exported including the drug name, dosage form, National Drug Code (NDC) number (in accordance with Food and Drug Administration regulations), the Administration Controlled Substance Code Number as set forth in Part 1308 of this chapter, the number and size of packages or containers, the name and quantity of the controlled substance contained in any finished dosage units, and the quantity of any controlled substance (expressed in anhydrous acid, base, or alkaloid) given in kilograms or parts thereof. The application shall include the name, address, and business of the consignee, foreign port of entry, the port of exportation, the approximate date of exportation, the name of the exporting carrier or vessel (if known, or if unknown it should be stated whether shipment will be made by express, freight, or otherwise, exports of controlled substances by mail being prohibited), the date and number, if any, of the supporting foreign import license or permit accompanying the application, and the authority by whom such foreign license or permit was issued. The application shall also contain an affidavit that the packages are labeled in conformance with obligations of the United States under international treaties, conventions, or protocols in effect on May 1, 1971. The affidavit shall further state that to the best of affiant's knowledge and belief, the controlled substances therein are to be applied exclusively to medical or scientific uses within the country to which exported, will not be reexported therefrom and that there is an actual need for the controlled substance for medical or scientific uses within such country, unless the application is submitted for reexport in accordance with paragraphs (c) and (d) of this section. In the case of exportation of crude cocaine, the affidavit may state that to the best of affiant's knowledge and belief, the controlled substances will be processed within the country to which exported, either for medical or scientific use within that country or for reexportation in accordance with the laws of that country to another for medical or scientific use within that country. The application shall be

154

signed and dated by the exporter and shall contain the address from which the substances will be shipped for exportation.

(b) There shall also be submitted with the application any import license or permit (and a translation thereof if in a foreign language) or a certified copy of any such license or permit issued by competent authorities in the country of destination, or other documentary evidence deemed adequate by the Administrator, showing that the merchandise is consigned to an authorized permittee, that it is to be applied exclusively to medical or scientific use within the country of destination, that it will not be reexported from such country, and that there is an actual need for the controlled substance for medical or scientific use within such country. (In the case of exportation of bulk coca leaf alkaloid, the submitted evidence need only show the material outlined in paragraph (a) of this section for such exportations.)

(c) Notwithstanding paragraphs (a) and (b) of this section, the Administration may authorize any controlled substance listed in Schedule I or II, or any narcotic drug listed in Schedule III or IV, to be exported from the United States to a country for subsequent export from that country to another country, if each of the following conditions is met, in accordance with §1003(f) of the Act (21 U.S.C. 953(f)):

(1) Both the country to which the controlled substance is exported from the United States (referred to in this section as the "first country") and the country to which the controlled substance is exported from the first country (referred to in this section as the "second country") are parties to the Single Convention on Narcotic Drugs, 1961, and the Convention on Psychotropic Substances, 1971;

(2) The first country and the second country have each instituted and maintain, in conformity with such Conventions, a system of controls of imports of controlled substances which the Administration deems adequate;

(3) With respect to the first country, the controlled substance is consigned to a holder of such permits or licenses as may be required under the laws of such country, and a permit or license

to import the controlled substance has been issued by the country;

(4) With respect to the second country, substantial evidence is furnished to the Administration by the applicant for the export permit that—

(i) The controlled substance is to be consigned to a holder of such permits or licenses as may be required under the laws of such country, and a permit or license to import the controlled substance is to be issued by the country; and

(ii) The controlled substance is to be applied exclusively to medical, scientific, or other legitimate uses within the country;

(5) The controlled substance will not be exported from the second country;

(6) The person who exported the controlled substance from the United States has complied with paragraph (d) of this section and a permit to export the controlled substance from the United States has been issued by the Administration; and

(7) Within 30 days after the controlled substance is exported from the first country to the second country, the person who exported the controlled substance from the United States must deliver to the Administration documentation certifying that such export from the first country has occurred. If the permit issued by the Administration authorized the reexport of a controlled substance from the first country to more than one second country, notification of each individual reexport shall be provided. This documentation shall be submitted on company letterhead, signed by a responsible company official, and shall include all of the following information:

(i) Name of second country;

(ii) Actual quantity shipped;

(iii) Actual date shipped; and

(iv) DEA export permit number for the original export.

(d) Where a person is seeking to export a controlled substance for reexport in accordance with paragraph (c) of this section, the following requirements shall apply in addition to (and not in lieu of) the requirements of paragraphs (a) and (b) of this section:

(1) Bulk substances will not be reexported in the same form as exported

from the United States, *i.e.*, the material must undergo further manufacturing process. This further manufactured material may only be reexported to a second country.

(2) Finished dosage units, if reexported, must be in a commercial package, properly sealed and labeled for legitimate medical use in the second country.

(3) Any proposed reexportation must be made known to the Administration at the time the initial DEA Form 161R is submitted. In addition, the following information must also be provided where indicated on the form:

(i) Whether the drug or preparation will be reexported in bulk or finished dosage units;

(ii) The product name, dosage strength, commercial package size, and quantity;

(iii) The name of consignee, complete address, and expected shipment date, as well as the name and address of the ultimate consignee in the second country.

(4) The application (DEA Form 161R) must also contain an affidavit that the consignee in the second country is authorized under the laws and regulations of the second country to receive the controlled substances. The affidavit must also contain the following statement, in addition to the statements required under paragraph (a) of this section:

(i) That the packages are labeled in conformance with the obligations of the United States under the Single Convention on Narcotic Drugs, 1961, the Convention on Psychotropic Substances, 1971, and any amendments to such treaties;

(ii) That the controlled substances are to be applied exclusively to medical or scientific uses within the second country;

(iii) That the controlled substances will not be further reexported from the second country, and

(iv) That there is an actual need for the controlled substances for medical or scientific uses within the second country.

(5) If the applicant proposes that the shipment of controlled substances will be separated into parts after it arrives in the first country and then reexported to more than one second country, the applicant shall so indicate on the DEA Form 161R, providing all the information required in this section for each second country.

(6) Within 30 days after the controlled substance is exported from the United States, the person who exported the controlled substance shall deliver to the Administration documentation on the DEA Form 161R initially completed for the transaction certifying that such export occurred. This documentation shall be signed by a responsible company official and shall include all of the following information:

(i) Actual quantity shipped;

(ii) Actual date shipped; and

(iii) DEA export permit number.

(7) The controlled substance will be reexported from the first country to the second country (or second countries) no later than 180 days after the controlled substance was exported from the United States.

(8) Shipments that have been exported from the United States and are refused by the consignee in either the first or second country, or are otherwise unacceptable or undeliverable, may be returned to the registered exporter in the United States upon authorization of the Administration. In these circumstances, the exporter in the United States shall file a written request for the return of the controlled substances to the United States with a brief summary of the facts that warrant the return, along with a completed DEA Form 357, Application for Import Permit, with the Drug Enforcement Administration, Import/Export Unit, Washington, DC 20537. The Administration will evaluate the request after considering all the facts as well as the exporter's registration status with the Administration. If the exporter provides sufficient documentation, the Administration will issue an import permit for the return of these drugs, and the exporter can then obtain an export permit from the country of original importation. The substance may be returned to the United States only after affirmative authorization is issued in writing by the Administration.

(e) In considering whether to grant an application for a permit under paragraphs (c) and (d) of this section, the Administration shall consider whether the applicant has previously obtained such a permit and, if so, whether the applicant complied fully with the requirements of this section with respect to that previous permit.

[36 FR 7815, Apr. 24, 1971. Redesignated at 38 FR 26609, Sept. 24, 1973, and amended at 52 FR 17290, May 7, 1987; 62 FR 13969, Mar. 24, 1997; 72 FR 72927, Dec. 26, 2007]

§1312.23 Issuance of export permit.

(a) The Administrator may authorize exportation of any controlled substance listed in Schedule I or II or any narcotic controlled substance listed in Schedule III or IV if he finds that such exportation is permitted by subsections 1003(a), (b), (c), (d), or (f) of the Act (21 U.S.C. 953(a), (b), (c), (d), or (f).

(b) The Administrator may require that such non-narcotic controlled substances in Schedule III as shall be designated by regulation in §1312.30 of this part be exported only pursuant to the issuance of an export permit. The Administrator may authorize the exportation of such substances if he finds that such exportation is permitted by section 1003(e) of the Act (21 U.S.C. 953(e)).

(c) If a non-narcotic substance listed in Schedule IV or V is also listed in Schedule I or II of the Convention on Psychotropic Substances, it shall be exported only pursuant to the issuance of an export permit. The Administrator may authorize the exportation of such substances if he finds that such exportation is permitted by section 1003(e) of the Act (21 U.S.C. 953(e)).

(d) The Administrator may require an applicant to submit such documents or written statements of fact relevant to the application as he deems necessary to determine whether the application should be granted. The failure of the applicant to provide such documents or statements within a reasonable time after being requested to do so shall be deemed to be a waiver by the applicant of an opportunity to present such documents or facts for consideration by the Administrator in granting or denying the application.

(e) Each export permit shall be issued in septuplet and serially numbered, with all seven copies bearing the same serial number and being designated "original" (Copy 1), "duplicate" (Copy 2), etc., respectively. Each export permit shall be predicated upon an import certificate or other documentary evidence. Export permits are not transferable.

(f) No export permit shall be issued for the exportation, or reexportation, of any controlled substance to any country when the Administration has information to show that the estimates or assessments submitted with respect to that country for the current period, under the Single Convention on Narcotic Drugs, 1961, or the Convention on Psychotropic Substances, 1971, have been, or, considering the quantity proposed to be imported, will be exceeded. If it shall appear through subsequent advice received from the International Narcotics Control Board of the United Nations that the estimates or assessments of the country of destination have been adjusted to permit further importation of the controlled substance, an export permit may then be issued if otherwise permissible.

[36 FR 23625, Dec. 11, 1971, as amended at 37 FR 15923, Aug. 8, 1972. Redesignated at 38 FR 26609, Sept. 24, 1973, and amended at 52 FR 17290, May 7, 1987; 72 FR 72929, Dec. 26, 2007]

§1312.24 Distribution of copies of export permit.

Copies of the export permit shall be distributed and serve purposes as follows:

(a) The original, duplicate, and triplicate copies (Copy 1, Copy 2, and Copy 3) shall be transmitted by the Administration to the exporter who will retain the triplicate copy (Copy 3) as his record of authority for the exportation. The exporter shall present to the District Director of the U.S. Customs Service at the port of export and at the time of shipment, the original and duplicate copies (Copy 1 and Copy 2). After endorsing the port of export on the reverse side of the original and duplicate copies (Copy 1 and Copy 2) the District Director shall forward the endorsed original copy (Copy 1) with the shipment, and return the endorsed duplicate copy (Copy 2) to the Drug Enforcement Administration, Drug Operations Section, Washington, DC 20537.

(b) The quadruplet copy (Copy 4) shall be forwarded by the Administrator to the District Director of the U.S. Customs Service at the port of export for comparison with the original copy (Copy 1) and for retention for the customs record.

(c) The quintuplet copy (Copy 5) shall be forwarded by the Administration to the officer in the country of destination who issued the import certificate, or other documentary evidence upon which the export permit is founded.

(d) The sextuplet and septuplet copies (Copy 6 and Copy 7) shall be retained by the Administration.

[36 FR 7815, Apr. 24, 1971, as amended at 36 FR 13387, July 21, 1971. Redesignated at 38 FR 26609, Sept. 24, 1973, and amended at 45 FR 74715, Nov. 12, 1980; 51 FR 5319, Feb. 13, 1986; 53 FR 48244, Nov. 30, 1988; 62 FR 13969, Mar. 24, 1997]

§ 1312.25   Expiration date.

An export permit shall not be valid after the date specified therein, which date shall conform to the expiration date specified in the supporting import certificate or other documentary evidence upon which the export permit is founded, but in no event shall the date be subsequent to 6 months after the date the permit is issued. Any unused export permit shall be returned by the permittee to the Drug Operations Section for cancellation.

[36 FR 7815, Apr. 24, 1971. Redesignated at 38 FR 26609, Sept. 24, 1973, and amended at 45 FR 74715, Nov. 12, 1980; 51 FR 5319, Feb. 13, 1986; 53 FR 48244, Nov. 30, 1988; 62 FR 13969, Mar. 24, 1997]

§ 1312.26   Records required of exporter.

The exporter shall keep a record of any serial numbers that might appear on packages of narcotic drugs in quantities of one ounce or more in such a manner as will identify the foreign consignee, along with Copy 3 of the export permit.

§ 1312.27   Contents of special controlled substances invoice.

(a) A person registered or authorized to export any non-narcotic controlled substance listed in Schedule III, IV, or V, which is not subject to the requirement of an export permit pursuant to § 1312.23 (b) or (c), or any person registered or authorized to export any controlled substance in Schedule V, must furnish a special controlled substances export invoice on DEA Form 236 to the Drug Enforcement Administration, Drug Operations Section, Washington, DC 20537, not less than 15 calendar days prior to the proposed date of exportation, and distribute four copies of same as hereinafter directed in § 1312.28 of this part.

(b) This invoice must be executed by the exporter in quintuplicate and include the following information.

(1) The name, address, and registration number, if any, of the exporter; and the name, address and registration number of the exporter broker, if any; and

(2) A complete description of the controlled substances to be exported including the drug name, dosage form, National Drug Code (NDC) number, the Administration Controlled Substances Code Number as set forth in part 1308 of this chapter, the number and size of packages or containers, the name and quantity of the controlled substance contained in finished dosage units, and the net quantity of any controlled substance (expressed in anhydrous acid, base, or alkaloid) given in kilograms or parts thereof; and

(3) The proposed export date, the port of exportation, the foreign port of entry, the carriers and shippers involved, method of shipment, the name of the vessel if applicable, and the name, address, and registration number, if any, of any forwarding agent utilized; and

(4) The name and address of the consignee in the country of destination, and any registration or license number if the consignee is required to have such numbers either by the country of destination or under United States law. In addition, documentation must be provided to show that:

(i) The consignee is authorized under the laws and regulations of the country of destination to receive the controlled substances, and that

(ii) The substance is being imported for consumption within the importing country to satisfy medical, scientific or other legitimate purposes, and that

(5) The reexport of non-narcotic controlled substances in Schedules III and IV, and controlled substances in Schedule V is not permitted under the authority of 21 U.S.C. 953(e), except as provided below:

(i) Bulk substances will not be reexported in the same form as exported from the United States, i.e, the material must undergo further manufacturing process. This further manufactured material may only be reexported to a country of ultimate consumption.

(ii) Finished dosage units, if reexported, will be in a commercial package, properly sealed and labeled for legitimate medical use in the country of destination.

(iii) Any reexportation be made known to DEA at the time the initial DEA Form 236, Controlled Substances Import/Export Declaration is completed, by checking the box marked "other" on the certification. The following information will be furnished in the remarks section:

(A) Indicate "for reexport".

(B) Indicate if reexport is bulk or finished dosage units.

(C) Indicate product name, dosage strength, commercial package size, and quantity.

(D) Indicate name of consignee, complete address, and expected shipment date, as well as, the name and address of the ultimate consignee in the country to where the substances will be reexported.

(E) A statement that the consignee in the country of ultimate destination is authorized under the laws and regulations of the country of ultimate destination to receive the controlled substances.

(iv) Shipments which have been exported from the United States and are refused by the consignee in the country of destination, or are otherwise unacceptable or undeliverable, may be returned to the registered exporter in the United States upon authorization of the Drug Enforcement Administration. In this circumstance, the exporter in the United States shall file a written request for reexport, along with a completed DEA Form 236, Import Declaration with the Drug Enforcement Ad-

ministration, Drug Operations Section, Washington, DC 20537. A brief summary of the facts that warrant the return of the substance to the United States along with an authorization from the country of export will be included with the request. DEA will evaluate the request after considering all the facts as well as the exporter's registration status with DEA. The substance may be returned to the United States only after affirmative authorization is issued in writing by DEA.

(c) Notwithstanding the time limitations included in paragraph (a) of this section, a registrant may obtain a special waiver of these time limitations in emergency or unusual instances; provided that a specific confirmation is received from the Administrator or his delegate advising the registrant to proceed pursuant to the special waiver.

[36 FR 7815, Apr. 24, 1971, as amended at 37 FR 15923, Aug. 8, 1972. Redesignated at 38 FR 26609, Sept. 24, 1973, and amended at 45 FR 74715, Nov. 12, 1980; 51 FR 5319, Feb. 13, 1986; 52 FR 17290, May 7, 1987; 62 FR 13969, Mar. 24, 1997]

§1312.28 Distribution of special controlled substances invoice.

The required five copies of the special controlled substances export invoice, DEA (or BND) Form 236, will be distributed as follows:

(a) Copy 1 shall accompany the shipment and remain with the shipment to its destination.

(b) Copy 2 shall accompany the shipment and will be detached and retained by appropriate customs officials at the foreign country of destination.

(c) Copy 3 shall accompany the shipment and will be detached by the District Director of the U.S. Customs Service at the port of exportation, who shall sign and date the certification of customs on such Copy 3, noting any changes from the entries made by the exporter, and shall then promptly forward Copy 3 to the Drug Control Section of the Administration.

(d) Copy 4 shall be forwarded, within the time limit required in §1312.27 of this part, directly to the Drug Enforcement Administration, Drug Operations Section, Washington, DC 20537. The documentation required by

§ 1312.27(b)(4) of this part must be attached to this copy.

(e) Copy 5 shall be retained by the exporter on file as his record of authority for the exportation.

[36 FR 7815, Apr. 24, 1971, as amended at 36 FR 13387, July 21, 1971. Redesignated at 38 FR 26609, Sept. 24, 1973, and amended at 45 FR 74715, Nov. 12, 1980; 51 FR 5319, Feb. 13, 1986; 52 FR 17291, May 7, 1987; 53 FR 48244, Nov. 30, 1988; 62 FR 13969, Mar. 24, 1997]

§ 1312.29 Domestic release prohibited.

An exporter or a forwarding agent acting for an exporter must either deliver the controlled substances to the port or border, or deliver the controlled substances to a bonded carrier approved by the consignor for delivery to the port or border, and may not, under any other circumstances, release a shipment of controlled substances to anyone, including the foreign consignee or his agent, within the United States.

§ 1312.30 Schedule III, IV, and V non-narcotic controlled substances requiring an import and export permit.

The following Schedule III, IV, and V non-narcotic controlled substances have been specifically designated by the Administrator of the Drug Enforcement Administration as requiring import and export permits pursuant to sections 1002(b)(2) and 1003(e)(3) of the Act (21 U.S.C. 952(b)(2) and 953(e)(3)):

(a) Dronabinol (synthetic) in sesame oil and encapsulated in a soft gelatin capsule in a U.S. Food and Drug Administration approved product.

(b) [Reserved]

[52 FR 17291, May 7, 1987, as amended at 64 FR 35930, July 2, 1999]

TRANSSHIPMENT AND IN-TRANSIT SHIPMENT OF CONTROLLED SUBSTANCES

§ 1312.31 Schedule I: Application for prior written approval.

(a) A controlled substance listed in schedule I may be imported into the United States for transshipment, or may be transferred or transshipped within the United States for immediate exportation, provided that:

(1) The controlled substance is necessary for scientific, medical, or other

legitimate purposes in the country of destination, and

(2) A transshipment permit has been issued by the Administrator.

(b) An application for a transshipment permit must be submitted to the Drug Enforcement Administration, Drug Operations Section, Washington, DC 20537, at least 30 days, or in the case of an emergency as soon as practicable, prior to the expected date of importation, transfer or transshipment. Each application shall contain the following:

(1) The date of execution;

(2) The identification and description of the controlled substance;

(3) The net quantity thereof;

(4) The number and size of the controlled substance containers;

(5) The name, address, and business of the foreign exporter;

(6) The foreign port of exportation;

(7) The approximate date of exportation;

(8) The identification of the exporting carrier;

(9) The name, address and business of the importer, transferor, or transshipper;

(10) The registration number, if any, of the importer, transferor or transshipper;

(11) The U.S. port of entry;

(12) The approximate date of entry;

(13) The name, address and business of the consignee at the foreign port of entry;

(14) The shipping route from the U.S. port of exportation to the foreign port of entry;

(15) The approximate date of receipt by the consignee at the foreign port of entry; and

(16) The signature of the importer, transferor or transshipper, or his agent accompanied by the agent's title.

(c) An application shall be accompanied by an export license, permit, or a certified copy of the export license, permit, or other authorization, issued by a competent authority of the country of origin (or other documentary evidence deemed adequate by the Administrator).

(d) An application shall be accompanied by an import license or permit or a certified copy of such license or permit issued by a competent authority of the country of destination (or other documentary evidence deemed adequate by the Administrator), indicating that the controlled substance:

(1) Is to be applied exclusively to scientific, medical or other legitimate uses within the country of destination;

(2) Will not be exported from such country; and

(3) Is needed therein because there is an actual shortage thereof and a demand therefor for scientific, medical or other legitimate uses within such country.

(e) Verification by an American consular officer of the signatures on a foreign import license or permit shall be required, if such license or permit does not bear the seal of the authority signing them.

(f) The Administrator may require an applicant to submit such documents or written statements of fact relevant to the application as he deems necessary to determine whether the application should be granted. The failure of the applicant to provide such documents or statements within a reasonable time after being requested to do so shall be deemed to be a waiver by the applicant of an opportunity to present such documents or facts for consideration by the Administrator in granting or denying the application.

(g) The Administrator shall, within 21 days from the date of receipt of the application, either grant or deny the application. The applicant shall be accorded an opportunity to amend the application, with the Administrator either granting or denying the amended application within 7 days of its receipt. If the Administrator does not grant or deny the application within 21 days of its receipt, or in the case of an amended application, within 7 days of its receipt, the application shall be deemed approved and the applicant may proceed.

[36 FR 7815, Apr. 24, 1971, as amended at 37 FR 15923, Aug. 8, 1972. Redesignated at 38 FR 26609, Sept. 24, 1973, and further amended at 45 FR 74715, Nov. 12, 1980; 51 FR 5319, Feb. 13, 1986; 53 FR 48244, Nov. 30, 1988; 62 FR 13969, Mar. 24, 1997]

§ 1312.32 Schedules II, III, IV: Advance notice.

(a) A controlled substance listed in Schedules II, III, or IV may be imported into the United States for transshipment, or may be transferred or transshipped within the United States for immediate exportation, provided that written notice is submitted to the Drug Enforcement Administration, Drug Operations Section, Washington, DC 20537, at least 15 days prior to the expected date of importation, transfer or transshipment.

(b) Each advance notice shall contain those items required by § 1312.31 (b) and (c).

[36 FR 7815, Apr. 24, 1971. Redesignated at 38 FR 26609, Sept. 24, 1973, and amended at 45 FR 74715, Nov. 12, 1980; 51 FR 5319, Feb. 13, 1986; 53 FR 48244, Nov. 30, 1988; 62 FR 13969, Mar. 24, 1997]

HEARINGS

§ 1312.41 Hearings generally.

(a) In any case where the Administrator shall hold a hearing regarding the denial of an application for an import, export or transshipment permit, the procedures for such hearing shall be governed generally by the adjudication procedures set forth in the Administrative Procedure Act (5 U.S.C. 551–559) and specifically by sections 1002 and 1003 of the Act (21 U.S.C. 952 and 953), by §§ 1312.42–1312.47, and by the procedures for administrative hearings under the Act set forth in §§ 1316.41–1316.67 of this chapter.

(b) [Reserved]

[36 FR 23625, Dec. 11, 1971, as amended at 37 FR 15923, Aug. 8, 1972. Redesignated at 38 FR 26609, Sept. 24, 1973]

§ 1312.42 Purpose of hearing.

(a) If requested by a person applying for an import, export, or transshipment permit, the Administrator shall hold a hearing for the purpose of receiving factual evidence regarding the issues involved in the issuance or denial of such permit to such person.

(b) Extensive argument should not be offered into evidence but rather presented in opening or closing statements of counsel or in memoranda or proposed findings of fact and conclusions of law.

[36 FR 23625, Dec. 11, 1971, as amended at 37 FR 15923, Aug. 8, 1972. Redesignated at 38 FR 26609, Sept. 24, 1973]

§ 1312.43 Waiver or modification of rules.

The Administrator of the presiding officer (with respect to matters pending before him) may modify or waive any rule in this part by notice in advance of the hearing, if he determines that no party in the hearing will be unduly prejudiced and the ends of justice will thereby be served. Such notice of modification or waiver shall be made a part of the record of the hearing.

[36 FR 23625, Dec. 11, 1971. Redesignated at 38 FR 26609, Sept. 24, 1973]

§ 1312.44 Request for hearing or appearance; waiver.

(a) Any applicant entitled to a hearing pursuant to § 1312.42 and who desires a hearing on the denial of his application for an import, export, or transshipment permit shall, within 30 days after the date of receipt of the denial of his application, file with the Administrator a written request for a hearing in the form prescribed in § 1316.47 of this chapter.

(b) Any applicant entitled to a hearing pursuant to § 1312.42 may, within the period permitted for filing a request for a hearing, file with the Administrator a waiver of an opportunity for a hearing, together with a written statement regarding his position on the matters of fact and law involved in such hearing. Such statement, if admissible, shall be made a part of the record and shall be considered in light of the lack of opportunity for cross-examination in determining the weight to be attached to matters of fact asserted therein.

(c) If any applicant entitled to a hearing pursuant to § 1312.42 fails to appear at the hearing, he shall be deemed to have waived his opportunity for the hearing unless he shows good cause for such failure.

(d) If the applicant waives or is deemed to have waived this opportunity for the hearing, the Administrator may cancel the hearing, if scheduled, and issue his final order pursuant to § 1312.47 without a hearing.

[37 FR 15923, Aug. 8, 1972. Redesignated at 38 FR 26609, Sept. 24, 1973]

§ 1312.45 Burden of proof.

At any hearing on the denial of an application for an import, export, or transshipment permit, the Administrator shall have the burden of proving that the requirements for such permit pursuant to sections 1002, 1003, and 1004 of the Act (21 U.S.C. 952, 953, and 954) are not satisfied.

[37 FR 15924, Aug. 8, 1972. Redesignated at 38 FR 26609, Sept. 24, 1973]

§ 1312.46 Time and place of hearing.

(a) If any applicant for an import, export, or transshipment permit requests a hearing on the issuance or denial of his application, the Administrator shall hold such hearing. Notice of the hearing shall be given to the applicant of the time and place at least 30 days prior to the hearing, unless the applicant waives such notice and requests the hearing be held at an earlier time, in which case the Administrator shall fix a date for such hearing as early as reasonably possible.

(b) The hearing will commence at the place and time designated in the notice given pursuant to paragraph (a) of this section but thereafter it may be moved to a different place and may be continued from day to day or recessed to a later day without notice other than announcement thereof by the presiding officer at the hearing.

[37 FR 15924, Aug. 8, 1972. Redesignated at 38 FR 26609, Sept. 24, 1973]

§ 1312.47 Final order.

As soon as practicable after the presiding officer has certified the record to the Administrator, the Administrator shall issue his order on the issuance or denial of the application for and import, export, or transshipment permit. The order shall include the findings of fact and conclusions of law upon which the order is based. The Administrator shall serve one copy of his order upon the applicant.

[37 FR 15924, Aug. 8, 1972. Redesignated at 38 FR 26609, Sept. 24, 1973]

PART 1313—IMPORTATION AND EXPORTATION OF LIST I AND LIST II CHEMICALS

AUTHORITY: 21 U.S.C. 802, 830, 871(b), 971.

SOURCE: 54 FR 31665, Aug. 1, 1989, unless otherwise noted.

§ 1313.01 Scope.

Procedures governing the importation, exportation, transshipment and in-transit shipment of listed chemicals pursuant to section 1018 of the Act (21 U.S.C. 971) are governed generally by that section and specifically by the sections of this part.

[54 FR 31665, Aug. 1, 1989, as amended at 60 FR 32465, June 22, 1995]

§ 1313.02 Definitions.

Any term used in this part shall have the definition set forth in section 102 of the Act (21 U.S.C. 802) or part 1300 of this chapter.

[62 FR 13969, Mar. 24, 1997]

§ 1313.05 Requirements for an established business relationship.

To document that an importer or exporter has an established business relationship with a customer, the importer or exporter must provide the Administrator with the following information in accordance with the waiver of 15-day advance notice requirements of § 1313.15 or § 1313.24:

(a) The name and street address of the chemical importer or exporter and of each regular customer;

(b) The telephone number, contact person, and where available, the facsimile number for the chemical importer or exporter and for each regular customer;

(c) The nature of the regular customer's business (*i.e.*, importer, exporter, distributor, manufacturer, etc.), and if known, the use to which the listed chemical or chemicals will be applied;

(d) The duration of the business relationship;

(e) The frequency and number of transactions occurring during the preceding 12-month period;

(f) The amounts and the listed chemical or chemicals involved in regulated transactions between the chemical importer or exporter and regular customer;

(g) The method of delivery (direct shipment or through a broker or forwarding agent); and

(h) Other information that the chemical importer or exporter considers relevant for determining whether a customer is a regular customer.

[72 FR 17407, Apr. 9, 2007]

§ 1313.08 Requirements for establishing a record as an importer.

To establish a record as an importer, the regulated person must provide the Administrator with the following information in accordance with the waiver of the 15-day advance notice requirements of § 1313.15:

(a) The name, DEA registration number (where applicable), street address, telephone number, and, where available, the facsimile number of the regulated person and of each foreign supplier; and

(b) The frequency and number of transactions occurring during the preceding 12 month period.

[72 FR 17407, Apr. 9, 2007]

IMPORTATION OF LISTED CHEMICALS

§ 1313.12 Requirement of authorization to import.

(a) Each regulated person who imports a listed chemical that meets or exceeds the threshold quantities identified in § 1310.04(f) or is a listed chemical for which no threshold has been established as identified in § 1310.04(g) of this chapter, shall notify the Administrator of the importation not later than 15 days before the transaction is to take place.

(b) A completed DEA Form 486 must be received at the following address not later than 15 days prior to the importation: Drug Enforcement Administration, P.O. Box 27284, Washington, DC 20038. A copy of the completed DEA Form 486 may be transmitted directly to the Drug Enforcement Administration, Chemical Control Section, through electronic facsimile media not later than 15 days prior to the importation.

(c) The 15-day advance notification requirement for listed chemical imports may be waived for the following:

(1) Any importation that meets both of the following requirements:

(i) The regulated person has satisfied the requirements for reporting to the Administration as a regular importer of the listed chemicals.

(ii) The importer intends to transfer the listed chemicals to a person who is a regular customer for the chemical, as defined in § 1300.02 of this chapter.

(2) A specific listed chemical, as set forth in paragraph (f) of this section, for which the Administrator determines that advance notification is not necessary for effective chemical diversion control.

(d) For imports where advance notification is waived pursuant to paragraph (c)(1) of this section, the DEA Form 486 must be received by the Drug Enforcement Administration, Chemical Operations Section, on or before the date of importation through use of the mailing address listed in § 1313.12(b) or through use of electronic facsimile media.

(e) For importations where advance notification is waived pursuant to paragraph (c)(2) of this section no DEA Form 486 is required, however, the regulated person shall submit quarterly reports to the Drug Enforcement Administration, Chemical Operations Section, P.O. Box 27284, Washington, DC 20038, by no later than the 15th day of the month following the end of each quarter. The report shall contain the following information regarding each individual importation:

(1) The name of the listed chemical;

(2) The quantity and date imported;

(3) The name and full business address of the supplier;

(4) The foreign port of embarkation; and

(5) The port of entry.

(f) The 15 day advance notification requirement set forth in paragraph (a) has been waived for imports of the following listed chemicals:

(1) Acetone.

(2) 2-Butanone (or Methyl Ethyl Ketone or MEK).

(3) Toluene.

[54 FR 31665, Aug. 1, 1989, as amended at 59 FR 51367, Oct. 11, 1994; 60 FR 32464, June 22, 1995; 66 FR 46520, Sept. 6, 2001; 67 FR 49569, July 31, 2002; 72 FR 17407, Apr. 9, 2007]

§ 1313.13 Contents of import declaration.

(a) Any List I or List II chemical listed in § 1310.02 of this chapter may be imported if that chemical is necessary for medical, commercial, scientific, or other legitimate uses within the United States. Chemical importations into the United States for immediate transfer/transshipment outside the United States must comply with the procedures set forth in § 1313.31.

(b) Any regulated person who desires to import a threshold or greater quantity of a listed chemical shall notify the Administration through procedures set forth in § 1313.12 and distribute three copies of DEA Form 486 as directed in § 1313.14.

(c) The DEA Form 486 must be executed in triplicate and must include the following information:

(1) The name, address, telephone number, telex number, and, where available, the facsimile number of the chemical importer; the name, address, telephone, telex, and where available, the facsimile number of the broker or forwarding agent (if any); and

(2) The name and description of each listed chemical as it appears on the label or container, the name of each chemical as it is designated in 1310.02 of this chapter, the size or weight of container, the number of containers, the net weight of each listed chemical given in kilograms or parts thereof; and the gross weight of the shipment given in kilograms or parts thereof; and

(3) The proposed import date, the foreign port of exportation and the first U.S. Customs Port of Entry; and

(4) The name, address, telephone number, telex number, and, where available, the facsimile number of the consigner in the foreign country of exportation; and

(5) The name, address, telephone number, and where available, the facsimile number of the person or persons to whom the importer intends to transfer the listed chemical and the quantity to be transferred to each transferee.

[54 FR 31665, Aug. 1, 1989, as amended at 60 FR 32465, June 22, 1995; 72 FR 17407, Apr. 9, 2007]

§ 1313.14 Distribution of import declaration.

The required three copies of the listed chemical import declaration (DEA Form 486) will be distributed as follows:

(a) Copy 1 shall be retained on file by the regulated person as the official record of import. Import declaration forms involving a List I chemical must be retained for four years; declaration forms for List II chemical must be retained for two years.

(b) Copy 2 is the Drug Enforcement Administration copy used to fulfill the notification requirements of Section 6053 of the Chemical Diversion and Trafficking Act of 1988, as specified in § 1313.12.

(c) Copy 3 shall be presented to the U.S. Customs Sevice along with the customs entry. If the import is a regulated transaction for which the 15-day advance notice requirement has been waived, the regulated person shall declare this information to the U.S. Customs Service Official by checking the block on the DEA Form 486 designated for this purpose.

[54 FR 31665, Aug. 1, 1989, as amended at 60 FR 32465, June 22, 1995]

§ 1313.15 Waiver of 15-day advance notice for regular importers.

(a) Each regulated person seeking designation as a "regular importer" shall provide, by certified mail return receipt requested, to the Administration such information as is required under § 1313.08 documenting their status as a regular importer.

(b) Each regulated person making application under paragraph (a) of this section shall be considered a "regular importer" for purposes of waiving the 15-day advance notice, 30 days after receipt of the application by the Administration, as indicated on the return receipt, unless the regulated person is otherwise notified in writing by the Administration.

(c) The Administrator, may, at any time, disqualify a regulated person's status as a regular importer on the grounds that the chemical being imported may be diverted to the clandestine manufacture of a controlled substance.

(d) Unless the Administration notifies the chemical importer to the contrary, the qualification of a regular importer of any one of these three chemicals, acetone, 2-Butanone (MEK), or toluene, qualifies that importer as a regular importer of all three of these chemicals.

(e) All chemical importers shall be required to file a DEA Form 486 as required by Section 1313.12.

[60 FR 32464, June 22, 1995, as amended at 62 FR 13969, Mar. 24, 1997; 72 FR 17407, Apr. 9, 2007]

§ 1313.16 Transfers following importation.

(a) In the case of a notice under § 1313.12(a) submitted by a regulated person, if the transferee identified in the notice is not a regular customer, the importer may not transfer the listed chemical until after the expiration of the 15-day period beginning on the date on which the notice is submitted to the Administration.

(b) After a notice under § 1313.12(a) or (d) is submitted to the Administration, if circumstances change and the importer will not be transferring the listed chemical to the transferee identified in the notice, or will be transferring a greater quantity of the chemical than specified in the notice, the importer must update the notice to identify the most recent prospective transferee or the most recent quantity or both (as the case may be) and may not transfer the listed chemical until after the expiration of the 15-day period beginning on the date on which the update is submitted to the Administration, except that the 15-day restriction does not apply if the prospective transferee identified in the update is a regular customer. The preceding sentence applies with respect to changing circumstances regarding a transferee or quantity identified in an update to the same extent and in the same manner as the sentence applies with respect to changing circumstances regarding a transferee or quantity identified in the original notice under § 1313.12(a) or (d).

(c) In the case of a transfer of a listed chemical that is subject to a 15-day restriction, the transferee involved shall, upon the expiration of the 15-day period, be considered to qualify as a regular customer, unless the Administration otherwise notifies the importer involved in writing.

(d) With respect to a transfer of a listed chemical with which a notice or update referred to in § 1313.12(a) or (d) is concerned:

(1) The Administration—

(i) May, in accordance with the same procedures as apply under §§ 1313.51 through 1313.57, order the suspension of the transfer of the listed chemical by the importer involved, except for a transfer to a regular customer, on the ground that the chemical may be diverted to the clandestine manufacture of a controlled substance (without regard to the form of the chemical that may be diverted, including the diversion of a finished drug product to be manufactured from bulk chemicals to be transferred), subject to the Administration ordering the suspension before the expiration of the 15-day period with respect to the importation (in any case in which such a period applies); and

(ii) May, for purposes of this paragraph (d), disqualify a regular customer on that ground.

(2) From and after the time when the Administration provides written notice of the order under paragraph (d)(1)(i) of this section (including a statement of the legal and factual basis for the order) to the importer, the importer may not carry out the transfer.

(e) For purposes of this section:

(1) The term *transfer*, with respect to a listed chemical, includes the sale of the chemical.

(2) The term *transferee* means a person to whom an importer transfers a listed chemical.

[72 FR 17407, Apr. 9, 2007]

§ 1313.17 Return declaration or amendment to Form 486 for imports.

(a) Within 30 days after a transaction is completed, the importer must send to the Administration a return declaration containing particulars of the transaction, including the date, quantity, chemical, container, name of transferees, and any other information as the Administration may specify. A single return declaration may include the particulars of both the importation and distribution. If the importer has not distributed all chemicals imported by the end of the initial 30-day period, the importer must file supplemental return declarations no later than 30 days from the date of any further distribution, until the distribution or other disposition of all chemicals imported under the import notification or any update are accounted for.

(b) If an importation for which a Form 486 has been filed fails to take place, the importer must file an amended Form 486 notifying the Administration that the importation did not occur.

[72 FR 17408, Apr. 9, 2007]

EXPORTATION OF LISTED CHEMICALS

§1313.21 Requirement of authorization to export.

(a) No person shall export or cause to be exported from the United States any chemical listed in §1310.02 of this chapter, which meets or exceeds the threshold quantities identified in §1310.04(f) or is a listed chemical for which no threshold has been established as identified in §1310.04(g) of this chapter, until such time as the Administrator has been notified. Notification must be made not later than 15 days before the transaction is to take place. In order to facilitate the export of listed chemicals and implement the purpose of the Act, regulated persons may wish to provide notification to the Administration as far in advance of the 15 days as possible.

(b) A completed DEA Form 486 must be received at the following address not later than 15 days prior to the exportation: Drug Enforcement Administration, P.O. Box 27284, Washington, DC 20038. A copy of the completed DEA Form 486 may be transmitted directly to the Drug Enforcement Administration, Chemical Control Section, through electronic facsimile media not later than 15 days prior to the exportation.

(c) The 15-day advance notification requirement for listed chemical exports may be waived for:

(1) Any regulated person who has satisfied the requirements of Section 1313.24 for reporting to the Administration an established business relationship with a foreign customer as defined in §1300.02(b)(12).

(2) A specific listed chemical to a specified country, as set forth in paragraph (f) of this section, for which the Administrator determines that advance notification is not necessary for effective chemical diversion control.

(d) For exports where advance notification is waived pursuant to paragraph (c)(1) of this section, the DEA Form 486 must be received by the Drug Enforcement Administration, Chemical Operations Section, on or before the date of exportation through use of the mailing address listed in Section 1313.12(b) or through use of electronic facsimile media.

(e) For exportations where advance notification is waived pursuant to paragraph (c)(2) of this section, no DEA Form 486 is required, however, the regulated person shall file quarterly reports to the Drug Enforcement Administration, Chemical Control Section, P.O. Box 27284, Washington, DC 20038, by no later than the 15th day of the month following the end of each quarter. The report shall contain the following information regarding each individual exportation:

(1) The name of the listed chemical;

(2) The quantity and date exported;

(3) The name and full business address of the foreign customer;

(4) The port of embarkation; and

(5) The foreign port of entry.

(f) The 15 day advance notification requirement set forth in paragraph (a) of this section has been waived for exports of the following listed chemicals to the following countries:

Name of Chemical	Country
[Reserved]	

(g) No person shall export or cause to be exported any listed chemical, knowing or having reasonable cause to believe the export is in violation of the laws of the country to which the chemical is exported or the chemical will be used to manufacture a controlled substance in violation of the Act or the laws of the country to which the chemical is exported. The Administration will publish a notice of foreign import restrictions for listed chemicals of which DEA has knowledge as provided in §1313.25.

[54 FR 31665, Aug. 1, 1989, as amended at 59 FR 51367, Oct. 11, 1994; 60 FR 32464, June 22, 1995; 62 FR 13969, Mar. 24, 1997; 66 FR 46520, Sept. 6, 2001; 67 FR 49569, July 31, 2002]

§ 1313.22 Contents of export declaration.

(a) Any List I or List II chemical listed in § 1310.02 of this chapter which meets or exceeds the quantitative threshold criteria established in § 1310.04(f) of this chapter may be exported if that chemical is needed for medical, commercial, scientific, or other legitimate uses.

(b) Any regulated person who desires to export a threshold or greater quantity of a listed chemical shall notify the Administration through procedures outlined in § 1313.21 and distribute three copies of DEA Form 486 as directed in § 1313.23.

(c) The DEA Form 486 must be executed in triplicate and must include all the following information:

(1) The name, address, telephone number, telex number, and, where available, the facsimile number of the chemical exporter; the name, address, telephone number, telex number, and, where available, the facsimile number of the export broker, if any;

(2) The name and description of each listed chemical as it appears on the label or container, the name of each listed chemical as it is designated in § 1310.02 of this chapter, the size or weight of container, the number of containers, the net weight of each listed chemical given in kilograms or parts thereof, and the gross weight of the shipment given in kilograms or parts thereof;

(3) The proposed export date, the U.S. Customs port of exportation, and the foreign port of entry; and

(4) The name, address, telephone, telex, and where available, the facsimile number of the consignee in the country where the chemical shipment is destined; the name(s) and address(es) of any intermediate consignee(s).

(d) Notwithstanding the time limitations included in paragraph (b) of this section, a regulated person may receive a waiver of the 15-day advance notification requirement following the procedures outlined in § 1313.24.

(e) Declared exports of listed chemicals which are refused, rejected, or otherwise deemed undeliverable may be returned to the U.S. chemical exporter of record. A brief written notification (this does not require a DEA Form 486)

outlining the circumstances must be sent to the Drug Enforcement Administration, P.O. Box 27284, Washington, DC 20038, following the return within a reasonable time. This provision does not apply to shipments that have cleared foreign customs, been delivered, and accepted by the foreign consignee. Returns to third parties in the United States will be regarded as imports.

[54 FR 31665, Aug. 1, 1989, as amended at 60 FR 32465, June 22, 1995; 67 FR 49569, July 31, 2002]

§ 1313.23 Distribution of export declaration.

The required three copies of the listed chemical export declaration (DEA Form 486) will be distributed as follows:

(a) Copy 1 shall be retained on file by the chemical exporters as the official record of export. Export declaration forms involving a List I chemical must be retained for four years; declaration forms for list II chemical must be retained for two years.

(b) Copy 2 is the Drug Enforcement Administration copy used to fulfill the notification requirements of Section 6053 of the Chemical Diversion and Trafficking Act of 1988, as specified in § 1313.21

(c) Copy 3 shall be presented to the U.S. Customs Service at the port of exit for each export of a listed chemical or chemicals on or before the day of exportation, and when possible, along with the Shippers Export Declaration.

[54 FR 31665, Aug. 1, 1989, as amended at 60 FR 32465, June 22, 1995; 61 FR 51004, Sept. 30, 1996]

§ 1313.24 Waiver of 15-day advance notice for chemical exporters.

(a) Each regulated person shall provide to the Administration the identity and information listed in § 1300.02(b)(12) for an established business relationship with a foreign customer not later than August 31, 1989.

(b) Not later than October 31, 1989, each regular customer so identified in notifications made under § 1313.24(a) shall be a regular customer for purposes of waiving the 15-day advance notice requirement, unless the regulated person is otherwise notified in writing by the Administration.

(c) Each foreign customer identified on an initial DEA Form 486 submitted after the effective date of the implementation of part 1313 shall, after the expiration of the 15-day period, qualify as a regular customer, unless the Administration otherwise notifies the regulated person in writing.

(d) Unless the Administration notifies the chemical exporter to the contrary, the qualification of a regular customer for any one of these three chemicals, acetone, 2-Butanone (MEK), or toluene, qualifies that customer as a regular customer for all three of these chemicals.

(e) The Administrator may notify any chemical exporter that a regular customer has been disqualified or that a new customer for whom a notification has been submitted is not to be accorded the status of a regular customer. In the event of a disqualification of an established regular customer, the chemical exporter will be notified in writing of the reasons for such action.

Public reporting (one-time) burden for this collection of information is estimated to average four hours per response, including the time for reviewing instructions, searching existing data sources, gathering and maintaining the data needed, and completing and reviewing and collection of information. Send comments regarding this burden estimate or any other aspect of this collection of information, including suggestions for reducing this burden to the Drug Enforcement Administration, Records Management Section, Washington, DC 20537; and to the Office of Management and Budget, Paperwork Reduction Project No. 1117–0025, Washington, DC 20503.

[54 FR 31665, Aug. 1, 1989, as amended at 56 FR 55077, Oct. 24, 1991; 62 FR 13969, Mar. 24, 1997]

§1313.25 Foreign import restrictions.

Any export from the United States in violation of the law of the country to which the chemical is exported is subject to the penalties of Title 21 United States Code 960(d).

§1313.26 Transfers following exportation.

(a) In the case of a notice under §1313.21(a) submitted by a regulated person, if the transferee identified in the notice, i.e., the foreign importer, is not a regular customer, the regulated person may not transfer the listed chemical until after the expiration of the 15-day period beginning on the date on which the notice is submitted to the Administration.

(b) After a notice under §1313.21(a) is submitted to the Administration, if circumstances change and the exporter will not be transferring the listed chemical to the transferee identified in the notice, or will be transferring a greater quantity of the chemical than specified in the notice, the exporter must update the notice to identify the most recent prospective transferee or the most recent quantity or both (as the case may be) and may not transfer the listed chemical until after the expiration of the 15-day period beginning on the date on which the update is submitted to the Administration, except that the 15-day restriction does not apply if the prospective transferee identified in the update is a regular customer. The preceding sentence applies with respect to changing circumstances regarding a transferee or quantity identified in an update to the same extent and in the same manner as the sentence applies with respect to changing circumstances regarding a transferee or quantity identified in the original notice under paragraph (a) of this section.

(c) In the case of a transfer of a listed chemical that is subject to a 15-day restriction, the transferee involved shall, upon the expiration of the 15-day period, be considered to qualify as a regular customer, unless the Administration otherwise notifies the exporter involved in writing.

(d) With respect to a transfer of a listed chemical with which a notice or update referred to in §1313.21(a) is concerned:

(1) The Administration—

(i) May, in accordance with the same procedures as apply under §§1313.51 through 1313.57, order the suspension of the transfer of the listed chemical by the exporter involved, except for a transfer to a regular customer, on the ground that the chemical may be diverted to the clandestine manufacture of a controlled substance (without regard to the form of the chemical that may be diverted, including the diversion of a finished drug product to be manufactured from bulk chemicals to be transferred), subject to the Administration ordering the suspension before the expiration of the 15-day period with respect to the exportation (in any case in which such a period applies); and

(ii) May, for purposes of this paragraph (d), disqualify a regular customer on that ground.

(2) From and after the time when the Administration provides written notice of the order under paragraph (d)(1)(i) of this section (including a statement of the legal and factual basis for the order) to the exporter, the exporter may not carry out the transfer.

(e) For purposes of this section:

(1) The term *transfer*, with respect to a listed chemical, includes the sale of the chemical.

(2) The term *transferee* means a person to whom an exporter transfers a listed chemical.

[72 FR 17408, Apr. 9, 2007]

§ 1313.27 Return declaration or amendment to Form 486 for exports.

(a) Within 30 days after a transaction is completed, the exporter must send to the Administration a return declaration containing particulars of the transaction, including the date, quantity, chemical, container, name of transferees, and any other information as the Administration may specify.

(b) If an exportation for which a Form 486 has been filed fails to take place, the exporter must file an amended Form 486 notifying the Administration that the exportation did not occur.

[72 FR 17408, Apr. 9, 2007]

TRANSSHIPMENTS, IN-TRANSIT SHIPMENTS AND INTERNATIONAL TRANSACTIONS INVOLVING LISTED CHEMICALS

§ 1313.31 Advance notice of importation for transshipment or transfer.

(a) A quantity of a chemical listed in § 1310.02 of this chapter that meets or exceeds the threshold reporting requirements found in § 1310.04(f) of this chapter may be imported into the United States for transshipment, or may be transferred or transshipped within the United States for immediate exportation, provided that advance notice is given to the Administration.

(b) Advance notification must be provided to the Drug Enforcement Administration, P.O. Box 27284, Washington, DC 20038, not later than 15 days prior to the proposed date the listed chemical will transship or transfer through the United States. The written notification (not a DEA Form 486) shall contain the following information:

(1) The date the notice was executed;

(2) The complete name and description of the listed chemical as it appears on the label or container.

(3) The name of the listed chemical as designated by § 1310.02 of this chapter.

(4) The number of containers and the size or weight of the container for each listed item;

(5) The new weight of each listed chemical given in kilograms or parts thereof;

(6) The gross weight of the shipment given in kilograms or parts thereof;

(7) The name, address, telephone number, telex number, business of the foreign exporter and, where available, the facsimile number;

(8) The foreign port of exportation;

(9) The approximate date of exportation;

(10) The complete identification of the exporting carrier;

(11) The name, address, business telephone number, telex number, and where available, the facsimile number of the importer, transferor, or transshipper;

(12) The U.S. port of entry;

(13) The approximate date of entry;

(14) The name, address, telephone number, telex number, business of the

consignee and, where available, facsimile number of the consignee at the foreign port of entry;

(15) The shipping route from the U.S. port of exportation to the foreign port of entry at final destination;

(16) The approximate date of receipt by the consignee at the foreign port of entry; and

(17) The signature of the importer, transferor or transshipper, or his agent, accompanied by the agent's title.

(c) Unless notified to the contrary prior to the expected date of delivery, the importation for transshipment or transfer is considered approved.

(d) No waiver of the 15-day advance notice will be given for imports of listed chemicals in quantities meeting or exceeding threshold quantities for transshipment or transfer outside the United States.

[54 FR 31665, Aug. 1, 1989, as amended at 67 FR 49569, July 31, 2002]

§ 1313.32 Requirement of authorization for international transactions.

(a) A broker or trader shall notify the Administrator prior to an international transaction involving a listed chemical which meets or exceeds the threshold amount identified in Section 1310.04 of this chapter, in which the broker or trader participates. Notification must be made no later than 15 days before the transaction is to take place. In order to facilitate an international transaction involving listed chemicals and implement the purpose of the Act, regulated persons may wish to provide advance notification to the Administration as far in advance of the 15 days as possible.

(b)(1) A completed DEA Form 486 must be received at the following address not later than 15 days prior to the international transaction:

Drug Enforcement Administration, P.O. Box 27284, Washington, D.C. 20038

(2) A copy of the DEA Form 486 may be transmitted directly to the Drug Enforcement Administration, Chemical Operations Section, through electronic facsimile media not later than 15 days prior to the exportation.

(c) No person shall serve as a broker or trader for an international transaction involving a listed chemical knowing or having reasonable cause to believe that the transaction is in violation of the laws of the country to which the chemical is exported or the chemical will be used to manufacture a controlled substance in violation of the laws of the country to which the chemical is exported. The Administration will publish a notice of foreign import restrictions for listed chemicals of which DEA has knowledge as provided in Section 1313.25.

(d) After a notice under paragraph (a) of this section is submitted to the Administration, if circumstances change and the broker or trader will not be transferring the listed chemical to the transferee identified in the notice, or will be transferring a greater quantity of the chemical than specified in the notice, the broker or trader must update the notice to identify the most recent prospective transferee or the most recent quantity or both (as the case may be). The preceding sentence applies with respect to changing circumstances regarding a transferee or quantity identified in an update to the same extent and in the same manner as the sentence applies with respect to changing circumstances regarding a transferee or quantity identified in the original notice under paragraph (a) of this section.

(e) For purposes of this section:

(1) The term *transfer*, with respect to a listed chemical, includes the sale of the chemical.

(2) The term *transferee* means a person to whom an exporter transfers a listed chemical.

[60 FR 32465, June 22, 1995; 61 FR 17566, Apr. 22, 1996; 67 FR 49569, July 31, 2002; 72 FR 17408, Apr. 9, 2007]

§ 1313.33 Contents of an international transaction declaration.

(a) An international transaction involving a chemical listed in § 1310.02 of this chapter which meets the threshold criteria established in § 1310.04 of this chapter may be arranged by a broker or trader if the chemical is needed for medical, commercial, scientific, or other legitimate uses.

(b) Any broker or trader who desires to arrange an international transaction involving a listed chemical which meets the criteria set forth in Section 1310.04 shall notify the Administration through the procedures outlined in Section 1313.32(b).

(c) The DEA Form 486 must be executed in triplicate and must include all the following information:

(1) The name, address, telephone number, telex number, and, where available, the facsimile number of the chemical exporter; the name, address, telephone number, telex number, and, where available, the facsimile number of the chemical importer;

(2) The name and description of each listed chemical as it appears on the label or container, the name of each listed chemical as it is designated in Section 1310.02 of this chapter, the size or weight of container, the number of containers, the net weight of each listed chemical given in kilograms or parts thereof, and the gross weight of the shipment given in kilograms or parts thereof;

(3) The proposed export date, the port of exportation, and the port of importation; and

(4) The name, address, telephone, telex, and where available, the facsimile number, of the consignee in the country where the chemical shipment is destined; the name(s) and address(es) of any intermediate consignee(s).

[60 FR 32465, June 22, 1995]

§ 1313.34 Distribution of the international transaction declaration.

The required three copies of the DEA Form 486 will be distributed as follows:

(a) Copies 1 and 3 shall be retained on file by the broker or trader as the official record of the international transaction. Declaration forms involving List I chemicals shall be retained for List II chemicals shall be retained for four years; declaration forms for two years.

(b) Copy 2 is the Drug Enforcement Administration copy used to fulfill the notification requirements of Section 1313.32.

[60 FR 32465, June 22, 1995; 60 FR 35264, July 6, 1995]

§ 1313.35 Return declaration or amendment to Form 486 for international transactions.

(a) Within 30 days after a transaction is completed, the broker or trader must send to the Administration a return declaration containing particulars of the transaction, including the date, quantity, chemical, container, name of transferees, and any other information as the Administration may specify.

(b) If a transaction for which a Form 486 has been filed fails to take place, the broker or trader must file an amended Form 486 notifying the Administration that the transaction did not occur.

[72 FR 17409, Apr. 9, 2007]

§ 1313.41 Suspension of shipments.

(a) The Administrator may suspend any importation or exportation of a chemical listed in § 1310.02 of this chapter based on evidence that the chemical proposed to be imported or exported may be diverted to the clandestine manufacture of a controlled substance. If the Administrator so suspends, he shall provide written notice of such suspension to the regulated person. Such notice shall contain a statement of the legal and factual basis for the order.

(b) Upon service of the order of suspension, the regulated person to whom the order applies under paragraph (a) of this section must, if he desires a hearing, file a written request for a hearing pursuant to §§ 1313.51–1313.57.

HEARINGS

§ 1313.51 Hearings generally.

In any case where a regulated person requests a hearing regarding the suspension of a shipment of a listed chemical, the procedures for such hearing shall be governed generally by the procedures set forth in the Administrative Procedure Act (5 U.S.C. 551–559) and specifically by section 6053 of the Chemical Diversion and Trafficking Act (Pub. L. 100–690), by 21 CFR 1313.52–1313.57, and by the procedures for administrative hearings under the Controlled Substances Act set forth in §§ 1316.41–1316.67 of this chapter.

§ 1313.52 Purpose of hearing.

If requested by a person entitled to a hearing, the Administrator shall cause a hearing to be held for the purpose of receiving factual evidence regarding the issues involved in the suspension of shipments within 45 days of the date of the request, unless the requesting party requests an extension of time.

§ 1313.53 Waiver of modification of rules.

The Administrator or the presiding officer (with respect to matters pending before him) may modify or waive any rule in this part by notice in advance of the hearing, if he determines that no party in the hearing will be unduly prejudiced and the ends of justice will thereby be served. Such notice of modification or waiver shall be made a part of the record of the hearing.

§ 1313.54 Request for hearing.

(a) Any person entitled to a hearing pursuant to § 1313.52 and desiring a hearing shall, within 30 days after receipt of the notice to suspend the shipment, file with the Administrator a written request for a hearing in the form prescribed in § 1316.47 of this chapter.

(b) If any person entitled to a hearing or to participate in a hearing pursuant to § 1313.41 fails to file a request for a hearing or a notice of appearance, or if he so files and fails to appear at the hearing, he shall be deemed to have waived his opportunity for the hearing or to participate in the hearing, unless he shows good cause for such failure.

(c) If all persons entitled to a hearing or to participate in a hearing waive or are deemed to waive their opportunity for the hearing or to participate in the hearing, the Administrator may cancel the hearing, if scheduled, and issue his final order pursuant to § 1313.57.

§ 1313.55 Burden of proof.

At any hearing regarding the suspension of shipments, the Agency shall have the burden of proving that the requirements of this part for such suspension are satisfied.

§ 1313.56 Time and place of hearing.

(a) If any regulated person requests a hearing on the suspension of shipments, a hearing will be scheduled no later than 45 days after the request is made, unless the regulated person requests an extension to this date.

(b) The hearing will commence at the place and time designated in the notice given pursuant to paragraph (a) of this section but thereafter it may be moved to a different place and may be continued from day to day or recessed to a later day without notice other than announcement thereof by the presiding officer at the hearing.

§ 1313.57 Final order.

As soon as practicable after the presiding officer has certified the record to the Administrator, the Administrator shall issue his order regarding the suspension of shipment. The order shall include the findings of fact and conclusions of law upon which the order is based. The Administrator shall serve one copy of his order upon each party in the hearing.

PART 1314—RETAIL SALE OF SCHEDULED LISTED CHEMICAL PRODUCTS

1314.115 Distributions not subject to reporting requirements.

Subpart D—Order To Show Cause

1314.150 Order to show cause.
1314.155 Suspension pending final order.

AUTHORITY: 21 U.S.C. 802, 830, 842, 871(b), 875, 877.

SOURCE: 71 FR 56024, Sept. 26, 2006, unless otherwise noted.

Subpart A—General

§ 1314.01 Scope.

This part specifies the requirements for retail sales of scheduled listed chemical products to individuals for personal use.

§ 1314.02 Applicability.

(a) This part applies to the following regulated persons who sell scheduled listed chemical products for personal use:

(1) Regulated sellers of scheduled listed chemical products sold at retail for personal use through face-to-face sales at stores or mobile retail vendors.

(2) Regulated persons who engage in a transaction with a non-regulated person and who ship the products to the non-regulated person by the U.S. Postal Service or by private or common carriers.

(b) The requirements in subpart A apply to all regulated persons subject to this part. The requirements in subpart B apply to regulated sellers as defined in § 1300.02 of this chapter. The requirements in subpart C apply to regulated persons who ship the products to the customer by the U.S. Postal Service or by private or common carriers.

§ 1314.03 Definitions.

As used in this part, the term "mail-order sale" means a retail sale of scheduled listed chemical products for personal use where a regulated person uses or attempts to use the U.S. Postal Service or any private or commercial carrier to deliver the product to the customer. Mail-order sale includes purchase orders submitted by phone, mail, fax, Internet, or any method other than face-to-face transaction.

§ 1314.05 Requirements regarding packaging of nonliquid forms.

A regulated seller or mail order distributor may not sell a scheduled listed chemical product in nonliquid form (including gel caps) unless the product is packaged either in blister packs, with each blister containing no more than two dosage units or, if blister packs are technically infeasible, in unit dose packets or pouches.

§ 1314.10 Effect on State laws.

Nothing in this part preempts State law on the same subject matter unless there is a positive conflict between this part and a State law so that the two cannot consistently stand together.

§ 1314.15 Loss reporting.

(a) Each regulated person must report to the Special Agent in Charge of the DEA Divisional Office for the area in which the regulated person making the report is located, any unusual or excessive loss or disappearance of a scheduled listed chemical product under the control of the regulated person. The regulated person responsible for reporting a loss in-transit is the supplier.

(b) Each report submitted under paragraph (a) of this section must, whenever possible, be made orally to the DEA Divisional Office for the area in which the regulated person making the report is located at the earliest practicable opportunity after the regulated person becomes aware of the circumstances involved.

(c) Written reports of losses must be filed within 15 days after the regulated person becomes aware of the circumstances of the event.

(d) A report submitted under this section must include a description of the circumstances of the loss (in-transit, theft from premises, etc.).

(e) A suggested format for the report is provided below:

Regulated Person

Registration number (if applicable) _____
Name _____
Business address _____
City _____
State _____
Zip _____
Business phone _____
Date of loss _____

Type of loss _____
Description of circumstances _____

Subpart B—Sales by Regulated Sellers

§1314.20 Restrictions on sales quantity.

(a) Without regard to the number of transactions, a regulated seller (including a mobile retail vendor) may not in a single calendar day sell any purchaser more than 3.6 grams of ephedrine base, 3.6 grams of pseudoephedrine base, or 3.6 grams of phenylpropanolamine base in scheduled listed chemical products.

(b) A mobile retail vendor may not in any 30-day period sell an individual purchaser more than 7.5 grams of ephedrine base, 7.5 grams of pseudoephedrine base, or 7.5 grams of phenylpropanolamine base in scheduled listed chemical products.

§1314.25 Requirements for retail transactions.

(a) Each regulated seller must ensure that sales of a scheduled listed chemical product at retail are made in accordance with this section and §1314.20.

(b) The regulated seller must place the product so that customers do not have direct access to the product before the sale is made (in this paragraph referred to as "behind-the-counter" placement). For purposes of this paragraph, a behind-the-counter placement of a product includes circumstances in which the product is stored in a locked cabinet that is located in an area of the facility where customers do have direct access. Mobile retail vendors must place the product in a locked cabinet.

(c) The regulated seller must deliver the product directly into the custody of the purchaser.

§1314.30 Recordkeeping for retail transactions.

(a)(1) Except for purchase by an individual of a single sales package containing not more than 60 milligrams of pseudoephedrine, the regulated seller must maintain, in accordance with criteria issued by the Administrator, a written or electronic list of each scheduled listed chemical product sale that identifies the products by name, the quantity sold, the names and addresses of the purchasers, and the dates and times of the sales (referred to as the "logbook"). The logbook may be maintained on paper or in electronic form.

(2) Effective November 27, 2006, if a logbook is maintained on paper, it must be created and maintained in a bound record book.

(b) The regulated seller must not sell a scheduled listed chemical product at retail unless the purchaser does the following:

(1) Presents an identification card that provides a photograph and is issued by a State or the Federal Government, or a document that, with respect to identification, is considered acceptable for purposes of 8 CFR 274a.2(b)(1)(v)(A) and 274a.2(b)(1)(v)(B).

(2) Signs the logbook and enters in the logbook his or her name, address, and the date and time of the sale.

(c) For records created electronically, the regulated seller may use an electronic signature system to capture the signature and may have the computer automatically enter the date and time of the sale. The regulated seller may ask the purchaser for their name and address and enter information if it is not feasible for the purchaser to enter the information electronically.

(d) The regulated seller must determine that the name entered in the logbook corresponds to the name provided on identification presented and that the date and time entered are correct.

(e) The regulated seller must enter in the logbook the name of the product and the quantity sold. Examples of methods of recording the quantity sold include the weight of the product per package and number of packages of each chemical, the cumulative weight of the product for each chemical, or quantity of product by Universal Product Code. These examples do not exclude other methods of displaying the quantity sold. For electronic records, the regulated seller may use a point-of-sale and bar code reader. Such electronic records must be provided pursuant to paragraph (i) of this section in a human readable form such that the requirements of paragraph (a)(1) of this section are satisfied.

(f) The regulated seller must include in the logbook or display by the logbook, the following notice:

WARNING: Section 1001 of Title 18, United States Code, states that whoever, with respect to the logbook, knowingly and willfully falsifies, conceals, or covers up by any trick, scheme, or device a material fact, or makes any materially false, fictitious, or fraudulent statement or representation, or makes or uses any false writing or document knowing the same to contain any materially false, fictitious, or fraudulent statement or entry, shall be fined not more than $250,000 if an individual or $500,000 if an organization, imprisoned not more than five years, or both.

(g) The regulated seller must maintain each entry in the logbook for not fewer than 2 years after the date on which the entry is made.

(h) A record under this section must be kept at the regulated seller's place of business where the transaction occurred, except that records may be kept at a single, central location of the regulated seller if the regulated seller has notified the Administration of the intention to do so. Written notification must be submitted by registered or certified mail, return receipt requested, to the Special Agent in Charge of the DEA Divisional Office for the area in which the records are required to be kept.

(i) The records required to be kept under this section must be readily retrievable and available for inspection and copying by authorized employees of the Administration under the provisions of 21 U.S.C. 880.

(j) A record developed and maintained to comply with a State law may be used to meet the requirements of this section if the record includes the information specified in this section.

§ 1314.35   Training of sales personnel.

Each regulated seller must ensure that its sales of a scheduled listed chemical product at retail are made in accordance with the following:

(a) In the case of individuals who are responsible for delivering the products into the custody of purchasers or who deal directly with purchasers by obtaining payments for the products, the regulated seller has submitted to the Administration a self-certification that all such individuals have, in accordance with criteria issued by the Administration, undergone training provided by the regulated seller to ensure that the individuals understand the requirements that apply under this part.

(b) The regulated seller maintains a copy of each self-certification and all records demonstrating that individuals referred to in paragraph (a) of this section have undergone the training.

§ 1314.40   Self-certification.

(a) A regulated seller must submit to the Administration the self-certification referred to in § 1314.35(a) in order to sell any scheduled listed chemical product. The certification is not effective for purposes of this section unless, in addition to provisions regarding the training of individuals referred to in § 1314.35(a), the certification includes a statement that the regulated seller understands each of the requirements that apply under this part and agrees to comply with the requirements.

(b) When a regulated seller files the initial self-certification, the Administration will assign the regulated seller to one of twelve groups. The expiration date of the self-certification for all regulated sellers in any group will be the last day of the month designated for that group. In assigning a regulated seller to a group, the Administration may select a group with an expiration date that is not less than 12 months or more than 23 months from the date of the self-certification. After the initial certification period, the regulated seller must update the self-certifications annually.

(c) The regulated seller must provide a separate certification for each place of business at which the regulated seller sells scheduled listed chemical products at retail.

§ 1314.45   Privacy protections.

To protect the privacy of individuals who purchase scheduled listed chemical products, the disclosure of information in logbooks under § 1314.15 is restricted as follows:

(a) The information shall be disclosed as appropriate to the Administration and to State and local law enforcement agencies.

(b) The information in the logbooks shall not be accessed, used, or shared for any purpose other than to ensure compliance with this title or to facilitate a product recall to protect public health and safety.

(c) A regulated seller who in good faith releases information in a logbook to Federal, State, or local law enforcement authorities is immune from civil liability for the release unless the release constitutes gross negligence or intentional, wanton, or willful misconduct.

§1314.50 Employment measures.

A regulated seller may take reasonable measures to guard against employing individuals who may present a risk with respect to the theft and diversion of scheduled listed chemical products, which may include, notwithstanding State law, asking applicants for employment whether they have been convicted of any crime involving or related to such products or controlled substances.

Subpart C—Mail-Order Sales

§1314.100 Sales limits for mail-order sales.

(a) Each regulated person who makes a sale at retail of a scheduled listed chemical product and is required under §1310.03(c) of this chapter to submit a report of the sales transaction to the Administration may not in a single calendar day sell to any purchaser more than 3.6 grams of ephedrine base, 3.6 grams of pseudoephedrine base, or 3.6 grams of phenylpropanolamine base in scheduled listed chemical products.

(b) Each regulated person who makes a sale at retail of a scheduled listed chemical product and is required under §1310.03(c) of this chapter to submit a report of the sales transaction to the Administration may not in any 30-day period sell to an individual purchaser more than 7.5 grams of ephedrine base, 7.5 grams of pseudoephedrine base, or 7.5 grams of phenylpropanolamine base in scheduled listed chemical products.

§1314.105 Verification of identity for mail-order sales.

(a) Each regulated person who makes a sale at retail of a scheduled listed

chemical product and is required under §1310.03(c) of this chapter to submit a report of the sales transaction to the Administration must, prior to shipping the product, receive from the purchaser a copy of an identification card that provides a photograph and is issued by a State or the Federal Government, or a document that, with respect to identification, is considered acceptable for purposes of 8 CFR 274a.2(b)(1)(v)(A) and 274a.2(b)(1)(v)(B). Prior to shipping the product, the regulated person must determine that the name and address on the identification correspond to the name and address provided by the purchaser as part of the sales transaction. If the regulated person cannot verify the identities of both the purchaser and the recipient, the person may not ship the scheduled listed chemical product.

(b) If the product is being shipped to a third party, the regulated person must comply with the requirements of paragraph (a) to verify that both the purchaser and the person to whom the product is being shipped live at the addresses provided. If the regulated person cannot verify the identities of both the purchaser and the recipient, the person may not ship the scheduled listed chemical product.

§1314.110 Reports for mail-order sales.

(a) Each regulated person required to report under §1310.03(c) of this chapter must either:

(1) Submit a written report, containing the information set forth in paragraph (b) of this section, on or before the 15th day of each month following the month in which the distributions took place. The report must be submitted under company letterhead, signed by the person authorized to sign on behalf of the regulated seller, to the Drug and Chemical Evaluation Section, Office of Diversion Control, Drug Enforcement Administration, Washington, DC 20537; or

(2) Upon request to and approval by the Administration, submit the report in electronic form, either via computer disk or direct electronic data transmission, in such form as the Administration shall direct. Requests to submit reports in electronic form should be submitted to the Drug and Chemical

Evaluation Section, Office of Diversion Control, Drug Enforcement Administration, Washington, DC 20537, ATTN: Electronic Reporting.

(b) Each monthly report must provide the following information for each distribution:

(1) Supplier name and registration number;

(2) Purchaser's name and address;

(3) Name/address shipped to (if different from purchaser's name/address);

(4) Method used to verify the identity of the purchaser and, where applicable, person to whom product is shipped;

(5) Name of the chemical contained in the scheduled listed chemical product and total quantity shipped (*e.g.* pseudoephedrine, 3 grams);

(6) Date of shipment;

(7) Product name;

(8) Dosage form (*e.g.*, tablet, liquid);

(9) Dosage strength (*e.g.*, 30mg, 60mg, per dose etc.);

(10) Number of dosage units (*e.g.*, 100 doses per package);

(11) Package type (blister pack, etc.);

(12) Number of packages;

(13) Lot number.

§ 1314.115   Distributions not subject to reporting requirements.

(a) The following distributions to nonregulated persons are not subject to the reporting requirements in § 1314.110:

(1) Distributions of sample packages when those packages contain not more than two solid dosage units or the equivalent of two dosage units in liquid form, not to exceed 10 milliliters of liquid per package, and not more than one package is distributed to an individual or residential address in any 30-day period.

(2) Distributions by retail distributors that may not include face-to-face transactions to the extent that such distributions are consistent with the activities authorized for a retail distributor as specified in § 1300.02(b)(29) of this chapter, except that this paragraph (a)(2) does not apply to sales of scheduled listed chemical products at retail.

(3) Distributions to a resident of a long term care facility or distributions to a long term care facility for dispensing to or for use by a resident of that facility.

(4) Distributions in accordance with a valid prescription.

(b) The Administrator may revoke any or all of the exemptions listed in paragraph (a) of this section for an individual regulated person if the Administrator finds that drug products distributed by the regulated person are being used in violation of the regulations in this chapter or the Controlled Substances Act.

Subpart D—Order to Show Cause

§ 1314.150   Order To show cause.

(a) If, upon information gathered by the Administration regarding any regulated seller or a distributor required to submit reports under § 1310.03(c) of this chapter, the Administrator determines that a regulated seller or distributor required to submit reports under § 1310.03(c) of this chapter has sold a scheduled listed chemical product in violation of Section 402 of the Act (21 U.S.C. 842(a)(12) or (13)), the Administrator will serve upon the regulated seller or distributor an order to show cause why the regulated seller or distributor should not be prohibited from selling scheduled listed chemical products.

(b) The order to show cause shall call upon the regulated seller or distributor to appear before the Administrator at a time and place stated in the order, which shall not be less than 30 days after the date of receipt of the order. The order to show cause shall also contain a statement of the legal basis for such hearing and for the prohibition and a summary of the matters of fact and law asserted.

(c) Upon receipt of an order to show cause, the regulated seller or distributor must, if he desires a hearing, file a request for a hearing as specified in subpart D of part 1316 of this chapter. If a hearing is requested, the Administrator shall hold a hearing at the time and place stated in the order, as provided in part 1316 of this chapter.

(d) When authorized by the Administrator, any agent of the Administration may serve the order to show cause.

§ 1314.155 Suspension pending final order.

(a) The Administrator may suspend the right to sell scheduled listed chemical products simultaneously with, or at any time subsequent to, the service upon the seller or distributor required to file reports under § 1310.03(c) of this chapter of an order to show cause why the regulated seller or distributor should not be prohibited from selling scheduled listed chemical products, in any case where he finds that there is an imminent danger to the public health or safety. If the Administrator so suspends, he shall serve with the order to show cause under § 1314.150 an order of immediate suspension that shall contain a statement of his findings regarding the danger to public health or safety.

(b) Upon service of the order of immediate suspension, the regulated seller or distributor shall, as instructed by the Administrator:

(1) Deliver to the nearest office of the Administration or to authorized agents of the Administration all of the scheduled listed chemical products in his or her possession; or

(2) Place all of the scheduled listed chemical products under seal as described in Section 304 of the Act (21 U.S.C. 824(f)).

(c) Any suspension shall continue in effect until the conclusion of all proceedings upon the prohibition, including any judicial review, unless sooner withdrawn by the Administrator or dissolved by a court of competent jurisdiction. Any regulated seller or distributor whose right to sell scheduled listed chemical products is suspended under this section may request a hearing on the suspension at a time earlier than specified in the order to show cause under § 1314.150, which request shall be granted by the Administrator, who shall fix a date for such hearing as early as reasonably possible.

PART 1315—IMPORTATION AND PRODUCTION QUOTAS FOR EPHEDRINE, PSEUDOEPHEDRINE, AND PHENYLPROPANOLAMINE

Subpart A—General Information

SOURCE: 72 FR 37448, July 10, 2007, unless otherwise noted.

AUTHORITY: 21 U.S.C. 802, 821, 826, 871(b), 952.

Subpart A—General Information

§ 1315.01 Scope.

This part specifies procedures governing the establishment of an assessment of annual needs, procurement and manufacturing quotas pursuant to section 306 of the Act (21 U.S.C. 826), and import quotas pursuant to section 1002 of the Act (21 U.S.C. 952) for ephedrine, pseudoephedrine, and phenylpropanolamine.

§ 1315.02 Definitions.

(a) Except as specified in paragraphs (b) and (c) of this section, any term contained in this part shall have the definition set forth in section 102 of the Act (21 U.S.C. 802) or part 1300 of this chapter.

(b) The term *net disposal* means, for a stated period, the sum of paragraphs (b)(1) through (b)(3) of this section minus the sum of paragraphs (b)(4) and (b)(5) of this section:

(1) The quantity of ephedrine, pseudoephedrine, or phenylpropanolamine distributed by the registrant to another person.

(2) The quantity of that chemical used by the registrant in the production of (or converted by the registrant into) another chemical or product.

(3) The quantity of that chemical otherwise disposed of by the registrant.

(4) The quantity of that chemical returned to the registrant by any purchaser.

(5) The quantity of that chemical distributed by the registrant to a registered manufacturer of that chemical for purposes other than use in the production of, or conversion into, another chemical or in the manufacture of dosage forms of that chemical.

(c) Ephedrine, pseudoephedrine, and phenylpropanolamine include their salts, optical isomers, and salts of optical isomers.

§ 1315.03 Personal use exemption.

A person need not register as an importer, file an import declaration, and obtain an import quota if both of the following conditions are met:

(a) The person purchases scheduled listed chemical products at retail and imports them for personal use, by means of shipping through any private or commercial carrier or the Postal Service.

(b) In any 30-day period, the person imports no more than 7.5 grams of ephedrine base, 7.5 grams of pseudoephedrine base, and 7.5 grams of phenylpropanolamine base in scheduled listed chemical products.

§ 1315.05 Applicability.

This part applies to all of the following:

(a) Persons registered to manufacture (including repackaging or relabeling) or to import ephedrine, pseudoephedrine, or phenylpropanolamine as bulk chemicals.

(b) Persons registered to manufacture (including repackaging or relabeling) or to import prescription and over-the-counter drug products containing ephedrine, pseudoephedrine, or phenylpropanolamine that may be lawfully marketed and distributed in the United States under the Federal Food, Drug, and Cosmetic Act.

Subpart B—Assessment of Annual Needs

§ 1315.11 Assessment of annual needs.

(a) The Administrator shall determine the total quantity of ephedrine, pseudoephedrine, and phenylpropanolamine, including drug products containing ephedrine, pseudoephedrine, and phenylpropanolamine, necessary to be manufactured and imported during the following calendar year to provide for the estimated medical, scientific, research, and industrial needs of the United States, for lawful export requirements, and for the establishment and maintenance of reserve stocks.

(b) In making his determinations, the Administrator shall consider the following factors:

(1) Total net disposal of the chemical by all manufacturers and importers during the current and 2 preceding years;

(2) Trends in the national rate of net disposal of each chemical;

(3) Total actual (or estimated) inventories of the chemical and of all substances manufactured from the chemical, and trends in inventory accumulation;

(4) Projected demand for each chemical as indicated by procurement and import quotas requested pursuant to § 1315.32; and

(5) Other factors affecting medical, scientific, research, and industrial

needs in the United States, lawful export requirements, and the establishment and maintenance of reserve stocks, as the Administrator finds relevant, including changes in the currently accepted medical use in treatment with the chemicals or the substances which are manufactured from them, the economic and physical availability of raw materials for use in manufacturing and for inventory purposes, yield and stability problems, potential disruptions to production (including possible labor strikes), and recent unforeseen emergencies such as floods and fires.

(c) The Administrator shall, on or before May 1 of each year, publish in the FEDERAL REGISTER, general notice of an assessment of annual needs for ephedrine, pseudoephedrine, and phenylpropanolamine determined by him under this section. A notice of the publication shall be mailed simultaneously to each person registered to manufacture or import the chemical.

(d) The Administrator shall permit any interested person to file written comments on or objections to the proposed assessment of annual needs and shall designate in the notice the time during which the filings may be made.

(e) The Administrator may, but is not required to, hold a public hearing on one or more issues raised by the comments and objections filed with him. In the event the Administrator decides to hold such a hearing, he shall publish a notice of the hearing in the FEDERAL REGISTER. The notice shall summarize the issues to be heard and set the time for the hearing, which shall not be less than 30 days after the date of publication of the notice.

(f) After consideration of any comments or objections, or after a hearing if one is ordered by the Administrator, the Administrator shall issue and publish in the FEDERAL REGISTER the final order determining the assessment of annual needs for the chemicals. The order shall include the findings of fact and conclusions of law upon which the order is based. The order shall specify the date on which it shall take effect. A notice of the publication shall be mailed simultaneously to each person registered as a manufacturer or importer of the chemical.

§ 1315.13 Adjustments of the assessment of annual needs.

(a) The Administrator may at any time increase or reduce the assessment of annual needs for ephedrine, pseudoephedrine, or phenylpropanolamine that has been previously fixed pursuant to § 1315.11.

(b) In determining to adjust the assessment of annual needs, the Administrator shall consider the following factors:

(1) Changes in the demand for that chemical, changes in the national rate of net disposal of the chemical, and changes in the rate of net disposal of the chemical by registrants holding individual manufacturing or import quotas for that chemical;

(2) Whether any increased demand for that chemical, the national and/or changes in individual rates of net disposal of that chemical are temporary, short term, or long term;

(3) Whether any increased demand for that chemical can be met through existing inventories, increased individual manufacturing quotas, or increased importation, without increasing the assessment of annual needs, taking into account production delays and the probability that other individual manufacturing quotas may be suspended pursuant to § 1315.24(b);

(4) Whether any decreased demand for that chemical will result in excessive inventory accumulation by all persons registered to handle that chemical (including manufacturers, distributors, importers, and exporters), notwithstanding the possibility that individual manufacturing quotas may be suspended pursuant to § 1315.24(b) or abandoned pursuant to § 1315.27;

(5) Other factors affecting medical, scientific, research, industrial, and importation needs in the United States, lawful export requirements, and reserve stocks, as the Administrator finds relevant, including changes in the currently accepted medical use in treatment with the chemical or the substances that are manufactured from it, the economic and physical availability of raw materials for use in manufacturing and for inventory purposes, yield and stability problems, potential disruptions to production (including

possible labor strikes), and recent unforeseen emergencies such as floods and fires.

(c) In the event that the Administrator determines to increase or reduce the assessment of annual needs for a chemical, the Administrator shall publish in the FEDERAL REGISTER general notice of an adjustment in the assessment of annual needs for that chemical as determined under this section. A notice of the publication shall be mailed simultaneously to each person registered as a manufacturer or importer of the chemical.

(d) The Administrator shall permit any interested person to file written comments on or objections to the proposal and shall designate in the notice the time during which such filings may be made.

(e) The Administrator may, but is not required to, hold a public hearing on one or more issues raised by the comments and objections filed with him. In the event the Administrator decides to hold such a hearing, he shall publish a notice of the hearing in the FEDERAL REGISTER. The notice shall summarize the issues to be heard and set the time for the hearing, which shall not be less than 10 days after the date of publication of the notice.

(f) After consideration of any comments or objections, or after a hearing if one is ordered by the Administrator, the Administrator shall issue and publish in the FEDERAL REGISTER the final order determining the assessment of annual needs for the chemical. The order shall include the findings of fact and conclusions of law upon which the order is based. The order shall specify the date on which it shall take effect. A notice of the publication shall be mailed simultaneously to each person registered as a manufacturer or importer of the chemical.

Subpart C—Individual Manufacturing Quotas

§ 1315.21 Individual manufacturing quotas.

The Administrator shall, on or before July 1 of each year, fix for and issue to each person registered to manufacture in bulk ephedrine, pseudoephedrine, or phenylpropanolamine who applies for a

manufacturing quota an individual manufacturing quota authorizing that person to manufacture during the next calendar year a quantity of that chemical. Any manufacturing quota fixed and issued by the Administrator is subject to his authority to reduce or limit it at a later date pursuant to § 1315.26 and to his authority to revoke or suspend it at any time pursuant to §§ 1301.36, 1309.43, 1309.44, or 1309.45 of this chapter.

§ 1315.22 Procedure for applying for individual manufacturing quotas.

Any person who is registered to manufacture ephedrine, pseudoephedrine, or phenylpropanolamine and who desires to manufacture a quantity of the chemical must apply on DEA Form 189 for a manufacturing quota for the quantity of the chemical. Copies of DEA Form 189 may be obtained from the Office of Diversion Control Web site, and must be filed (on or before April 1 of the year preceding the calendar year for which the manufacturing quota is being applied) with the Drug & Chemical Evaluation Section, Drug Enforcement Administration, Department of Justice, Washington, DC 20537. A separate application must be made for each chemical desired to be manufactured. The applicant must state the following:

(a) The name and DEA Chemical Code Number, as set forth in part 1310 of this chapter, of the chemical.

(b) For the chemical in each of the current and preceding 2 calendar years,

(1) The authorized individual manufacturing quota, if any;

(2) The actual or estimated quantity manufactured;

(3) The actual or estimated net disposal;

(4) The actual or estimated inventory allowance pursuant to § 1315.24; and

(5) The actual or estimated inventory as of December 31.

(c) For the chemical in the next calendar year,

(1) The desired individual manufacturing quota; and

(2) Any additional factors that the applicant finds relevant to the fixing of the individual manufacturing quota including any of the following:

(i) The trend of (and recent changes in) the applicant's and the national rates of net disposal.

(ii) The applicant's production cycle and current inventory position.

(iii) The economic and physical availability of raw materials for use in manufacturing and for inventory purposes.

(iv) Yield and stability problems.

(v) Potential disruptions to production (including possible labor strikes).

(vi) Recent unforeseen emergencies such as floods and fires.

§ 1315.23 Procedure for fixing individual manufacturing quotas.

(a) In fixing individual manufacturing quotas for ephedrine, pseudoephedrine, and phenylpropanolamine, the Administrator shall allocate to each applicant who is currently manufacturing the chemical a quota equal to 100 percent of the estimated net disposal of that applicant for the next calendar year, adjusted—

(1) By the amount necessary to increase or reduce the estimated inventory of the applicant on December 31 of the current year to his estimated inventory allowance for the next calendar year, pursuant to § 1315.24, and

(2) By any other factors which the Administrator deems relevant to the fixing of the individual manufacturing quota of the applicant, including:

(i) The trend of (and recent changes in) the applicant's and the national rates of net disposal,

(ii) The applicant's production cycle and current inventory position,

(iii) The economic and physical availability of raw materials for use in manufacturing and for inventory purposes,

(iv) Yield and stability problems,

(v) Potential disruptions to production (including possible labor strikes), and

(vi) Recent unforeseen emergencies such as floods and fires.

(b) In fixing individual manufacturing quotas for a chemical, the Administrator shall allocate to each applicant who is not currently manufacturing the chemical a quota equal to 100 percent of the reasonably estimated net disposal of that applicant for the next calendar year, as determined by the Administrator, adjusted—

(1) By the amount necessary to provide the applicant his estimated inventory allowance for the next calendar year, pursuant to § 1315.24; and

(2) By any other factors which the Administrator deems relevant to the fixing of the individual manufacturing quota of the applicant, including any of the following:

(i) The trend of (and recent changes in) the national rate of net disposal.

(ii) The applicant's production cycle and current inventory position.

(iii) The economic and physical availability of raw materials for use in manufacturing and for inventory purposes.

(iv) Yield and stability problems.

(v) Potential disruptions to production (including possible labor strikes).

(vi) Recent unforeseen emergencies such as floods and fires.

(c) On or before March 1 of each year the Administrator shall adjust the individual manufacturing quota allocated for that year to each applicant in paragraph (a) of this section by the amount necessary to increase or reduce the actual inventory of the applicant to December 31 of the preceding year to his estimated inventory allowance for the current calendar year, pursuant to § 1315.24.

§ 1315.24 Inventory allowance.

(a) For the purpose of determining individual manufacturing quotas pursuant to § 1315.23, each registered manufacturer shall be allowed as a part of the quota an amount sufficient to maintain an inventory equal to either of the following:

(1) For current manufacturers, 50 percent of his average estimated net disposal for the current calendar year and the last preceding calendar year; or

(2) For new manufacturers, 50 percent of his reasonably estimated net disposal for the next calendar year as determined by the Administrator.

(b) During each calendar year each registered manufacturer shall be allowed to maintain an inventory of a chemical not exceeding 65 percent of his estimated net disposal of that chemical for that year, as determined at the time his quota for that year was determined. At any time the inventory of a chemical held by a manufacturer exceeds 65 percent of his estimated net disposal, his quota for that chemical is automatically suspended and shall remain suspended until his inventory is less than 60 percent of his estimated net disposal. The Administrator may, upon application and for good cause shown, permit a manufacturer whose quota is, or is likely to be, suspended under this paragraph to continue manufacturing and to accumulate an inventory in excess of 65 percent of his estimated net disposal, upon such conditions and within such limitations as the Administrator may find necessary or desirable.

(c) If, during a calendar year, a registrant has manufactured the entire quantity of a chemical allocated to him under an individual manufacturing quota, and his inventory of that chemical is less than 40 percent of his estimated net disposal of that chemical for that year, the Administrator may, upon application pursuant to § 1315.25, increase the quota of such registrant sufficiently to allow restoration of the inventory to 50 percent of the estimated net disposal for that year.

§ 1315.25   Increase in individual manufacturing quotas.

(a) Any registrant who holds an individual manufacturing quota for a chemical may file with the Administrator an application on DEA Form 189 for an increase in the registrant's quota to meet the registrant's estimated net disposal, inventory, and other requirements during the remainder of that calendar year.

(b) The Administrator, in passing upon a registrant's application for an increase in the individual manufacturing quota, shall take into consideration any occurrences since the filing of the registrant's initial quota application that may require an increased manufacturing rate by the registrant during the balance of the calendar year. In passing upon the application the Administrator may also take into consideration the amount, if any, by which his determination of the total quantity for the chemical to be manufactured under § 1315.11 exceeds the aggregate of all the individual manufacturing quotas for the chemical, and the equitable distribution of such excess among other registrants.

§ 1315.26   Reduction in individual manufacturing quotas.

The Administrator may at any time reduce an individual manufacturing quota for a chemical that he has previously fixed to prevent the aggregate of the individual manufacturing quotas and import quotas outstanding or to be granted from exceeding the assessment of annual needs that has been established for that chemical pursuant to § 1315.11, as adjusted pursuant to § 1315.13. If a quota assigned to a new manufacturer pursuant to § 1315.23(b), or if a quota assigned to any manufacturer is increased pursuant to § 1315.24(c), or if an import quota issued to an importer pursuant to § 1315.34, causes the total quantity of a chemical to be manufactured and imported during the year to exceed the assessment of annual needs that has been established for that chemical pursuant to § 1315.11, as adjusted pursuant to § 1315.13, the Administrator may proportionately reduce the individual manufacturing quotas and import quotas of all other registrants to keep the assessment of annual needs within the limits originally established, or, alternatively, the Administrator may reduce the individual manufacturing quota of any registrant whose quota is suspended pursuant to § 1315.24(b) or §§ 1301.36, 1309.43, 1309.44, or 1309.45 of this chapter or is abandoned pursuant to § 1315.27.

§ 1315.27   Abandonment of quota.

Any manufacturer assigned an individual manufacturing quota for a chemical pursuant to § 1315.23 may at any time abandon his right to manufacture all or any part of the quota by filing with the Drug & Chemical Evaluation Section a written notice of the abandonment, stating the name and DEA Chemical Code Number, as set forth in part 1310 of this chapter, of the chemical and the amount which he has chosen not to manufacture. The Administrator may, in his discretion, allocate the amount among the other manufacturers in proportion to their respective quotas.

Subpart D—Procurement and Import Quotas

§1315.30 Procurement and import quotas.

(a) To determine the estimated needs for, and to insure an adequate and uninterrupted supply of, ephedrine, pseudoephedrine, and phenylpropanolamine the Administrator shall issue procurement and import quotas.

(b) A procurement quota authorizes a registered manufacturer to procure and use quantities of each chemical for the following purposes:

(1) Manufacturing the bulk chemical into dosage forms.

(2) Manufacturing the bulk chemical into other substances.

(3) Repackaging or relabeling the chemical or dosage forms.

(c) An import quota authorizes a registered importer to import quantities of the chemical for the following purposes:

(1) Distribution of the chemical to a registered manufacturer that has a procurement quota for the chemical.

(2) Other distribution of the chemical consistent with the legitimate medical and scientific needs of the United States.

§1315.32 Obtaining a procurement quota.

(a) Any person who is registered to manufacture ephedrine, pseudoephedrine, or phenylpropanolamine, or whose requirement of registration is waived pursuant to §1309.24 of this chapter, and who desires to use during the next calendar year any ephedrine, pseudoephedrine, or phenylpropanolamine for purposes of manufacturing (including repackaging or relabeling), must apply on DEA Form 250 for a procurement quota for the chemical. A separate application must be made for each chemical desired to be procured or used.

(b) The applicant must state separately all of the following:

(1) Each purpose for which the chemical is desired.

(2) The quantity desired for each purpose during the next calendar year.

(3) The quantities used and estimated to be used, if any, for that purpose during the current and preceding 2 calendar years.

(c) If the purpose is to manufacture the chemical into dosage form, the applicant must state the official name, common or usual name, chemical name, or brand name of that form. If the dosage form produced is a controlled substance listed in any schedule, the applicant must also state the schedule number and National Drug Code Number, of the substance.

(d) If the purpose is to manufacture another chemical, the applicant must state the official name, common or usual name, chemical name, or brand name of the substance and the DEA Chemical Code Number, as set forth in part 1310 of this chapter.

(e) DEA Form 250 must be filed on or before April 1 of the year preceding the calendar year for which the procurement quota is being applied. Copies of DEA Form 250 may be obtained from the Office of Diversion Control Web site, and must be filed with the Drug & Chemical Evaluation Section, Drug Enforcement Administration, Department of Justice, Washington, DC 20537.

(f) The Administrator shall, on or before July 1 of the year preceding the calendar year during which the quota shall be effective, issue to each qualified applicant a procurement quota authorizing him to procure and use:

(1) All quantities of the chemical necessary to manufacture products that the applicant is authorized to manufacture pursuant to §1315.23; and

(2) Such other quantities of the chemical as the applicant has applied to procure and use and are consistent with his past use, his estimated needs, and the total quantity of the chemical that will be produced.

(g) Any person to whom a procurement quota has been issued may at any time request an adjustment in the quota by applying to the Administrator with a statement showing the need for the adjustment. The application must be filed with the Drug & Chemical Evaluation Section, Drug Enforcement Administration, Department of Justice, Washington, DC 20537. The Administrator shall increase or decrease the procurement quota of the person if and to the extent that he finds, after considering the factors enumerated in paragraph (f) of this section and any occurrences since the issuance of the procurement quota, that the need justifies an adjustment.

(h) Any person to whom a procurement quota has been issued, authorizing that person to procure and use a quantity of ephedrine, pseudoephedrine, or phenylpropanolamine during the current calendar year, must, at or before the time of placing an order with another manufacturer or importer requiring the distribution of a quantity of the chemical, certify in writing to the other registrant that the quantity of ephedrine, pseudoephedrine, or phenylpropanolamine ordered does not exceed the person's unused and available procurement quota of the chemical for the current calendar year. The written certification must be executed by a person authorized to sign the registration application pursuant to § 1301.13 or § 1309.32(g) of this chapter. Registrants must not fill an order from persons required to apply for a procurement quota under paragraph (b) of this section unless the order is accompanied by a certification as required under this section.

(i) The certification required by paragraph (h) of this section must contain all of the following:

(1) The date of the certification.

(2) The name and address of the registrant to whom the certification is directed.

(3) A reference to the purchase order number to which the certification applies.

(4) The name of the person giving the order to which the certification applies.

(5) The name of the chemical to which the certification applies.

(6) A statement that the quantity (expressed in grams) of the chemical to which the certification applies does not exceed the unused and available procurement quota of the chemical, issued to the person giving the order, for the current calendar year.

(7) The signature of the individual authorized to sign a certification as provided in paragraph (h) of this section.

§ 1315.34 Obtaining an import quota.

(a) Any person who is registered to import ephedrine, pseudoephedrine, or phenylpropanolamine, or whose requirement of registration is waived pursuant to § 1309.24(c) of this chapter, and who desires to import during the next calendar year any ephedrine, pseudoephedrine, or phenylpropanolamine or drug products containing these chemicals, must apply on DEA Form 488 for an import quota for the chemical. A separate application must be made for each chemical desired to be imported.

(b) The applicant must provide the following information in the application:

(1) The applicant's name and DEA registration number.

(2) The name and address of a contact person and contact information (telephone number, fax number, e-mail address).

(3) Name of the chemical and DEA Chemical Code number.

(4) Type of product (bulk or finished dosage forms).

(5) For finished dosage forms, the official name, common or usual name, chemical name, or brand name, NDC number, and the authority to market the drug product under the Federal Food, Drug and Cosmetic Act of each form to be imported.

(6) The amount requested expressed in terms of base.

(7) For the current and preceding two calendar years, expressed in terms of base:

(i) Distribution/Sales—name, address, and registration number (if applicable) of each customer and the amount sold.

(ii) Inventory as of December 31 (each form—bulk, in-process, finished dosage form).

(iii) Acquisition—imports.

(c) For each form of the chemical (bulk or dosage unit), the applicant must state the quantity desired for import during the next calendar year.

(d) DEA Form 488 must be filed on or before April 1 of the year preceding the calendar year for which the import quota is being applied. Copies of DEA Form 488 may be obtained from the Office of Diversion Control Web site, and must be filed with the Drug & Chemical Evaluation Section, Drug Enforcement Administration, Department of Justice, Washington, DC 20537.

(e) The Administrator may at his discretion request additional information from an applicant.

(f) On or before July 1 of the year preceding the calendar year during which the quota shall be effective, the Administrator shall issue to each qualified applicant an import quota authorizing him to import:

(1) All quantities of the chemical necessary to manufacture products that registered manufacturers are authorized to manufacture pursuant to § 1315.23; and

(2) Such other quantities of the chemical that the applicant has applied to import and that are consistent with his past imports, the estimated medical, scientific, and industrial needs of the United States, the establishment and maintenance of reserve stocks, and the total quantity of the chemical that will be produced.

§ 1315.36 Amending an import quota.

(a) An import quota authorizes the registered importer to import up to the set quantity of ephedrine, pseudoephedrine, or phenylpropanolamine and distribute the chemical or drug products on the DEA Form 488. An importer must apply to change the quantity to be imported.

(b) Any person to whom an import quota has been issued may at any time request an increase in the quota quantity by applying to the Administrator with a statement showing the need for the adjustment. The application must be filed with the Drug & Chemical Evaluation Section, Drug Enforcement Administration, Department of Justice, Washington, DC 20537. The Administrator may increase the import quota of the person if and to the extent that he determines that the approval is necessary to provide for medical, scientific, or other legitimate purposes regarding the chemical. The Administrator shall specify a period of time for which the approval is in effect or shall provide that the approval is in effect until the Administrator notifies the applicant in writing that the approval is terminated.

(c) With respect to the application under paragraph (b) of this section, the Administrator shall approve or deny the application within 60 days of receiving the application. If the Administrator does not approve or deny the application within 60 days of receiving it, the application is deemed to be approved and the approval remains in effect until the Administrator notifies the applicant in writing that the approval is terminated.

Subpart E—Hearings

§ 1315.50 Hearings generally.

The procedures for the hearing related to assessment of annual needs or to the issuance, adjustment, suspension, or denial of a manufacturing, procurement, or import quota are governed generally by the adjudication procedures set forth in the Administrative Procedure Act (5 U.S.C. 551–559) and specifically by section 1002 of the Act (21 U.S.C. 952), by §§ 1315.52 through 1315.62 of this part, and by the procedures for administrative hearings under the Act set forth in §§ 1316.41 through 1316.67 of this chapter.

§ 1315.52 Purpose of hearing.

(a) The Administrator may, in his sole discretion, hold a hearing for the purpose of receiving factual evidence regarding any one or more issues (to be specified by him) involved in the determination or adjustment of any assessment of national needs.

(b) If requested by a person applying for or holding a procurement, import, or individual manufacturing quota, the Administrator shall hold a hearing for the purpose of receiving factual evidence regarding the issues involved in the issuance, adjustment, suspension, or denial of the quota to the person, but the Administrator need not hold a hearing on suspension of a quota under § 1301.36 or § 1309.43 of this chapter separate from a hearing on the suspension of registration under that section.

(c) Extensive argument should not be offered into evidence, but rather presented in opening or closing statements of counsel or in memoranda or proposed findings of fact and conclusions of law.

187

§ 1315.54 Waiver or modification of rules.

The Administrator or the presiding officer (with respect to matters pending before him) may modify or waive any rule in this part by notice in advance of the hearing, if he determines that no party in the hearing will be unduly prejudiced and the ends of justice will thereby be served. Such notice of modification or waiver shall be made a part of the record of the hearing.

§ 1315.56 Request for hearing or appearance; waiver.

(a) Any applicant or registrant entitled to a hearing under § 1315.52 and who desires a hearing on the issuance, adjustment, suspension or denial of a procurement, import, or individual manufacturing quota must, within 30 days after the date of receipt of the issuance, adjustment, suspension or denial of the application, file with the Administrator a written request for a hearing in the form prescribed in § 1316.47 of this chapter.

(b) Any interested person who desires a hearing on the determination of an assessment of annual needs must, within the time prescribed in § 1315.11(c), file with the Administrator a written request for a hearing in the form prescribed in § 1316.47 of this chapter, including in the request a statement of the grounds for the hearing.

(c) Any interested person who desires to participate in a hearing on the determination or adjustment of an assessment of annual needs, which hearing is ordered by the Administrator under § 1315.11(c) or § 1315.13(c), may do so by filing with the Administrator, within 30 days of the date of publication of notice of the hearing in the FEDERAL REGISTER, a written notice of his intention to participate in the hearing in the form prescribed in § 1316.48 of this chapter.

(d) Any person entitled to a hearing under § 1315.52 or entitled to participate in a hearing under paragraph (c) of this section may, within the period permitted for filing a request for a hearing or notice of appearance, file with the Administrator a waiver of an opportunity for a hearing, together with a written statement regarding his position on the matters of fact and law involved in such hearing. The statement, if admissible, shall be made a part of the record and shall be considered in light of the lack of opportunity for cross-examination in determining the weight to be attached to matters of fact asserted.

(e) If any person entitled to a hearing under § 1315.52 or entitled to participate in a hearing under paragraph (c) of this section fails to file a request for a hearing or notice of appearance or if he so files and fails to appear at the hearing, he shall be deemed to have waived his opportunity for the hearing unless he shows good cause for such failure.

(f) If all persons entitled to a hearing or to participate in a hearing waive or are deemed to waive their opportunity for the hearing or to participate in the hearing, the Administrator may cancel the hearing, if scheduled, and issue his final order under § 1315.62 without a hearing.

§ 1315.58 Burden of proof.

(a) At any hearing regarding the determination or adjustment of an assessment of annual needs each interested person participating in the hearing shall have the burden of proving any propositions of fact or law asserted by him in the hearing.

(b) At any hearing regarding the issuance, adjustment, suspension, or denial of a procurement, import, or individual manufacturing quota, the Administration shall have the burden of proving that the requirements of this part for such issuance, adjustment, suspension, or denial are satisfied.

§ 1315.60 Time and place of hearing.

(a) If any applicant or registrant requests a hearing on the issuance, adjustment, suspension, or denial of his procurement, import, or individual manufacturing quota under § 1315.54, the Administrator shall hold a hearing.

(b) Notice of the hearing shall be given to the applicant or registrant of the time and place at least 30 days prior to the hearing, unless the applicant or registrant waives such notice and requests the hearing be held at an earlier time, in which case the Administrator shall fix a date for such hearing as early as reasonably possible.

(c) The hearing shall commence at the place and time designated in the notice given under paragraph (b) of this section or in the notice of hearing published in the FEDERAL REGISTER pursuant to §1315.11(c) or §1315.13(c), but thereafter it may be moved to a different place and may be continued from day to day or recessed to a later day without notice other than announcement by the presiding officer at the hearing.

§ 1315.62 Final order.

As soon as practicable after the presiding officer has certified the record to the Administrator, the Administrator shall issue his order on the determination or adjustment of the assessment of annual needs or on the issuance, adjustment, suspension, or denial of the procurement, import, or individual manufacturing quota, as the case may be. The order shall include the findings of fact and conclusions of law upon which the order is based. The order shall specify the date on which it shall take effect. The Administrator shall serve one copy of his order upon each party in the hearing.

PART 1316—ADMINISTRATIVE FUNCTIONS, PRACTICES, AND PROCEDURES

Subpart A—Administrative Inspections

Subpart B—Protection of Researchers and Research Subjects

Subpart C—Enforcement Proceedings

Subpart D—Administrative Hearings

Subpart E—Seizure, Forfeiture, and Disposition of Property

SOURCE: 36 FR 7820, Apr. 24, 1971, unless otherwise noted. Redesignated at 38 FR 26609, Sept. 24, 1973.

Subpart A—Administrative Inspections

AUTHORITY: 21 U.S.C. 822(f), 830(a), 871(b), 880, 958(f), 965.

§ 1316.01 Scope of subpart A.

Procedures regarding administrative inspections and warrants pursuant to sections 302(f), 510, 1008(d), and 1015 of the Act (21 U.S.C. 822(f), 880, 958(d), and 965) are governed generally by those sections and specifically by the sections of this subpart.

§ 1316.02 Definitions.

As used in this subpart, the following terms shall have the meanings specified:

(a) The term *Act* means the Controlled Substances Act (84 Stat. 1242; 21 U.S.C. 801) and/or the Controlled Substances Import and Export Act (84 Stat. 1285; 21 U.S.C. 951).

(b) The term *Administration* means the Drug Enforcement Administration.

(c) The term *controlled premises* means—

(1) Places where original or other records or documents required under the Act are kept or required to be kept, and

(2) Places, including factories, warehouses, or other establishments and conveyances, where persons registered under the Act or exempted from registration under the Act, or regulated persons may lawfully hold, manufacture, or distribute, dispense, administer, or otherwise dispose of controlled substances or listed chemicals or where records relating to those activities are maintained.

(d) The term *Administrator* means the Administrator of the Administration. The Administrator has been delegated authority under the Act by the Attorney General (28 CFR 0.100).

(e) The term *inspector* means an officer or employee of the Administration authorized by the Administrator to make inspections under the Act.

(f) The term *register* and *registration* refer to registration required and permitted by sections 303 and 1008 of the Act (21 U.S.C. 823 and 958).

(g) Any term not defined in this part shall have the definition set forth in section 102 of the Act (21 U.S.C. 802) or part 1300 of this chapter.

[36 FR 7820, Apr. 24, 1971. Redesignated at 38 FR 26609, Sept. 24, 1973, as amended at 60 FR 32465, June 22, 1995; 60 FR 36334, July 14, 1995; 62 FR 13969, Mar. 24, 1997]

§ 1316.03 Authority to make inspections.

In carrying out his functions under the Act, the Administrator, through his inspectors, is authorized in accordance with sections 510 and 1015 of the Act (21 U.S.C. 880 and 965) to enter controlled premises and conduct administrative inspections thereof, for the purpose of:

(a) Inspecting, copying, and verifying the correctness of records, reports, or other documents required to be kept or made under the Act and regulations promulgated under the Act, including, but not limited to, inventory and other records required to be kept pursuant to part 1304 of this chapter, order form records required to be kept pursuant to part 1305 of this chapter, prescription and distribution records required to be kept pursuant to part 1306 of this chapter, records of listed chemicals, tableting machines, and encapsulating machines required to be kept pursuant to part 1310 of this chapter, import/export records of listed chemicals required to be kept pursuant to part 1313 of this chapter, shipping records identifying the name of each carrier used and the date and quantity of each shipment, and storage records identifying the name of each warehouse used and the date and quantity of each storage.

(b) Inspecting within reasonable limits and to a reasonable manner all pertinent equipment, finished and unfinished controlled substances, listed chemicals, and other substances or materials, containers, and labeling found at the controlled premises relating to this Act;

(c) Making a physical inventory of all controlled substances and listed chemicals on-hand at the premises;

(d) Collecting samples of controlled substances or listed chemicals (in the event any samples are collected during an inspection, the inspector shall issue a receipt for such samples on DEA Form 84 to the owner, operator, or agent in charge of the premises);

(e) Checking of records and information on distribution of controlled substances or listed chemicals by the registrant or regulated person (i.e., has the distribution of controlled substances or listed chemicals increased markedly within the past year, and if so why);

(f) Except as provided in §1316.04, all other things therein (including records, files, papers, processes, controls and facilities) appropriate for verification of the records, reports, documents referred to above or otherwise bearing on the provisions of the Act and the regulations thereunder.

[36 FR 7820, Apr. 24, 1971. Redesignated at 38 FR 26609, Sept. 24, 1973, and amended at 51 FR 5319, Feb. 13, 1986; 55 FR 50827, Dec. 11, 1990; 60 FR 32465, June 22, 1995]

§1316.04 Exclusion from inspection.

(a) Unless the owner, operator or agent in charge of the controlled premises so consents in writing, no inspection authorized by these regulations shall extend to:

(1) Financial data;

(2) Sales data other than shipping data; or

(3) Pricing data.

(b) [Reserved]

§1316.05 Entry.

An inspection shall be carried out by an inspector. Any such inspector, upon (a) stating his purpose and (b) presenting to the owner, operator or agent in charge of the premises to be inspected (1) appropriate credentials, and (2) written notice of his inspection authority under §1316.06 of this chapter, and (c) receiving informed consent under §1316.08 or through the use of administrative warrant issued under §§1316.09–1316.13, shall have the right to enter such premises and conduct inspections at reasonable times and in a reasonable manner.

[36 FR 7820, Apr. 24, 1971, as amended at 36 FR 13387, July 21, 1971. Redesignated at 38 FR 26609, Sept. 24, 1973; 62 FR 13970, Mar. 24, 1997]

§1316.06 Notice of inspection.

The notice of inspection (DEA (or DNB) Form 82) shall contain:

(a) The name and title of the owner, operator, or agent in charge of the controlled premises;

(b) The controlled premises name;

(c) The address of the controlled premises to be inspected;

(d) The date and time of the inspection;

(e) A statement that a notice of inspection is given pursuant to section 510 of the Act (21 U.S.C. 880);

(f) A reproduction of the pertinent parts of section 510 of the Act; and

(g) The signature of the inspector.

§1316.07 Requirement for administrative inspection warrant; exceptions.

In all cases where an inspection is contemplated, an administrative inspection warrant is required pursuant to section 510 of the Act (21 U.S.C. 880), except that such warrant shall not be required for establishments applying for initial registration under the Act, for the inspection of books and records pursuant to an administrative subpoena issued in accordance with section 506 of the Act (21 U.S.C. 876) nor for entries in administrative inspections (including seizures of property):

(a) With the consent of the owner, operator, or agent in charge of the controlled premises as set forth in §1316.08;

(b) In situations presenting imminent danger to health or safety;

(c) In situations involving inspection of conveyances where there is reasonable cause to obtain a warrant;

(d) In any other exceptional or emergency circumstance or time or opportunity to apply for a warrant is lacking; or

(e) In any other situations where a warrant is not constitutionally required.

§ 1316.08 Consent to inspection.

(a) An administrative inspection warrant shall not be required if informed consent is obtained from the owner, operator, or agent in charge of the controlled premises to be inspected.

(b) Wherever possible, informed consent shall consist of a written statement signed by the owner, operator, or agent in charge of the premises to be inspected and witnessed by two persons. The written consent shall contain the following information:

(1) That he (the owner, operator, or agent in charge of the premises) has been informed of his constitutional right not to have an administrative inspection made without an administrative inspection warrant;

(2) That he has right to refuse to consent to such an inspection;

(3) That anything of an incriminating nature which may be found may be seized and used against him in a criminal prosecution;

(4) That he has been presented with a notice of inspection as set forth in § 1316.06;

(5) That the consent given by him is voluntary and without threats of any kind; and

(6) That he may withdraw his consent at any time during the course of inspection.

(c) The written consent shall be produced in duplicate and be distributed as follows:

(1) The original will be retained by the inspector; and

(2) The duplicate will be given to the person inspected.

[36 FR 7820, Apr. 24, 1971, as amended at 37 FR 15924, Aug. 8, 1972. Redesignated at 38 FR 26609, Sept. 24, 1973]

§ 1316.09 Application for administrative inspection warrant.

(a) An administrative inspection warrant application shall be submitted to any judge of the United States or of a State court of record, or any United States magistrate and shall contain the following information:

(1) The name and address of the controlled premises to be inspected;

(2) A statement of statutory authority for the administrative inspection warrant, and that the fact that the particular inspection in question is designed to insure compliance with the Act and the regulations promulgated thereunder;

(3) A statement relating to the nature and extent of the administrative inspection, including, where necessary, a request to seize specified items and/or to collect samples of finished or unfinished controlled substances or listed chemicals;

(4) A statement that the establishment either:

(i) Has not been previously inspected, or

(ii) Was last inspected on a particular date.

(b) The application shall be submitted under oath to an appropriate judge or magistrate.

[36 FR 7820, Apr. 24, 1971, as amended at 36 FR 13387, July 21, 1971. Redesignated at 38 FR 26609, Sept. 24, 1973; 60 FR 32466, June 22, 1995]

§ 1316.10 Administrative probable cause.

If the judge or magistrate is satisfied that "administrative probable cause," as defined in section 510(d)(1) of the Act (21 U.S.C. 880(d)(1)) exists, he shall issue an administrative warrant. Administrative probable cause shall not mean criminal probable cause as defined by Federal statute or case law.

§ 1316.11 Execution of warrants.

An administrative inspection warrant shall be executed and returned as required by, and any inventory or seizure made shall comply with the requirements of, section 510(d)(3) of the Act (21 U.S.C. 880(d)(3)). The inspection shall begin as soon as is practicable after the issuance of the administrative inspection warrant and shall be completed with reasonable promptness.

The inspection shall be conducted during regular business hours and shall be completed in a reasonable manner.

§1316.12 Refusal to allow inspection with an administrative warrant.

If a registrant or any person subject to the Act refuses to permit execution of an administrative warrant or impedes the inspector in the execution of that warrant, he shall be advised that such refusal or action constitutes a violation of section 402(a)(6) of the Act (21 U.S.C. 842(a)(6)). If he persists and the circumstances warrant, he shall be arrested and the inspection shall commence or continue.

[36 FR 7820, Apr. 24, 1971. Redesignated at 38 FR 26609, Sept. 24, 1973, as amended at 62 FR 13970, Mar. 24, 1997]

§1316.13 Frequency of administrative inspections.

Except where circumstances otherwise dictate, it is the intent of the Administration to inspect all manufacturers of controlled substances listed in Schedules I and II and distributors of controlled substances listed in Schedule I once each year. Distributors of controlled substances listed in Schedules II through V and manufacturers of controlled substances listed in Schedules III through V shall be inspected as circumstances may require, based in part on the registrant's history of compliance with the requirements of this chapter and maintenance of effective controls and procedures to guard against the diversion of controlled substances.

[62 FR 13969, Mar. 24, 1997]

Subpart B—Protection of Researchers and Research Subjects

AUTHORITY: 21 U.S.C. 830, 871(b).

§1316.21 Definitions.

As used in this part, the following terms shall have the meanings specified:

(a) The term *investigative personnel* includes managers, Diversion Investigators, attorneys, analysts and support personnel employed by the Drug Enforcement Administration who are involved in the processing, reviewing and analyzing of declarations and other relevant documents or data relative to regulated transactions or are involved in conducting investigations initiated pursuant to the receipt of such declarations, documents or data.

(b) The term *law enforcement personnel* means Special Agents employed by the Drug Enforcement Administration who, in the course of their official duties, gain knowledge of information which is confidential under such section.

[54 FR 31670, Aug. 1, 1989]

§1316.22 Exemption.

(a) Any person who is aggrieved by a disclosure of information in violation of subsection (c)(1) of Section 310 of the Controlled Substances Act (21 U.S.C. 830) may bring a civil action against the violator for appropriate relief.

(b) Notwithstanding the provision of paragraph (a), a civil action may not be brought under such paragraph against investigative or law enforcement personnel of the Drug Enforcement Administration.

[54 FR 31670, Aug. 1, 1989]

§1316.23 Confidentiality of identity of research subjects.

(a) Any person conducting a bona fide research project directly related to the enforcement of the laws under the jurisdiction of the Attorney General concerning drugs or other substances which are or may be subject to control under the Controlled Substances Act (84 Stat. 1242; 21 U.S.C. 801) who intends to maintain the confidentiality of the identity of those persons who are the subjects of such research may petition the Administrator of the Drug Enforcement Administration for a grant of confidentiality: *Providing*, That:

(1) The Attorney General is authorized to carry out such research under the provisions of Section 502(a) (2–6) of the Controlled Substances Act of 1970 (21 U.S.C. 872(a) (2–6)); and the research is being conducted with funds provided in whole or in part by the Department of Justice; or

(2) The research is of a nature that the Attorney General would be authorized to carry out under the provisions

of Section 502(a) (2–6) of the Controlled Substances Act (21 U.S.C. 872(a) (2–6), and is being conducted with funds provided from sources outside the Department of Justice.

(b) All petitions for Grants of Confidentiality shall be addressed to the Administrator, Drug Enforcement Administration, Washington, DC 20537, and shall contain the following:

(1) A statement as to whether the research protocol requires the manufacture, production, import, export, distribution, dispensing, administration, or possession of controlled substances, and if so the researcher's registration number or a statement that an application for such registration has been submitted to DEA;

(2) The location of the research project;

(3) The qualifications of the principal investigator;

(4) A general description of the research or a copy of the research protocol;

(5) The source of funding for the research project;

(6) A statement as to the risks posed to the research subjects by the research procedures and what protection will be afforded to the research subjects;

(7) A statement as to the risks posed to society in general by the research procedures and what measures will be taken to protect the interests of society;

(8) A specific request to withhold the names and/or any other identifying characteristics of the research subjects; and

(9) Statements establishing that a grant of confidentiality is necessary to the successful completion of the research project.

(c) The grant of confidentiality of identity of research subjects shall consist of a letter issued by the Administrator, which shall include:

(1) The researcher's name and address.

(2) The researcher's registration number, if applicable.

(3) The title and purpose of the research.

(4) The location of the research project.

(5) An authorization for all persons engaged in the research to withhold the names and identifying characteristics of persons who are the subjects of such research, stating that persons who obtain this authorization may not be compelled in any Federal, State, or local civil, criminal, administrative, legislative, or other proceeding to identify the subjects of such research for which this authorization was obtained.

(6) The limits of this authorization, if any.

(7) A statement to the effect that the grant of confidentiality of identity of research subjects shall be perpetual but shall pertain only to the subjects of the research described in the research protocol, the description of the research submitted to DEA, or as otherwise established by DEA.

(d) Within 30 days of the date of completion of the research project, the researcher shall so notify the Administrator. The Administrator shall issue another letter including the information required in paragraph (c) of this section and stating the starting and finishing dates of the research for which the confidentiality of identity of research subjects was granted; upon receipt of this letter, the research shall return the original letter of exemption.

[42 FR 54946, Oct. 12, 1977. Redesignated at 54 FR 31670, Aug. 1, 1989, as amended at 62 FR 13970, Mar. 24, 1997]

§ 1316.24 Exemption from prosecution for researchers.

(a) Upon registration of an individual to engage in research in controlled substances under the Controlled Substances Act (84 Stat. 1242; 21 U.S.C. 801), the Administrator of the Drug Enforcement Administration, on his own motion or upon request in writing from the Secretary or from the researcher or researching practitioner, may exempt the registrant when acting within the scope of his registration, from prosecution under Federal, State, or local laws for offenses relating to possession, distribution or dispensing of those controlled substances within the scope of his exemption. However, this exemption does not diminish any requirement of compliance with the Federal Food, Drug and Cosmetic Act (21 U.S.C. 301).

(b) All petitions for Grants of Exemption from Prosecution for the Researcher shall be addressed to the Administrator, Drug Enforcement Administration, 1405 I Street NW., Washington, DC 20537 and shall contain the following:

(1) The researcher's registration number if any, for the project;

(2) The location of the research project;

(3) The qualifications of the principal investigator;

(4) A general description of the research or a copy of the research protocol;

(5) The source of funding for the research project;

(6) A statement as to the risks posed to the research subjects by the research procedures and what protection will be afforded to the research subjects;

(7) A statement as to the risks posed to society in general by the research procedures and what measures will be taken to protect the interests of society;

(8) A specific request for exemption from prosecution by Federal, State, or local authorities for offenses related to the possession, distribution, and dispensing of controlled substances in accord with the procedures described in the research protocol;

(9) A statement establishing that a grant of exemption from prosecution is necessary to the successful completion of the research project.

(c) Any researcher or practitioner proposing to engage in research requesting both exemption from prosecution and confidentiality of identity of research subjects may submit a single petition incorporating the information required in §§1316.23(b) and 1316.24(b).

(d) The exemption shall consist of a letter issued by the Administrator, which shall include:

(1) The researcher's name and address;

(2) The researcher's registration number for the research project;

(3) The location of the research project;

(4) A concise statement of the scope of the researcher's registration;

(5) Any limits of the exemption; and

(6) A statement that the exemption shall apply to all acts done in the scope of the exemption while the exemption is in effect. The exemption shall remain in effect until completion of the research project or until the registration of the researcher is either revoked or suspended or his renewal of registration is denied. However, the protection afforded by the grant of exemption from prosecution during the research period shall be perpetual.

(e) Within 30 days of the date of completion of the research project, the researcher shall so notify the Administrator. The Administrator shall issue another letter including the information required in paragraph (d) of this section and stating the date of which the period of exemption concluded; upon receipt of this letter the researcher shall return the original letter of exemption.

[42 FR 54946, Oct. 12, 1977. Redesignated at 54 FR 31670, Aug. 1, 1989, as amended at 62 FR 13970, Mar. 24, 1997]

Subpart C—Enforcement Proceedings

AUTHORITY: 21 U.S.C. 871(b), 883.

§1316.31 Authority for enforcement proceeding.

A hearing may be ordered or granted by any Special Agent in Charge of the Drug Enforcement Administration, at his discretion, to permit any person against whom criminal and/or civil action is contemplated under the Controlled Substances Act (84 Stat. 1242; 21 U.S.C. 801) or the Controlled Substances Import and Export Act (84 Stat. 1285; 21 U.S.C. 951) an opportunity to present his views and his proposals for bringing his alleged violations into compliance with the law. Such hearing will also permit him to show cause why prosecution should not be instituted, or to present his views on the contemplated proceeding.

[36 FR 7820, Apr. 24, 1971. Redesignated at 38 FR 26609, Sept. 24, 1973, and amended at 47 FR 41735, Sept. 22, 1982]

§ 1316.32 Notice of proceeding; time and place.

Appropriate notice designating the time and place for the hearing shall be given to the person. Upon request, timely and properly made, by the person to whom notice has been given, the time or place of the hearing, or both, may be changed if the request states reasonable grounds for such change. Such request shall be addressed to the Special Agent in Charge who issued the notice.

[36 FR 7820, Apr. 24, 1971. Redesignated at 38 FR 26609, Sept. 24, 1973, and amended at 47 FR 41735, Sept. 22, 1982]

§ 1316.33 Conduct of proceeding.

Presentation of views at a hearing under this subpart shall be private and informal. The views presented shall be confined to matters relevant to bringing violations into compliance with the Act or to other contemplated proceedings under the Act. These views may be presented orally or in writing by the person to whom the notice was given, or by his authorized representative.

§ 1316.34 Records of proceeding.

A formal record, either verbatim or summarized, of the hearing may be made at the discretion of the Special Agent in Charge. If a verbatim record is to be made, the person attending the hearing will be so advised prior to the start of the hearing.

[37 FR 15924, Aug. 8, 1972. Redesignated at 38 FR 26609, Sept. 24, 1973, and amended at 47 FR 41735, Sept. 22, 1982]

Subpart D—Administrative Hearings

AUTHORITY: 21 U.S.C. 811, 812, 871(b), 875, 958(d), 965.

§ 1316.41 Scope of subpart D.

Procedures in any administrative hearing held under the Act are governed generally by the rule making and/or adjudication procedures set forth in the Administrative Procedure Act (5 U.S.C. 551–559) and specifically by the procedures set forth in this subpart, except where more specific regulations (set forth in §§ 1301.51–1301.57,

§§ 1303.31–1303.37, §§ 1308.41–1308.51, §§ 1311.51–1311.53, §§ 1312.41–1312.47, or §§ 1313.51–1313.57) apply.

[36 FR 7820, Apr. 24, 1971, as amended at 37 FR 15924, Aug. 8, 1972. Redesignated at 38 FR 26609, Sept. 24, 1973, as amended at 62 FR 13970, Mar. 24, 1997]

§ 1316.42 Definitions.

As used in this subpart, the following terms shall have the meanings specified:

(a) The term *Act* means the Controlled Substances Act (84 Stat. 1242; 21 U.S.C. 801) and/or the Controlled Substances Import and Export Act (84 Stat. 1285; 21 U.S.C. 951).

(b) The term *Administrator* means the Administrator of the Administration. The Administrator has been delegated authority under the Act by the Attorney General (28 CFR 0.100).

(c) The term *hearing* means any hearing held pursuant to the Act.

(d) The term *Hearing Clerk* means the hearing clerk of the Administration.

(e) The term *person* includes an individual, corporation, government or governmental subdivision or agency, business trust, partnership, association or other legal entity.

(f) The term *presiding officer* means an administrative law judge qualified and appointed as provided in the Administrative Procedure Act (5 U.S.C. 556).

(g) The term *proceeding* means all actions involving a hearing, colmencing with the publication by the Administrator of the notice of proposed rule making or the issuance of an order to show cause.

(h) Any term not defined in this part shall have the definition set forth in section 102 of the Act (21 U.S.C. 802) or part 1300 of this chapter.

[36 FR 7820, Apr. 24, 1971, as amended at 38 FR 757, Jan. 4, 1973. Redesignated at 38 FR 26609, Sept. 24, 1973, as amended at 62 FR 13969, Mar. 24, 1997]

§ 1316.43 Information; special instructions.

Information regarding procedure under these rules and instructions supplementing these rules in special instances will be furnished by the Hearing Clerk upon request.

§ 1316.44 Waiver or modification of rules.

The Administrator or the presiding officer (with respect to matters pending before him) may modify or waive any rule in this subpart by notice in advance of the hearing, if he determines that no party in the hearing will be unduly prejudiced and the ends of justice will thereby be served. Such notice of modification or waiver shall be made a part of the record of the hearing.

§ 1316.45 Filings; address; hours.

Documents required or permitted to be filed in, and correspondence relating to, hearings governed by the regulations in this chapter shall be filed with the Hearing Clerk, Drug Enforcement Administration, Department of Justice, Washington, DC 20537. This office is open Monday through Friday from 8:30 a.m. to 5 p.m. eastern standard or daylight saving time, whichever is effective in the District of Columbia at the time, except on national legal holidays. Documents shall be dated and deemed filed upon receipt by the Hearing Clerk.

[36 FR 7820, Apr. 24, 1971. Redesignated at 38 FR 26609, Sept. 24, 1973, and amended at 55 FR 27464, July 3, 1990]

§ 1316.46 Inspection of record.

(a) The record bearing on any proceeding, except for material described in subsection (b) of this section, shall be available for inspection and copying by any person entitled to participate in such proceeding, during office hours in the office of the Hearing Clerk, Drug Enforcement Administration, Department of Justice, Washington, DC 20537.

(b) The following material shall not be available for inspection as part of the record:

(1) A research protocol filed with an application for registration to conduct research with controlled substances listed in Schedule I, pursuant to § 1301.32 (a)(6) of this chapter, if the applicant requests that the protocol be kept confidential;

(2) An outline of a production or manufacturing process filed with an application for registration to manufacture a new narcotic controlled substance, pursuant to § 1301.33 of this chapter, if the applicant requests that the outline be kept confidential;

(3) Any confidential or trade secret information disclosed in conjunction with an application for registration, or in reports filed while registered, or acquired in the course of an investigation, entitled to protection under subsection 402(a) (8) of the Act (21 U.S.C. 842(a) (8)) or any other law restricting public disclosure of information; and

(4) Any material contained in any investigatory report, memorandum, or file, or case report compiled by the Administration.

[36 FR 7820, Apr. 24, 1971. Redesignated at 38 FR 26609, Sept. 24, 1973, as amended at 62 FR 13970, Mar. 24, 1997]

§ 1316.47 Request for hearing.

(a) Any person entitled to a hearing and desiring a hearing shall, within the period permitted for filing, file a request for a hearing in the following form:

_____ (Date)

Administrator, Drug Enforcement Administration, United States Department of Justice, Washington, DC 20537, Attention: DEA Federal Register Representative.

DEAR SIR: The undersigned _____ (Name of person) hereby requests a hearing in the matter of: _____ (Identification of the proceeding).

(A) (State with particularity the interest of the person in the proceeding.)

(B) (State with particularity the objections or issues, if any, concerning which the person desires to be heard.)

(C) (State briefly the position of the person with regard to the particular objections or issues.)

All notices to be sent pursuant to the proceeding should be addressed to:

_____

(Name)

_____

(Street address)

_____

(City and State)

Respectfully yours,

_____

(Signature of person)

(b) The Administrative Law Judge, upon request and showing of good cause, may grant a reasonable extension of the time allowed for response to an Order to Show Cause.

[36 FR 7820, Apr. 24, 1971, as amended at 36 FR 13387, July 21, 1971. Redesignated at 38 FR 26609, Sept. 24, 1973]

EDITORIAL NOTE: For FEDERAL REGISTER citations affecting § 1316.47, see the List of CFR Sections Affected, which appears in the Finding Aids section of the printed volume and on GPO Access.

§ 1316.48 Notice of appearance.

Any person entitled to a hearing and desiring to appear in any hearing, shall, if he has not filed a request for hearing, file within the time specified in the notice of proposed rule making, a written notice of appearance in the following form:

_____ (Date)

Administrator, Drug Enforcement Administration, United States Department of Justice, Washington, DC 20537, Attention: DEA Federal Register Representative.

DEAR SIR: Please take notice that _____ (Name of person) will appear in the matter of: _____
(Identification of the proceeding).
  (A) (State with particularity the interest of the person in the proceeding.)
  (B) (State with particularity the objections or issues, if any, concerning which the person desires to be heard.)
  (C) (State briefly the position of the person with regard to the particular objections or issues.)
  All notices to be sent pursuant to this appearance should be addressed to:

_____

(Name)

_____

(Street address)

_____

(City and State)

Respectfully yours,

_____

(Signature of person)

[36 FR 7820, Apr. 24, 1971, as amended at 36 FR 13387, July 21, 1971. Redesignated at 38 FR 26609, Sept. 24, 1973, and amended at 40 FR 57210, Dec. 8, 1975]

§ 1316.49 Waiver of hearing.

Any person entitled to a hearing may, within the period permitted for filing a request for hearing or notice of appearance, waiver of an opportunity for a hearing, together with a written statement regarding his position on the matters of fact and law involved in such hearing. Such statement, if admissible, shall be made a part of the record and shall be considered in light of the lack of opportunity for cross-examination in determining the weight to be attached to matters of fact asserted therein.

§ 1316.50 Appearance; representation; authorization.

Any person entitled to appear in a hearing may appear in person or by a representative in any proceeding or hearing and may be heard with respect to matters relevant to the issues under consideration. A representative must either be an employee of the person or an attorney at law who is a member of the bar, in good standing, of any State, territory, or the District of Columbia, and admitted to practice before the highest court of that jurisdiction. Any representative may be required by the Administrator or the presiding officer to present a notarized power of attorney showing his authority to act in such representative capacity and/or an affidavit or certificate of admission to practice.

[36 FR 7820, Apr. 24, 1971, as amended at 36 FR 13387, July 21, 1971. Redesignated at 38 FR 26609, Sept. 24, 1973]

§ 1316.51 Conduct of hearing and parties; ex parte communications.

(a) Hearings shall be conducted in an informal but orderly manner in accordance with law and the directions of the presiding officer.

(b) Participants in any hearing and their representatives, whether or not members of the bar, shall conduct themselves in accordance with judicial standards of practice and ethics and the directions of the presiding officer. Refusal to comply with this section shall constitute grounds for immediate exclusion from any hearing.

(c) If any official of the Administration is contacted by any individual in private or public life concerning any substantive matter which is the subject of any hearing, at any time after the date on which the proceedings commence, the official who is contacted shall prepare a memorandum setting forth the substance of the conversation and shall file this memorandum in the appropriate public docket file. The presiding officer and employees of the Administration shall comply with the requirements of 5 U.S.C. 554(d) regarding ex parte communications and participation in any hearing.

§1316.52 Presiding officer.

A presiding officer, designated by the Administrator, shall preside over all hearings. The functions of the presiding officer shall commence upon his designation and terminate upon the certification of the record to the Administrator. The presiding officer shall have the duty to conduct a fair hearing, to take all necessary action to avoid delay, and to maintain order. He shall have all powers necessary to these ends, including (but not limited to) the power to:

(a) Arrange and change the date, time, and place of hearings (other than the time and place prescribed in §1301.56) and prehearing conferences and issue notice thereof.

(b) Hold conferences to settle, simplify, or determine the issues in a hearing, or to consider other matters that may aid in the expeditious disposition of the hearing.

(c) Require parties to state their position in writing with respect to the various issues in the hearing and to exchange such statements with all other parties.

(d) Sign and issue subpoenas to compel the attendance of witnesses and the production of documents and materials to the extent necessary to conduct administrative hearings pending before him.

(e) Examine witnesses and direct witnesses to testify.

(f) Receive, rule on, exclude, or limit evidence.

(g) Rule on procedural items pending before him.

(h) Take any action permitted to the presiding officer as authorized by this part or by the provisions of the Administrative Procedure Act (5 U.S.C. 551–559).

[36 FR 7820, Apr. 24, 1971. Redesignated at 38 FR 26609, Sept. 24, 1973, and amended at 42 FR 57457, Nov. 3, 1977; 62 FR 13970, Mar. 24, 1997]

§1316.53 Time and place of hearing.

The hearing will commence at the place and time designated in the notice of hearing published in the FEDERAL REGISTER but thereafter it may be moved to a different place and may be continued from day to day or recessed to a later day without notice other than announcement thereof by the presiding officer at the hearing.

§1316.54 Prehearing conference.

The presiding officer on his own motion, or on the motion of any party for good cause shown, may direct all parties to appear at a specified time and place for a conference for:

(a) The simplification of the issues.

(b) The possibility of obtaining stipulations, admission of facts, and documents.

(c) The possibility of limiting the number of expert witnesses.

(d) The identification and, if practicable, the scheduling of all witnesses to be called.

(e) The advance submission at the prehearing conference of all documentary evidence and affidavits to be marked for identification.

(f) Such other matters as may aid in the expeditious disposition of the hearing.

§1316.55 Prehearing ruling.

The presiding officer may have the prehearing conference reported verbatim and shall make a ruling reciting the action taken at the conference, the agreements made by the parties, the schedule of witnesses, and a statement of the issues for hearing. Such ruling shall control the subsequent course of the hearing unless modified by a subsequent ruling.

§1316.56 Burden of proof.

At any hearing, the proponent for the issuance, amendment, or repeal of any rule shall have the burden of proof.

§ 1316.57 Submission of documentary evidence and affidavits and identification of witnesses subsequent to prehearing conference.

All documentary evidence and affidavits not submitted and all witnesses not identified at the prehearing conference shall be submitted or identified to the presiding officer as soon as possible, with a showing that the offering party had good cause for failing to so submit or identify at the prehearing conference. If the presiding officer determines that good cause does exist, the documents or affidavits shall be submitted or witnesses identified to all parties sufficiently in advance of the offer of such documents or affidavits or witnesses at the hearing to avoid prejudice or surprise to the other parties. If the presiding officer determines that good cause does not exist, he may refuse to admit as evidence such documents or affidavits or the testimony of such witnesses.

§ 1316.58 Summary of testimony; affidavits.

(a) The presiding officer may direct that summaries of the direct testimony of witnesses be prepared in writing and served on all parties in advance of the hearing. Witnesses will not be permitted to read summaries of their testimony into the record and all witnesses shall be available for cross-examination. Each witness shall, before proceeding to testify, be sworn or make affirmation.

(b) Affidavits submitted at the prehearing conference or pursuant to § 1316.57 with good cause may be examined by all parties and opposing affidavits may be submitted to the presiding officer within a period of time fixed by him. Affidavits admitted into evidence shall be considered in light of the lack of opportunity for cross-examination in determining the weight to be attached to statements made therein.

[36 FR 7820, Apr. 24, 1971, as amended at 36 FR 13387, July 21, 1971. Redesignated at 38 FR 26609, Sept. 24, 1973]

§ 1316.59 Submission and receipt of evidence.

(a) The presiding officer shall admit only evidence that is competent, relevant, material and not unduly repetitious.

(b) Opinion testimony shall be admitted when the presiding officer is satisfied that the witness is properly qualified.

(c) The authenticity of all documents submitted in advance shall be deemed admitted unless written objection thereto is filed with the presiding officer, except that a party will be permitted to challenge such authenticity at a later time upon a showing of good cause for failure to have filed such written objection.

(d) Samples, if otherwise admissible into evidence, may be displayed at the hearing and may be described for purposes of the record, or may be admitted in evidence as exhibits.

(e) Where official notice is taken or is to be taken of a material fact not appearing in the evidence of record, any party, on timely request, shall be afforded opportunity to controvert such fact.

(f) The presiding officer shall file as exhibits copies of the following documents:

(1) The order to show cause or notice of hearing;

(2) Any notice of waiver or modification of rules made pursuant to § 1316.44 or otherwise;

(3) Any waiver of hearing (together with any statement filed therewith) filed pursuant to § 1316.49 or otherwise;

(4) The prehearing ruling, if any, made pursuant to § 1316.55;

(5) Any other document necessary to show the basis for the hearing.

§ 1316.60 Objections; offer of proof.

If any party in the hearing objects to the admission or rejection of any evidence or to other limitation of the scope of any examination or cross-examination, he shall state briefly the grounds for such objection without extended argument or debate thereon except as permitted by the presiding officer. A ruling of the presiding officer on any such objection shall be a part of the transcript together with such offer of proof as has been made if a proper foundation has been laid for its admission. An offer of proof made in connection with an objection taken to any ruling of the presiding officer rejecting or excluding proffered oral testimony shall consist of a statement of the substance of the evidence which the party contends would be adduced by such testimony; and, if the excluded evidence consists of evidence in documentary or written form a copy of such evidence shall be marked for identification and shall accompany the records as the offer of proof.

§ 1316.61 Exceptions to rulings.

Exceptions to rulings of the presiding officer are unnecessary. It is sufficient that a party, at the time the ruling of the presiding officer is sought, makes known the action that he desires the presiding officer to take, or his objection to an action taken, and his grounds therefor.

§ 1316.62 Appeal from ruling of presiding officer.

Rulings of the presiding officer may not be appealed to the Administrator prior to his consideration of the entire hearing, except with the consent of the presiding officer and where he certifies on the record or in writing that the allowance of an interlocutory appeal is clearly necessary to prevent exceptional delay, expense, or prejudice to any party or substantial detriment to the public interest. If an appeal is allowed, any party in the hearing may file a brief in quintuplicate with the Administrator within such period that the presiding officer directs. No oral argument will be heard unless the Administrator directs otherwise.

§ 1316.63 Official transcript; index; corrections.

(a) Testimony given at a hearing shall be reported verbatim. The Administration will make provision for a stenographic record of the testimony and for such copies of the transcript thereof as it requires for its own purpose.

(b) At the close of the hearing, the presiding officer shall afford the parties and witnesses time (not longer than 30 days, except in unusual cases) in which to submit written proposed corrections of the transcript, pointing out errors that may have been made in transcribing the testimony. The presiding officer shall promptly thereafter

order such corrections made as in his judgment are required to make the transcript conform to the testimony.

[36 FR 7820, Apr. 24, 1971, as amended at 36 FR 13387, July 21, 1971. Redesignated at 38 FR 26609, Sept. 24, 1973, and amended at 50 FR 2046, Jan. 15, 1985]

§ 1316.64 Proposed findings of fact and conclusions of law.

Any party in the hearing may file in quintuplicate proposed findings of fact and conclusions of law within the time fixed by the presiding officer. Any party so filing shall also serve one copy of his proposed findings and conclusion upon each other party in the hearing. The party shall include a statement of supporting reasons for the proposed findings and conclusions, together with evidence of record (including specific and complete citations of the pages of the transcript and exhibits) and citations of authorities relied upon.

§ 1316.65 Report and record.

(a) As soon as practicable after the time for the parties to file proposed findings of fact and conclusions of law has expired, the presiding officer shall prepare a report containing the following:

(1) His recommended rulings on the proposed findings of fact and conclusions of law;

(2) His recommended findings of fact and conclusions of law, with the reasons therefore; and

(3) His recommended decision.

(b) The presiding officer shall serve a copy of his report upon each party in the hearing. The report shall be considered to have been served when it is mailed to such party or its attorney of record.

(c) Not less than twenty-five days after the date on which he caused copies of his report to be served upon the parties, the presiding officer shall certify to the Administrator the record, which shall contain the transcript of testimony, exhibits, the findings of fact and conclusions of law proposed by the parties, the presiding officer's report, and any exceptions thereto which may have been filed by the parties.

[36 FR 7778, Apr. 24, 1971. Redesignated at 38 FR 26609, Sept. 24, 1973 and amended at 44 FR 55332, Sept. 26, 1979]

§ 1316.66 Exceptions.

(a) Within twenty days after the date upon which a party is served a copy of the report of the presiding officer, such party may file with the Hearing Clerk, Office of the Administrative Law Judge, exceptions to the recommended decision, findings of fact and conclusions of law contained in the report. The party shall include a statement of supporting reasons for such exceptions, together with evidence of record (including specific and complete citations of the pages of the transcript and exhibits) and citations of the authorities relied upon.

(b) The Hearing Clerk shall cause such filings to become part of the record of the proceeding.

(c) The Administrative Law Judge may, upon the request of any party to a proceeding, grant time beyond the twenty days provided in paragraph (a) of this section for the filing of a response to the exceptions filed by another party if he determines that no party in the hearing will be unduly prejudiced and that the ends of justice will be served thereby. Provided however, that each party shall be entitled to only one filing under this section; that is, either a set of exceptions or a response thereto.

[44 FR 55332, Sept. 26, 1979]

§ 1316.67 Final order.

As soon as practicable after the presiding officer has certified the record to the Administrator, the Administrator shall cause to be published in the FEDERAL REGISTER his final order in the proceeding, which shall set forth the final rule and the findings of fact and conclusions of law upon which the rule is based. This order shall specify the date on which it shall take effect, which date shall not be less than 30 days from the date of publication in the FEDERAL REGISTER unless the Administrator finds that the public interest in the matter necessitates an earlier effective date, in which event the Administrator shall specify in the order his findings as to the conditions which led him to conclude that an earlier effective date was required.

[44 FR 42179, July 19, 1979, as amended at 44 FR 55332, Sept. 26, 1979]

§ 1316.68 Copies of petitions for judicial review.

Copies of petitions for judicial review, filed pursuant to section 507 of the Act (21 U.S.C. 877) shall be delivered to and served upon the Administrator in quintuplicate. The Administrator shall certify the record of the hearing and shall file the certified record in the appropriate U.S. Court of Appeals.

[36 FR 7820, Apr. 24, 1971. Redesignated at 44 FR 42179, July 19, 1979]

Subpart E—Seizure, Forfeiture, and Disposition of Property

AUTHORITY: 21 U.S.C 871(b), 881, 965, 19 U.S.C. 1606, 1607, 1608, 1610, 1613, 1618, 28 U.S.C. 509, 510.

§ 1316.71 Definitions.

As used in this subpart, the following terms shall have the meanings specified:

(a) The term *Act* means the Controlled Substances Act (84 Stat. 1242; 21 U.S.C. 801) and/or the Controlled Substances Import and Export Act (84 Stat. 1285; 21 U.S.C. 951).

(b) The term *custodian* means the officer required under § 1316.72 to take custody of particular property which has been seized pursuant to the Act.

(c) The term *property* means a controlled substance, raw material, product, container, equipment, money or other asset, vessel, vehicle, or aircraft within the scope of the Act.

(d) The terms *seizing officer, officer seizing,* etc., mean any officer, authorized and designated by § 1316.72 to carry out the provisions of the Act, who initially seizes property or adopts a seizure initially made by any other officer or by a private person.

(e) The term *Special Agents-in-Charge* means Drug Enforcement Administration Special Agents-in-Charge or Resident Agents in Charge and Federal Bureau of Investigation Special Agents-in-Charge.

(f) Any term not defined in this section shall have the definition set forth in section 102 of the Act (21 U.S.C. 802) or part 1300 of this chapter.

[36 FR 7820, Apr. 24, 1971. Redesignated at 38 FR 26609, Sept. 24, 1973, and amended at 45 FR 20096, Mar. 27, 1980; 47 FR 43370, Oct. 1, 1982; 49 FR 28701, July 16, 1984; 62 FR 13969, Mar. 24, 1997]

§1316.72 Officers who will make seizures.

For the purpose of carrying out the provisions of the Act, all special agents of the Drug Enforcement Administration and the Federal Bureau of Investigation are authorized and designated to seize such property as may be subject to seizure.

[47 FR 43370, Oct. 1, 1982]

§1316.73 Custody and other duties.

An officer seizing property under the Act shall store the property in a location designated by the custodian, generally in the judicial district of seizure. The Special Agents-in-Charge are designated as custodians to receive and maintain in storage all property seized pursuant to the Act, are authorized to dispose of any property pursuant to the Act and any other applicable statutes or regulations relative to disposal, and to perform such other duties regarding such seized property as are appropriate, including the impound release of property pursuant to 28 CFR 0.101(c).

[47 FR 43370, Oct. 1, 1982]

§1316.74 Appraisement.

The custodian shall appraise the property to determine the domestic value at the time and place of seizure. The domestic value shall be considered the price at which such or similar property is freely offered for sale. If there is no market for the property at the place of seizure, the domestic value shall be considered the value in the principal market nearest the place of seizure.

(Authority: Sec. 606, 46 Stat. 754 (19 U.S.C. 1606))

[36 FR 7820, Apr. 24, 1971. Redesignated at 38 FR 26609, Sept. 24, 1973, and amended at 52 FR 41418, Oct. 28, 1987]

§1316.75 Advertisement.

(a) If the appraised value does not exceed the monetary amount set forth in title 19, United States Code, Section 1607; the seized merchandise is any monetary instrument within the meaning of section 5312(a)(3) of title 31 of the United States Code; or if a conveyance used to import, export or otherwise transport or store any controlled substance is involved, the custodian or DEA Asset Forfeiture Section shall cause a notice of the seizure and of the intention to forfeit and sell or otherwise dispose of the property to be published once a week for at least 3 successive weeks in a newspaper of general circulation in the judicial district in which the processing for forfeiture is brought.

(b) The notice shall: (1) Describe the property seized and show the motor and serial numbers, if any; (2) state the time, cause, and place of seizure; and (3) state that any person desiring to claim the property may, within 20 days from the date of first publication of the notice, file with the custodian or DEA Asset Forfeiture Section a claim to the property and a bond with satisfactory sureties in the sum of $5,000 or ten percent of the value of the claimed property whichever is lower, but not less than $250.

(Authority: Sec. 607, 46 Stat. 754, as amended (19 U.S.C. 1607); Pub. L. 98–473, Pub. L. 98–573)

[36 FR 7820, Apr. 24, 1971. Redesignated at 38 FR 26609, Sept. 24, 1973 and amended at 44 FR 56324, Oct. 1, 1979; 49 FR 1178, Jan. 10, 1984; 49 FR 50643, Dec. 31, 1984; 52 FR 24446, July 1, 1987; 56 FR 8686, Mar. 1, 1991]

§1316.76 Requirements as to claim and bond.

(a) The bond shall be rendered to the United States, with sureties to be approved by the custodian or DEA Asset Forfeiture Section, conditioned that in the case of condemnation of the property the obligor shall pay all costs and expenses of the proceedings to obtain such condemnation. When the claim and bond are received by the custodian or DEA Asset Forfeiture Section, he shall, after finding the documents in proper form and the sureties satisfactory, transmit the documents, together with a description of the property and a complete statement of the facts and circumstances surrounding the seizure, to the United States Attorney for the judicial district in which the proceeding for forfeiture is brought. If the documents are not in satisfactory condition when first received, a reasonable time for correction may be allowed. If correction is not made within a reasonable time the documents may be treated as nugatory, and the case shall proceed as though they had not been tendered.

(b) The filing of the claim and the posting of the bond does not entitle the claimant to possession of the property, however, it does stop the administrative forfeiture proceedings. The bond posted to cover corts may be in cash, certified check, or satisfactory sureties. The costs and expenses secured by the bond are such as are incurred after the filing of the bond including storage cost, safeguarding, court fees, marshal's costs, etc.

(Authority: Sec. 608, 46 Stat. 755 (19 U.S.C. 1608); Pub. L. 98–473, Pub. L. 98–573)

[36 FR 7820, Apr. 24, 1971. Redesignated at 38 FR 26609, Sept. 24, 1973 and amended at 49 FR 1178, Jan. 10, 1984; 49 FR 50643, Dec. 31, 1984; 56 FR 8686, Mar. 1, 1991]

§ 1316.77   Administrative forfeiture.

(a) For property seized by officers of the Drug Enforcement Administration, if the appraised value does not exceed the jurisdictional limits in § 1316.75(a), and a claim and bond are not filed within the 20 days hereinbefore mentioned, the DEA Special Agent-in-Charge or DEA Asset Forfeiture Section shall declare the property forfeited. The DEA Special Agent-in-Charge or DEA Asset Forfeiture Section shall prepare the Declaration of Forfeiture and forward it to the Administrator of the Administration as notification of the action he has taken. Thereafter, the property shall be retained in the district of the DEA Special Agent-in-Charge or DEA Asset Forfeiture Section or delivered elsewhere for official use, or otherwise disposed of, in accordance with official instructions received by the DEA Special Agent-in-Charge or DEA Asset Forfeiture Section.

(b) For property seized by officers of the Federal Bureau of Investigation, if the appraised value does not exceed the jurisdictional limits in § 1316.75(a), and a claim and bond are not filed within the 20 days hereinbefore mentioned, the FBI Property Management Officer shall declare the property forfeited. The FBI Property Management Officer shall prepare the Declaration of Forfeiture. Thereafter, the property shall be retained in the field office or delivered elsewhere for official use, or otherwise disposed of, in accordance with the official instructions of the FBI Property Management Officer.

(Authority: 28 U.S.C. 509 and 510; 21 U.S.C. 871 and 881(d); Pub. L. 98–473, Pub. L. 98–573)

[48 FR 35087, Aug. 3, 1983, as amended at 49 FR 1178, Jan. 10, 1984; 49 FR 50643, Dec. 31, 1984; 56 FR 8686, Mar. 1, 1991; 62 FR 13970, Mar. 24, 1997]

§ 1316.78   Judicial forfeiture.

If the appraised value is greater than the jurisdictional limits in § 1316.75(a) or a claim and satisfactory bond have been received for property the jurisdictional limits in § 1316.76, the custodian or DEA Asset Forfeiture Section shall transmit a description of the property and a complete statement of the facts and circumstances surrounding the seizure to the U.S. Attorney for the judicial district in which the proceeding for forfeiture is sought for the purpose of instituting condemnation proceedings. The U.S. Attorney shall also be furnished the newspaper advertisements required by § 1316.75. The Forfeiture Counsel of DEA shall make applications to the U.S. District Courts to place property in official DEA use.

(Authority: Sec. 610, 46 Stat. 755 (19 U.S.C. 1610); Pub. L. 98–473, Pub. L. 98–573)

[36 FR 7820, Apr. 24, 1971. Redesignated at 38 FR 26609, Sept. 24, 1973 and amended at 44 FR 56324, Oct. 1, 1979; 49 FR 1178, Jan. 10, 1984; 49 FR 32174, Aug. 13, 1984; 49 FR 50643, Dec. 31, 1984; 56 FR 8686, Mar. 1, 1991]

§ 1316.79   Petitions for remission or mitigation of forfeiture.

(a) Any person interested in any property which has been seized, or forfeited either administratively or by court proceedings, may file a petition for remission or mitigation of the forfeiture. Such petition shall be filed in triplicate with the DEA Asset Forfeiture Section or Special Agent-in-Charge of the DEA or FBI, depending upon which agency seized the property, for the judicial district in which the proceeding for forfeiture is brought. It shall be addressed to the Director of the FBI or the Administrator of the DEA, depending upon which agency seized the property, if the property is subject to administrative forfeiture pursuant to §1316.77, and addressed to the Attorney General if the property is subject to judicial forfeiture pursuant to §1316.78. The petition must be executed and sworn to by the person alleging interest in the property.

(b) The petition shall include the following: (1) A complete description of the property, including motor and serial numbers, if any, and the date and place of seizure; (2) the petitioner's interest in the property, which shall be supported by bills of sale, contracts, mortgages, or other satisfactory documentary evidence; and, (3) the facts and circumstances, to be established by satisfactory proof, relied upon by the petitioner to justify remission or mitigation.

(c) Where the petition is for restoration of the proceeds of sale, or for value of the property placed in official use, it must be supported by satisfactory proof that the petitioner did not know of the seizure prior to the declaration of condemnation of forfeiture and was in such circumstances as prevented him from knowing of the same.

(Authority: Secs. 613, 618, 46 Stat. 756, 757, as amended (19 U.S.C. 1613, 1618; 28 U.S.C. 509 and 510; 21 U.S.C. 871 and 881(d)); Pub. L. 98–473, Pub. L. 98–573)

[36 FR 7820, Apr. 24, 1971. Redesignated at 38 FR 26609, Sept. 24, 1973, and amended at 48 FR 35088, Aug. 3, 1983; 49 FR 1178, Jan. 10, 1984; 49 FR 50643, Dec. 31, 1984; 56 FR 8686, Mar. 1, 1991]

§1316.80 Time for filing petitions.

(a) In order to be considered as seasonably filed, a petition for remission or mitigation of forfeiture should be filed within 30 days of the receipt of the notice of seizure. If a petition for remission or mitigation of forfeiture has not been received within 30 days of the notice of seizure, the property will either be placed in official service or sold as soon as it is forfeited. Once property is placed in official use, or is sold, a petition for remission or mitigation of forfeiture can no longer be accepted.

(b) A petition for restoration of proceeds of sale, or for the value of property placed in official use, must be filed within 90 days of the sale of the property, or within 90 days of the date the property is placed in official use.

(Authority: Secs. 613, 618, 46 Stat. 756, 757, as amended (19 U.S.C. 1613, 1618); Pub. L. 98–473, Pub. L. 98–573)

[36 FR 7820, Apr. 24, 1971. Redesignated at 38 FR 26609, Sept. 24, 1973, and amended at 49 FR 50643, Dec. 31, 1984]

§1316.81 Handling of petitions.

Upon receipt of a petition, the custodian or DEA Asset Forfeiture System shall request an appropriate investigation. The petition and the report of investigation shall be forwarded to the Director of the FBI or to the Administrator of the DEA, depending upon which agency seized the property. If the petition involves a case which has been referred to the U.S. Attorney for the institution of court proceedings, the custodian or DEA Asset Forfeiture System shall transmit the petition to the U.S. Attorney for the judicial district in which the proceeding for forfeiture is brought. He shall notify the petitioner of this action.

(Authority: 28 U.S.C. 509 and 510; 21 U.S.C. 871 and 881(d); Pub. L. 98–473, Pub. L. 98–573)

[48 FR 35088, Aug. 3, 1983, as amended at 49 FR 1178, Jan. 10, 1984; 49 FR 50643, Dec. 31, 1984; 56 FR 8686, Mar. 1, 1991; 62 FR 13970, Mar. 24, 1997]

Subpart F—Expedited Forfeiture Proceedings for Certain Property

AUTHORITY: 21 U.S.C. 822, 871, 872, 880, 881, 881–1, 883, 958, 965; 19 U.S.C. 1606, 1607, 1608, 1610, 1613, 1618; 28 U.S.C. 509, 510; Pub. L. No. 100–690, sec. 6079, 6080.

SOURCE: 54 FR 37610, Sept. 11, 1989, unless otherwise noted.

§1316.90 Purpose and scope.

(a) The following definitions, regulations, and criteria are designed to establish and implement procedures required by sections 6079 and 6080 of the Anti-Drug Abuse Act of 1988, Public Law No. 100–690 (102 Stat. 4181). They are intended to supplement existing law and procedures relative to the forfeiture of property under the identified statutory authority. The provisions of these regulations do not affect the existing legal and equitable rights and remedies of those with an interest in property seized for forfeiture, nor do these provisions relieve interested parties from their existing obligations and responsibilities in pursuing their interests through such courses of action. These regulations are intended to reflect the intent of Congress to minimize the adverse impact on those entitled to legal or equitable relief occasioned by the prolonged detention of property subject to forfeiture due to violations of law involving personal use quantities of controlled substances, and conveyances seized for drug-related offenses. The definition of personal use quantities of a controlled substance as contained herein is intended to distinguish between those quantities small in amount which are generally considered to be possessed for personal consumption and not for further distribution, and those larger quantities generally considered to be subject to further distribution.

(b) In this regard, for violations involving the possession of personal use quantities of a controlled substance, section 6079(b)(2) requires either that administrative forfeiture be completed within 21 days of the seizure of the property, or alternatively, that procedures are established that provide a means by which an individual entitled to relief may initiate an expedited administrative review of the legal and factual basis of the seizure for forfeiture. Should an individual request relief pursuant to these regulations and be entitled to the return of the seized property, such property shall be returned immediately following that determination, and the administrative forfeiture process shall cease. Should the individual not be entitled to the return of the seized property, however, the administrative forfeiture of that property shall proceed. The owner may, in any event, obtain release of property pending the administrative forfeiture by submitting to the agency making the determination, property sufficient to preserve the government's vested interest for purposes of the administrative forfeiture.

(c) Section 6080 requires a similar expedited review by the Attorney General or his representative in those instances where a conveyance is being forfeited in a civil judicial proceeding following its seizure for a drug-related offense.

§ 1316.91   Definitions.

As used in this subpart, the following terms shall have the meanings specified:

(a) The term *Appraised Value* means the estimated domestic price at the time of seizure at which such or similar property is freely offered for sale.

(b) The term *Commercial Fishing Industry Vessel* means a vessel that:

(1) Commercially engages in the catching, taking, or harvesting of fish or an activity that can reasonably be expected to result in the catching, taking, or harvesting of fish;

(2) Commercially prepares fish or fish products other than by gutting, decapitating, gilling, skinning, shucking, icing, freezing, or brine chilling; or

(3) Commercially supplies, stores, refrigerates, or transports fish, fish products, or materials directly related to fishing or the preparation of fish to or from a fishing, fish processing, or fish tender vessel or fish processing facility.

(c) The term *Controlled Substance* has the meaning given in section 802 of title 21, United States Code (U.S.C.).

(d) The term *Drug-Related Offense* means any proscribed offense which involves the possession, distribution, manufacture, cultivation, sale, transfer, or the attempt or conspiracy to possess, distribute, manufacture, cultivate, sell or transfer any substance the possession of which is prohibited by Title 21, U.S.C.

(e) The term *Immediately* means within 20 days of the filing of a petition for expedited release by an owner.

(f) The term *Interested Party* means one who was in legal possession of the property at the time of seizure and is entitled to legal possession at the time of the granting of the petition for expedited release. This includes a lienholder (to the extent of his interest in the property) whose claim is in writing (except for a maritime lien which need not be in writing), unless the collateral is in the possession of the secured party. The agreement securing such lien must create or provide for a security interest in the collateral, describe the collateral, and be signed by the debtor.

(g) The term *Legal and Factual Basis of the Seizure* means a statement of the applicable law under which the property is seized, and a statement of the circumstances of the seizure sufficiently precise to enable an owner or other interested party to identify the date, place, and use or acquisition which makes the property subject to forfeiture.

(h) The term *Normal and Customary Manner* means that inquiry suggested by particular facts and circumstances which would customarily be undertaken by a reasonably prudent individual in a like or similar situation. Actual knowledge of such facts and circumstances is unnecessary, and implied, imputed, or constructive knowledge is sufficient. An established norm, standard, or custom is persuasive but not conclusive or controlling in determining whether an owner acted in a normal and customary manner to ascertain how property would be used by another legally in possession of the property. The failure to act in a normal and customary manner as defined herein will result in the denial of a petition for expedited release of the property and is intended to have the desirable effect of inducing owners of the property to exercise greater care in transferring possession of their property.

(i) The term *Owner* means one having a legal and possessory interest in the property seized for forfeiture. Even though one may hold primary and direct title to the property seized, such person may not have sufficient actual beneficial interest in the property to support a petition as owner if the facts indicate that another person had dominion and control over the property.

(j) The term *Personal Use Quantities* means possession of controlled substances in circumstances where there is no other evidence of an intent to distribute, of to facilitate the manufacturing, compounding, processing, delivering, importing or exporting of any controlled substance. Evidence of personal use quantities shall not include weepings or other evidence of possession of quantities of a controlled substance for other than personal use.

(1) Such other evidence shall include:

(i) Evidence, such as drug scales, drug distribution paraphernalia, drug records, drug packaging material, method of drug packaging, drug "cutting" agents and other equipment, that indicates an intent to process, package or distribute a controlled substance;

(ii) Information from reliable sources indicating possession of a controlled substance with intent to distribute;

(iii) The arrest and/or conviction record of the person or persons in actual or constructive possession of the controlled substance for offenses under Federal, State or local law that indicates an intent to distribute a controlled substance;

(iv) The controlled substance is related to large amounts of cash or any amount of prerecorded government funds;

(v) The controlled substance is possessed under circumstances that indicate such a controlled substance is a sample intended for distribution in anticipation of a transaction involving large quantities, or is part of a larger delivery; or

(vi) Statements by the possessor, or otherwise attributable to the possessor, including statements of conspirators, that indicate possession with intent to distribute.

(2) Possession of a controlled substance shall be presumed to be for personal use when there are no indicia of illicit drug trafficking or distribution such as, but not limited to, the factors listed above and the amounts do not exceed the following quantities:

(i) One gram of a mixture of substance containing a detectable amount of heroin;

(ii) One gram of a mixture or substance containing a detectable amount of—

(A) Coca leaves, except coba leaves and extracts of coca leaves frol which cocaine, ecgonine, and derivations of ecgonine or their salts have been removed;

(B) Cocaine, its salts, optical and geometric isomers, and salts of isomers;

(C) Ecgonine, its derivatives, their salts, isomers, and salts of isomers; or

(D) Any compound, mixture or preparation which contains any quantity of any of the substances referred to in paragraphs (j)(2)(ii)(A) through (j)(2)(ii)(C) of this section;

(iii) 1/10th gram of a mixture or substance described in paragraph (j)(2)(ii) of this section which contains cocaine base;

(iv) 1/10th gram of a mixture or substance containing a detectable amount of phencyclidine (PCP);

(v) 500 micrograms of a mixture or substance containing a detectable amount of lysergic acid diethylamide (LSD);

(vi) One ounce of a mixture of substance containing a detectable amount of marihuana;

(vii) One gram of methamphetamine, its salts, isomers, and salts of its isomers, or one gram of a mixture or substance containing a detectable amount of methamphetamine, its salts, isomers, or salts of its isomers.

(3) The possession of a narcotic, a depressant, a stimulant, a hallucinogen or cannabis-controlled substance will be considered in excess of personal use quantities if the dosage unit amount possessed provides the same or greater equivalent efficacy as described in paragraph (j)(2) of this section.

(k) The term *Property* means property subject to forfeiture under title 21, U.S.C., sections 881(a) (4), (6), and (7); title 19, U.S.C., section 1595a, and; title 49, U.S.C. App., section 782.

(l) The term *Seizing Agency* means the Federal agency which has seized the property or adopted the seizure of another agency, and has the responsibility for administratively forfeiting the property;

(m) The term *Statutory Rights or Defenses to the Forfeiture* means all legal and equitable rights and remedies available to a claimant of property seized for forfeiture.

(n) The term *Sworn to* as used in §§ 1316.92(e) and 1316.95(c) refers to the oath as provided by Title 28, U.S.C., section 1746.

§ 1316.92 Petition for expedited release in an administrative forfeiture action.

(a) Where property is seized for administrative forfeiture involving con-
trolled substances in personal use quantities the owner may petition the seizing agency for expedited release of the property.

(b) Where property described in paragraph (a) of this section is a commercial fishing industry vessel proceeding to or from a fishing area or intermediate port of call or actually engaged in fishing operations, which would be subject to seizure for administrative forfeiture for a violation of law involving controlled substances in personal use quantities, a summons to appear shall be issued in lieu of a physical seizure. The vessel shall report to the port designated in the summons. The seizing agency shall be authorized to effect administrative forfeiture as if the vessel had been physically seized. Upon answering the summons to appear on or prior to the last reporting date specified in the summons, the owner of the vessel may file a petition for expedited release pursuant to paragraph (a) of this section and the provisions of paragraph (a) of this section and other provishons in this subpart pertaining to a petition for expedited release shall apply as if the vessel had been physically seized.

(c) The owner filing the petition for expedited release shall establish the following:

(1) The owner has a valid, good faith interest in the seized property as owner or otherwise;

(2) The owner reasonably attempted to ascertain the use of the property in a normal and customary manner; and

(3) The owner did not know or consent to the illegal use of the property, or in the event that the owner knew or should have known of the illegal use, the owner did what reasonably could be expected to prevent the violation.

(d) In addition to those factors listed in paragraph (c) of this section, if an owner can demonstrate that the owner has other statutory rights or defenses that would cause the owner to prevail on the issue of forfeiture, such factor shall also be considered in ruling on the petition for expedited release.

(e) A petition for expedited release must be filed in a timely manner to be considered by the seizing agency. In order to be filed in a timely manner the petition must be received by the appropriate seizing agency within 20 days from the date of the first publication of the notice of seizure. The petition must be executed and sworn to by the owner and both the envelope and the request must be clearly marked "PETITION FOR EXPEDITED RELEASE." Such petition shall be filed in triplicate with the Special Agent in Charge of the Drug Enforcement Administration (DEA) or Federal Bureau of Investigation (FBI) field office in the judicial district in which the property was seized, depending upon which agency seized the property. The petition shall be addressed to the Director of the FBI or to the Administrator of the DEA, depending upon which agency seized the property.

(f) The petition shall include the following:

(1) A complete description of the property, including identification numbers, if any, and the date and place of seizure;

(2) The petitioner's interest in the property, which shall be supported by title documentation, bills of sale, contracts, mortgages, or other satisfactory documentary evidence; and

(3) A statement of the facts and circumstances, to be established by satisfactory proof, relied upon by the petitioner to justify expedited release of the seized property.

§1316.93 Ruling on petition for expedited release in an administrative forfeiture action.

(a) Upon receipt of a petition for expedited release filed pursuant to §1316.92(a), the seizing agency shall determine first whether a final administrative determination of the case, without regard to the provisions of this subpart, can be made within 21 days of the seizure. If such a final administrative determination is made within 21 days, no further action need be taken under this subpart.

(b) If no such final administrative determination is made within 21 days of the seizure, the following procedure shall apply. The seizing agency shall, within 20 days after the receipt of the petition for expedited release, determine whether the petition filed by the owner has established the factors listed in §1316.92(c) and:

(1) If the seizing agency determines that those factors have been established, it shall terminate the administrative proceedings and return the property to the owner (or in the case of a commercial fishing industry vessel for which a summons has been issued shall dismiss the summons), except where it is evidence of a violation of law; or

(2) If the seizing agency determines that those factors have not been established, the agency shall proceed with the administrative forfeiture.

§1316.94 Posting of substitute res in an administrative forfeiture action.

(a) Where property is seized for administrative forfeiture involving controlled substances in personal use quantities, the owner may obtain release of the property by posting a substitute res with the seizing agency. The property will be released to the owner upon the payment of an amount equal to the appraised value of the property if it is not evidence of a violation of law or has design or other characteristics that particularly suit it for use in illegal activities. This payment must be in the form of a traveler's check, a money order, a cashier's check or an irrevocable letter of credit made payable to the seizing agency. A bond in the form of a cashier's check will be considered as paid once the check has been accepted for payment by the financial institution which issued the check.

(b) If a substitute res is posted and the property is administratively forfeited, the seizing agency will forfeit the substitute res in lieu of the property.

§1316.95 Petition for expedited release of a conveyance in a judicial forfeiture action.

(a) Where a conveyance has been seized and is being forfeited in a judicial proceeding for a drug-related offense, the owner may petition the United States Attorney for an expedited release of the conveyance.

(b) The owner filing the petition for expedited release shall establish the following:

(1) The owner has a valid, good faith interest in the seized conveyance as owner or otherwise;

(2) The owner has statutory rights or defenses that would show to a substantial probability that the owner would prevail on the issue of forfeiture;

(3) The owner reasonably attempted to ascertain the use of the conveyance in a normal and customary manner; and

(4) The owner did not know or consent to the illegal use of the conveyance; or in the event that the owner knew or should have known of the illegal use, the owner did what reasonably could be expected to prevent the violation.

(c) A petition for expedited release must be filed in a timely manner in order to be considered by the United States Attorney. To be considered as filed in a timely manner, the petition must be received by the appropriate United States Attorney within 20 days from the date of the first publication of the notice of the action and arrest of the property, or within 30 days after filing of the claim, whichever occurs later. The petition must be executed and sworn to by the owner, and both the envelope and the request must be clearly marked "PETITION FOR EXPEDITED RELEASE." Such petition shall be filed in triplicate and addressed to and filed with the United States Attorney prosecuting the conveyance for forfeiture with a copy to the seizing agency.

(d) The petition shall include the following:

(1) A complete description of the conveyance, including the identification number, and the date and place of seizure;

(2) The petitioner's interest in the conveyance, which shall be supported by bills of sale, contracts, mortgages, or other satisfactory documentary evidence; and,

(3) The facts and circumstances, to be established by satisfactory proof, relied upon by the petitioner to justify expedited release of the seized conveyance.

§1316.96 Ruling on a petition for expedited release of a conveyance in a judicial forfeiture action.

(a) Upon receipt of a petition for expedited release filed pursuant to §1316.95, the United States Attorney shall rule on the petition within 20

days of receipt. A petition shall be deemed filed on the date it is received by the United States Attorney.

(b) If the United States Attorney does not rule on the petition for expedited release within 20 days after the date on which it is filed, the conveyance shall be returned to the owner or interested party pending further forfeiture proceedings, except where it is evidence of a violation of law. Release of conveyance under provisions of this paragraph shall not affect the forfeiture action with respect to that conveyance.

(c) Upon a favorable ruling on the petition for expedited release, the United States Attorney shall, where necessary, move to terminate the judicial proceedings against the conveyance and immediately direct the return of the conveyance except where it is evidence of a violation of law.

(d) If, within 20 days, the United States Attorney denies the petition for expedited release, the government shall retain possession of the conveyance until the owner provides a substitute res bond pursuant to §1316.98 or the forfeiture is finalized.

§1316.97 Initiating judicial forfeiture proceeding against a conveyance within 60 days of the filing of a claim and cost bond.

(a) The United States Attorney shall file a complaint for forfeiture of the conveyance within 60 days of the filing of the claim and cost bond.

(b) Upon the failure of the United States Attorney to file a complaint for forfeiture of a conveyance within 60 days unless the court extends the 60-day period following a showing of good cause, or unless the owner and the United States Attorney agree to such an extension, the court shall order the return of the conveyance and the return of any bond.

§1316.98 Substitute res bond in a judicial forfeiture action against a conveyance.

(a) Where a conveyance is being forfeited in a judicial proceeding for a drug-related offense, the owner may obtain release of the property by filing a substitute res bond with the seizing agency. The conveyance will be released to the owner upon the payment of a bond in the amount of the appraised value of the conveyance if it is not evidence of a violation of law or has design or other characteristics that particularly suit it for use in illegal activities. This bond must be in the form of a traveler's check, a money order, a cashier's check or an irrevocable letter of credit made payable to the Department of Justice or to the United States Customs Service depending on which agency seized the conveyance. A bond in the form of a cashier's check will be considered as paid once the check has been accepted for payment by the financial institution which issued the check.

(b) If a substitute res bond is filed and the conveyance is judicially forfeited, the court will forfeit the bond in lieu of the property.

§ 1316.99 Notice provisions.

(a) *Special notice provision.* At the time of seizure of property defined in §1316.91 for violations involving the possession of personal use quantities of a controlled substance and conveyances seized pursuant to §1316.95, written notice must be provided to the possessor of the property regarding applicable statutes and Federal regulations including the procedures established for the filing of a petition for expedited release and for the posting of a substitute res bond as set forth in sections 6079 and 6080 of the Anti-Drug Abuse Act of 1988 and implementing regulations.

(b) *Standard notice provision.* The standard notice to the owner as required by title 19, U.S.C., section 1607 and applicable regulations, shall be made at the earliest practicable opportunity after determining ownership of the seized property or conveyance and shall include the legal and factual basis of the seizure.

CHAPTER III—OFFICE OF NATIONAL DRUG CONTROL POLICY

PART 1400 [RESERVED]

PART 1401—PUBLIC AVAILABILITY OF INFORMATION

AUTHORITY: 5 U.S.C. 552, as amended.

SOURCE: 64 FR 69901, Dec. 15, 1999, unless otherwise noted.

§ 1401.1 Purpose.

The purpose of this part is to prescribe rules, guidelines and procedures to implement the Freedom of Information Act (FOIA), as amended, 5 U.S.C. 552.

§ 1401.2 The Office of National Drug Control Policy—organization and functions.

(a) The Office of National Drug Control Policy (ONDCP) was created by the Anti-Drug Abuse Act of 1988, 21 U.S.C. 1501 *et seq.*, and reestablished under 21 U.S.C. 1701 *et seq.* The mission of ONDCP is to coordinate the anti-drug efforts of the various agencies and departments of the Federal government, to consult with States and localities and assist their anti-drug efforts, to conduct a national media campaign, and to annually promulgate the National Drug Control Strategy.

(b) ONDCP is headed by the Director of National Drug Control Policy. The Director is assisted by a Deputy Director of National Drug Control Policy, a Deputy Director for Supply Reduction, a Deputy Director for Demand Reduction, and a Deputy Director for State and Local Affairs.

(c) Offices within ONDCP include Chief of Staff, and the Offices of Legal Counsel, Strategic Planning, Legislative Affairs, Programs Budget and Evaluation, Supply Reduction, Demand Reduction, Public Affairs, State and Local Affairs, and the Financial Management Office.

(d) The Office of Public Affairs is responsible for providing information to the press and to the general public. If members of the public have general questions about ONDCP that can be answered by telephone, they may call the Office of Public Affairs at (202) 395–6618. This number should not be used to make FOIA requests. All oral requests for information under FOIA will be rejected.

§ 1401.3 Definitions.

For the purpose of this part:

(a) All the terms defined in the Freedom of Information Act apply.

(b) *Commercial-use request* means a request from or on behalf of one who seeks information for a cause or purpose that furthers the commercial, trade or profit interests of the requester or the person or institution on whose behalf the request is made. In determining whether a requester properly belongs in this category, ONDCP will consider the intended use of the information.

(c) *Direct costs* means the expense actually expended to search, review, or duplicate in response to a FOIA request. For example, direct costs include 116% of the salary of the employee performing work and the actual costs incurred while operating equipment.

(d) *Duplicate* means the process of making a copy of a document. Such copies may take the form of paper, microform, audio-visual materials, or machine-readable documentation. ONDCP will provide a copy of the material in a form that is usable by the requester.

(e) *Educational institution* means preschool, a public or private elementary or secondary school, an institution of undergraduate higher education, an institution of graduate higher education, an institution of professional education, or an institution of vocational education that operates a program or programs of scholarly research.

215

(f) *Noncommercial scientific institution* means an institution that is not operated on a commercial basis as that term is defined in this section, and that is operated solely for the purpose of conducting scientific research not intended to promote any particular product or industry.

(g) *Records* and any other terms used in this part in reference to information includes any information that would be an agency record subject to the requirements of this part when maintained in any format, including electronic format.

(h) *Representative of the news media* means any person actively gathering news for an entity that is organized and operated to publish or broadcast news to the public. News is information about current events or information that would be of interest to the public. Examples of the news media include television or radio stations that broadcast to the public at large and publishers of news periodicals that make their products available to the general public for purchase or subscription. Freelance journalists may be regarded as working for the news media where they demonstrate a reasonable basis for expecting publication through that organization, even though not actually employed by it.

(i) *Request* means a letter or other written communication seeking records or information under FOIA.

(j) *Review* means the process of examining documents that are located during a search to determine if any portion should lawfully be withheld. It is the processing of determining disclosability.

(k) *Search* means to review, manually or by automated means, agency records for the purpose of locating those records responsive to a request.

§ 1401.4 Access to information.

The Office of National Drug Control Policy makes available information pertaining to matters issued, adopted, or promulgated by ONDCP, that are within the scope of 5 U.S.C. 552(a)(2). A public reading area and the ONDCP FOIA Handbook are located at *http://www.whitehousedrugpolicy.gov/about/about.html.*

§ 1401.5 How to request records.

(a) Each request must reasonably describe the record(s) sought including the type of document, specific event or action, originator of the record, date or time period, subject matter, location, and all other pertinent data.

(b) Requests must be received by ONDCP through the mail or by electronic facsimile transmission. Mailed requests must be addressed to Executive Office of the President, Office of National Drug Control Policy, Office of Legal Counsel, Washington, DC 20503. The applicable fax number is (202) 395-5543.

(c) The words "FOIA REQUEST" or "REQUEST FOR RECORDS" must be clearly marked on the cover-letter, letter and envelope. The time limitations imposed by § 1401.7 will not begin until the Office of the General Counsel identifies a letter or fax as a FOIA request.

§ 1401.6 Expedited process.

(a) Requests and appeals will be given expedited treatment whenever ONDCP determines either:

(1) The lack of expedited treatment could reasonably be expected to pose an imminent threat to the life or physical safety of an individual; or

(2) An urgency to inform the public about an actual or alleged federal government activity occurs and the request is made by a person primarily engaged in disseminating information.

(b) A request for expedited processing may be made at the time of the initial request for records or at a later time.

(c) A requester who seeks expedited processing must submit a statement, certified to be true and correct to the best of that person's knowledge and belief, explaining in detail the basis for requesting expedited processing. A requester within the category in paragraph (a)(2) of this section also must establish a particular urgency to inform the public about the government activity involved in the request, beyond the public's right to know about government activity generally. The formality of certification may be waived as a matter of administrative discretion.

(d) Within ten days of receipt of a request for expedited processing, ONDCP will decide whether to grant it and will notify the requester of the decision. If a request for expedited treatment is granted, the request will be given priority and will be processed as soon as practicable. If a request for expedited processing is denied, any appeal of that decision will be acted on expeditiously.

§1401.7 Prompt response.

The General Counsel, or designee, will determine within 20 days (excepting Saturdays, Sundays and legal public holidays) after the receipt of a FOIA request whether it is appropriate to grant the request and will provide written notification to the person making the request. If the request is denied, the written notification will include the names of the individuals who participated in the determination, the reasons for the denial, and that an appeal may be lodged within the Office of National Drug Control Policy.

§1401.8 Extension of time.

(a) In unusual circumstances, the Office of General Counsel may extend the time limit prescribed in §1401.7 or §1401.9 by written notice to the FOIA requester. The notice will state the reasons for the extension and the date a determination is expected. The extension period may be divided among the initial request and an appeal but will not exceed a total of 10 working days (excepting Saturdays, Sundays, or legal public holidays).

(b) The phrase "unusual circumstances" means:

(1) The requested records are located in establishments that are separated from the office processing the request;

(2) A voluminous amount of separate and distinct records are demanded in a single request; or

(3) Another agency or two or more components in the same agency have substantial interest in the determination of the request.

(c) Where unusual circumstance exist, ONDCP may provide an opportunity for amendment of the initial request so that the request may be timely processed. Refusal by the person to reasonably modify the request or arrange an alternative time frame shall be considered as a factor for purposes of 5 U.S.C. 552 (a)(6)(C).

(d) ONDCP may aggregate requests by a requester or a group of requestors where multiple requests reasonably appear to be a single request.

§1401.9 Appeals.

An appeal to the ONDCP must explain in writing the legal and factual basis for the appeal. It must be received by mail at the address specified in §1401.5 within 30 days of receipt of a denial. The Director or designee will decide the appeal within 20 days (excepting Saturdays, Sundays, and legal public holidays). If the Director or designee deny an appeal in whole or in part, the written determination will contain the reason for the denial, the names of the individuals who participated in the determination, and the provisions for judicial review.

§1401.10 Fees to be charged—general.

ONDCP will recoup the full allowable costs it incurs in response to a FOIA request.

(a) *Manual search for records.* ONDCP will charge 116% of the salary of the individual(s) making a search.

(b) *Computerized search for records.* ONDCP will charge 116% of the salary of the programmer/operator and the apportionable time of the central processing unit directly attributed to the search.

(c) *Review of records.* ONDCP will charge 116% of the salary of the individual(s) conducting a review. Records or portions of records withheld under an exemption subsequently determined not to apply may be reviewed to determine the applicability of exemptions not considered. The cost for a subsequent review is assessable.

(d) *Duplication of records.* Request for copies prepared by computer will cost 116% of the apportionable operator time and the cost of the tape or disk. Other methods of duplication will cost 116% of the salary of the individual copying the data plus 15 cents per copy of 8½×11 inch original.

(e) *Other charges.* ONDCP will recover the costs of providing other services such as certifying records or sending records by special methods.

§ 1401.11   Fees to be charged—miscellaneous provisions.

(a) Remittance shall be mailed to the Office of Legal Counsel, ONDCP, Washington DC 20503, and made payable to the order of the Treasury of the United States on a postal money order or personal check or bank draft drawn on a bank in the United States.

(b) ONDCP may require advance payment where the estimated fee exceeds $250, or a requester previously failed to pay within 30 days of the billing date.

(c) ONDCP may assess interest charges beginning the 31st day of billing. Interest will be at the rate prescribed in section 3717 of title 31 of the United States Code and will accrue from the date of the billing.

(d) ONDCP may assess search charges where records are not located or where records are exempt from disclosure.

(e) ONDCP may aggregate individual requests and charge accordingly for requests seeking portions of a document or documents.

§ 1401.12   Fees to be charged—categories of requesters.

(a) There are four categories of FOIA requesters: commercial use requesters; educational and non-commercial scientific institutions; representatives of the news media; and all other requesters.

(b) The specific levels of fees for each of these categories are:

(1) *Commercial use requesters.* ONDCP will recover the full direct cost of providing search, review and duplication services. Commercial use requesters will not receive free search-time or free reproduction of documents.

(2) *Educational and non-commercial scientific institution requesters.* ONDCP will charge the cost of reproduction, excluding charges for the first 100 pages. Requesters must demonstrate the request is authorized by and under the auspices of a qualifying institution and that the records are sought for scholarly or scientific research not a commercial use.

(3) *Requesters who are representatives of the news media.* ONDCP will charge the cost of reproduction, excluding charges for the first 100 pages. Requesters must meet the criteria in § 1401.3(h), and the request must not be made for a commercial use. A request that supports the news dissemination function of the requester shall not be considered a commercial use.

(4) *All other requesters.* ONDCP will recover the full direct cost of the search and the reproduction of records, excluding the first 100 pages of reproduction and the first two hours of search time. Requests for records concerning the requester will be treated under the fee provisions of the Privacy Act of 1974, 5 U.S.C. 552a, which permits fees only for reproduction.

§ 1401.13   Waiver or reduction of fees.

Fees chargeable in connection with a request may be waived or reduced where ONDCP determines that disclosure is in the public interest because it is likely to contribute significantly to public understanding of the operations or activities of the Government and is not primarily in the commercial interest of the requester.

PART 1402—MANDATORY DECLASSIFICATION REVIEW

Sec.
1402.1   Purpose.
1402.2   Responsibility.
1402.3   Information in the custody of ONDCP.
1402.4   Information classified by another agency.
1402.5   Appeal procedure.
1402.6   Fees.
1402.7   Suggestions and complaints.

AUTHORITY: Section 3.4, E.O. 12356 (3 CFR, 1982 Comp., p. 166), and Information Security Oversight Office Directive No. 1 (32 CFR 2001.32).

SOURCE: 57 FR 55089, Nov. 24, 1992, unless otherwise noted.

§ 1402.1   Purpose.

Other government agencies, U.S. citizens or permanent resident aliens may request that classified information in files of the Office of National Drug Control Policy (ONDCP) be reviewed for possible declassification and release. This part prescribes the procedures for such review and subsequent release or denial.

§ 1402.2 Responsibility.

All requests for the mandatory declassification review of classified information in ONDCP files should be addressed to the Security Officer, Office of National Drug Control Policy, Executive Office of the President, Washington, DC 20500, who will acknowledge receipt of the request. When a request does not reasonably describe the information sought, the requester shall be notified that unless additional information is provided, or the scope of the request is narrowed, no further action will be taken.

§ 1402.3 Information in the custody of ONDCP.

Information contained in ONDCP files and under the exclusive declassification jurisdiction of ONDCP will be reviewed by the Director of the Office of Planning, Budget, and Administration of ONDCP and/or the office of primary interest to determine whether, under the declassification provisions of section 3.1 of Executive Order 12356 (3 CFR, 1982 Comp., p. 166), the requested information may be declassified. If the information may not be released, in whole or in part, the requester shall be given a brief statement as to the reasons for denial, a notice of the right to appeal the determination to the Director of ONDCP, and a notice that such an appeal must be filed within 60 days in order to be considered.

§ 1402.4 Information classified by another agency.

When a request is received for information that was classified by another agency, the Director of the Office of Planning, Budget, and Administration of ONDCP will forward the request and a copy of the document(s) along with any other related materials, to the appropriate agency for review and determination as to release. Recommendations as to release or denial may be made if appropriate. The requester will be notified of the referral, unless the receiving agency objects on the grounds that its association with the information requires protection.

§ 1402.5 Appeal procedure.

Appeals reviewed as a result of a denial will be routed to the Director of ONDCP, who will take action as necessary to determine whether any part of the information may be declassified. If so, the Director shall notify the requester of this determination and shall make any information available that is declassified and is otherwise releasable. If continued classification is required, the requester shall be notified by the Director of ONDCP of the reasons therefore.

§ 1402.6 Fees.

There will normally be no fees charged for the mandatory review of classified material for declassification under this part.

§ 1402.7 Suggestions and complaints.

Suggestions and complaints regarding the information security program of ONDCP should be submitted, in writing, to the Security Officer, Office of National Drug Control Policy, Washington, DC 20500.

PART 1403—UNIFORM ADMINISTRATIVE REQUIREMENTS FOR GRANTS AND COOPERATIVE AGREEMENTS TO STATE AND LOCAL GOVERNMENTS

Subpart A—General

AUTHORITY: 5 U.S.C. 301.

SOURCE: 57 FR 55092, Nov. 24, 1992, unless otherwise noted.

Subpart A—General

§ 1403.1 Purpose and scope of this part.

This part establishes uniform administrative rules for Federal grants and cooperative agreements and subawards to State, local and Indian tribal governments.

§ 1403.2 Scope of subpart.

This subpart contains general rules pertaining to this part and procedures for control of exceptions from this part.

§ 1403.3 Definitions.

As used in this part:

Accrued expenditures mean the charges incurred by the grantee during a given period requiring the provision of funds for:

(1) Goods and other tangible property received;

(2) Services performed by employees, contractors, subgrantees, subcontractors, and other payees; and

(3) Other amounts becoming owed under programs for which no current services or performance is required, such as annuities, insurance claims, and other benefit payments.

Accrued income means the sum of:

(1) Earnings during a given period from services performed by the grantee and goods and other tangible property delivered to purchasers, and

(2) Amounts becoming owed to the grantee for which no current services or performance is required by the grantee.

Acquisition cost of an item of purchased equipment means the net invoice unit price of the property including the cost of modifications, attachments, accessories, or auxiliary apparatus necessary to make the property usable for the purpose for which it was acquired. Other charges such as the cost of installation, transportation, taxes, duty or protective in-transit insurance, shall be included or excluded from the unit acquisition cost in accordance with the grantee's regular accounting practices.

Administrative requirements mean those matters common to grants in general, such as financial management, kinds and frequency of reports, and retention of records. These are distinguished from "programmatic" requirements, which concern matters that can be treated only on a program-by-program or grant-by-grant basis, such as kinds of activities that can be supported by grants under a particular program.

Awarding agency means:

(1) With respect to a grant, the Federal agency, and

(2) With respect to a subgrant, the party that awarded the subgrant.

Cash contributions means the grantee's cash outlay, including the outlay of money contributed to the grantee or subgrantee by other public agencies and institutions, and private organizations and individuals. When authorized by Federal legislation, Federal funds received from other assistance agreements may be considered as grantee or subgrantee cash contributions.

Contract means (except as used in the definitions for "grant" and "subgrant" in this section and except where qualified by "Federal") a procurement contract under a grant or subgrant, and means a procurement subcontract under a contract.

Cost sharing or matching means the value of the third party in-kind contributions and the portion of the costs of a federally assisted project or program not borne by the Federal Government.

Cost-type contract means a contract or subcontract under a grant in which the contractor or subcontractor is paid on the basis of the costs it incurs, with or without a fee.

Equipment means tangible, non-expendable, personal property having a useful life of more than one year and an acquisition cost of $5,000 or more per unit. A grantee may use its own definition of equipment provided that such definition would at least include all equipment defined above.

Expenditure report means:

(1) For nonconstruction grants, the SF–269 "Financial Status Report" (or other equivalent report);

(2) For construction grants, the SF–271 "Outlay Report and Request for Reimbursement" (or other equivalent report).

Federally recognized Indian tribal government means the governing body or a governmental agency of any Indian tribe, band, nation, or other organized group or community (including any Native village as defined in section 3 of the Alaska Native Claims Settlement Act, 85 Stat. 688) certified by the Secretary of the Interior as eligible for the special programs and services provided by him through the Bureau of Indian Affairs.

Government means a State or local government or a federally recognized Indian tribal government.

Grant means an award of financial assistance, including cooperative agreements, in the form of money, or property in lieu of money, by the Federal Government to an eligible grantee. The term does not include technical assistance which provides services instead of money, or other assistance in the form of revenue sharing, loans, loan guarantees, interest subsidies, insurance, or direct appropriations. Also, the term does not include assistance, such as a fellowship or other lump sum award, which the grantee is not required to account for.

Grantee means the government to which a grant is awarded and which is accountable for the use of the funds provided. The grantee is the entire legal entity even if only a particular component of the entity is designated in the grant award document.

Local government means a county, municipality, city, town, township, local public authority (including any public and Indian housing agency under the United States Housing Act of 1937) school district, special district, intrastate district, council of governments (whether or not incorporated as a nonprofit corporation under state law), any other regional or interstate government entity, or any agency or instrumentality of a local government.

Obligations means the amounts of orders placed, contracts and subgrants awarded, goods and services received, and similar transactions during a given period that will require payment by the grantee during the same or a future period.

OMB means the United States Office of Management and Budget.

Outlays (expenditures) means charges made to the project or program. They may be reported on a cash or accrual basis. For reports prepared on a cash basis, outlays are the sum of actual cash disbursement for direct charges for goods and service, the amount of indirect expense incurred, the value of in-kind contributions applied, and the amount of cash advances and payments made to contractors and subgrantees. For reports prepared on an accrued expenditure basis, outlays are the sum of actual cash disbursements, the amount of indirect expense incurred, the value of in-kind contributions applied, and the new increase (or decrease) in the amounts owed by the grantee for goods and other property received, for services performed by employees, contractors, subgrantees, subcontractors, and other payees, and other amounts becoming owed under programs for which no current services or performance are required, such as annuities, insurance claims, and other benefit payments.

Percentage of completion method refers to a system under which payments are made for construction work according to the percentage of completion of the work, rather than to the grantee's cost incurred.

Prior approval means documentation evidencing consent prior to incurring specific cost.

Real property means land, including land improvements, structures and appurtenances thereto, excluding movable machinery and equipment.

Share, when referring to the awarding agency's portion of real property, equipment or supplies, means the same percentage as the awarding agency's portion of the acquiring party's total costs under the grant to which the acquisition costs under the grant to which the acquisition cost of the property was charged. Only costs are to be counted—not the value of third-party in-kind contributions.

State means any of the several States of the United States, the District of Columbia, the Commonwealth of Puerto Rico, any territory or possession of the United States, or any agency or instrumentality of a State exclusive of local governments. The term does not include any public and Indian housing agency under United States Housing Act of 1937.

Subgrant means an award of financial assistance in the form of money, or property in lieu of money, made under a grant by a grantee to an eligible subgrantee. The term includes financial assistance when provided by contractual legal agreement, but does not include procurement purchases, nor does it include any form of assistance which is excluded from the definition of "grant" in this part.

Subgrantee means the government or other legal entity to which a subgrant is awarded and which is accountable to the grantee for the use of the funds provided.

Supplies means all tangible personal property other than "equipment" as defined in this part.

Suspension means depending on the context, either

(1) Temporary withdrawal of the authority to obligate grant funds pending corrective action by the grantee or subgrantee or a decision to terminate the grant, or

(2) In action taken by a suspending official in accordance with agency regulations implementing E.O. 12549 to immediately exclude a person from participating in grant transactions for a period, pending completion of an investigation and such legal or debarment proceedings as may ensue.

Termination means permanent withdrawal of the authority to obligate previously-awarded grant funds before that authority would otherwise expire. It also means the voluntary relinquishment of that authority by the grantee or subgrantee. "Termination" does not include:

(1) Withdrawal of funds awarded on the basis of the grantee's underestimate of the unobligated balance in a prior period;

(2) Withdrawal of the unobligated balance as of the expiration of a grant;

(3) Refusal to extend a grant or award additional funds, to make a competing or noncompeting continuation, renewal, extension, or supplemental award; or

(4) Voiding of a grant upon determination that the award was obtained fraudulently, or was otherwise illegal or invalid from inception.

Terms of a grant or subgrant mean all requirements of the grant or subgrant, whether in statute, regulations, or the award document.

Third party in-kind contributions mean property or services which benefit a federally assisted project or program and which are contributed by non-Federal third parties without charge to the grantee, or a cost-type contractor under the grant agreement.

Unliquidated obligations for reports prepared on a cash basis mean the amount of obligations incurred by the grantee that has not been paid. For reports prepared on an accrued expenditure basis, they represent the amount of obligations incurred by the grantee for which an outlay has not been recorded.

Unobligated balance means the portion of the funds authorized by the Federal agency that has not been obligated by the grantee and is determined

by deducting the cumulative obligations from the cumulative funds authorized.

§ 1403.4 **Applicability.**

(a) *General.* Subparts A–D of this part
apply to all grants and subgrants to
governments, except where inconsistent with Federal statutes or with
regulations authorized in accordance
with the exception provision of § 1403.6,
or:

(1) Grants and subgrants to State and
local institutions of higher education
or State and local hospitals;

(2) The block grants authorized by
the Omnibus Budget Reconciliation
Act of 1981 (Community Services; Pre-
ventive Health and Health Services; Alcohol, Drug Abuse, and Mental Health
Services; Maternal and Child Health
Services; Social Services; Low-Income
Home Energy Assistance; States' Pro-
gram of Community Development
Block Grants for Small Cities; and Ele-
mentary and Secondary Education
other than programs administered by
the Secretary of Education under title
V, subtitle D, chapter 2, section 583—
the Secretary's discretionary grant
program) and titles I–III of the Job
Training Partnership Act of 1982 and
under the Public Health Services Act
(Section 1921), Alcohol and Drug Abuse
Treatment and Rehabilitation Block
Grant and part C of title V, Mental
Health Service for the Homeless Block
Grant);

(3) Entitlement grants to carry out
the following programs of the Social
Security Act:

(i) Aid to Needy Families with Dependent Children (title IV–A of the
Act, not including the Work Incentive
Program (WIN) authorized by section
402(a)19(G); HHS grants for WIN are
subject to this part);

(ii) Child Support Enforcement and
Establishment of Paternity (title IV–D
of the Act);

(iii) Foster Care and Adoption Assistance (title IV–E of the Act);

(iv) Aid to the Aged, Blind, and Dis-
abled (titles I, X, XIV, and XVI–AABD
of the Act); and

(v) Medical Assistance (Medicaid)
(title XIX of the Act) not including the
State Medicaid Fraud Control program
authorized by section 1903(a)(6)(B);

(4) Entitlement grants under the following programs of The National
School Lunch Act:

(i) School Lunch (section 4 of the
Act),

(ii) Commodity Assistance (section 6
of the Act),

(iii) Special Meal Assistance (section
11 of the Act),

(iv) Summer Food Service for Children (section 13 of the Act), and

(v) Child Care Food Program (section
17 of the Act);

(5) Entitlement grants under the following programs of The Child Nutrition Act of 1966:

(i) Special Milk (section 3 of the Act),
and

(ii) School Breakfast (section 4 of the
Act);

(6) Entitlement grants for State Ad-
ministrative expenses under The Food
Stamp Act of 1977 (section 16 of the
Act);

(7) A grant for an experimental, pilot,
or demonstration project that is also
supported by a grant listed in paragraph (a)(3) of this section;

(8) Grant funds awarded under subsection 412(e) of the Immigration and
Nationality Act (8 U.S.C. 1522(e)) and
subsection 501(a) of the Refugee Education Assistance Act of 1980 (Pub. L.
96–422, 94 Stat. 1809), for cash assistance, medical assistance, and supplemental security income benefits to ref-
ugees and entrants and the administrative costs of providing the assistance
and benefits;

(9) Grants to local education agencies
under 20 U.S.C. 236 through 241–1(a),
and 242 through 244 (portions of the Impact Aid program), except for 20 U.S.C.
238(d)(2)(c) and 240(f) (Entitlement Increase for Handicapped Children); and

(10) Payments under the Veterans
Administration's State Home Per Diem
Program (38 U.S.C. 641(a)).

(b) *Entitlement programs.* Entitlement
programs enumerated above in
§ 1403.4(a) (3) through (8) are subject to
subpart E.

§ 1403.5 **Effect on other issuances.**

All other grants administration provisions of codified program regulations, program manuals, handbooks
and other nonregulatory materials
which are inconsistent with this part

are superseded, except to the extent they are required by statute, or authorized in accordance with the exception provision in § 1403.6.

§ 1403.6 Additions and exceptions.

(a) For classes of grants and grantees subject to this part, Federal agencies may not impose additional administrative requirements except in codified regulations published in the FEDERAL REGISTER.

(b) Exceptions for classes of grants or grantees may be authorized only by OMB.

(c) Exceptions on a case-by-case basis and for subgrantees may be authorized by the affected Federal agencies.

Subpart B—Pre-Award Requirements

§ 1403.10 Forms for applying for grants.

(a) *Scope.* (1) This section prescribes forms and instructions to be used by governmental organizations (except hospitals and institutions of higher education operated by a government) in applying for grants. This section is not applicable, however, to formula grant programs which do not require applicants to apply for funds on a project basis.

(2) This section applies only to applications to Federal agencies for grants, and is not required to be applied by grantees in dealing with applicants for subgrants. However, grantees are encouraged to avoid more detailed or burdensome application requirements for subgrants.

(b) *Authorized forms and instructions for governmental organizations.* (1) In applying for grants, applicants shall only use standard application forms or those prescribed by the granting agency with the approval of OMB under the Paperwork Reduction Act of 1980.

(2) Applicants are not required to submit more than the original and two copies of preapplications or applications.

(3) Applicants must follow all applicable instructions that bear OMB clearance numbers. Federal agencies may specify and describe the programs, functions, or activities that will be used to plan, budget, and evaluate the

work under a grant. Other supplementary instructions may be issued only with the approval of OMB to the extent required under the Paperwork Reduction Act of 1980. For any standard form, except the SF–424 facesheet, Federal agencies may shade out or instruct the applicant to disregard any line item that is not needed.

(4) When a grantee applies for additional funding (such as a continuation or supplemental award) or amends a previously submitted application, only the affected pages need be submitted. Previously submitted pages with information that is still current need not be resubmitted.

§ 1403.11 State plans.

(a) *Scope.* The statutes for some programs require States to submit plans before receiving grants. Under regulations implementing Executive Order 12372, "Intergovernmental Review of Federal Programs," States are allowed to simplify, consolidate and substitute plans. This section contains additional provisions for plans that are subject to regulations implementing the Executive Order.

(b) *Requirements.* A State need meet only Federal administrative or programmatic requirements for a plan that are in statutes or codified regulations.

(c) *Assurances.* In each plan the States will include an assurance that the State shall comply with all applicable Federal statutes and regulations in effect with respect to the periods for which it receives grant funding. For this assurance and other assurances required in the plan, the State may:

(1) Cite by number the statutory or regulatory provisions requiring the assurances and affirm that it gives the assurances required by those provisions,

(2) Repeat the assurance language in the statutes or regulations, or

(3) Develop its own language to the extent permitted by law.

(d) *Amendments.* A State will amend a plan whenever necessary to reflect: (1) New or revised Federal statutes or regulations or (2) a material change in any State law, organization, policy, or State agency operation. The State will obtain approval for the amendment and its effective date but need submit for approval only the amended portions of the plan.

§ 1403.12 Special grant or subgrant conditions for "high-risk" grantees.

(a) A grantee or subgrantee may be considered "high risk" if an awarding agency determines that a grantee or subgrantee:

(1) Has a history of unsatisfactory performance, or

(2) Is not financially stable, or

(3) Has a management system which does not meet the management standards set forth in this part, or

(4) Has not conformed to terms and conditions of previous awards, or

(5) Is otherwise not responsible; and if the awarding agency determines that an award will be made, special conditions and/or restrictions shall correspond to the high risk condition and shall be included in the award.

(b) Special conditions or restrictions may include:

(1) Payment on a reimbursement basis;

(2) Withholding authority to proceed to the next phase until receipt of evidence of acceptable performance within a given funding period;

(3) Requiring additional, more detailed financial reports;

(4) Additional project monitoring;

(5) Requiring the grantee or subgrantee to obtain technical or management assistance; or

(6) Establishing additional prior approvals;

(c) If an awarding agency decides to impose such conditions, the awarding official will notify the grantee or subgrantee as early as possible, in writing, of:

(1) The nature of the special conditions/restrictions;

(2) The reason(s) for imposing them;

(3) The corrective actions which must be taken before they will be removed and the time allowed for completing the corrective actions; and

(4) The method of requesting reconsideration of the conditions/restrictions imposed.

Subpart C—Post-Award Requirements

FINANCIAL ADMINISTRATION

§ 1403.20 Standards for financial management systems.

(a) A State must expend and account for grant funds in accordance with State laws and procedures for expending and accounting for its own funds. Fiscal control and accounting procedures of the State, as well as its subgrantees and cost-type contractors, must be sufficient to—

(1) Permit preparation of reports required by this part and the statutes authorizing the grant, and

(2) Permit the tracing of funds to a level of expenditures adequate to establish that such funds have not been used in violation of the restrictions and prohibitions of applicable statutes.

(b) The financial management systems of other grantees and subgrantees must meet the following standards:

(1) *Financial reporting.* Accurate, current, and complete disclosure of the financial results of financially assisted activities must be made in accordance with the financial reporting requirements of the grant or subgrant.

(2) *Accounting records.* Grantees and subgrantees must maintain records which adequately identify the source and application of funds provided for financially-assisted activities. These records must contain information pertaining to grant or subgrant awards and authorizations, obligations, unobligated balances, assets, liabilities, outlays or expenditures, and income.

(3) *Internal control.* Effective control and accountability must be maintained for all grant and subgrant cash, real and personal property, and other assets. Grantees and subgrantees must adequately safeguard all such property and must assure that it is used solely for authorized purposes.

(4) *Budget control.* Actual expenditures or outlays must be compared with budgeted amounts for each grant or subgrant. Financial information

must be related to performance or productivity data, including the development of unit cost information whenever appropriate or specifically required in the grant or subgrant agreement. If unit cost data are required, estimates based on available documentation will be accepted whenever possible.

(5) *Allowable cost.* Applicable OMB cost principles, agency program regulations, and the terms of grant and subgrant agreements will be followed in determining the reasonableness, allowability, and allocability of costs.

(6) *Source documentation.* Accounting records must be supported by such source documentation as canceled checks, paid bills, payrolls, time and attendance records, contract and subgrant award documents, etc.

(7) *Cash management.* Procedures for minimizing the time elapsing between the transfer of funds from the U.S. Treasury and disbursement by grantees and subgrantees must be followed whenever advance payment procedures are used. Grantees must establish reasonable procedures to ensure the receipt of reports on subgrantees' cash balances and cash disbursements in sufficient time to enable them to prepare complete and accurate cash transactions reports to the awarding agency. When advances are made by letter-of-credit or electronic transfer of funds methods, the grantee must make drawdowns as close as possible to the time of making disbursements. Grantees must monitor cash drawdowns by their subgrantees to assure that they conform substantially to the same standards of timing and amount as apply to advances to the grantees.

(c) An awarding agency may review the adequacy of the financial management system of any applicant for financial assistance as part of a preaward review or at any time subsequent to award.

§ 1403.21 Payment.

(a) *Scope.* This section prescribes the basic standard and the methods under which a Federal agency will make payments to grantees, and grantees will make payments to subgrantees and contractors.

(b) *Basic standard.* Methods and procedures for payment shall minimize the time elapsing between the transfer of funds and disbursement by the grantee or subgrantee, in accordance with Treasury regulations at 31 CFR part 205.

(c) *Advances.* Grantees and subgrantees shall be paid in advance, provided they maintain or demonstrate the willingness and ability to maintain procedures to minimize the time elapsing between the transfer of the funds and their disbursement by the grantee or subgrantee.

(d) *Reimbursement.* Reimbursement shall be the preferred method when the requirements in paragraph (c) of this section are not met. Grantees and subgrantees may also be paid by reimbursement for any construction grant. Except as otherwise specified in regulation, Federal agencies shall not use the percentage of completion method to pay construction grants. The grantee or subgrantee may use that method to pay its construction contractor, and if it does, the awarding agency's payments to the grantee or subgrantee will be based on the grantee's or subgrantee's actual rate of disbursement.

(e) *Working capital advances.* If a grantee cannot meet the criteria for advance payments described in paragraph (c) of this section, and the Federal agency has determined that reimbursement is not feasible the grantee lacks sufficient working capital, the awarding agency may provide cash or a working capital advance basis. Under this procedure the awarding agency shall advance cash to the grantee to cover its estimated disbursement needs for an initial period generally geared to the grantee's disbursing cycle. Thereafter, the awarding agency shall reimburse the grantee for its actual cash disbursements. The working capital advance method of payment shall not be used by grantees or subgrantees if the reason for using such method is the unwillingness or inability of the grantee to provide timely advances to the subgrantee to meet the subgrantee's actual cash disbursements.

(f) *Effect of program income, refunds, and audit recoveries on payment.* (1) Grantees and subgrantees shall disburse repayments to and interest earned on a revolving fund before requesting additional cash payments for the same activity.

(2) Except as provided in paragraph (f)(1) of this section, grantees and subgrantees shall disburse program income, rebates, refunds, contract settlements, audit recoveries and interest earned on such funds before requesting additional cash payments.

(g) *Withholding payments.* (1) Unless otherwise required by Federal statute, awarding agencies shall not withhold payments for proper charges incurred by grantees or subgrantees unless—

(i) The grantee or subgrantee has failed to comply with grant award conditions or

(ii) The grantee or subgrantee is indebted to the United States.

(2) Cash withheld for failure to comply with grant award condition, but without suspension of the grant, shall be released to the grantee upon subsequent compliance. When a grant is suspended, payment adjustments will be made in accordance with § 1403.43(c).

(3) A Federal agency shall not make payment to grantees for amounts that are withheld by grantees or subgrantees from payment to contractors to assure satisfactory completion of work. Payments shall be made by the Federal agency when the grantees or subgrantees actually disburse the withheld funds to the contractors or to escrow accounts established to assure satisfactory completion of work.

(h) *Cash depositories.* (1) Consistent with the national goal of expanding the opportunities for minority business enterprises, grantees and subgrantees are encouraged to use minority banks (a bank which is owned at least 50 percent by minority group members). A list of minority owned banks can be obtained from the Minority Business Development Agency, Department of Commerce, Washington, DC 20230.

(2) A grantee or subgrantee shall maintain a separate bank account only when required by Federal-State agreement.

(i) *Interest earned on advances.* Except for interest earned on advances of funds exempt under the Intergovernmental Cooperation Act (31 U.S.C. 6501 et seq.) and the Indian Self-Determination Act (23 U.S.C. 450), grantees and subgrantees shall promptly, but at least quarterly, remit interest earned on advances to the Federal agency. The grantee or subgrantee may keep interest amounts up to $100 per year for administrative expenses.

§ 1403.22 **Allowable costs.**

(a) *Limitation on use of funds.* Grant funds may be used only for:

(1) The allowable costs of the grantees, subgrantees and cost-type contractors, including allowable costs in the form of payments to fixed-price contractors; and

(2) Reasonable fees or profit to cost-type contractors but not any fee or profit (or other increment above allowable costs) to the grantee or subgrantee.

(b) *Applicable cost principles.* For each kind of organization, there is a set of Federal principles for determining allowable costs. Allowable costs will be determined in accordance with the cost principles applicable to the organization incurring the costs. The following chart lists the kinds of organizations and the applicable cost principles.

For the costs of a—	Use the principles in—
State, local or Indian tribal government.	OMB Circular A–87.
Private nonprofit organization other than (1) institution of higher education, (2) hospital, or (3) organization named in OMB Circular A–122 as not subject to that circular.	OMB Circular A–122.
Educational institutions	OMB Circular A–21.
For-profit organizations other than a hospital and an organization named in OMB Circular A–122 as not subject to that circular.	48 CFR part 31. Contract Cost Principles and Procedures, or uniform cost accounting standards that comply with cost principles acceptable to the Federal agency.

§ 1403.23 **Period of availability of funds.**

(a) *General.* Where a funding period is specified, a grantee may charge to the award only costs resulting from obligations of the funding period unless carryover of unobligated balances is permitted, in which case the carryover balances may be charged for costs resulting from obligations of the subsequent funding period.

(b) *Liquidation of obligations.* A grantee must liquidate all obligations incurred under the award not later than 90 days after the end of the funding period (or as specified in a program regulation) to coincide with the submission of the annual Financial Status Report (SF–269). The Federal agency may extend this deadline at the request of the grantee.

§ 1403.24   **Matching or cost sharing.**

(a) *Basic rule: Costs and contributions acceptable.* With the qualifications and exceptions listed in paragraph (b) of this section, a matching or cost sharing requirement may be satisfied by either or both of the following:

(1) Allowable costs incurred by the grantee, subgrantee or a cost-type contractor under the assistance agreement. This includes allowable costs borne by non-Federal grants or by others cash donations from non-Federal third parties.

(2) The value of third party in-kind contributions applicable to the period to which the cost sharing or matching requirements applies.

(b) *Qualifications and exceptions*—(1) *Costs borne by other Federal grant agreements.* Except as provided by Federal statute, a cost sharing or matching requirement may not be met by costs borne by another Federal grant. This prohibition does not apply to income earned by a grantee or subgrantee from a contract awarded under another Federal grant.

(2) *General revenue sharing.* For the purpose of this section, general revenue sharing funds distributed under 31 U.S.C. 6702 are not considered Federal grant funds.

(3) *Cost or contributions counted towards other Federal cost-sharing requirements.* Neither costs nor the values of third party in-kind contributions may count towards satisfying a cost sharing or matching requirement of a grant agreement if they have been or will be counted towards satisfying a cost sharing or matching requirement of another Federal grant agreement, a Federal procurement contract, or any other award of Federal funds.

(4) *Costs financed by program income.* Costs financed by program income, as defined in § 1403.25, shall not count towards satisfying a cost sharing or matching requirement unless they are expressly permitted in the terms of the assistant agreement. (This use of general program income is described in § 1403.25(g).)

(5) *Services or property financed by income earned by contractors.* Contractors under a grant may earn income from the activities carried out under the contract in addition to the amounts earned from the party awarding the contract. No costs of services or property supported by this income may count toward satisfying cost sharing or matching requirement unless other provisions of the grant agreement expressly permit this kind of income to be used to meet the requirement.

(6) *Records.* Costs and third party in-kind contributions counting towards satisfying a cost sharing or matching requirement must be verifiable from the records of grantees and subgrantee or cost-type contractors. These records must show how the value placed on third party in-kind contributions was derived. To the extent feasible, volunteer services will be supported by the same methods that the organization uses to support the allocability of regular personnel costs.

(7) *Special standards for third party in-kind contributions.* (i) Third party in-kind contributions count towards satisfying a cost sharing or matching requirement only where, if the party receiving the contributions were to pay for them, the payments would be allowable costs.

(ii) Some third party in-kind contributions are goods and services that, if the grantee, subgrantee, or contractor receiving the contribution had to pay for them, the payments would have been an indirect costs. Costs sharing or matching credit for such contributions shall be given only if the grantee, subgrantee, or contractor has established, along with its regular indirect cost rate, a special rate for allocating to individual projects or programs the value of the contributions.

(iii) A third party in-kind contribution to a fixed-price contract may count towards satisfying a cost sharing or matching requirement only if it results in:

(A) An increase in the services or property provided under the contract (without additional cost to the grantee or subgrantee) or

(B) A cost savings to the grantee or subgrantee.

(iv) The values placed on third party in-kind contributions for cost sharing or matching purposes will conform to the rules in the succeeding sections of this part. If a third party in-kind contribution is a type not treated in those sections, the value placed upon it shall be fair and reasonable.

(c) *Valuation of donated services*—(1) *Volunteer services.* Unpaid services provided to a grantee or subgrantee by individuals will be valued at rates consistent with those ordinarily paid for similar work in the grantee's or subgrantee's organization. If the grantee or subgrantee does not have employees performing similar work, the rates will be consistent with those ordinarily paid by other employers for similar work in the same labor market. In either case, a reasonable amount for fringe benefits may be included in the valuation.

(2) *Employees of other organizations.* When an employer other than a grantee, subgrantee, or cost-type contractor furnishes free of charge the services of an employee in the employee's normal line of work, the services will be valued at the employee's regular rate of pay exclusive of the employee's fringe benefits and overhead costs. If the services are in a different line of work, paragraph (c)(1) of this section applies.

(d) *Valuation of third party donated supplies and loaned equipment or space.* (1) If a third party donates supplies, the contribution will be valued at the market value of the supplies at the time of donation.

(2) If a third party donates the use of equipment or space in a building but retains title, the contribution will be valued at the fair rental rate of the equipment or space.

(e) *Valuation of third party donated equipment, buildings, and land.* If a third party donates equipment, buildings, or land, and title passes to a grantee or subgrantee, the treatment of the donated property will depend upon the purpose of the grant or subgrant, as follows:

(1) *Awards for capital expenditures.* If the purpose of the grant or subgrant is to assist the grantee or subgrantee in the acquisition of property, the market value of that property at the time of donation may be counted as cost sharing or matching.

(2) *Other awards.* If assisting in the acquisition of property is not the purpose of the grant or subgrant, paragraphs (e)(2) (i) and (ii) of this section apply:

(i) If approval is obtained from the awarding agency, the market value at the time of donation of the donated equipment or buildings and the fair rental rate of the donated land may be counted as cost sharing or matching. In the case of a subgrant, the terms of the grant agreement may require that the approval be obtained from the Federal agency as well as the grantee. In all cases, the approval may be given only if a purchase of the equipment or rental of the land would be approved as an allowable direct cost. If any part of the donated property was acquired with Federal funds, only the non-federal share of the property may be counted as cost-sharing or matching.

(ii) If approval is not obtained under paragraph (e)(2)(i) of this section, no amount may be counted for donated land, and only depreciation or use allowances may be counted for donated equipment and buildings. The depreciation or use allowances for this property are not treated as third party in-kind contributions. Instead, they are treated as costs incurred by the grantee or subgrantee. They are computed and allocated (usually as indirect costs) in accordance with the cost principles specified in § 1403.22, in the same way as depreciation or use allowances for purchased equipment and buildings. The amount of depreciation or use allowances for donated equipment and buildings is based on the property's market value at the time it was donated.

(f) *Valuation of grantee or subgrantee donates real property for construction/acquisition.* If a grantee or subgrantee donates real property for a construction or facilities acquisition project, the current market value of that property may be counted as cost sharing or matching. If any part of the donated property was acquired with Federal funds, only the non-federal share of the property may be counted as cost sharing or matching.

(g) *Appraisal of real property.* In some cases under paragraphs (d), (e) and (f) of this section, it will be necessary to establish the market value of land or a building or the fair rental rate of land or of space in a building. In these cases, the Federal agency may require the market value or fair rental value be set by an independent appraiser, and that the value or rate be certified by the grantee. This requirement will also be imposed by the grantee on subgrantees.

§ 1403.25   Program income.

(a) *General.* Grantees are encouraged to earn income to defray program costs. Program income includes income from fees for services performed, from the use of rental of real or personal property acquired with grant funds, from the sale of commodities or items fabricated under a grant agreement, and from payments of principal and interest on loans made with grant funds. Except as otherwise provided in regulations of the Federal agency, program income does not include interest on grant funds, rebates, credits, discounts, refunds, etc., and interest earned on any of them.

(b) *Definition of program income.* Program income means gross income received by the grantee or subgrantee directly generated by a grant supported activity, or earned only as a result of the grant agreement during the grant period. "During the grant period" is the time between the effective date of the award and the ending date of the award reflected in the final financial report.

(c) *Cost of generating program income.* If authorized by Federal regulations or the grant agreement, costs incident to the generation of program income may be deducted from gross income to determine program income.

(d) *Governmental revenues.* Taxes, special assessments levies, fines, and other such revenues raised by a grantee or subgrantee are not program income unless the revenues are specifically identified in the grant agreement or Federal agency regulations as program income.

(e) *Royalties.* Income from royalties and license fees for copyrighted material, patents, and inventions developed by a grantee or subgrantee is program income only if the revenues are specifically identified in the grant agreement or Federal agency regulations as program income. (See § 1403.34.)

(f) *Property.* Proceeds from the sale of real property or equipment will be handled in accordance with the requirements of § 1403.31 and § 1403.32.

(g) *Use of program income.* Program income shall be deducted from outlays which may be both Federal and non-Federal as described below, unless the Federal agency regulations or the grant agreement specify another alternative (or a combination of the alternatives). In specifying alternatives, the Federal agency may distinguish between income earned by the grantee and income earned by subgrantees and between the sources, kinds, or amounts of income. When Federal agencies authorize the alternatives in paragraphs (g) (2) and (3) of this section, program income in excess of any limits stipulated shall also be deducted from outlays.

(1) *Deduction.* Ordinarily program income shall be deducted from total allowable costs to determine the net allowable costs. Program income shall be used for current costs unless the Federal agency authorizes otherwise. Program income which the grantee did not anticipate at the time of the award shall be used to reduce the Federal agency and grantee contributions rather than to increase the funds committed to the project.

(2) *Addition.* When authorized, program income may be added to the funds committed to the grant agreement by the Federal agency and the grantee. The program income shall be used for the purposes and under the conditions of the grant agreement.

(3) *Cost sharing or matching.* When authorized, program income may be used to meet the cost sharing or matching requirement of the grant agreement. The amount of the Federal grant award remains the same.

(h) *Income after the award period.* There are no Federal requirements governing the disposition of program income earned after the end of the award period (i.e., until the ending date of the final financial report, see paragraph (a) of this section), unless the terms of the agreement or the Federal agency regulations provide otherwise.

§ 1403.26 Non-Federal audit.

(a) *Basic rule.* Grantees and subgrantees are responsible for obtaining audits in accordance with the Single Audit Act Amendments of 1996 (31 U.S.C. 7501–7507) and revised OMB Circular A–133, "Audits of States, Local Governments, and Non-Profit Organizations." The audits shall be made by an independent auditor in accordance with generally accepted government auditing standards covering financial audits.

(b) *Subgrantees.* State or local governments, as those terms are defined for purposes of the Single Audit Act Amendments of 1996, that provide Federal awards to a subgrantee, which expends $300,000 or more (or other amount as specified by OMB) in Federal awards in a fiscal year, shall:

(1) Determine whether State or local subgrantees have met the audit requirements of the Act and whether subgrantees covered by OMB Circular A–110, "Uniform Administrative Requirements for Grants and Agreements with Institutions of Higher Education, Hospitals, and Other Non-Profit Organizations," have met the audit requirements of the Act. Commercial contractors (private for-profit and private and governmental organizations) providing goods and services to State and local governments are not required to have a single audit performed. State and local governments should use their own procedures to ensure that the contractor has complied with laws and regulations affecting the expenditure of Federal funds;

(2) Determine whether the subgrantee spent Federal assistance funds provided in accordance with applicable laws and regulations. This may be accomplished by reviewing an audit of the subgrantee made in accordance with the Act, Circular A–110, or through other means (e.g., program reviews) if the subgrantee has not had such an audit;

(3) Ensure that appropriate corrective action is taken within six months

after receipt of the audit report in instance of noncompliance with Federal laws and regulations;

(4) Consider whether subgrantee audits necessitate adjustment of the grantee's own records; and

(5) Require each subgrantee to permit independent auditors to have access to the records and financial statements.

(c) *Auditor selection.* In arranging for audit services, § 1403.36 shall be followed.

[57 FR 55092, Nov. 24, 1992, as amended at 62 FR 45939, 45941, Aug. 29, 1997]

CHANGES, PROPERTY, AND SUBAWARDS

§ 1403.30 Changes.

(a) *General.* Grantees and subgrantees are permitted to rebudget within the approved direct cost budget to meet unanticipated requirements and may make limited program changes to the approved project. However, unless waived by the awarding agency, certain types of post-award changes in budgets and projects shall require the prior written approval of the awarding agency.

(b) *Relation to cost principles.* The applicable cost principles (see § 1403.22) contain requirements for prior approval of certain types of costs. Except where waived, those requirements apply to all grants and subgrants even if paragraphs (c) through (f) of this section do not.

(c) *Budget changes—(1) Nonconstruction projects.* Except as stated in other regulations or an award document, grantees or subgrantees shall obtain the prior approval of the awarding agency whenever any of the following changes is anticipated under a nonconstruction award:

(i) Any revision which would result in the need for additional funding.

(ii) Unless waived by the awarding agency, cumulative transfers among direct cost categories, or, if applicable, among separately budgeted programs, projects, functions, or activities which exceed or are expected to exceed ten percent of the current total approved budget, whenever the awarding agency's share exceeds $100,000.

(iii) Transfer of funds allotted for training allowances (i.e., from direct payments to trainees to other expense categories).

(2) *Construction projects.* Grantees and subgrantees shall obtain prior written approval for any budget revision which would result in the need for additional funds.

(3) *Combined construction and nonconstruction projects.* When a grant or subgrant provides funding for both construction and nonconstruction activities, the grantee or subgrantee must obtain prior written approval from the awarding agency before making any fund or budget transfer from nonconstruction to construction or vice versa.

(d) *Programmatic changes.* Grantees or subgrantees must obtain the prior approval of the awarding agency whenever any of the following actions is anticipated:

(1) Any revision of the scope or objectives of the project (regardless of whether there is an associated budget revision requiring prior approval).

(2) Need to extend the period of availability of funds.

(3) Changes in key persons in cases where specified in an application or a grant award. In research projects, a change in the project director or principal investigator shall always require approval unless waived by the awarding agency.

(4) Under nonconstruction projects, contracting out, subgranting (if authorized by law) or otherwise obtaining the services of a third party to perform activities which are central to the purposes of the award. This approval requirement is in addition to the approval requirements of § 1403.36 but does not apply to the procurement of equipment, supplies, and general support services.

(e) *Additional prior approval requirements.* The awarding agency may not require prior approval for any budget revision which is not described in paragraph (c) of this section.

(f) *Requesting prior approval.* (1) A request for prior approval of any budget revision will be in the same budget format the grantee used in its application and shall be accompanied by a narrative justification for the proposed revision.

(2) A request for a prior approval under the applicable Federal cost principles (see § 1403.22) may be made by letter.

(3) A request by a subgrantee for prior approval will be addressed in writing to the grantee. The grantee will promptly review such request and shall approve or disapprove the request in writing. A grantee will not approve any budget or project revision which is inconsistent with the purpose or terms and conditions of the Federal grant to the grantee. If the revision requested by the subgrantee would result in a change to the grantee's approved project which requires Federal prior approval, the grantee will obtain the Federal agency's approval before approving the subgrantee's request.

§ 1403.31 Real property.

(a) *Title.* Subject to the obligations and conditions set forth in this section, title to real property acquired under a grant or subgrant will vest upon acquisition in the grantee or subgrantee respectively.

(b) *Use.* Except as otherwise provided by Federal statutes, real property will be used for the originally authorized purposes as long as needed for those purposes, and the grantee or subgrantee shall not dispose of or encumber its title or other interests.

(c) *Disposition.* When real property is no longer needed for the originally authorized purpose, the grantee or subgrantee will request disposition instructions from the awarding agency. The instructions will provide for one of the following alternatives:

(1) *Retention of title.* Retain title after compensating the awarding agency. The amount paid to the awarding agency will be computed by applying the awarding agency's percentage of participation in the cost of the original purchase to the fair market value of the property. However, in those situations were a grantee or subgrantee is disposing of real property acquired with grant funds and acquiring replacement real property under the same program, the net proceeds from the disposition may be used as an offset to the cost of the replacement property.

(2) *Sale of property.* Sell the property and compensate the awarding agency.

The amount due to the awarding agency will be calculated by applying the awarding agency's percentage of participation in the cost of the original purchase to the proceeds of the sale after deduction of any actual and reasonable selling and fixing-up expenses. If the grant is still active, the net proceeds from sale may be offset against the original cost of the property. When a grantee or subgrantee is directed to sell property, sales procedures shall be followed that provide for competition to the extent practicable and result in the highest possible return.

(3) *Transfer of title.* Transfer title to the awarding agency or to a third-party designated/approved by the awarding agency. The grantee or subgrantee shall be paid an amount calculated by applying the grantee or subgrantee's percentage of participation in the purchase of the real property to the current fair market value of the property.

§ 1403.32 Equipment.

(a) *Title.* Subject to the obligations and conditions set forth in this section, title to equipment acquired under a grant or subgrant will vest upon acquisition in the grantee or subgrantee respectively.

(b) *States.* A State will use, manage, and dispose of equipment acquired under a grant by the State in accordance with State laws and procedures. Other grantees and subgrantees will follow paragraphs (c) through (e) of this section.

(c) *Use.* (1) Equipment shall be used by the grantee or subgrantee in the program or project for which it was acquired as long as needed, whether or not the project or program continues to be supported by Federal funds. When no longer needed for the original program or project, the equipment may be used in other activities currently or previously supported by a Federal agency.

(2) The grantee or subgrantee shall also make equipment available for use on other projects or programs currently or previously supported by the Federal Government, providing such use will not interfere with the work on the projects or program for which it was originally acquired. First pref-

erence for other use shall be given to other programs or projects supported by the awarding agency. User fees should be considered if appropriate.

(3) Notwithstanding the encouragement in § 1403.25(a) to earn program income, the grantee or subgrantee must not use equipment acquired with grant funds to provide services for a fee to compete unfairly with private companies that provide equivalent services, unless specifically permitted or contemplated by Federal statute.

(4) When acquiring replacement equipment, the grantee or subgrantee may use the equipment to be replaced as a trade-in or sell the property and use the proceeds to offset the cost of the replacement property, subject to the approval of the awarding agency.

(d) *Management requirements.* Procedures for managing equipment (including replacement equipment), whether acquired in whole or in part with grant funds, until disposition takes place will, as a minimum, meet the following requirements:

(1) Property records must be maintained that include a description of the property, a serial number or other identification number, the source of property, who holds title, the acquisition date, and cost of the property, percentage of Federal participation in the cost of the property, the location, use and condition of the property, and any ultimate disposition data including the date of disposal and sale price of the property.

(2) A physical inventory of the property must be taken and the results reconciled with the property records at least once every two years.

(3) A control system must be developed to ensure adequate safeguards to prevent loss, damage, or theft of the property. Any loss, damage, or theft shall be investigated.

(4) Adequate maintenance procedures must be developed to keep the property in good condition.

(5) If the grantee or subgrantee is authorized or required to sell the property, proper sales procedures must be established to ensure the highest possible return.

(e) *Disposition.* When original or replacement equipment acquired under a grant or subgrant is no longer needed for the original project or program or for other activities currently or previously supported by a Federal agency, disposition of the equipment will be made as follows:

(1) Items of equipment with a current per-unit fair market value of less than $5,000 may be retained, sold or otherwise disposed of with no further obligation to the awarding agency.

(2) Items of equipment with a current per unit fair market value in excess of $5,000 may be retained or sold and the awarding agency shall have a right to an amount calculated by multiplying the current market value or proceeds from sale by the awarding agency's share of the equipment.

(3) In cases where a grantee or subgrantee fails to take appropriate disposition actions, the awarding agency may direct the grantee or subgrantee to take excess and disposition actions.

(f) *Federal equipment.* In the event a grantee or subgrantee is provided federally-owned equipment:

(1) Title will remain vested in the Federal Government.

(2) Grantees or subgrantees will manage the equipment in accordance with Federal agency rules and procedures, and submit an annual inventory listing.

(3) When the equipment is no longer needed, the grantee or subgrantee will request disposition instructions from the Federal agency.

(g) *Right to transfer title.* The Federal awarding agency may reserve the right to transfer title to the Federal Government or a third party named by the awarding agency when such a third party is otherwise eligible under existing statutes. Such transfers shall be subject to the following standards:

(1) The property shall be identified in the grant or otherwise made known to the grantee in writing.

(2) The Federal awarding agency shall issue disposition instruction within 120 calendar days after the end of the Federal support of the project for which it was acquired. If the federal awarding agency fails to issue disposition instructions within the 120 calendar-day period the grantee shall follow § 1403.32(e).

(3) When title to equipment is transferred, the grantee shall be paid an amount calculated by applying the percentage of participation in the purchase to the current fair market value of the property.

§ 1403.33 Supplies.

(a) *Title.* Title to supplies acquired under a grant or subgrant will vest, upon acquisition, in the grantee or subgrantee respectively.

(b) *Disposition.* If there is a residual inventory of unused supplies exceeding $5,000 in total aggregate fair market value upon termination or completion of the award, and if the supplies are not needed for any other federally sponsored programs or projects, the grantee or subgrantee shall compensate the awarding agency for its share.

§ 1403.34 Copyrights.

The Federal awarding agency reserves a royalty-free, nonexclusive, and irrevocable license to reproduce, publish or otherwise use, and to authorize others to use, for Federal Government purposes:

(a) The copyright in any work developed under a grant, subgrant, or contract under a grant or subgrant; and

(b) Any rights of copyright to which a grantee, subgrantee or a contractor purchases ownership with grant support.

§ 1403.35 Subawards to debarred and suspended parties.

Grantees and subgrantees must not make any award or permit any award (subgrant or contract) at any tier to any party which is debarred or suspended or is otherwise excluded from or ineligible for participation in Federal assistance programs under Executive Order 12549, "Debarment and Suspension."

§ 1403.36 Procurement.

(a) *States.* When procuring property and services under a grant, a State will follow the same policies and procedures it uses for procurements from its non-Federal funds. The State will ensure that every purchase order or other contract includes any clauses required by Federal statutes and executive orders and their implementing regulations. Other grantees and subgrantees will follow paragraphs (b) through (i) of this section.

(b) *Procurement standards.* (1) Grantees and subgrantees will use their own procurement procedures which reflect applicable State and local laws and regulations, provided that the procurements conform to applicable Federal law and the standards identified in this section.

(2) Grantees and subgrantees will maintain a contract administration system which ensures that contractors perform in accordance with the terms, conditions, and specifications of their contracts or purchase orders.

(3) Grantees and subgrantees will maintain a written code of standards of conduct governing the performance of their employees engaged in the award and administration of contracts. No employee, officer or agent of the grantee or subgrantee shall participate in selection, or in the award or administration of a contract supported by Federal funds if a conflict of interest, real or apparent, would be involved. Such a conflict would arise when:

(i) The employee, officer or agent,

(ii) Any member of his immediate family,

(iii) His or her partner, or

(iv) An organization which employs, or is about to employ, any of the above, has a financial or other interest in the firm selected for award. The grantee's or subgrantee's officers, employees or agents will neither solicit nor accept gratuities, favors or anything of monetary value from contractors, potential contractors, or parties to subagreements. Grantee and subgrantees may set minimum rules where the financial interest is not substantial or the gift is an unsolicited item of nominal intrinsic value. To the extent permitted by State or local law or regulations, such standards or conduct will provide for penalties, sanctions, or other disciplinary actions for violations of such standards by the grantee's and subgrantee's officers, employees, or agents, or by contractors or their agents. The awarding agency may in regulation provide additional prohibitions relative to real, apparent, or potential conflicts of interest.

(4) Grantee and subgrantee procedures will provide for a review of proposed procurements to avoid purchase of unnecessary or duplicative items. Consideration should be given to consolidating or breaking out procurements to obtain a more economical purchase. Where appropriate, an analysis will be made of lease versus purchase alternatives, and any other appropriate analysis to determine the most economical approach.

(5) To foster greater economy and efficiency, grantees and subgrantees are encouraged to enter into State and local intergovernmental agreements for procurement or use of common goods and services.

(6) Grantees and subgrantees are encouraged to use Federal excess and surplus property in lieu of purchasing new equipment and property whenever such use is feasible and reduces project costs.

(7) Grantees and subgrantees are encouraged to use value engineering clauses in contracts for construction projects of sufficient size to offer reasonable opportunities for cost reductions. Value engineering is a systematic and creative analysis of each contract item or task to ensure that its essential function is provided at the overall lower cost.

(8) Grantees and subgrantees will make awards only to responsible contractors possessing the ability to perform successfully under the terms and conditions of a proposed procurement. Consideration will be given to such matters as contractor integrity, compliance with public policy, record of past performance, and financial and technical resources.

(9) Grantees and subgrantees will maintain records sufficient to detail the significant history of a procurement. These records will include, but are not necessarily limited to the following: rationale for the method of procurement, selection of contract type, contractor selection or rejection, and the basis for the contract price.

(10) Grantees and subgrantees will use time and material type contracts only—

(i) After a determination that no other contract is suitable, and

(ii) If the contract includes a ceiling price that the contractor exceeds at its own risk.

235

(11) Grantees and subgrantees alone will be responsible, in accordance with good administrative practice and sound business judgment, for the settlement of all contractual and administrative issues arising out of procurements. These issues include, but are not limited to source evaluation, protests, disputes, and claims. These standards do not relieve the grantee or subgrantee of any contractual responsibilities under its contracts. Federal agencies will not substitute their judgment for that of the grantee or subgrantee unless the matter is primarily a Federal concern. Violations of law will be referred to the local, State, or Federal authority having proper jurisdiction.

(12) Grantees and subgrantees will have protest procedures to handle and resolve disputes relating to their procurements and shall in all instances disclose information regarding the protest to the awarding agency. A protestor must exhaust all administrative remedies with the grantee and subgrantee before pursuing a protest with the Federal agency. Reviews of protests by the Federal agency will be limited to:

(i) Violations of Federal law or regulations and the standards of this section (violations of State or local law will be under the jurisdiction of State or local authorities) and

(ii) Violations of the grantee's or subgrantee's protest procedures for failure to review a complaint or protest. Protests received by the Federal agency other than those specified above will be referred to the grantee or subgrantee.

(c) *Competition.* (1) All procurement transactions will be conducted in a manner providing full and open competition consistent with the standards of § 1403.36. Some of the situations considered to be restrictive of competition include but are not limited to:

(i) Placing unreasonable requirements on firms in order for them to qualify to do business,

(ii) Requiring unnecessary experience and excessive bonding,

(iii) Noncompetitive pricing practices between firms or between affiliated companies,

(iv) Noncompetitive awards to consultants that are on retainer contracts,

(v) Organizational conflicts of interest,

(vi) Specifying only a "brand name" product instead of allowing "an equal" product to be offered and describing the performance of other relevant requirements of the procurement, and

(vii) Any arbitrary action in the procurement process.

(2) Grantees and subgrantees will conduct procurements in a manner that prohibits the use of statutorily or administratively imposed in-State or local geographical preferences in the evaluation of bids or proposals, except in those cases where applicable Federal statutes expressly mandate or encourage geographic preference. Nothing in this section preempts State licensing laws. When contracting for architectural and engineering (A/E) services, geographic location may be a selection criteria provided its application leaves an appropriate number of qualified firms, given the nature and size of the project, to compete for the contract.

(3) Grantees will have written selection procedures for procurement transactions. These procedures will ensure that all solicitations:

(i) Incorporate a clear and accurate description of the technical requirements for the material, product, or service to be procured. Such description shall not, in competitive procurements, contain features which unduly restrict competition. The description may include a statement of the qualitative nature of the material, product or service to be procured, and when necessary, shall set forth those minimum essential characteristics and standards to which it must conform if it is to satisfy its intended use. Detailed product specifications should be avoided if at all possible. When it is impractical or uneconomical to make a clear and accurate description of the technical requirements, a "brand name or equal" description may be used as a means to define the performance or other salient requirements of a procurement. The specific features of the named brand which must be met by offerors shall be clearly stated; and

(ii) Identify all requirements which the offerors must fulfill and all other factors to be used in evaluating bids or proposals.

(4) Grantees and subgrantees will ensure that all prequalified lists of persons, firms, or products which are used in acquiring goods and services are current and include enough qualified sources to ensure maximum open and free competition. Also, grantees and subgrantees will not preclude potential bidders from qualifying during the solicitation period.

(d) *Methods of procurement to be followed.* (1) Procurement by *small purchase procedures.* Small purchase procedures are those relatively simple and informal procurement methods for securing services, supplies, or other property that do not cost more than the simplified acquisition threshold fixed at 41 U.S.C. 403(11) (currently set at $100,000). If small purchase procedures are used, price or rate quotations shall be obtained from an adequate number of qualified sources.

(2) Procurement by *sealed bids* (formal advertising). Bids are publicly solicited and a firm-fixed-price contract (lump sum or unit price) is awarded to the responsible bidder whose bid, conforming with all the material terms and conditions of the invitation for bids, is the lowest in price. The sealed bid method is the preferred method for procuring construction, if the conditions in §1403.36(d)(2)(i) apply.

(i) In order for sealed bidding to be feasible, the following conditions should be present:

(A) A complete, adequate, and realistic specification or purchase description is available;

(B) Two or more responsible bidders are willing and able to compete effectively and for the business; and

(C) The procurement lends itself to a firm fixed price contract and the selection of the successful bidder can be made principally on the basis of price.

(ii) If sealed bids are used, the following requirements apply:

(A) The invitation for bids will be publicly advertised and bids shall be solicited from an adequate number of known suppliers, providing them sufficient time prior to the date set for opening the bids;

(B) The invitation for bids, which will include any specifications and pertinent attachments, shall define the items or services in order for the bidder to properly respond;

(C) All bids will be publicly opened at the time and place prescribed in the invitation for bids;

(D) A firm fixed-price contract award will be made in writing to the lowest responsive and responsible bidder. Where specified in bidding documents, factors such as discounts, transportation cost, and life cycle costs shall be considered in determining which bid is lowest. Payment discounts will only be used to determine the low bid when prior experience indicates that such discounts are usually taken advantage of; and

(E) Any or all bids may be rejected if there is a sound documented reason.

(3) Procurement by *competitive proposals.* The technique of competitive proposals is normally conducted with more than one source submitting an offer, and either a fixed-price or cost-reimbursement type contract is awarded. It is generally used when conditions are not appropriate for the use of sealed bids. If this method is used, the following requirements apply:

(i) Requests for proposals will be publicized and identify all evaluation factors and their relative importance. Any response to publicized requests for proposals shall be honored to the maximum extent practical;

(ii) Proposals will be solicited from an adequate number of qualified sources;

(iii) Grantees and subgrantees will have a method for conducting technical evaluations of the proposals received and for selecting awardees;

(iv) Awards will be made to the responsible firm whose proposal is most advantageous to the program, with price and other factors considered; and

(v) Grantees and subgrantees may use competitive proposal procedures for qualifications-based procurement of architectural/engineering (A/E) professional services whereby competitors' qualifications are evaluated and the most qualified competitor is selected, subject to negotiation of fair and reasonable compensation. The method, where price is not used as a selection factor, can only be used in procurement of A/E professional services. It cannot be used to purchase other types of services though A/E firms are a potential source to perform the proposed effort.

(4) Procurement by *noncompetitive proposals* is procurement through solicitation of a proposal from only one source, or after solicitation of a number of sources, competition is determined inadequate.

(i) Procurement by noncompetitive proposals may be used only when the award of a contract is infeasible under small purchase procedures, sealed bids or competitive proposals and one of the following circumstances applies:

(A) The item is available only from a single source;

(B) The public exigency or emergency for the requirement will not permit a delay resulting from competitive solicitation;

(C) The awarding agency authorizes noncompetitive proposals; or

(D) After solicitation of a number of sources, competition is determined inadequate.

(ii) Cost analysis, i.e., verifying the proposed cost data, the projections of the data, and the evaluation of the specific elements of costs and profits, is required.

(iii) Grantees and subgrantees may be required to submit the proposed procurement to the awarding agency for pre-award review in accordance with paragraph (g) of this section.

(e) *Contracting with small and minority firms, women's business enterprise and labor surplus area firms.* (1) The grantee and subgrantee will take all necessary affirmative steps to assure that minority firms, women's business enterprises, and labor surplus area firms are used when possible.

(2) Affirmative steps shall include:

(i) Placing qualified small and minority businesses and women's business enterprises on solicitation lists;

(ii) Assuring that small and minority businesses, and women's business enterprises are solicited whenever they are potential sources;

(iii) Dividing total requirements, when economically feasible, into smaller tasks or quantities to permit maximum participation by small and minority business, and women's business enterprises;

(iv) Establishing delivery schedules, where the requirement permits, which encourage participation by small and minority business, and women's business enterprises;

(v) Using the services and assistance of the Small Business Administration, and the Minority Business Development Agency of the Department of Commerce; and

(vi) Requiring the prime contractor, if subcontracts are to be let, to take the affirmative steps listed in paragraphs (e)(2) (i) through (v) of this section.

(f) *Contract cost and price.* (1) Grantees and subgrantees must perform a cost or price analysis in connection with every procurement action including contract modifications. The method and degree of analysis is dependent on the facts surrounding the particular procurement situation, but as a starting point, grantees must make independent estimates before receiving bids or proposals. A cost analysis must be performed when the offeror is required to submit the elements of his estimated cost, e.g., under professional, consulting, and architectural engineering services contracts. A cost analysis will be necessary when adequate price competition is lacking, and for sole source procurements, including contract modifications or change orders, unless price reasonableness can be established on the basis of a catalog or market price of a commercial product sold in substantial quantities to the general public or based on prices set by law or regulation. A price analysis will be used in all other instances to determine the reasonableness of the proposed contract price.

(2) Grantees and subgrantees will negotiate profit as a separate element of the price for each contract in which there is no price competition and in all cases where cost analysis is performed. To establish a fair and reasonable profit, consideration will be given to the complexity of the work to be performed, the risk borne by the contractor, the contractor's investment, the amount of subcontracting, the quality of its record of past performance, and industry profit rates in the surrounding geographical area for similar work.

(3) Costs or prices based on estimated costs for contracts under grants will be allowable only to the extent that costs incurred or cost estimates included in negotiated prices are consistent with Federal cost principles (see §1403.22). Grantees may reference their own cost principles that comply with the applicable Federal cost principles.

(4) The cost plus a percentage of cost and percentage of constructing cost methods of contracting shall not be used.

(g) *Awarding agency review.* (1) Grantees and subgrantees must make available, upon request of the awarding agency, technical specifications on proposed procurements where the awarding agency believes such review is needed to ensure that the item and/or service specified is the one being proposed for purchase. This review generally will take place prior to the time the specification is incorporated into a solicitation document. However, if the grantee or subgrantee desires to have the review accomplished after a solicitation has been developed, the awarding agency may still review the specifications, with such review usually limited to the technical aspects of the proposed purchase.

(2) Grantees and subgrantees must on request make available for awarding agency pre-award review procurement documents, such as requests for proposals or invitations for bids, independent cost estimates, etc. when:

(i) A grantee's or subgrantee's procurement procedures or operation fails to comply with the procurement standards in this section; or

(ii) The procurement is expected to exceed the simplified acquisition threshold and is to be awarded without competition or only one bid or offer is received in response to a solicitation; or

(iii) The procurement, which is expected to exceed the simplified acquisition threshold, specifies a "brand name" product; or

(iv) The proposed award is more than the simplified acquisition threshold and is to be awarded to other than the apparent low bidder under a sealed bid procurement; or

(v) A proposed contract modification changes the scope of a contract or increases the contract amount by more than the simplified acquisition threshold.

(3) A grantee or subgrantee will be exempt from the pre-award review in paragraph (g)(2) of this section if the awarding agency determines that its procurement systems comply with the standards of this section.

(i) A grantee or subgrantee may request that its procurement system be reviewed by the awarding agency to determine whether its system meets these standards in order for its system to be certified. Generally, these reviews shall occur where there is a continuous high-dollar funding, and third-party contracts are awarded on a regular basis.

(ii) A grantee or subgrantee may self-certify its procurement system. Such self-certification shall not limit the awarding agency's right to survey the system. Under a self-certification procedure, awarding agencies may wish to rely on written assurances from the grantee or subgrantee that it is complying with these standards. A grantee or subgrantee will cite specific procedures, regulations, standards, etc., as being in compliance with these requirements and have its system available for review.

(h) *Bonding requirements.* For construction or facility improvement contracts or subcontracts exceeding the simplified acquisition threshold, the awarding agency may accept the bonding policy and requirements of the grantee or subgrantee provided the awarding agency has made a determination that the awarding agency's interest is adequately protected. If such a determination has not been made, the minimum requirements shall be as follows:

(1) *A bid guarantee from each bidder equivalent to five percent of the bid price.* The "bid guarantee" shall consist of a firm commitment such as a bid bond, certified check, or other negotiable instrument accompanying a bid as assurance that the bidder will, upon acceptance of his bid, execute such contractual documents as may be required within the time specified.

(2) *A performance bond on the part of the contractor for 100 percent of the contract price.* A "performance bond" is

one executed in connection with a contract to secure fulfillment of all the contractor's obligations under such contract.

(3) *A payment bond on the part of the contractor for 100 percent of the contract price.* A "payment bond" is one executed in connection with a contract to assure payment as required by law of all persons supplying labor and material in the execution of the work provided for in the contract.

(i) *Contract provisions.* A grantee's and subgrantee's contracts must contain provisions in paragraph (i) of this section. Federal agencies are permitted to require changes, remedies, changed conditions, access and records retention, suspension of work, and other clauses approved by the Office of Federal Procurement Policy.

(1) Administrative, contractual, or legal remedies in instances where contractors violate or breach contract terms, and provide for such sanctions and penalties as may be appropriate. (Contracts more than the simplified acquisition threshold)

(2) Termination for cause and for convenience by the grantee or subgrantee including the manner by which it will be effected and the basis for settlement. (All contracts in excess of $10,000)

(3) Compliance with Executive Order 11246 of September 24, 1965, entitled "Equal Employment Opportunity," as amended by Executive Order 11375 of October 13, 1967, and as supplemented in Department of Labor regulations (41 CFR chapter 60). (All construction contracts awarded in excess of $10,000 by grantees and their contractors or subgrantees)

(4) Compliance with the Copeland "Anti-Kickback" Act (18 U.S.C. 874) as supplemented in Department of Labor regulations (29 CFR Part 3). (All contracts and subgrants for construction or repair)

(5) Compliance with the Davis-Bacon Act (40 U.S.C. 276a to 276a–7) as supplemented by Department of Labor regulations (29 CFR Part 5). (Construction contracts in excess of $2000 awarded by grantees and subgrantees when required by Federal grant program legislation)

(6) Compliance with Sections 103 and 107 of the Contract Work Hours and Safety Standards Act (40 U.S.C. 327–330) as supplemented by Department of Labor regulations (29 CFR Part 5). (Construction contracts awarded by grantees and subgrantees in excess of $2000, and in excess of $2500 for other contracts which involve the employment of mechanics or laborers)

(7) Notice of awarding agency requirements and regulations pertaining to reporting.

(8) Notice of awarding agency requirements and regulations pertaining to patent rights with respect to any discovery or invention which arises or is developed in the course of or under such contract.

(9) Awarding agency requirements and regulations pertaining to copyrights and rights in data.

(10) Access by the grantee, the subgrantee, the Federal grantor agency, the Comptroller General of the United States, or any of their duly authorized representatives to any books, documents, papers, and records of the contractor which are directly pertinent to that specific contract for the purpose of making audit, examination, excerpts, and transcriptions.

(11) Retention of all required records for three years after grantees or subgrantees make final payments and all other pending matters are closed.

(12) Compliance with all applicable standards, orders, or requirements issued under section 306 of the Clean Air Act (42 U.S.C. 1857(h)), section 508 of the Clean Water Act (33 U.S.C. 1368), Executive Order 11738, and Environmental Protection Agency regulations (40 CFR part 15). (Contracts, subcontracts, and subgrants of amounts in excess of $100,000).

(13) Mandatory standards and policies relating to energy efficiency which are contained in the state energy conservation plan issued in compliance with the Energy Policy and Conservation Act (Pub. L. 94–163, 89 Stat. 871).

[57 FR 55092, Nov. 24, 1992, as amended at 60 FR 19639, 19642, Apr. 19, 1995]

§ 1403.37   Subgrants.

(a) *States.* States shall follow state law and procedures when awarding and administering subgrants (whether on a cost reimbursement or fixed amount basis) of financial assistance to local and Indian tribal governments. States shall:

(1) Ensure that every subgrant includes any clauses required by Federal statute and executive orders and their implementing regulations;

(2) Ensure that subgrantees are aware of requirements imposed upon them by Federal statute and regulation;

(3) Ensure that a provision for compliance with §1403.42 is placed in every cost reimbursement subgrant; and

(4) Conform any advances of grant funds to subgrantees substantially to the same standards of timing and amount that apply to cash advances by Federal agencies.

(b) *All other grantees.* All other grantees shall follow the provisions of this part which are applicable to awarding agencies when awarding and administering subgrants (whether on a cost reimbursement or fixed amount basis) of financial assistance to local and Indian tribal governments. Grantees shall:

(1) Ensure that every subgrant includes a provision for compliance with this part;

(2) Ensure that every subgrant includes any clauses required by Federal statute and executive orders and their implementing regulations; and

(3) Ensure that subgrantees are aware of requirements imposed upon them by Federal statutes and regulations.

(c) *Exceptions.* By their own terms, certain provisions of this part do not apply to the award and administration of subgrants:

(1) Section 1403.10;

(2) Section 1403.11;

(3) The letter-of-credit procedures specified in Treasury Regulations at 31 CFR part 205, cited in §1403.21; and

(4) Section 1403.50.

REPORTS, RECORDS, RETENTION, AND ENFORCEMENT

§1403.40 Monitoring and reporting program performance.

(a) *Monitoring by grantees.* Grantees are responsible for managing the day-to-day operations of grant and subgrant supported activities. Grantees must monitor grant and subgrant supported activities to assure compliance with applicable Federal requirements and that performance goals are being achieved. Grantee monitoring must cover each program, function or activity.

(b) *Nonconstruction performance reports.* The Federal agency may, if it decides that performance information available from subsequent applications contains sufficient information to meet its programmatic needs, require the grantee to submit a performance report only upon expiration or termination of grant support. Unless waived by the Federal agency this report will be due on the same date as the final Financial Status Report.

(1) Grantees shall submit annual performance reports unless the awarding agency requires quarterly or semi-annual reports. However, performance reports will not be required more frequently than quarterly. Annual reports shall be due 90 days after the grant year, quarterly or semi-annual reports shall be due 30 days after the reporting period. The final performance report will be due 90 days after the expiration or termination of grant support. If a justified request is submitted by a grantee, the Federal agency may extend the due date for any performance report. Additionally, requirements for unnecessary performance reports may be waived by the Federal agency.

(2) Performance reports will contain, for each grant, brief information on the following:

(i) A comparison of actual accomplishments to the objectives established for the period. Where the output of the project can be quantified, a computation of the cost per unit of output may be required if that information will be useful.

(ii) The reasons for slippage if established objectives were not met.

(iii) Additional pertinent information including, when appropriate, analysis and explanation of cost overruns or high unit costs.

(3) Grantees will not be required to submit more than the original and two copies of performance reports.

(4) Grantees will adhere to the standards in this section in prescribing performance reporting requirements for subgrantees.

(c) *Construction performance reports.* For the most part, on-site technical inspections and certified percentage-of-completion data are relied on heavily by Federal agencies to monitor progress under construction grants and subgrants. The Federal agency will require additional formal performance reports only when considered necessary, and never more frequently than quarterly.

(d) *Significant developments.* Events may occur between the scheduled performance reporting dates which have significant impact upon the grant or subgrant supported activity. In such cases, the grantee must inform the Federal agency as soon as the following types of conditions become known:

(1) Problems, delays, or adverse conditions which will materially impair the ability to meet the objective of the award. This disclosure must include a statement of the action taken, or contemplated, and any assistance needed to resolve the situation.

(2) Favorable developments which enable meeting time schedules and objectives sooner or at less cost than anticipated or producing more beneficial results than originally planned.

(e) Federal agencies may make site visits as warranted by program needs.

(f) *Waivers, extensions.* (1) Federal agencies may waive any performance report required by this part if not needed.

(2) The grantee may waive any performance report from a subgrantee when not needed. The grantee may extend the due date for any performance report from a subgrantee if the grantee will still be able to meet its performance reporting obligations to the Federal agency.

§ 1403.41 Financial reporting.

(a) *General.* (1) Except as provided in paragraphs (a) (2) and (5) of this section, grantees will use only the forms specified in paragraphs (a) through (e) of this section, and such supplementary or other forms as may from time to time be authorized by OMB, for:

(i) Submitting financial reports to Federal agencies, or

(ii) Requesting advances or reimbursements when letters of credit are not used.

(2) Grantees need not apply the forms prescribed in this section in dealing with their subgrantees. However, grantees shall not impose more burdensome requirements on subgrantees.

(3) Grantees shall follow all applicable standard and supplemental Federal agency instructions approved by OMB to the extent required under the Paperwork Reduction Act of 1980 for use in connection with forms specified in paragraphs (b) through (e) of this section. Federal agencies may issue substantive supplementary instructions only with the approval of OMB. Federal agencies may shade out or instruct the grantee to disregard any line item that the Federal agency finds unnecessary for its decision making purposes.

(4) Grantees will not be required to submit more than the original and two copies of forms required under this part.

(5) Federal agencies may provide computer outputs to grantees to expedite or contribute to the accuracy of reporting. Federal agencies may accept the required information from grantees in machine usable format or computer printouts instead of prescribed forms.

(6) Federal agencies may waive any report required by this section if not needed.

(7) Federal agencies may extend the due date of any financial report upon receiving a justified request from a grantee.

(b) *Financial Status Report*—(1) *Form.* Grantees will use Standard Form 269 or 269A, Financial Status Report, to report the status of funds for all nonconstruction grants and for construction grants when required in accordance with paragraph § 1403.41(e)(2)(iii) of this section.

(2) *Accounting basis.* Each grantee will report program outlays and program income on a cash or accrual basis as prescribed by the awarding agency. If the Federal agency requires accrual information and the grantee's accounting records are not normally kept on the accrual basis, the grantee shall not be

required to convert its accounting system but shall develop such accrual information through an analysis of the documentation on hand.

(3) *Frequency.* The Federal agency may prescribe the frequency of the report for each project or program. However, the report will not be required more frequently than quarterly. If the Federal agency does not specify the frequency of the report, it will be submitted annually. A final report will be required upon expiration or termination of grant support.

(4) *Due date.* When reports are required on a quarterly or semiannual basis, they will be due 30 days after the reporting period. When required on an annual basis, they will be due 90 days after the grant year. Final reports will be due 90 days after the expiration or termination of grant support.

(c) *Federal Cash Transactions Report*—(1) *Form.* (i) For grants paid by letter of credit, Treasury check advances or electronic transfer of funds, the grantee will submit the Standard Form 272, Federal Cash Transactions Report, and when necessary, its continuation sheet, Standard Form 272a, unless the terms of the award exempt the grantee from this requirement.

(ii) These reports will be used by the Federal agency to monitor cash advanced to grantees and to obtain disbursement or outlay information for each grant from grantees. The format of the report may be adapted as appropriate when reporting is to be accomplished with the assistance of automatic data processing equipment provided that the information to be submitted is not changed in substance.

(2) *Forecasts of Federal cash requirements.* Forecasts of Federal cash requirements may be required in the 'Remarks'' section of the report.

(3) *Cash in hands of subgrantees.* When considered necessary and feasible by the Federal agency, grantees may be required to report the amount of cash advances in excess of three days' needs in the hands of their subgrantees or contractors and to provide short narrative explanations of actions taken by the grantee to reduce the excess balances.

(4) *Frequency and due date.* Grantees must submit the report no later than 15 working days following the end of each quarter. However, where an advance either by letter of credit or electronic transfer of funds is authorized at an annualized rate of one million dollars or more, the Federal agency may require the report to be submitted within 15 working days following the end of each month.

(d) *Request for advance or reimbursement*—(1) *Advance payments.* Requests for Treasury check advance payments will be submitted on Standard Form 270, Request for Advance or Reimbursement. (This form will not be used for drawdowns under a letter of credit, electronic funds transfer or when Treasury check advance payments are made to the grantee automatically on a predetermined basis.)

(2) *Reimbursements.* Requests for reimbursement under nonconstruction grants will also be submitted on Standard Form 270. (For reimbursement requests under construction grants, see paragraph (e)(1) of this section.)

(3) The frequency for submitting payment requests is treated in § 1403.41(b)(3).

(e) *Outlay report and request for reimbursement for construction programs*—(1) *Grants that support construction activities paid by reimbursement method.* (i) Requests for reimbursement under construction grants will be submitted on Standard Form 271, Outlay Report and Request for Reimbursement for Construction Programs. Federal agencies may, however, prescribe the Request for Advance or Reimbursement form, specified in § 1403.41(d), instead of this form.

(ii) The frequency for submitting reimbursement requests is treated in § 1403.41(b)(3).

(2) *Grants that support construction activities paid by letter of credit, electronic funds transfer or Treasury check advance.* (i) When a construction grant is paid by letter of credit, electronic funds transfer or Treasury check advances, the grantee will report its outlays to the Federal agency using Standard Form 271, Outlay Report and Request for Reimbursement for Construction Programs. The Federal agency will provide any necessary special instruction. However, frequency and

243

due date shall be governed by § 1403.41(b) (3) and (4).

(ii) When a construction grant is paid by Treasury check advances based on periodic requests from the grantee, the advances will be requested on the form specified in § 1403.41(d).

(iii) The Federal agency may substitute the Financial Status Report specified in § 1403.41(b) for the Outlay Report and Request for Reimbursement for Construction Programs.

(3) *Accounting basis.* The accounting basis for the Outlay Report and Request for Reimbursement for Construction Programs shall be governed by § 1403.41(b)(2).

§ 1403.42 Retention and access requirements for records.

(a) *Applicability.* (1) This section applies to all financial and programmatic records, supporting documents, statistical records, and other records of grantees or subgrantees which are:

(i) Required to be maintained by the terms of this Part, program regulations or the grant agreement, or

(ii) Otherwise reasonably considered as pertinent to program regulations or the grant agreement.

(2) This section does not apply to records maintained by contractors or subcontractors. For a requirement to place a provision concerning records in certain kinds of contracts, see § 1403.36(i)(10).

(b) *Length of retention period.* (1) Except as otherwise provided, records must be retained for three years from the starting date specified in paragraph (c) of this section.

(2) If any litigation, claim, negotiation, audit or other action involving the records has been started before the expiration of the 3-year period, the records must be retained until completion of the action and resolution of all issues which arise from it, or until the end of the regular 3-year period, whichever is later.

(3) To avoid duplicate recordkeeping, awarding agencies may make special arrangements with grantees and subgrantees to retain any records which are continuously needed for joint use. The awarding agency will request transfer of records to its custody when it determines that the records possess long-term retention value. When the records are transferred to or maintained by the Federal agency, the 3-year retention requirement is not applicable to the grantee or subgrantees.

(c) *Starting date of retention period*—(1) *General.* When grant support is continued or renewed at annual or other intervals, the retention period for the records of each funding period starts on the day the grantee or subgrantee submits to the awarding agency its single or last expenditure report for that period. However, if grant support is continued or renewed quarterly, the retention period for each year's records starts on the day the grantee submits its expenditure report for the last quarter of the Federal fiscal year. In all other cases, the retention period starts on the day the grantee submits its final expenditure report. If an expenditure report has been waived, the retention period starts on the day the report would have been due.

(2) *Real property and equipment records.* The retention period for real property and equipment records starts from the date of the disposition or replacement or transfer at the direction of the awarding agency.

(3) *Records for income transactions after grant or subgrant support.* In some cases grantees must report income after the period of grant support. Where there is such a requirement, the retention period for the records pertaining to the earning of the income starts from the end of the grantee's fiscal year in which the income is earned.

(4) *Indirect cost rate proposals, cost allocations plans, etc.* This paragraph applies to the following types of documents, and their supporting records: indirect cost rate computations or proposals, cost allocation plans, and any similar accounting computations of the rate at which a particular group of costs is chargeable (such as computer usage chargeback rates or composite fringe benefit rates).

(i) *If submitted for negotiation.* If the proposal, plan, or other computation is required to be submitted to the Federal Government (or to the grantee) to form the basis for negotiation of the rate, then the 3-year retention period for its supporting records starts from the date of such submission.

(ii) *If not submitted for negotiation.* If the proposal, plan, or other computation is not required to be submitted to the Federal Government (or to the grantee) for negotiation purposes, then the 3-year retention period for the proposal plan, or computation and its supporting records starts from end of the fiscal year (or other accounting period) covered by the proposal, plan, or other computation.

(d) *Substitution of microfilm.* Copies made by microfilming, photocopying, or similar methods may be substituted for the original records.

(e) *Access to records*—(1) *Records of grantees and subgrantees.* The awarding agency and the Comptroller General of the United States, or any of their authorized representatives, shall have the right of access to any pertinent books, documents, papers, or other records of grantees and subgrantees which are pertinent to the grant, in order to make audits, examinations, excerpts, and transcripts.

(2) *Expiration of right of access.* The rights of access in this section must not be limited to the required retention period but shall last as long as the records are retained.

(f) *Restrictions on public access.* The Federal Freedom of Information Act (5 U.S.C. 552) does not apply to records. Unless required by Federal, State, or local law, grantees and subgrantees are not required to permit public access to their records.

§1403.43 Enforcement.

(a) *Remedies for noncompliance.* If a grantee or subgrantee materially fails to comply with any term of an award, whether stated in a Federal statute or regulation, an assurance, in a State plan or application, a notice of award, or elsewhere, the awarding agency may take one or more of the following actions, as appropriate in the circumstances:

(1) Temporarily withhold cash payments pending correction of the deficiency by the grantee or subgrantee or more severe enforcement action by the awarding agency,

(2) Disallow (that is, deny both use of funds and matching credit for) all or part of the cost of the activity or action not in compliance,

(3) Wholly or partly suspend or terminate the current award for the grantee's or subgrantee's program,

(4) Withhold further awards for the program, or

(5) Take other remedies that may be legally available.

(b) *Hearings, appeals.* In taking an enforcement action, the awarding agency will provide the grantee or subgrantee an opportunity for such hearing, appeal, or other administrative proceeding to which the grantee or subgrantee is entitled under any statute or regulation applicable to the action involved.

(c) *Effects of suspension and termination.* Costs of grantee or subgrantee resulting from obligations incurred by the grantee or subgrantee during a suspension or after termination of an award are not allowable unless the awarding agency expressly authorizes them in the notice of suspension or termination or subsequently. Other grantee or subgrantee costs during suspension or after termination which are necessary and not reasonably avoidable are allowable if:

(1) The costs result from obligations which were properly incurred by the grantee or subgrantee before the effective date of suspension or termination, are not in anticipation of it, and, in the case of a termination, are noncancellable, and,

(2) The costs would be allowable if the award were not suspended or expired normally at the end of the funding period in which the termination takes effect.

(d) *Relationship to Debarment and Suspension.* The enforcement remedies identified in this section, including suspension and termination, do not preclude grantee or subgrantee from being subject to "Debarment and Suspension" under E.O. 12549 (see §1403.35).

§1403.44 Termination for convenience.

Except as provided in §1403.43 awards may be terminated in whole or in part only as follows:

(a) By the awarding agency with the consent of the grantee or subgrantee in which case the two parties shall agree upon the termination conditions, including the effective date and in the case of partial termination, the portion to be terminated, or

(b) By the grantee or subgrantee upon written notification to the awarding agency, setting forth the reasons for such termination, the effective date, and in the case of partial termination, the portion to be terminated. However, if, in the case of a partial termination, the awarding agency determines that the remaining portion of the award will not accomplish the purposes for which the award was made, the awarding agency may terminate the award in its entirety under either § 1403.43 or paragraph (a) of this section.

Subpart D—After-The-Grant Requirements

§ 1403.50   Closeout.

(a) *General.* The Federal agency will close out the award when it determines that all applicable administrative actions and all required work of the grant has been completed.

(b) *Reports.* Within 90 days after the expiration or termination of the grant, the grantee must submit all financial, performance, and other reports required as a condition of the grant. Upon request by the grantee, Federal agencies may extend this time frame. These may include but are not limited to:

(1) Final performance or progress report.

(2) Financial Status Report (SF 269) or Outlay Report and Request for Reimbursement for Construction Programs (SF–271) (as applicable).

(3) Final request for payment (SF–270) (if applicable).

(4) Invention disclosure (if applicable).

(5) Federally-owned property report: In accordance with § 1403.32(f), a grantee must submit an inventory of all federally owned property (as distinct from property acquired with grant funds) for which it is accountable and request disposition instructions from the Federal agency of property no longer needed.

(c) *Cost adjustment.* The Federal agency will, within 90 days after receipt of reports in paragraph (b) of this section, make upward or downward adjustments to the allowable costs.

(d) *Cash adjustments.* (1) The Federal agency will make prompt payment to the grantee for allowable reimbursable costs.

(2) The grantee must immediately refund to the Federal agency any balance of unobligated (unencumbered) cash advanced that is not authorized to be retained for use on other grants.

§ 1403.51   Later disallowances and adjustments.

The closeout of a grant does not affect:

(a) The Federal agency's right to disallow costs and recover funds on the basis of a later audit or other review;

(b) The grantee's obligation to return any funds due as a result of later refunds, corrections, or other transactions;

(c) Records retention as required in § 1403.42;

(d) Property management requirements in § 1403.31 and § 1403.32; and

(e) Audit requirements in § 1403.26.

§ 1403.52   Collection of amounts due.

(a) Any funds paid to a grantee in excess of the amount to which the grantee is finally determined to be entitled under the terms of the award constitute a debt to the Federal Government. If not paid within a reasonable period after demand, the Federal agency may reduce the debt by:

(1) Making an administrative offset against other requests for reimbursement,

(2) Withholding advance payments otherwise due to the grantee, or

(3) Other action permitted by law.

(b) Except where otherwise provided by statutes or regulations, the Federal agency will charge interest on an overdue debt in accordance with the Federal Claims Collection Standards (4 CFR ch. II). The date from which interest is computed is not extended by litigation or the filing of any form of appeal.

Subpart E—Entitlement [Reserved]

APPENDIX A TO PART 1403—OMB CIR-
    CULAR A–128, "AUDITS OF STATE AN
    LOCAL GOVERNMENTS"

Circular No. A–128
April 12, 1985.

To the Heads of Executive Departments and Establishments

Subject: Audits of State and Local Governments.

1. Purpose. This Circular is issued pursuant to the Single Audit Act of 1984, Pub. L. 98–502. It establishes audit requirements for State and local governments that receive Federal aid, and defines Federal responsibilities for implementing and monitoring those requirements.

2. Supersession. The Circular supersedes Attachment P, "Audit Requirements," of Circular A–102, "Uniform requirements for grants to State and local governments."

3. Background. The Single Audit Act builds upon earlier efforts to improve audits of Federal aid programs. The Act requires State or local governments that receive $100,000 or more a year in Federal funds to have an audit made for that year. Section 7505 of the Act requires the Director of the Office of Management and Budget to prescribe policies, procedures and guidelines to implement the Act. It specifies that the Director shall designate "cognizant" Federal agencies, determine criteria for making appropriate charges to federal programs for the cost of audits, and provide procedures to assure that small firms or firms owned and controlled by disadvantaged individuals have the opportunity to participate in contracts for single audits.

4. Policy. The Single Audit Act requires the following:

a. State or local governments that receive $100,000 or more a year in Federal financial assistance shall have an audit made in accordance with this Circular.

b. State or local governments that receive between $25,000 and $100,000 a year shall have an audit made in accordance with this Circular, or in accordance with Federal laws and regulations governing the programs they participate in.

c. State or local governments that receive less than $25,000 a year shall be exempt from compliance with the Act and other Federal audit requirements. These State and local governments shall be governed by audit requirements prescribed by State or local law or regulation.

d. Nothing in this paragraph exempts State or local governments from maintaining records of Federal financial assistance or from providing access to such records to Federal agencies, as provided for in Federal law or in Circular A–102, "Uniform requirements for grants to state or local governments."

5. Definitions. For the purposes of this Circular the following definitions from the Single Audit Act apply:

a. *Cognizant agency* means the Federal agency assigned by the Office of Management and Budget to carry out the responsibilities described in paragraph 11 of this Circular.

b. *Federal financial assistance* means assistance provided by a Federal agency in the form of grants, contracts, cooperative agreements, loans, loan guarantees, property, interest subsidies, insurance, or direct appropriations, but does not include direct Federal cash assistance to individuals. It includes awards received directly from Federal agencies, or indirectly through other units of States and local governments.

c. *Federal agency* has the same meaning as the term "agency" in section 551(1) of Title 5, United States Code.

d. *Generally accepted accounting principles* has the meaning specified in the generally accepted government auditing standards.

e. *Generally accepted government auditing standards* means the Standards For Audit of Government Organizations, Programs, Activities, and Functions, developed by the Comptroller General, dated February 27, 1981.

f. *Independent auditor* means:

(1) A State or local government auditor who meets the independence standards specified in generally accepted government auditing standards; or

(2) A public accountant who meets such independence standards.

g. *Internal controls* means the plan of organization and methods and procedures adopted by management to ensure that:

(1) Resource use is consistent with laws, regulations, and policies;

(2) Resources are safeguarded against waste, loss, and misuse; and

(3) Reliable data are obtained, maintained, and fairly disclosed in reports.

h. *Indian tribe* means any Indian tribe, band, nations, or other organized group or community, including any Alaskan Native village or regional or village corporations (as defined in, or established under, the Alaskan Native Claims Settlement Act) that is recognized by the United States as eligible for the special programs and services provided by the United States to Indians because of their status as Indians.

i. *Local government* means any unit of local government within a State, including a county, a borough, municipality, city, town, township, parish, local public authority, special district, school district, intrastate district, council of government, and any other instrumentality of local government.

j. *Major Federal Assistance Program*, as defined by Pub. L. 98–502, is described in the Attachment to this Circular.

k. *Public accountants* means those individuals who meet the qualification standards included in generally accepted government auditing standards for personnel performing government audits.

1. *State* means any State of the United States, the District of Columbia, the Commonwealth of Puerto Rico, the Virgin Islands, Guam, American Samoa, the Commonwealth of the Northern Mariana Islands, and the Trust Territory of the Pacific Islands, any instrumentality thereof, and any multi-State, regional, or interstate entity that has governmental functions and any Indian tribe.

m. *Subrecipient* means any person or government department, agency, or establishment that receives Federal financial assistance to carry out a program through a State or local government, but does not include an individual that is a beneficiary of such a program. A subrecipient may also be a direct recipient of Federal financial assistance.

6. Scope of audit. The Single Act provides that:

a. The audit shall be made by an independent auditor in accordance with generally accepted government auditing standards covering financial and compliance audits.

b. The audit shall cover the entire operations of a State or local government or, at the option of that government, it may cover departments, agencies or establishments that received, expended, or otherwise administered Federal financial assistance during the year. However, if a State or local government receives $25,000 or more in General Revenue Sharing Funds in a fiscal year, it shall have an audit of its entire operations. A series of audits of individual departments, agencies, and establishments for the same fiscal year may be considered a single audit.

c. Public hospitals and public colleges and universities may be excluded from State and local audits and the requirements of this Circular. However, if such entities are excluded, audits of these entities shall be made in accordance with statutory requirements and the provisions of Circular A–110, "Uniform requirements for grants to universities, hospitals, and other nonprofit organizations."

d. The auditor shall determine whether:

(1) The financial statements of the government, department, agency or establishment present fairly its financial position and the results of its financial operations in accordance with generally accepted accounting principles;

(2) The organization has internal accounting and other control systems to provide reasonable assurance that it is managing Federal financial assistance programs in compliance with applicable laws and regulations; and

(3) The organization has complied with laws and regulations that may have material effect on its financial statements and on each major Federal assistance program.

7. Frequency of audit. Audits shall be made annually unless the State or local government has, by January 1, 1987, a constitutional or statutory requirement for less frequent audits. For those governments, the cognizant agency shall permit biennial audits, covering both years, if the government so requests. It shall also honor requests for biennial audits by governments that have an administrative policy calling for audits less frequent than annual, but only for fiscal years beginning before January 1, 1987.

8. Internal control and compliance reviews. The Single Audit Act requires that the independent auditor determine and report on whether the organization has internal control systems to provide reasonable assurance that it is managing Federal assistance programs in compliance with applicable laws and regulations.

a. Internal control review. In order to provide this assurance the auditor must make a study and evaluation of internal control systems used in administering Federal assistance programs. The study and evaluation must be made whether or not the auditor intends to place reliance on such systems. As part of this review, the auditor shall:

(1) Test whether these internal control systems are functioning in accordance with prescribed procedures.

(2) Examine the recipient's system for monitoring subrecipients and obtaining and acting on subrecipient audit reports.

b. Compliance review. The law also requires the auditor to determine whether the organization has complied with laws and regulations that may have a material effect on each major Federal assistance program.

(1) In order to determine which major programs are to be tested for compliance, State and local governments shall identify in their accounts all Federal funds received and expended and the programs under which they were received. This shall include funds received directly from Federal agencies and through other State and local governments.

(2) The review must include the selection and testing of a representative number of charges from each major Federal assistance program. The selection and testing of transactions shall be based on the auditor's professional judgment considering such factors as the amount of expenditures for the program and the individual awards; the newness of the program or changes in its conditions; prior experience with the program, particularly as revealed in audits and other evaluations (e.g., inspections program reviews); the extent to which the program is carried out through subrecipients; the extent to which the program contracts for goods or services; the level to which the program is already subject to program reviews or other forms of independent oversight; the adequacy of the controls for ensuring compliance; the exception of adherence or lack of adherence to the applicable laws and regulations; and the potential impact of adverse findings.

(a) In making the test of transactions, the auditor shall determine whether:

—The amounts reported as expenditures were for allowable services, and

—The records show that those who received services or benefits were eligible to receive them.

(b) In addition to transaction testing, the auditor shall determine whether:

—Matching requirements, levels of effort and earmarking limitations were met,

—Federal financial reports and claims for advances and reimbursements contain information that is supported by the books and records from which the basic financial statements have been prepared, and

—Amounts claimed or used for matching were determined in accordance with OMB Circular A–87, "Cost principles for State and local governments," and Attachment F of Circular A–102, "Uniform requirements for grants to State and local governments."

(c) The principal compliance requirements of the largest Federal aid programs may be ascertained by referring to the Compliance Supplement for Single Audits of State and Local Governments, issued by OMB and available from the Government Printing Office. For those programs not covered in the Compliance Supplement, the auditor may ascertain compliance requirements by researching the statutes, regulations, and agreements governing individual programs.

(3) Transactions related to other Federal assistance programs that are selected in connection with examinations of financial statements and evaluations of internal controls shall be tested for compliance with Federal laws and regulations that apply to such transactions.

9. Subrecipients. State or local governments that receive Federal financial assistance and provide $25,000 or more of it in a fiscal year to a subrecipient shall:

a. Determine whether State or local subrecipients have met the audit requirements of this Circular and whether subrecipients covered by Circular A–110, "Uniform requirements for grants to universities, hospitals, and other nonprofit organizations," have met that requirement;

b. Determine whether the subrecipient spent Federal assistance funds provided in accordance with applicable laws and regulations. This may be accomplished by reviewing an audit of the subrecipient made in accordance with this Circular, Circular A–110, or through other means (e.g., program reviews) if the subrecipient has not yet had such an audit;

c. Ensure that appropriate corrective action is taken within six months after receipt of the audit report in instances of noncompliance with Federal laws and regulations;

d. Consider whether subrecipient audits necessitate adjustment of the recipient's own records; and

e. Require each subrecipient to permit independent auditors to have access to the records and financial statements as necessary to comply with this Circular.

10. Relation to other audit requirements. The Single Audit Act provides that an audit made in accordance with this Circular shall be in lieu of any financial or financial compliance audit required under individual Federal assistance programs. To the extent that a single audit provides Federal agencies with information and assurances they need to carry out their overall responsibilities, they shall rely upon and use such information. However, a Federal agency shall make any additional audits which are necessary to carry out its responsibilities under Federal law and regulation. Any additional Federal audit effort shall be planned and carried out in such a way as to avoid duplication.

a. The provisions of this Circular do not limit the authority of Federal agencies to make, or contract for audits and evaluations of Federal financial assistance programs, nor do they limit the authority of any Federal agency Inspector General or other Federal audit official.

b. The provisions of this Circular do not authorize any State or local government or subrecipient thereof to constrain Federal agencies, in any manner, from carrying out additional audits.

c. A Federal agency that makes or contracts for audits in addition to the audits made by recipients pursuant to this Circular shall, consistent with other applicable laws and regulations, arrange for funding the cost of such additional audits. Such additional audits include economy and efficiency audits, program results audits, and program evaluations.

11. Cognizant agency responsibilities. The Single Audit Act provides for cognizant Federal agencies to oversee the implementation of this Circular.

a. The Office of Management and Budget will assign cognizant agencies for States and their subdivisions and larger local governments and their subdivisions. Other Federal agencies may participate with an assigned cognizant agency, in order to fulfill the cognizance responsibilities. Smaller governments not assigned a cognizant agency will be under the general oversight of the Federal agency that provides them the most funds whether directly or indirectly.

b. A cognizant agency shall have the following responsibilities:

(1) Ensure that audits are made and reports are received in a timely manner and in accordance with the requirements of this Circular.

(2) Provide technical advice and liaison to State and local governments and independent auditors.

(3) Obtain or make quality control reviews of selected audits made by non-Federal audit organizations, and provide the results, when appropriate, to other interested organizations.

(4) Promptly inform other affected Federal agencies and appropriate Federal law enforcement officials of any reported illegal acts or irregularities. They should also inform State or local law enforcement and prosecuting authorities, if not advised by the recipient, of any violation of law within their jurisdiction.

(5) Advise the recipient of audits that have been found not to have met the requirements set forth in this Circular. In such instances, the recipient will be expected to work with the auditor to take corrective action. If corrective action is not taken, the cognizant agency shall notify the recipient and Federal awarding agencies of the facts and make recommendations for followup action. Major inadequacies or repetitive substandard performance of independent auditors shall be referred to appropriate professional bodies for disciplinary action.

(6) Coordinate, to the extent practicable, audits made by or for Federal agencies that are in addition to the audits made pursuant to this Circular; so that the additional audits build upon such audits.

(7) Oversee the resolution of audit findings that affect the programs of more than one agency.

12. Illegal acts or irregularities. If the auditor becomes aware of illegal acts or other irregularities, prompt notice shall be given to recipient management officials above the level of involvement. (See also paragraph 13(a)(3) below for the auditor's reporting responsibilities.) The recipient, in turn, shall promptly notify the cognizant agency of the illegal acts or irregularities and of proposed and actual actions, if any. Illegal acts and irregularities include such matters as conflicts of interest, falsification of records or reports, and misappropriations of funds or other assets.

13. Audit reports. Audit reports must be prepared at the completion of the audit. Reports serve many needs of State and local governments as well as meeting the requirements of the Single Audit Act.

a. The audit report shall state that the audit was made in accordance with the provisions of this Circular. The report shall be made up of at least:

(1) The auditor's report on financial statements and on a schedule of Federal assistance; the financial statements; and a schedule of Federal assistance, showing the total expenditures for each Federal assistance program as identified in the Catalog of Federal Domestic Assistance. Federal programs or grants that have not been assigned a catalog number shall be identified under the caption "other Federal assistance."

(2) The auditor's report on the study and evaluation of internal control systems must identify the organization's significant internal accounting controls, and those controls designed to provide reasonable assurance that Federal programs are being managed in compliance with laws and regulations. It must also identify the controls that were evaluated, the controls that were not evaluated, and the material weaknesses identified as a result of the evaluation.

(3) The auditor's report on compliance containing:

—A statement of positive assurance with respect to those items tested for compliance, including compliance with law and regulations pertaining to financial reports and claims for advances and reimbursements;

—Negative assurance on those items not tested;

—A summary of all instances of noncompliance; and

—An identification of total amounts questioned, if any, for each Federal assistance award, as a result of noncompliance.

b. The three parts of the audit report may be bound into a single report, or presented at the same time as separate documents.

c. All fraud abuse, or illegal acts or indications of such acts, including all questioned costs found as the result of these acts that auditors become aware of, should normally be covered in a separate written report submitted in accordance with paragraph 13f.

d. In addition to the audit report, the recipient shall provide comments on the findings and recommendations in the report, including a plan for corrective action taken or planned and comments on the status of corrective action taken on prior findings. If corrective action is not necessary, a statement describing the reason it is not should accompany the audit report.

e. The reports shall be made available by the State or local government for public inspection within 30 days after the completion of the audit.

f. In accordance with generally accepted government audit standards, reports shall be submitted by the auditor to the organization audited and to those requiring or arranging for the audit. In addition, the recipient shall submit copies of the reports to each Federal department or agency that provided Federal assistance funds to the recipient. Subrecipients shall submit copies to recipients that provided them Federal assistance funds. The reports shall be sent within 30 days after the completion of the audit, but no later than one year after the end of the audit period unless a longer period is agreed to with the cognizant agency.

g. Recipients of more than $100,000 in Federal funds shall submit one copy of the audit report within 30 days after issuance to a central clearinghouse to be designated by the Office of Management and Budget. The clearinghouse will keep completed audits on file and follow up with State and local governments that have not submitted required audit reports.

h. Recipients shall keep audit reports on file for three years from their issuance.

14. Audit Resolution. As provided in paragraph 11, the cognizant agency shall be responsible for monitoring the resolution of audit findings that affect the programs of more than one Federal agency. Resolution of findings that relate to the programs of a single Federal agency will be the responsibility of the recipient and that agency. Alternate arrangements may be made on a case-by-case basis by agreement among the agencies concerned.

Resolution shall be made within six months after receipt of the report by the Federal departments and agencies. Corrective action should proceed as rapidly as possible.

15. Audit workpapers and reports. Workpapers and reports shall be retained for a minimum of three years from the date of the audit report, unless the auditor is notified in writing by the cognizant agency to extend the retention period. Audit workpapers shall be made available upon request to the cognizant agency or its designee or the General Accounting Office, at the completion of the audit.

16. Audit Costs. The cost of audits made in accordance with the provisions of this Circular are allowable charges to Federal assistance programs.

a. The charges may be considered a direct cost or an allocated indirect cost, determined in accordance with the provision of Circular A-87, "Cost principles for State and local governments."

b. Generally, the percentage of costs charged to Federal assistance programs for a single audit shall not exceed the percentage that Federal funds expended represent of total funds expended by the recipient during the fiscal year. The percentage may be exceeded, however, if appropriate documentation demonstrates higher actual cost.

17. Sanctions. The Single Audit Act provides that no cost may be charged to Federal assistance programs for audits required by the Act that are not made in accordance with this Circular. In cases of continued inability or unwillingness to have a proper audit, Federal agencies must consider other appropriate sanctions including:

—Withhodling a percentage of assistance payments until the audit is completed satisfactorily,

—Withholding or disallowing overhead costs, and

—Suspending the Federal assistance agreement until the audit is made.

18. Auditor Selection. In arranging for audit services State and local governments shall follow the procurement standards prescribed by Attachment O of Circular A-102, "Uniform requirements for grants to State and local governments." The standards provide that while recipients are encouraged to enter into intergovernmental agreements for audit and other services, analysis should be made to determine whether it would be more economical to purchase the services from private firms. In instances where use of such intergovernmental agreements are required by State statutes (e.g., audit services) these statutes will take precedence.

19. Small and Minority Audit Firms. Small audit firms and audit firms owned and controlled by socially and economically disadvantaged individuals shall have the maximum practicable opportunity to participate in contracts awarded to fulfill the requirements of this Circular. Recipients of Federal assistance shall take the following steps to further this goal:

a. Assure that small audit firms and audit firms owned and controlled by socially and economically disadvantaged individuals are used to the fullest extent practicable.

b. Make information on forthcoming opportunities available and arrange time frames for the audit so as to encourage and facilitate participation by small audit firms and audit firms owned and controlled by socially and economically disadvantaged individuals.

c. Consider in the contract process whether firms competing for larger audits intend to subcontract with small audit firms and audit firms owned and controlled by socially and economically disadvantaged individuals.

d. Encourage contracting with small audit firms or audit firms owned and controlled by socially and economically disadvantaged individuals which have traditionally audited government programs and, in such cases where this is not possible, assure that these firms are given consideration for audit subcontracting opportunities.

e. Encourage contracting with consortiums of small audit firms as described in paragraph (a) above when a contract is too large for an individual small audit firm or audit firm owned and controlled by socially and economically disadvantaged individuals.

f. Use the services and assistance, as appropriate, of such organizations as the Small Business Administration in the solicitation and utilization of small audit firms or audit firms owned and controlled by socially and economically disadvantaged individuals.

20. Reporting. Each Federal agency will report to the Director of OMB on or before March 1, 1987, and annually thereafter on the effectiveness of State and local governments in carrying out the provisions of this Circular. The report must identify each State or local government or Indian tribe that, in the

opinion of the agency, is failing to comply with Circular.

21. Regulations. Each Federal agency shall include the provisions of this Circular in its regulations implementing the Single Audit Act.

22. Effective date. This Circular is effective upon publication and shall apply to fiscal years of State and local governments that begin after December 31, 1984. Earlier implementation is encouraged. However, until it is implemented, the audit provisions of Attachment P to Circular A–102 shall continue to be observed.

23. Inquiries. All questions or inquiries should be addressed to Financial Management Division, Office of Management and Budget, telephone number (202) 395–3993.

24. Sunset review date. This Circular shall have an independent policy review to ascertain its effectiveness three years from the date of issuance.

David A. Stockman,
Director.

CIRCULAR A–128 ATTACHMENT

DEFINITION OF MAJOR PROGRAM AS PROVIDED
IN PUB. L. 98–502

"Major Federal Assistance Program," for State and local governments having Federal assistance expenditures between $100,000 and $100,000,000. means any program for which Federal expenditures during the applicable year exceed the larger of $300,000, or 3 percent of such total expenditures.

Where total expenditures of Federal assistance exceed $100,000,000, the following criteria apply:

Total expenditures of Federal financial assistance for all programs		Major Federal assistance program means any program that exceeds
More than	But less than	
$100 million	1 billion	$3 million
1 billion	2 billion	4 million
2 billion	3 billion	7 million
3 billion	4 billion	10 million
4 billion	5 billion	13 million
5 billion	6 billion	16 million
6 billion	7 billion	19 million
Over 7 billion		20 million

[57 FR 55092, Nov. 24, 1992; 58 FR 26185, Apr. 30, 1993]

PART 1404—GOVERNMENTWIDE DEBARMENT AND SUSPENSION (NONPROCUREMENT)

Sec.
1404.25   How is this part organized?
1404.50   How is this part written?
1404.75   Do terms in this part have special meanings?

Subpart A—General

1404.100   What does this part do?
1404.105   Does this part apply to me?
1404.110   What is the purpose of the nonprocurement debarment and suspension system?
1404.115   How does an exclusion restrict a person's involvement in covered transactions?
1404.120   May we grant an exception to let an excluded person participate in a covered transaction?
1404.125   Does an exclusion under the nonprocurement system affect a person's eligibility for Federal procurement contracts?
1404.130   Does exclusion under the Federal procurement system affect a person's eligibility to participate in nonprocurement transactions?
1404.135   May the Office of National Drug Control Policy exclude a person who is not currently participating in a nonprocurement transaction?
1404.140   How do I know if a person is excluded?
1404.145   Does this part address persons who are disqualified, as well as those who are excluded from nonprocurement transactions?

Subpart B—Covered Transactions

1404.200   What is a covered transaction?
1404.205   Why is it important to know if a particular transaction is a covered transaction?
1404.210   Which nonprocurement transactions are covered transactions?
1404.215   Which nonprocurement transactions are not covered transactions?
1404.220   Are any procurement contracts included as covered transactions?
1404.225   How do I know if a transaction in which I may participate is a covered transaction?

Subpart C—Responsibilities of Participants Regarding Transactions

DOING BUSINESS WITH OTHER PERSONS

1404.300   What must I do before I enter into a covered transaction with another person at the next lower tier?
1404.305   May I enter into a covered transaction with an excluded or disqualified person?
1404.310   What must I do if a Federal agency excludes a person with whom I am already doing business in a covered transaction?
1404.315   May I use the services of an excluded person as a principal under a covered transaction?

Office of National Drug Control Policy

ctt 144

1404.320 Must I verify that principals of my covered transactions are eligible to participate?

1404.325 What happens if I do business with an excluded person in a covered transaction?

1404.330 What requirements must I pass down to persons at lower tiers with whom I intend to do business?

DISCLOSING INFORMATION—PRIMARY TIER PARTICIPANTS

1404.335 What information must I provide before entering into a covered transaction with the Office of National Drug Control Policy?

1404.340 If I disclose unfavorable information required under §1404.335, will I be prevented from participating in the transaction?

1404.345 What happens if I fail to disclose the information required under §1404.335?

1404.350 What must I do if I learn of the information required under §1404.335 after entering into a covered transaction with the Office of National Drug Control Policy?

DISCLOSING INFORMATION—LOWER TIER PARTICIPANTS

1404.355 What information must I provide to a higher tier participant before entering into a covered transaction with that participant?

1404.360 What happens if I fail to disclose the information required under §1404.355?

1404.365 What must I do if I learn of information required under §1404.355 after entering into a covered transaction with a higher tier participant?

Subpart D—Responsibilities of Office of National Drug Control Policy Officials Regarding Transactions

1404.400 May I enter into a transaction with an excluded or disqualified person?

1404.405 May I enter into a covered transaction with a participant if a principal of the transaction is excluded?

1404.410 May I approve a participant's use of the services of an excluded person?

1404.415 What must I do if a Federal agency excludes the participant or a principal after I enter into a covered transaction?

1404.420 May I approve a transaction with an excluded or disqualified person at a lower tier?

1404.425 When do I check to see if a person is excluded or disqualified?

1404.430 How do I check to see if a person is excluded or disqualified?

1404.435 What must I require of a primary tier participant?

1404.440 What method do I use to communicate those requirements to participants?

1404.445 What action may I take if a primary tier participant knowingly does business with an excluded or disqualified person?

1404.450 What action may I take if a primary tier participant fails to disclose the information required under §1404.335?

1404.455 What may I do if a lower tier participant fails to disclose the information required under §1404.355 to the next higher tier?

Subpart E—Excluded Parties List System

1404.500 What is the purpose of the Excluded Parties List System (EPLS)?

1404.505 Who uses the EPLS?

1404.510 Who maintains the EPLS?

1404.515 What specific information is in the EPLS?

1404.520 Who places the information into the EPLS?

1404.525 Whom do I ask if I have questions about a person in the EPLS?

1404.530 Where can I find the EPLS?

Subpart F—General Principles Relating to Suspension and Debarment Actions

1404.600 How do suspension and debarment actions start?

1404.605 How does suspension differ from debarment?

1404.610 What procedures does the Office of National Drug Control Policy use in suspension and debarment actions?

1404.615 How does the Office of National Drug Control Policy notify a person of a suspension and debarment action?

1404.620 Do Federal agencies coordinate suspension and debarment actions?

1404.625 What is the scope of a suspension or debarment action?

1404.630 May the Office of National Drug Control Policy impute the conduct of one person to another?

1404.635 May the Office of National Drug Control Policy settle a debarment or suspension action?

1404.640 May a settlement include a voluntary exclusion?

1404.645 Do other Federal agencies know if the Office of National Drug Control Policy agrees to a voluntary exclusion?

Subpart G—Suspension

1404.700 When may the suspending official issue a suspension?

1404.705 What does the suspending official consider in issuing a suspension?

1404.710 When does a suspension take effect?

1404.715 What notice does the suspending official give me if I am suspended?

253

Subpart H—Debarment

Subpart I—Definitions

Subpart J [Reserved]

APPENDIX TO PART 1404—COVERED TRANSACTIONS

AUTHORITY: E.O. 12549 3 CFR 1986 Comp., p. 189; E.O. 12689 3 CFR 1989 Comp., p. 235; sec. 2455, Pub. L. 103–355, 108 Stat. 3327 (31 U.S.C. 6101 note); 21 U.S.C. 1701.

SOURCE: 68 FR 66544, 66580, 66581, Nov. 26 2003, unless otherwise noted.

§ 1404.25   How is this part organized?

(a) This part is subdivided into ten subparts. Each subpart contains information related to a broad topic or specific audience with special responsibilities, as shown in the following table:

In subpart . . .	You will find provisions related to . . .
A	general information about this rule.
B	the types of Office of National Drug Control Policy transactions that are covered by the Governmentwide nonprocurement suspension and debarment system.
C	the responsibilities of persons who participate in covered transactions.
D	the responsibilities of Office of National Drug Control Policy officials who are authorized to enter into covered transactions.
E	the responsibilities of Federal agencies for the Excluded Parties List System (Disseminated by the General Services Administration).
F	the general principles governing suspension, debarment, voluntary exclusion and settlement.
G	suspension actions.
H	debarment actions.
I	definitions of terms used in this part.

In subpart . . .	You will find provisions related to . . .
J	[Reserved]

(b) The following table shows which subparts may be of special interest to you, depending on who you are:

If you are . . .	See subpart(s) . . .
(1) a participant or principal in a non-procurement transaction.	A, B, C, and I.
(2) a respondent in a suspension action	A, B, F, G and I.
(3) a respondent in a debarment action	A, B, F, H and I.
(4) a suspending official	A, B, D, E, F, G and I.
(5) a debarring official	A, B, D, E, F, H and I.
(6) a (n) Office of National Drug Control Policy official authorized to enter into a covered transaction.	A, B, D, E and I.
(7) Reserved	J.

§ 1404.50 How is this part written?

(a) This part uses a "plain language" format to make it easier for the general public and business community to use. The section headings and text, often in the form of questions and answers, must be read together.

(b) Pronouns used within this part, such as "I" and "you," change from subpart to subpart depending on the audience being addressed. The pronoun "we" always is the Office of National Drug Control Policy.

(c) The "Covered Transactions" diagram in the appendix to this part shows the levels or "tiers" at which the Office of National Drug Control Policy enforces an exclusion under this part.

§ 1404.75 Do terms in this part have special meanings?

This part uses terms throughout the text that have special meaning. Those terms are defined in Subpart I of this part. For example, three important terms are—

(a) *Exclusion or excluded*, which refers only to discretionary actions taken by a suspending or debarring official under this part or the Federal Acquisition Regulation (48 CFR part 9, subpart 9.4);

(b) *Disqualification or disqualified*, which refers to prohibitions under specific statutes, executive orders (other than Executive Order 12549 and Executive Order 12689), or other authorities.

Disqualifications frequently are not subject to the discretion of an agency official, may have a different scope than exclusions, or have special conditions that apply to the disqualification; and

(c) *Ineligibility or ineligible*, which generally refers to a person who is either excluded or disqualified.

Subpart A—General

§ 1404.100 What does this part do?

This part adopts a governmentwide system of debarment and suspension for Office of National Drug Control Policy nonprocurement activities. It also provides for reciprocal exclusion of persons who have been excluded under the Federal Acquisition Regulation, and provides for the consolidated listing of all persons who are excluded, or disqualified by statute, executive order, or other legal authority. This part satisfies the requirements in section 3 of Executive Order 12549, "Debarment and Suspension" (3 CFR 1986 Comp., p. 189), Executive Order 12689, "Debarment and Suspension" (3 CFR 1989 Comp., p. 235) and 31 U.S.C. 6101 note (Section 2455, Public Law 103–355, 108 Stat. 3327).

§ 1404.105 Does this part apply to me?

Portions of this part (see table at § 1404.25(b)) apply to you if you are a(n)—

(a) Person who has been, is, or may reasonably be expected to be, a participant or principal in a covered transaction;

(b) Respondent (a person against whom the Office of National Drug Control Policy has initiated a debarment or suspension action);

(c) Office of National Drug Control Policy debarring or suspending official; or

(d) Office of National Drug Control Policy official who is authorized to enter into covered transactions with non-Federal parties.

§ 1404.110 What is the purpose of the nonprocurement debarment and suspension system?

(a) To protect the public interest, the Federal Government ensures the integrity of Federal programs by conducting business only with responsible persons.

(b) A Federal agency uses the nonprocurement debarment and suspension system to exclude from Federal programs persons who are not presently responsible.

(c) An exclusion is a serious action that a Federal agency may take only to protect the public interest. A Federal agency may not exclude a person or commodity for the purposes of punishment.

§ 1404.115 How does an exclusion restrict a person's involvement in covered transactions?

With the exceptions stated in §§ 1404.120, 1404.315, and 1404.420, a person who is excluded by the Office of National Drug Control Policy or any other Federal agency may not:

(a) Be a participant in a(n) Office of National Drug Control Policy transaction that is a covered transaction under subpart B of this part;

(b) Be a participant in a transaction of any other Federal agency that is a covered transaction under that agency's regulation for debarment and suspension; or

(c) Act as a principal of a person participating in one of those covered transactions.

§ 1404.120 May we grant an exception to let an excluded person participate in a covered transaction?

(a) The Director of National Drug Control Policy may grant an exception permitting an excluded person to participate in a particular covered transaction. If the Director of National Drug Control Policy grants an exception, the exception must be in writing and state the reason(s) for deviating from the governmentwide policy in Executive Order 12549.

(b) An exception granted by one agency for an excluded person does not extend to the covered transactions of another agency.

§ 1404.125 Does an exclusion under the nonprocurement system affect a person's eligibility for Federal procurement contracts?

If any Federal agency excludes a person under its nonprocurement common rule on or after August 25, 1995, the excluded person is also ineligible to participate in Federal procurement transactions under the FAR. Therefore, an exclusion under this part has reciprocal effect in Federal procurement transactions.

§ 1404.130 Does exclusion under the Federal procurement system affect a person's eligibility to participate in nonprocurement transactions?

If any Federal agency excludes a person under the FAR on or after August 25, 1995, the excluded person is also ineligible to participate in nonprocurement covered transactions under this part. Therefore, an exclusion under the FAR has reciprocal effect in Federal nonprocurement transactions.

§ 1404.135 May the Office of National Drug Control Policy exclude a person who is not currently participating in a nonprocurement transaction?

Given a cause that justifies an exclusion under this part, we may exclude any person who has been involved, is currently involved, or may reasonably be expected to be involved in a covered transaction.

§ 1404.140 How do I know if a person is excluded?

Check the *Excluded Parties List System* (EPLS) to determine whether a person is excluded. The General Services Administration (GSA) maintains the *EPLS* and makes it available, as detailed in subpart E of this part. When a Federal agency takes an action to exclude a person under the nonprocurement or procurement debarment and suspension system, the agency enters the information about the excluded person into the *EPLS*.

§ 1404.145 Does this part address persons who are disqualified, as well as those who are excluded from nonprocurement transactions?

Except if provided for in Subpart J of this part, this part—

(a) Addresses disqualified persons only to—

(1) Provide for their inclusion in the *EPLS;* and

(2) State responsibilities of Federal agencies and participants to check for disqualified persons before entering into covered transactions.

(b) Does not specify the—

(1) Office of National Drug Control Policy transactions for which a disqualified person is ineligible. Those transactions vary on a case-by-case basis, because they depend on the language of the specific statute, Executive order, or regulation that caused the disqualification;

(2) Entities to which the disqualification applies; or

(3) Process that the agency uses to disqualify a person. Unlike exclusion, disqualification is frequently not a discretionary action that a Federal agency takes.

Subpart B—Covered Transactions

§ 1404.200 What is a covered transaction?

A covered transaction is a nonprocurement or procurement transaction that is subject to the prohibitions of this part. It may be a transaction at—

(a) The primary tier, between a Federal agency and a person (see appendix to this part); or

(b) A lower tier, between a participant in a covered transaction and another person.

§ 1404.205 Why is it important if a particular transaction is a covered transaction?

The importance of a covered transaction depends upon who you are.

(a) As a participant in the transaction, you have the responsibilities laid out in Subpart C of this part. Those include responsibilities to the person or Federal agency at the next higher tier from whom you received the transaction, if any. They also include responsibilities if you subsequently enter into other covered transactions with persons at the next lower tier.

(b) As a Federal official who enters into a primary tier transaction, you

have the responsibilities laid out in subpart D of this part.

(c) As an excluded person, you may not be a participant or principal in the transaction unless—

(1) The person who entered into the transaction with you allows you to continue your involvement in a transaction that predates your exclusion, as permitted under § 1404.310 or § 1404.415; or

(2) A(n) Office of National Drug Control Policy official obtains an exception from the Director of National Drug Control Policy to allow you to be involved in the transaction, as permitted under § 1404.120.

§ 1404.210 Which nonprocurement transactions are covered transactions?

All nonprocurement transactions, as defined in § 1404.970, are covered transactions unless listed in § 1404.215. (See appendix to this part.)

§ 1404.215 Which nonprocurement transactions are not covered transactions?

The following types of nonprocurement transactions are not covered transactions:

(a) A direct award to—

(1) A foreign government or foreign governmental entity;

(2) A public international organization;

(3) An entity owned (in whole or in part) or controlled by a foreign government; or

(4) Any other entity consisting wholly or partially of one or more foreign governments or foreign governmental entities.

(b) A benefit to an individual as a personal entitlement without regard to the individual's present responsibility (but benefits received in an individual's business capacity are not excepted). For example, if a person receives social security benefits under the Supplemental Security Income provisions of the Social Security Act, 42 U.S.C. 1301 et seq., those benefits are not covered transactions and, therefore, are not affected if the person is excluded.

(c) Federal employment.

(d) A transaction that the Office of National Drug Control Policy needs to respond to a national or agency-recognized emergency or disaster.

(e) A permit, license, certificate, or similar instrument issued as a means to regulate public health, safety, or the environment, unless the Office of National Drug Control Policy specifically designates it to be a covered transaction.

(f) An incidental benefit that results from ordinary governmental operations.

(g) Any other transaction if the application of an exclusion to the transaction is prohibited by law.

§ 1404.220 **Are any procurement contracts included as covered transactions?**

(a) Covered transactions under this part—

(1) Do not include any procurement contracts awarded directly by a Federal agency; but

(2) Do include some procurement contracts awarded by non-Federal participants in nonprocurement covered transactions (see appendix to this part).

(b) Specifically, a contract for goods or services is a covered transaction if any of the following applies:

(1) The contract is awarded by a participant in a nonprocurement transaction that is covered under § 1404.210, and the amount of the contract is expected to equal or exceed $25,000.

(2) The contract requires the consent of a(n) Office of National Drug Control Policy official. In that case, the contract, regardless of the amount, always is a covered transaction, and it does not matter who awarded it. For example, it could be a subcontract awarded by a contractor at a tier below a nonprocurement transaction, as shown in the appendix to this part.

(3) The contract is for federally-required audit services.

§ 1404.225 **How do I know if a transaction in which I may participate is a covered transaction?**

As a participant in a transaction, you will know that it is a covered transaction because the agency regulations governing the transaction, the appropriate agency official, or participant at the next higher tier who enters into the transaction with you, will tell you that you must comply with applicable portions of this part.

Subpart C—Responsibilities of Participants Regarding Transactions

DOING BUSINESS WITH OTHER PERSONS

§ 1404.300 **What must I do before I enter into a covered transaction with another person at the next lower tier?**

When you enter into a covered transaction with another person at the next lower tier, you must verify that the person with whom you intend to do business is not excluded or disqualified. You do this by:

(a) Checking the *EPLS;* or

(b) Collecting a certification from that person if allowed by this rule; or

(c) Adding a clause or condition to the covered transaction with that person.

§ 1404.305 **May I enter into a covered transaction with an excluded or disqualified person?**

(a) You as a participant may not enter into a covered transaction with an excluded person, unless the Office of National Drug Control Policy grants an exception under § 1404.120.

(b) You may not enter into any transaction with a person who is disqualified from that transaction, unless you have obtained an exception under the disqualifying statute, Executive order, or regulation.

§ 1404.310 **What must I do if a Federal agency excludes a person with whom I am already doing business in a covered transaction?**

(a) You as a participant may continue covered transactions with an excluded person if the transactions were in existence when the agency excluded the person. However, you are not required to continue the transactions, and you may consider termination. You should make a decision about whether to terminate and the type of termination action, if any, only after a thorough review to ensure that the action is proper and appropriate.

(b) You may not renew or extend covered transactions (other than no-cost time extensions) with any excluded person, unless the Office of National Drug Control Policy grants an exception under §1404.120.

§1404.315 May I use the services of an excluded person as a principal under a covered transaction?

(a) You as a participant may continue to use the services of an excluded person as a principal under a covered transaction if you were using the services of that person in the transaction before the person was excluded. However, you are not required to continue using that person's services as a principal. You should make a decision about whether to discontinue that person's services only after a thorough review to ensure that the action is proper and appropriate.

(b) You may not begin to use the services of an excluded person as a principal under a covered transaction unless the Office of National Drug Control Policy grants an exception under §1404.120.

§1404.320 Must I verify that principals of my covered transactions are eligible to participate?

Yes, you as a participant are responsible for determining whether any of your principals of your covered transactions is excluded or disqualified from participating in the transaction. You may decide the method and frequency by which you do so. You may, but you are not required to, check the *EPLS*.

§1404.325 What happens if I do business with an excluded person in a covered transaction?

If as a participant you knowingly do business with an excluded person, we may disallow costs, annul or terminate the transaction, issue a stop work order, debar or suspend you, or take other remedies as appropriate.

§1404.330 What requirements must I pass down to persons at lower tiers with whom I intend to do business?

Before entering into a covered transaction with a participant at the next lower tier, you must require that participant to—

(a) Comply with this subpart as a condition of participation in the transaction. You may do so using any method(s), unless §1404.440 requires you to use specific methods.

(b) Pass the requirement to comply with this subpart to each person with whom the participant enters into a covered transaction at the next lower tier.

DISCLOSING INFORMATION—PRIMARY TIER PARTICIPANTS

§1404.335 What information must I provide before entering into a covered transaction with the Office of National Drug Control Policy?

Before you enter into a covered transaction at the primary tier, you as the participant must notify the Office of National Drug Control Policy office that is entering into the transaction with you, if you know that you or any of the principals for that covered transaction:

(a) Are presently excluded or disqualified;

(b) Have been convicted within the preceding three years of any of the offenses listed in §1404.800(a) or had a civil judgment rendered against you for one of those offenses within that time period;

(c) Are presently indicted for or otherwise criminally or civilly charged by a governmental entity (Federal, State or local) with commission of any of the offenses listed in §1404.800(a); or

(d) Have had one or more public transactions (Federal, State, or local) terminated within the preceding three years for cause or default.

§1404.340 If I disclose unfavorable information required under §1404.335, will I be prevented from participating in the transaction?

As a primary tier participant, your disclosure of unfavorable information about yourself or a principal under §1404.335 will not necessarily cause us to deny your participation in the covered transaction. We will consider the information when we determine whether to enter into the covered transaction. We also will consider any additional information or explanation that you elect to submit with the disclosed information.

259

§ 1404.345 What happens if I fail to disclose information required under § 1404.335?

If we later determine that you failed to disclose information under § 1404.335 that you knew at the time you entered into the covered transaction, we may—

(a) Terminate the transaction for material failure to comply with the terms and conditions of the transaction; or

(b) Pursue any other available remedies, including suspension and debarment.

§ 1404.350 What must I do if I learn of information required under § 1404.335 after entering into a covered transaction with the Office of National Drug Control Policy?

At any time after you enter into a covered transaction, you must give immediate written notice to the Office of National Drug Control Policy office with which you entered into the transaction if you learn either that—

(a) You failed to disclose information earlier, as required by § 1404.335; or

(b) Due to changed circumstances, you or any of the principals for the transaction now meet any of the criteria in § 1404.335.

DISCLOSING INFORMATION—LOWER TIER PARTICIPANTS

§ 1404.355 What information must I provide to a higher tier participant before entering into a covered transaction with that participant?

Before you enter into a covered transaction with a person at the next higher tier, you as a lower tier participant must notify that person if you know that you or any of the principals are presently excluded or disqualified.

§ 1404.360 What happens if I fail to disclose the information required under § 1404.355?

If we later determine that you failed to tell the person at the higher tier that you were excluded or disqualified at the time you entered into the covered transaction with that person, we may pursue any available remedies, including suspension and debarment.

§ 1404.365 What must I do if I learn of information required under § 1404.355 after entering into a covered transaction with a higher tier participant?

At any time after you enter into a lower tier covered transaction with a person at a higher tier, you must provide immediate written notice to that person if you learn either that—

(a) You failed to disclose information earlier, as required by § 1404.355; or

(b) Due to changed circumstances, you or any of the principals for the transaction now meet any of the criteria in § 1404.355.

Subpart D—Responsibilities of Office of National Drug Control Policy Officials Regarding Transactions

§ 1404.400 May I enter into a transaction with an excluded or disqualified person?

(a) You as an agency official may not enter into a covered transaction with an excluded person unless you obtain an exception under § 1404.120.

(b) You may not enter into any transaction with a person who is disqualified from that transaction, unless you obtain a waiver or exception under the statute, Executive order, or regulation that is the basis for the person's disqualification.

§ 1404.405 May I enter into a covered transaction with a participant if a principal of the transaction is excluded?

As an agency official, you may not enter into a covered transaction with a participant if you know that a principal of the transaction is excluded, unless you obtain an exception under § 1404.120.

§ 1404.410 May I approve a participant's use of the services of an excluded person?

After entering into a covered transaction with a participant, you as an agency official may not approve a participant's use of an excluded person as a principal under that transaction, unless you obtain an exception under § 1404.120.

§ 1404.415 What must I do if a Federal agency excludes the participant or a principal after I enter into a covered transaction?

(a) You as an agency official may continue covered transactions with an excluded person, or under which an excluded person is a principal, if the transactions were in existence when the person was excluded. You are not required to continue the transactions, however, and you may consider termination. You should make a decision about whether to terminate and the type of termination action, if any, only after a thorough review to ensure that the action is proper.

(b) You may not renew or extend covered transactions (other than no-cost time extensions) with any excluded person, or under which an excluded person is a principal, unless you obtain an exception under § 1404.120.

§ 1404.420 May I approve a transaction with an excluded or disqualified person at a lower tier?

If a transaction at a lower tier is subject to your approval, you as an agency official may not approve—

(a) A covered transaction with a person who is currently excluded, unless you obtain an exception under § 1404.120; or

(b) A transaction with a person who is disqualified from that transaction, unless you obtain a waiver or exception under the statute, Executive order, or regulation that is the basis for the person's disqualification.

§ 1404.425 When do I check to see if a person is excluded or disqualified?

As an agency official, you must check to see if a person is excluded or disqualified before you—

(a) Enter into a primary tier covered transaction;

(b) Approve a principal in a primary tier covered transaction;

(c) Approve a lower tier participant if agency approval of the lower tier participant is required; or

(d) Approve a principal in connection with a lower tier transaction if agency approval of the principal is required.

§ 1404.430 How do I check to see if a person is excluded or disqualified?

You check to see if a person is excluded or disqualified in two ways:

(a) You as an agency official must check the *EPLS* when you take any action listed in § 1404.425.

(b) You must review information that a participant gives you, as required by § 1404.335, about its status or the status of the principals of a transaction.

§ 1404.435 What must I require of a primary tier participant?

You as an agency official must require each participant in a primary tier covered transaction to—

(a) Comply with subpart C of this part as a condition of participation in the transaction; and

(b) Communicate the requirement to comply with Subpart C of this part to persons at the next lower tier with whom the primary tier participant enters into covered transactions.

§ 1404.440 What method do I use to communicate those requirements to participants?

You must obtain certifications from participants that they will comply with subpart C of this part and that they will obtain similar certifications from lower-tier participants.

[68 FR 66581, Nov. 26, 2003]

§ 1404.445 What action may I take if a primary tier participant knowingly does business with an excluded or disqualified person?

If a participant knowingly does business with an excluded or disqualified person, you as an agency official may refer the matter for suspension and debarment consideration. You may also disallow costs, annul or terminate the transaction, issue a stop work order, or take any other appropriate remedy.

§ 1404.450 What action may I take if a primary tier participant fails to disclose the information required under § 1404.335?

If you as an agency official determine that a participant failed to disclose information, as required by § 1404.335, at the time it entered into a covered transaction with you, you may—

(a) Terminate the transaction for material failure to comply with the terms and conditions of the transaction; or

(b) Pursue any other available remedies, including suspension and debarment.

§ 1404.455 What may I do if a lower tier participant fails to disclose the information required under § 1404.355 to the next higher tier?

If you as an agency official determine that a lower tier participant failed to disclose information, as required by § 1404.355, at the time it entered into a covered transaction with a participant at the next higher tier, you may pursue any remedies available to you, including the initiation of a suspension or debarment action.

Subpart E—Excluded Parties List System

§ 1404.500 What is the purpose of the Excluded Parties List System (EPLS)?

The *EPLS* is a widely available source of the most current information about persons who are excluded or disqualified from covered transactions.

§ 1404.505 Who uses the EPLS?

(a) Federal agency officials use the *EPLS* to determine whether to enter into a transaction with a person, as required under § 1404.430.

(b) Participants also may, but are not required to, use the *EPLS* to determine if—

(1) Principals of their transactions are excluded or disqualified, as required under § 1404.320; or

(2) Persons with whom they are entering into covered transactions at the next lower tier are excluded or disqualified.

(c) The *EPLS* is available to the general public.

§ 1404.510 Who maintains the EPLS?

In accordance with the OMB guidelines, the General Services Administration (GSA) maintains the *EPLS*. When a Federal agency takes an action to exclude a person under the nonprocurement or procurement debarment and suspension system, the agency enters the information about the excluded person into the *EPLS*.

§ 1404.515 What specific information is in the EPLS?

(a) At a minimum, the *EPLS* indicates—

(1) The full name (where available) and address of each excluded or disqualified person, in alphabetical order, with cross references if more than one name is involved in a single action;

(2) The type of action;

(3) The cause for the action;

(4) The scope of the action;

(5) Any termination date for the action;

(6) The agency and name and telephone number of the agency point of contact for the action; and

(7) The Dun and Bradstreet Number (DUNS), or other similar code approved by the GSA, of the excluded or disqualified person, if available.

(b)(1) The database for the *EPLS* includes a field for the Taxpayer Identification Number (TIN) (the social security number (SSN) for an individual) of an excluded or disqualified person.

(2) Agencies disclose the SSN of an individual to verify the identity of an individual, only if permitted under the Privacy Act of 1974 and, if appropriate, the Computer Matching and Privacy Protection Act of 1988, as codified in 5 U.S.C. 552(a).

§ 1404.520 Who places the information into the EPLS?

Federal officials who take actions to exclude persons under this part or officials who are responsible for identifying disqualified persons must enter the following information about those persons into the *EPLS*:

(a) Information required by § 1404.515(a);

(b) The Taxpayer Identification Number (TIN) of the excluded or disqualified person, including the social security number (SSN) for an individual, if the number is available and may be disclosed under law;

(c) Information about an excluded or disqualified person, generally within five working days, after—

(1) Taking an exclusion action;

(2) Modifying or rescinding an exclusion action;

(3) Finding that a person is disqualified; or

(4) Finding that there has been a change in the status of a person who is listed as disqualified.

§ 1404.525 Whom do I ask if I have questions about a person in the EPLS?

If you have questions about a person in the *EPLS*, ask the point of contact for the Federal agency that placed the person's name into the *EPLS*. You may find the agency point of contact from the *EPLS*.

§ 1404.530 Where can I find the EPLS?

(a) You may access the *EPLS* through the Internet, currently at *http:// epls.arnet.gov.*

(b) As of November 26, 2003, you may also subscribe to a printed version. However, we anticipate discontinuing the printed version. Until it is discontinued, you may obtain the printed version by purchasing a yearly subscription from the Superintendent of Documents, U.S. Government Printing Office, Washington, DC 20402, or by calling the Government Printing Office Inquiry and Order Desk at (202) 783–3238.

Subpart F—General Principles Relating to Suspension and Debarment Actions

§ 1404.600 How do suspension and debarment actions start?

When we receive information from any source concerning a cause for suspension or debarment, we will promptly report and investigate it. We refer the question of whether to suspend or debar you to our suspending or debarring official for consideration, if appropriate.

§ 1404.605 How does suspension differ from debarment?

Suspension differs from debarment in that—

A suspending official . . .	A debarring official . . .
(a) Imposes suspension as a temporary status of ineligibility for procurement and nonprocurement transactions, pending completion of an investigation or legal proceedings.	Imposes debarment for a specified period as a final determination that a person is not presently responsible.
(b) Must—	Must conclude, based on a *preponderance of the evidence,* that the person has engaged in conduct that warrants debarment.
(1) Have *adequate evidence* that there may be a cause for debarment of a person; and.	
(2) Conclude that *immediate action* is necessary to protect the Federal interest.	
(c) Usually imposes the suspension *first,* and then promptly notifies the suspended person, giving the person an opportunity to contest the suspension and have it lifted.	Imposes debarment *after* giving the respondent notice of the action and an opportunity to contest the proposed debarment.

§ 1404.610 What procedures does the Office of National Drug Control Policy use in suspension and debarment actions?

In deciding whether to suspend or debar you, we handle the actions as informally as practicable, consistent with principles of fundamental fairness.

(a) For suspension actions, we use the procedures in this subpart and subpart G of this part.

(b) For debarment actions, we use the procedures in this subpart and subpart H of this part.

§ 1404.615 How does the Office of National Drug Control Policy notify a person of a suspension or debarment action?

(a) The suspending or debarring official sends a written notice to the last known street address, facsimile number, or e-mail address of—

(1) You or your identified counsel; or

(2) Your agent for service of process, or any of your partners, officers, directors, owners, or joint venturers.

(b) The notice is effective if sent to any of these persons.

§ 1404.620 Do Federal agencies coordinate suspension and debarment actions?

Yes, when more than one Federal agency has an interest in a suspension or debarment, the agencies may consider designating one agency as the lead agency for making the decision. Agencies are encouraged to establish methods and procedures for coordinating their suspension and debarment actions.

§ 1404.625 What is the scope of a suspension or debarment?

If you are suspended or debarred, the suspension or debarment is effective as follows:

(a) Your suspension or debarment constitutes suspension or debarment of all of your divisions and other organizational elements from all covered transactions, unless the suspension or debarment decision is limited—

(1) By its terms to one or more specifically identified individuals, divisions, or other organizational elements; or

(2) To specific types of transactions.

(b) Any affiliate of a participant may be included in a suspension or debarment action if the suspending or debarring official—

(1) Officially names the affiliate in the notice; and

(2) Gives the affiliate an opportunity to contest the action.

§ 1404.630 May the Office of National Drug Control Policy impute conduct of one person to another?

For purposes of actions taken under this rule, we may impute conduct as follows:

(a) *Conduct imputed from an individual to an organization.* We may impute the fraudulent, criminal, or other improper conduct of any officer, director, shareholder, partner, employee, or other individual associated with an organization, to that organization when the improper conduct occurred in connection with the individual's performance of duties for or on behalf of that organization, or with the organization's knowledge, approval or acquiescence. The organization's acceptance of the benefits derived from the conduct is evidence of knowledge, approval or acquiescence.

(b) *Conduct imputed from an organization to an individual, or between individuals.* We may impute the fraudulent, criminal, or other improper conduct of any organization to an individual, or from one individual to another individual, if the individual to whom the improper conduct is imputed either participated in, had knowledge of, or reason to know of the improper conduct.

(c) *Conduct imputed from one organization to another organization.* We may impute the fraudulent, criminal, or other improper conduct of one organization to another organization when the improper conduct occurred in connection with a partnership, joint venture, joint application, association or similar arrangement, or when the organization to whom the improper conduct is imputed has the power to direct, manage, control or influence the activities of the organization responsible for the improper conduct. Acceptance of the benefits derived from the conduct is evidence of knowledge, approval or acquiescence.

§ 1404.635 May the Office of National Drug Control Policy settle a debarment or suspension action?

Yes, we may settle a debarment or suspension action at any time if it is in the best interest of the Federal Government.

§ 1404.640 May a settlement include a voluntary exclusion?

Yes, if we enter into a settlement with you in which you agree to be excluded, it is called a voluntary exclusion and has governmentwide effect.

§ 1404.645 Do other Federal agencies know if the Office of National Drug Control Policy agrees to a voluntary exclusion?

(a) Yes, we enter information regarding a voluntary exclusion into the *EPLS*.

(b) Also, any agency or person may contact us to find out the details of a voluntary exclusion.

Subpart G—Suspension

§ 1404.700 When may the suspending official issue a suspension?

Suspension is a serious action. Using the procedures of this subpart and subpart F of this part, the suspending official may impose suspension only when that official determines that—

(a) There exists an indictment for, or other adequate evidence to suspect, an offense listed under § 1404.800(a), or

(b) There exists adequate evidence to suspect any other cause for debarment listed under § 1404.800(b) through (d); and

(c) Immediate action is necessary to protect the public interest.

§ 1404.705 What does the suspending official consider in issuing a suspension?

(a) In determining the adequacy of the evidence to support the suspension, the suspending official considers how much information is available, how credible it is given the circumstances, whether or not important allegations are corroborated, and what inferences can reasonably be drawn as a result. During this assessment, the suspending official may examine the basic documents, including grants, cooperative agreements, loan authorizations, contracts, and other relevant documents.

(b) An indictment, conviction, civil judgment, or other official findings by Federal, State, or local bodies that determine factual and/or legal matters, constitutes adequate evidence for purposes of suspension actions.

(c) In deciding whether immediate action is needed to protect the public interest, the suspending official has wide discretion. For example, the suspending official may infer the necessity for immediate action to protect the public interest either from the nature of the circumstances giving rise to a cause for suspension or from potential business relationships or involvement with a program of the Federal Government.

§ 1404.710 When does a suspension take effect?

A suspension is effective when the suspending official signs the decision to suspend.

§ 1404.715 What notice does the suspending official give me if I am suspended?

After deciding to suspend you, the suspending official promptly sends you a Notice of Suspension advising you—

(a) That you have been suspended;

(b) That your suspension is based on—

(1) An indictment;

(2) A conviction;

(3) Other adequate evidence that you have committed irregularities which seriously reflect on the propriety of further Federal Government dealings with you; or

(4) Conduct of another person that has been imputed to you, or your affiliation with a suspended or debarred person;

(c) Of any other irregularities in terms sufficient to put you on notice without disclosing the Federal Government's evidence;

(d) Of the cause(s) upon which we relied under § 1404.700 for imposing suspension;

(e) That your suspension is for a temporary period pending the completion of an investigation or resulting legal or debarment proceedings;

(f) Of the applicable provisions of this subpart, Subpart F of this part, and any other Office of National Drug Control Policy procedures governing suspension decision making; and

(g) Of the governmentwide effect of your suspension from procurement and nonprocurement programs and activities.

§ 1404.720 How may I contest a suspension?

If you as a respondent wish to contest a suspension, you or your representative must provide the suspending official with information in opposition to the suspension. You may do this orally or in writing, but any information provided orally that you consider important must also be submitted in writing for the official record.

§ 1404.725 How much time do I have to contest a suspension?

(a) As a respondent you or your representative must either send, or make rrangements to appear and present, the

265

information and argument to the suspending official within 30 days after you receive the Notice of Suspension.

(b) We consider the notice to be received by you—

(1) When delivered, if we mail the notice to the last known street address, or five days after we send it if the letter is undeliverable;

(2) When sent, if we send the notice by facsimile or five days after we send it if the facsimile is undeliverable; or

(3) When delivered, if we send the notice by e-mail or five days after we send it if the e-mail is undeliverable.

§ 1404.730 What information must I provide to the suspending official if I contest a suspension?

(a) In addition to any information and argument in opposition, as a respondent your submission to the suspending official must identify—

(1) Specific facts that contradict the statements contained in the Notice of Suspension. A general denial is insufficient to raise a genuine dispute over facts material to the suspension;

(2) All existing, proposed, or prior exclusions under regulations implementing E.O. 12549 and all similar actions taken by Federal, state, or local agencies, including administrative agreements that affect only those agencies;

(3) All criminal and civil proceedings not included in the Notice of Suspension that grew out of facts relevant to the cause(s) stated in the notice; and

(4) All of your affiliates.

(b) If you fail to disclose this information, or provide false information, the Office of National Drug Control Policy may seek further criminal, civil or administrative action against you, as appropriate.

§ 1404.735 Under what conditions do I get an additional opportunity to challenge the facts on which the suspension is based?

(a) You as a respondent will not have an additional opportunity to challenge the facts if the suspending official determines that—

(1) Your suspension is based upon an indictment, conviction, civil judgment, or other finding by a Federal, State, or local body for which an opportunity to contest the facts was provided;

(2) Your presentation in opposition contains only general denials to information contained in the Notice of Suspension;

(3) The issues raised in your presentation in opposition to the suspension are not factual in nature, or are not material to the suspending official's initial decision to suspend, or the official's decision whether to continue suspension; or

(4) On the basis of advice from the Department of Justice, an office of the United States Attorney, a State attorney general's office, or a State or local prosecutor's office, that substantial interests of the government in pending or contemplated legal proceedings based on the same facts as the suspension would be prejudiced by conducting fact-finding.

(b) You will have an opportunity to challenge the facts if the suspending official determines that—

(1) The conditions in paragraph (a) of this section do not exist; and

(2) Your presentation in opposition raises a genuine dispute over facts material to the suspension.

(c) If you have an opportunity to challenge disputed material facts under this section, the suspending official or designee must conduct additional proceedings to resolve those facts.

§ 1404.740 Are suspension proceedings formal?

(a) Suspension proceedings are conducted in a fair and informal manner. The suspending official may use flexible procedures to allow you to present matters in opposition. In so doing, the suspending official is not required to follow formal rules of evidence or procedure in creating an official record upon which the official will base a final suspension decision.

(b) You as a respondent or your representative must submit any documentary evidence you want the suspending official to consider.

§ 1404.745 How is fact-finding conducted?

(a) If fact-finding is conducted—

(1) You may present witnesses and other evidence, and confront any witness presented; and

(2) The fact-finder must prepare written findings of fact for the record.

(b) A transcribed record of fact-finding proceedings must be made, unless you as a respondent and the Office of National Drug Control Policy agree to waive it in advance. If you want a copy of the transcribed record, you may purchase it.

§ 1404.750 What does the suspending official consider in deciding whether to continue or terminate my suspension?

(a) The suspending official bases the decision on all information contained in the official record. The record includes—

(1) All information in support of the suspending official's initial decision to suspend you;

(2) Any further information and argument presented in support of, or opposition to, the suspension; and

(3) Any transcribed record of fact-finding proceedings.

(b) The suspending official may refer disputed material facts to another official for findings of fact. The suspending official may reject any resulting findings, in whole or in part, only after specifically determining them to be arbitrary, capricious, or clearly erroneous.

§ 1404.755 When will I know whether the suspension is continued or terminated?

The suspending official must make a written decision whether to continue, modify, or terminate your suspension within 45 days of closing the official record. The official record closes upon the suspending official's receipt of final submissions, information and findings of fact, if any. The suspending official may extend that period for good cause.

§ 1404.760 How long may my suspension last?

(a) If legal or debarment proceedings are initiated at the time of, or during your suspension, the suspension may continue until the conclusion of those proceedings. However, if proceedings are not initiated, a suspension may not exceed 12 months.

(b) The suspending official may extend the 12 month limit under paragraph (a) of this section for an additional 6 months if an office of a U.S. Assistant Attorney General, U.S. Attorney, or other responsible prosecuting official requests an extension in writing. In no event may a suspension exceed 18 months without initiating proceedings under paragraph (a) of this section.

(c) The suspending official must notify the appropriate officials under paragraph (b) of this section of an impending termination of a suspension at least 30 days before the 12 month period expires to allow the officials an opportunity to request an extension.

Subpart H—Debarment

§ 1404.800 What are the causes for debarment?

We may debar a person for—

(a) Conviction of or civil judgment for—

(1) Commission of fraud or a criminal offense in connection with obtaining, attempting to obtain, or performing a public or private agreement or transaction;

(2) Violation of Federal or State antitrust statutes, including those proscribing price fixing between competitors, allocation of customers between competitors, and bid rigging;

(3) Commission of embezzlement, theft, forgery, bribery, falsification or destruction of records, making false statements, tax evasion, receiving stolen property, making false claims, or obstruction of justice; or

(4) Commission of any other offense indicating a lack of business integrity or business honesty that seriously and directly affects your present responsibility;

(b) Violation of the terms of a public agreement or transaction so serious as to affect the integrity of an agency program, such as—

(1) A willful failure to perform in accordance with the terms of one or more public agreements or transactions;

(2) A history of failure to perform or of unsatisfactory performance of one or more public agreements or transactions; or

(3) A willful violation of a statutory or regulatory provision or requirement applicable to a public agreement or transaction;

(c) Any of the following causes:

(1) A nonprocurement debarment by any Federal agency taken before October 1, 1988, or a procurement debarment by any Federal agency taken pursuant to 48 CFR part 9, subpart 9.4, before August 25, 1995;

(2) Knowingly doing business with an ineligible person, except as permitted under § 1404.120;

(3) Failure to pay a single substantial debt, or a number of outstanding debts (including disallowed costs and overpayments, but not including sums owed the Federal Government under the Internal Revenue Code) owed to any Federal agency or instrumentality, provided the debt is uncontested by the debtor or, if contested, provided that the debtor's legal and administrative remedies have been exhausted;

(4) Violation of a material provision of a voluntary exclusion agreement entered into under § 1404.640 or of any settlement of a debarment or suspension action; or

(5) Violation of the provisions of the Drug-Free Workplace Act of 1988 (41 U.S.C. 701); or

(d) Any other cause of so serious or compelling a nature that it affects your present responsibility.

§ 1404.805 What notice does the debarring official give me if I am proposed for debarment?

After consideration of the causes in § 1404.800 of this subpart, if the debarring official proposes to debar you, the official sends you a Notice of Proposed Debarment, pursuant to § 1404.615, advising you—

(a) That the debarring official is considering debarring you;

(b) Of the reasons for proposing to debar you in terms sufficient to put you on notice of the conduct or transactions upon which the proposed debarment is based;

(c) Of the cause(s) under § 1404.800 upon which the debarring official relied for proposing your debarment;

(d) Of the applicable provisions of this subpart, Subpart F of this part, and any other Office of National Drug Control Policy procedures governing debarment; and

(e) Of the governmentwide effect of a debarment from procurement and nonprocurement programs and activities.

§ 1404.810 When does a debarment take effect?

A debarment is not effective until the debarring official issues a decision. The debarring official does not issue a decision until the respondent has had an opportunity to contest the proposed debarment.

§ 1404.815 How may I contest a proposed debarment?

If you as a respondent wish to contest a proposed debarment, you or your representative must provide the debarring official with information in opposition to the proposed debarment. You may do this orally or in writing, but any information provided orally that you consider important must also be submitted in writing for the official record.

§ 1404.820 How much time do I have to contest a proposed debarment?

(a) As a respondent you or your representative must either send, or make arrangements to appear and present, the information and argument to the debarring official within 30 days after you receive the Notice of Proposed Debarment.

(b) We consider the Notice of Proposed Debarment to be received by you—

(1) When delivered, if we mail the notice to the last known street address, or five days after we send it if the letter is undeliverable;

(2) When sent, if we send the notice by facsimile or five days after we send it if the facsimile is undeliverable; or

(3) When delivered, if we send the notice by e-mail or five days after we send it if the e-mail is undeliverable.

§ 1404.825 What information must I provide to the debarring official if I contest a proposed debarment?

(a) In addition to any information and argument in opposition, as a respondent your submission to the debarring official must identify—

(1) Specific facts that contradict the statements contained in the Notice of

Proposed Debarment. Include any information about any of the factors listed in §1404.860. A general denial is insufficient to raise a genuine dispute over facts material to the debarment;

(2) All existing, proposed, or prior exclusions under regulations implementing E.O. 12549 and all similar actions taken by Federal, State, or local agencies, including administrative agreements that affect only those agencies;

(3) All criminal and civil proceedings not included in the Notice of Proposed Debarment that grew out of facts relevant to the cause(s) stated in the notice; and

(4) All of your affiliates.

(b) If you fail to disclose this information, or provide false information, the Office of National Drug Control Policy may seek further criminal, civil or administrative action against you, as appropriate.

§1404.830 Under what conditions do I get an additional opportunity to challenge the facts on which a proposed debarment is based?

(a) You as a respondent will not have an additional opportunity to challenge the facts if the debarring official determines that—

(1) Your debarment is based upon a conviction or civil judgment;

(2) Your presentation in opposition contains only general denials to information contained in the Notice of Proposed Debarment; or

(3) The issues raised in your presentation in opposition to the proposed debarment are not factual in nature, or are not material to the debarring official's decision whether to debar.

(b) You will have an additional opportunity to challenge the facts if the debarring official determines that—

(1) The conditions in paragraph (a) of this section do not exist; and

(2) Your presentation in opposition raises a genuine dispute over facts material to the proposed debarment.

(c) If you have an opportunity to challenge disputed material facts under this section, the debarring official or designee must conduct additional proceedings to resolve those facts.

§1404.835 Are debarment proceedings formal?

(a) Debarment proceedings are conducted in a fair and informal manner. The debarring official may use flexible procedures to allow you as a respondent to present matters in opposition. In so doing, the debarring official is not required to follow formal rules of evidence or procedure in creating an official record upon which the official will base the decision whether to debar.

(b) You or your representative must submit any documentary evidence you want the debarring official to consider.

§1404.840 How is fact-finding conducted?

(a) If fact-finding is conducted—

(1) You may present witnesses and other evidence, and confront any witness presented; and

(2) The fact-finder must prepare written findings of fact for the record.

(b) A transcribed record of fact-finding proceedings must be made, unless you as a respondent and the Office of National Drug Control Policy agree to waive it in advance. If you want a copy of the transcribed record, you may purchase it.

§1404.845 What does the debarring official consider in deciding whether to debar me?

(a) The debarring official may debar you for any of the causes in §1404.800. However, the official need not debar you even if a cause for debarment exists. The official may consider the seriousness of your acts or omissions and the mitigating or aggravating factors set forth at §1404.860.

(b) The debarring official bases the decision on all information contained in the official record. The record includes—

(1) All information in support of the debarring official's proposed debarment;

(2) Any further information and argument presented in support of, or in opposition to, the proposed debarment; and

(3) Any transcribed record of fact-finding proceedings.

(c) The debarring official may refer disputed material facts to another official for findings of fact. The debarring

269

official may reject any resultant findings, in whole or in part, only after specifically determining them to be arbitrary, capricious, or clearly erroneous.

§ 1404.850 What is the standard of proof in a debarment action?

(a) In any debarment action, we must establish the cause for debarment by a preponderance of the evidence.

(b) If the proposed debarment is based upon a conviction or civil judgment, the standard of proof is met.

§ 1404.855 Who has the burden of proof in a debarment action?

(a) We have the burden to prove that a cause for debarment exists.

(b) Once a cause for debarment is established, you as a respondent have the burden of demonstrating to the satisfaction of the debarring official that you are presently responsible and that debarment is not necessary.

§ 1404.860 What factors may influence the debarring official's decision?

This section lists the mitigating and aggravating factors that the debarring official may consider in determining whether to debar you and the length of your debarment period. The debarring official may consider other factors if appropriate in light of the circumstances of a particular case. The existence or nonexistence of any factor, such as one of those set forth in this section, is not necessarily determinative of your present responsibility. In making a debarment decision, the debarring official may consider the following factors:

(a) The actual or potential harm or impact that results or may result from the wrongdoing.

(b) The frequency of incidents and/or duration of the wrongdoing.

(c) Whether there is a pattern or prior history of wrongdoing. For example, if you have been found by another Federal agency or a State agency to have engaged in wrongdoing similar to that found in the debarment action, the existence of this fact may be used by the debarring official in determining that you have a pattern or prior history of wrongdoing.

(d) Whether you are or have been excluded or disqualified by an agency of the Federal Government or have not been allowed to participate in State or local contracts or assistance agreements on a basis of conduct similar to one or more of the causes for debarment specified in this part.

(e) Whether you have entered into an administrative agreement with a Federal agency or a State or local government that is not governmentwide but is based on conduct similar to one or more of the causes for debarment specified in this part.

(f) Whether and to what extent you planned, initiated, or carried out the wrongdoing.

(g) Whether you have accepted responsibility for the wrongdoing and recognize the seriousness of the misconduct that led to the cause for debarment.

(h) Whether you have paid or agreed to pay all criminal, civil and administrative liabilities for the improper activity, including any investigative or administrative costs incurred by the government, and have made or agreed to make full restitution.

(i) Whether you have cooperated fully with the government agencies during the investigation and any court or administrative action. In determining the extent of cooperation, the debarring official may consider when the cooperation began and whether you disclosed all pertinent information known to you.

(j) Whether the wrongdoing was pervasive within your organization.

(k) The kind of positions held by the individuals involved in the wrongdoing.

(l) Whether your organization took appropriate corrective action or remedial measures, such as establishing ethics training and implementing programs to prevent recurrence.

(m) Whether your principals tolerated the offense.

(n) Whether you brought the activity cited as a basis for the debarment to the attention of the appropriate government agency in a timely manner.

(o) Whether you have fully investigated the circumstances surrounding the cause for debarment and, if so, made the result of the investigation available to the debarring official.

(p) Whether you had effective standards of conduct and internal control systems in place at the time the questioned conduct occurred.

(q) Whether you have taken appropriate disciplinary action against the individuals responsible for the activity which constitutes the cause for debarment.

(r) Whether you have had adequate time to eliminate the circumstances within your organization that led to the cause for the debarment.

(s) Other factors that are appropriate to the circumstances of a particular case.

§1404.865 How long may my debarment last?

(a) If the debarring official decides to debar you, your period of debarment will be based on the seriousness of the cause(s) upon which your debarment is based. Generally, debarment should not exceed three years. However, if circumstances warrant, the debarring official may impose a longer period of debarment.

(b) In determining the period of debarment, the debarring official may consider the factors in §1404.860. If a suspension has preceded your debarment, the debarring official must consider the time you were suspended.

(c) If the debarment is for a violation of the provisions of the Drug-Free Workplace Act of 1988, your period of debarment may not exceed five years.

§1404.870 When do I know if the debarring official debars me?

(a) The debarring official must make a written decision whether to debar within 45 days of closing the official record. The official record closes upon the debarring official's receipt of final submissions, information and findings of fact, if any. The debarring official may extend that period for good cause.

(b) The debarring official sends you written notice, pursuant to §1404.615 that the official decided, either—

(1) Not to debar you; or

(2) To debar you. In this event, the notice:

(i) Refers to the Notice of Proposed Debarment;

(ii) Specifies the reasons for your debarment;

(iii) States the period of your debarment, including the effective dates; and

(iv) Advises you that your debarment is effective for covered transactions and contracts that are subject to the Federal Acquisition Regulation (48 CFR chapter 1), throughout the executive branch of the Federal Government unless an agency head or an authorized designee grants an exception.

§1404.875 May I ask the debarring official to reconsider a decision to debar me?

Yes, as a debarred person you may ask the debarring official to reconsider the debarment decision or to reduce the time period or scope of the debarment. However, you must put your request in writing and support it with documentation.

§1404.880 What factors may influence the debarring official during reconsideration?

The debarring official may reduce or terminate your debarment based on—

(a) Newly discovered material evidence;

(b) A reversal of the conviction or civil judgment upon which your debarment was based;

(c) A bona fide change in ownership or management;

(d) Elimination of other causes for which the debarment was imposed; or

(e) Other reasons the debarring official finds appropriate.

§1404.885 May the debarring official extend a debarment?

(a) Yes, the debarring official may extend a debarment for an additional period, if that official determines that an extension is necessary to protect the public interest.

(b) However, the debarring official may not extend a debarment solely on the basis of the facts and circumstances upon which the initial debarment action was based.

(c) If the debarring official decides that a debarment for an additional period is necessary, the debarring official must follow the applicable procedures in this subpart, and subpart F of this part, to extend the debarment.

Subpart I—Definitions

§ 1404.900 Adequate evidence.

Adequate evidence means information sufficient to support the reasonable belief that a particular act or omission has occurred.

§ 1404.905 Affiliate.

Persons are *affiliates* of each other if, directly or indirectly, either one controls or has the power to control the other or a third person controls or has the power to control both. The ways we use to determine control include, but are not limited to—

(a) Interlocking management or ownership;

(b) Identity of interests among family members;

(c) Shared facilities and equipment;

(d) Common use of employees; or

(e) A business entity which has been organized following the exclusion of a person which has the same or similar management, ownership, or principal employees as the excluded person.

§ 1404.910 Agency.

Agency means any United States executive department, military department, defense agency, or any other agency of the executive branch. Other agencies of the Federal government are not considered "agencies" for the purposes of this part unless they issue regulations adopting the governmentwide Debarment and Suspension system under Executive orders 12549 and 12689.

§ 1404.915 Agent or representative.

Agent or representative means any person who acts on behalf of, or who is authorized to commit, a participant in a covered transaction.

§ 1404.920 Civil judgment.

Civil judgment means the disposition of a civil action by any court of competent jurisdiction, whether by verdict, decision, settlement, stipulation, other disposition which creates a civil liability for the complained of wrongful acts, or a final determination of liability under the Program Fraud Civil Remedies Act of 1988 (31 U.S.C. 3801–3812).

§ 1404.925 Conviction.

Conviction means—

(a) A judgment or any other determination of guilt of a criminal offense by any court of competent jurisdiction, whether entered upon a verdict or plea, including a plea of nolo contendere; or

(b) Any other resolution that is the functional equivalent of a judgment, including probation before judgment and deferred prosecution. A disposition without the participation of the court is the functional equivalent of a judgment only if it includes an admission of guilt.

§ 1404.930 Debarment.

Debarment means an action taken by a debarring official under subpart H of this part to exclude a person from participating in covered transactions and transactions covered under the Federal Acquisition Regulation (48 CFR chapter 1). A person so excluded is debarred.

§ 1404.935 Debarring official.

(a) *Debarring official* means an agency official who is authorized to impose debarment. A debarring official is either—

(1) The agency head; or

(2) An official designated by the agency head.

(b) [Reserved]

§ 1404.940 Disqualified.

Disqualified means that a person is prohibited from participating in specified Federal procurement or nonprocurement transactions as required under a statute, Executive order (other than Executive Orders 12549 and 12689) or other authority. Examples of disqualifications include persons prohibited under—

(a) The Davis-Bacon Act (40 U.S.C. 276(a));

(b) The equal employment opportunity acts and Executive orders; or

(c) The Clean Air Act (42 U.S.C. 7606), Clean Water Act (33 U.S.C. 1368) and Executive Order 11738 (3 CFR, 1973 Comp., p. 799).

§ 1404.945 Excluded or exclusion.

Excluded or exclusion means—

(a) That a person or commodity is prohibited from being a participant in covered transactions, whether the person has been suspended; debarred; proposed for debarment under 48 CFR part 9, subpart 9.4; voluntarily excluded; or

(b) The act of excluding a person.

§ 1404.950 Excluded Parties List System

Excluded Parties List System (EPLS) means the list maintained and disseminated by the General Services Administration (GSA) containing the names and other information about persons who are ineligible. The *EPLS* system includes the printed version entitled, "List of Parties Excluded or Disqualified from Federal Procurement and Nonprocurement Programs," so long as published.

§ 1404.955 Indictment.

Indictment means an indictment for a criminal offense. A presentment, information, or other filing by a competent authority charging a criminal offense shall be given the same effect as an indictment.

§ 1404.960 Ineligible or ineligibility.

Ineligible or ineligibility means that a person or commodity is prohibited from covered transactions because of an exclusion or disqualification.

§ 1404.965 Legal proceedings.

Legal proceedings means any criminal proceeding or any civil judicial proceeding, including a proceeding under the Program Fraud Civil Remedies Act (31 U.S.C. 3801–3812), to which the Federal Government or a State or local government or quasi-governmental authority is a party. The term also includes appeals from those proceedings.

§ 1404.970 Nonprocurement transaction.

(a) *Nonprocurement transaction* means any transaction, regardless of type (except procurement contracts), including, but not limited to the following:

(1) Grants.
(2) Cooperative agreements.
(3) Scholarships.
(4) Fellowships.
(5) Contracts of assistance.
(6) Loans.
(7) Loan guarantees.
(8) Subsidies.

(9) Insurances.
(10) Payments for specified uses.
(11) Donation agreements.

(b) A nonprocurement transaction at any tier does not require the transfer of Federal funds.

§ 1404.975 Notice.

Notice means a written communication served in person, sent by certified mail or its equivalent, or sent electronically by e-mail or facsimile. (See § 1404. 615.)

§ 1404.980 Participant.

Participant means any person who submits a proposal for or who enters into a covered transaction, including an agent or representative of a participant.

§ 1404.985 Person.

Person means any individual, corporation, partnership, association, unit of government, or legal entity, however organized.

§ 1404.990 Preponderance of the evidence.

Preponderance of the evidence means proof by information that, compared with information opposing it, leads to the conclusion that the fact at issue is more probably true than not.

§ 1404.995 Principal.

Principal means—

(a) An officer, director, owner, partner, principal investigator, or other person within a participant with management or supervisory responsibilities related to a covered transaction; or

(b) A consultant or other person, whether or not employed by the participant or paid with Federal funds, who—

(1) Is in a position to handle Federal funds;

(2) Is in a position to influence or control the use of those funds; or,

(3) Occupies a technical or professional position capable of substantially influencing the development or outcome of an activity required to perform the covered transaction.

§ 1404.1000 Respondent.

Respondent means a person against whom an agency has initiated a debarment or suspension action.

273

§ 1404.1005   State.

(a) *State* means—

(1) Any of the states of the United States;

(2) The District of Columbia;

(3) The Commonwealth of Puerto Rico;

(4) Any territory or possession of the United States; or

(5) Any agency or instrumentality of a state.

(b) For purposes of this part, *State* does not include institutions of higher education, hospitals, or units of local government.

§ 1404.1010   Suspending official.

(a) *Suspending official* means an agency official who is authorized to impose suspension. The suspending official is either:

(1) The agency head; or

(2) An official designated by the agency head.

(b) [Reserved]

§ 1404.1015   Suspension.

Suspension is an action taken by a suspending official under subpart G of this part that immediately prohibits a person from participating in covered transactions and transactions covered under the Federal Acquisition Regulation (48 CFR chapter 1) for a temporary period, pending completion of an agency investigation and any judicial or administrative proceedings that may ensue. A person so excluded is suspended.

§ 1404.1020   Voluntary exclusion or voluntarily excluded.

(a) *Voluntary exclusion* means a person's agreement to be excluded under the terms of a settlement between the person and one or more agencies. Voluntary exclusion must have governmentwide effect.

(b) *Voluntarily excluded* means the status of a person who has agreed to a voluntary exclusion.

Subpart J [Reserved]

APPENDIX TO PART 1404—COVERED TRANSACTIONS

COVERED TRANSACTIONS

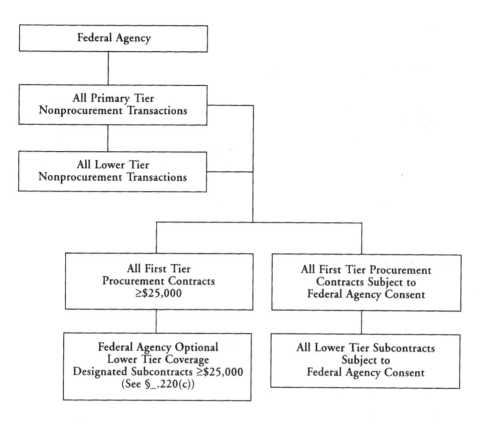

PART 1405—GOVERNMENTWIDE REQUIREMENTS FOR DRUG-FREE WORKPLACE (FINANCIAL ASSISTANCE)

Subpart A—Purpose and Coverage

Sec.

Subpart B—Requirements for Recipients Other Than Individuals

Subpart C—Requirements for Recipients Who Are Individuals

1405.301 [Reserved]

Subpart D—Responsibilities of Office of National Drug Control Policy Awarding Officials

1405.400 What are my responsibilities as an Office of National Drug Control Policy awarding official?

Subpart E—Violations of This Part and Consequences

1405.500 How are violations of this part determined for recipients other than individuals?
1405.505 How are violations of this part determined for recipients who are individuals?
1405.510 What actions will the Federal Government take against a recipient determined to have violated this part?
1405.515 Are there exceptions to those actions?

Subpart F—Definitions

1405.605 Award.
1405.610 Controlled substance.
1405.615 Conviction.
1405.620 Cooperative agreement.
1405.625 Criminal drug statute.
1405.630 Debarment.
1405.635 Drug-free workplace.
1405.640 Employee.
1405.645 Federal agency or agency.
1405.650 Grant.
1405.655 Individual.

1405.660 Recipient.
1405.665 State.
1405.670 Suspension.

AUTHORITY: 21 U.S.C. 1701; 41 U.S.C. 701, *et seq.*

SOURCE: 68 FR 66557, 66581, 66582, Nov. 26, 2003, unless otherwise noted.

Subpart A—Purpose and Coverage

§ 1405.100 What does this part do?

This part carries out the portion of the Drug-Free Workplace Act of 1988 (41 U.S.C. 701 *et seq.*, as amended) that applies to grants. It also applies the provisions of the Act to cooperative agreements and other financial assistance awards, as a matter of Federal Government policy.

§ 1405.105 Does this part apply to me?

(a) Portions of this part apply to you if you are either—

(1) A recipient of an assistance award from the Office of National Drug Control Policy; or

(2) A(n) Office of National Drug Control Policy awarding official. (See definitions of award and recipient in §§ 1405.605 and 1405.660, respectively.)

(b) The following table shows the subparts that apply to you:

If you are . . .	see subparts . . .
(1) A recipient who is not an individual	A, B and E.
(2) A recipient who is an individual	A, C and E.
(3) A(n) Office of National Drug Control Policy awarding official	A, D and E.

§ 1405.110 Are any of my Federal assistance awards exempt from this part?

This part does not apply to any award that the Director of National Drug Control Policy determines that the application of this part would be inconsistent with the international obligations of the United States or the laws or regulations of a foreign government.

§ 1405.115 Does this part affect the Federal contracts that I receive?

It will affect future contract awards indirectly if you are debarred or suspended for a violation of the requirements of this part, as described in § 1405.510(c). However, this part does not apply directly to procurement contracts. The portion of the Drug-Free Workplace Act of 1988 that applies to Federal procurement contracts is carried out through the Federal Acquisition Regulation in chapter 1 of Title 48 of the Code of Federal Regulations (the drug-free workplace coverage currently is in 48 CFR part 23, subpart 23.5).

Subpart B—Requirements for Recipients Other Than Individuals

§ 1405.200 What must I do to comply with this part?

There are two general requirements if you are a recipient other than an individual.

(a) First, you must make a good faith effort, on a continuing basis, to maintain a drug-free workplace. You must agree to do so as a condition for receiving any award covered by this part. The specific measures that you must take in this regard are described in more detail in subsequent sections of this subpart. Briefly, those measures are to—

(1) Publish a drug-free workplace statement and establish a drug-free awareness program for your employees (see §§ 1405.205 through 1405.220); and

(2) Take actions concerning employees who are convicted of violating drug statutes in the workplace (see § 1405.225).

(b) Second, you must identify all known workplaces under your Federal awards (see § 1405.230).

§ 1405.205 What must I include in my drug-free workplace statement?

You must publish a statement that—

(a) Tells your employees that the unlawful manufacture, distribution, dispensing, possession, or use of a controlled substance is prohibited in your workplace;

(b) Specifies the actions that you will take against employees for violating that prohibition; and

(c) Lets each employee know that, as a condition of employment under any award, he or she:

(1) Will abide by the terms of the statement; and

(2) Must notify you in writing if he or she is convicted for a violation of a criminal drug statute occurring in the workplace and must do so no more than five calendar days after the conviction.

§ 1405.210 To whom must I distribute my drug-free workplace statement?

You must require that a copy of the statement described in § 1405.205 be given to each employee who will be engaged in the performance of any Federal award.

§ 1405.215 What must I include in my drug-free awareness program?

You must establish an ongoing drug-free awareness program to inform employees about—

(a) The dangers of drug abuse in the workplace;

(b) Your policy of maintaining a drug-free workplace;

(c) Any available drug counseling, rehabilitation, and employee assistance programs; and

(d) The penalties that you may impose upon them for drug abuse violations occurring in the workplace.

§ 1405.220 By when must I publish my drug-free workplace statement and establish my drug-free awareness program?

If you are a new recipient that does not already have a policy statement as described in § 1405.205 and an ongoing awareness program as described in § 1405.215, you must publish the statement and establish the program by the time given in the following table:

. . .	then you . . .
a) The performance period of the award is less than 30 days	must have the policy statement and program in place as soon as possible, but before the date on which performance is expected to be completed.
b) The performance period of the award is 30 days or more ...	must have the policy statement and program in place within 30 days after award.
c) You believe there are extraordinary circumstances that will require more than 30 days for you to publish the policy statement and establish the awareness program.	may ask the Office of National Drug Control Policy awarding official to give you more time to do so. The amount of additional time, if any, to be given is at the discretion of the awarding official.

§ 1405.225 What actions must I take concerning employees who are convicted of drug violations in the workplace?

There are two actions you must take if an employee is convicted of a drug violation in the workplace:

(a) First, you must notify Federal agencies if an employee who is engaged in the performance of an award informs you about a conviction, as required by § 1405.205(c)(2), or you otherwise learn of the conviction. Your notification to the Federal agencies must—

(1) Be in writing;

(2) Include the employee's position title;

(3) Include the identification number(s) of each affected award;

(4) Be sent within ten calendar days after you learn of the conviction; and

(5) Be sent to every Federal agency on whose award the convicted employee was working. It must be sent to every awarding official or his or her official designee, unless the Federal agency has specified a central point for the receipt of the notices.

(b) Second, within 30 calendar days of learning about an employee's conviction, you must either—

(1) Take appropriate personnel action against the employee, up to and including termination, consistent with the requirements of the Rehabilitation Act of 1973 (29 U.S.C. 794), as amended; or

(2) Require the employee to participate satisfactorily in a drug abuse assistance or rehabilitation program approved for these purposes by a Federal, State or local health, law enforcement, or other appropriate agency.

§ 1405.230 How and when must I identify workplaces?

(a) You must identify all known workplaces under each Office of National Drug Control Policy award. A failure to do so is a violation of your drug-free workplace requirements. You may identify the workplaces—

(1) To the Office of National Drug Control Policy official that is making the award, either at the time of application or upon award; or

(2) In documents that you keep on file in your offices during the performance of the award, in which case you must make the information available for inspection upon request by Office of National Drug Control Policy officials or their designated representatives.

(b) Your workplace identification for an award must include the actual address of buildings (or parts of buildings) or other sites where work under the award takes place. Categorical descriptions may be used (*e.g.*, all vehicles of a mass transit authority or State highway department while in operation, State employees in each local unemployment office, performers in concert halls or radio studios).

(c) If you identified workplaces to the Office of National Drug Control Policy awarding official at the time of application or award, as described in paragraph (a)(1) of this section, and any workplace that you identified changes during the performance of the award, you must inform the Office of National Drug Control Policy awarding official.

Subpart C—Requirements for Recipients Who Are Individuals

§ 1405.300 What must I do to comply with this part if I am an individual recipient?

As a condition of receiving a(n) Office of National Drug Control Policy award, if you are an individual recipient, you must agree that—

(a) You will not engage in the unlawful manufacture, distribution, dispensing, possession, or use of a controlled substance in conducting any activity related to the award; and

(b) If you are convicted of a criminal drug offense resulting from a violation occurring during the conduct of any award activity, you will report the conviction:

(1) In writing.

(2) Within 10 calendar days of the conviction.

(3) To the Office of National Drug Control Policy awarding official or other designee for each award that you currently have, unless § 1405.301 or the award document designates a central point for the receipt of the notices. When notice is made to a central point it must include the identification number(s) of each affected award.

§ 1405.301 [Reserved]

Subpart D—Responsibilities of Office of National Drug Control Policy Awarding Officials

§ 1405.400 What are my responsibilities as a(n) Office of National Drug Control Policy awarding official?

As a(n) Office of National Drug Control Policy awarding official, you must obtain each recipient's agreement, as a condition of the award, to comply with the requirements in—

(a) Subpart B of this part, if the recipient is not an individual; or

(b) Subpart C of this part, if the recipient is an individual.

Subpart E—Violations of this Part and Consequences

§ 1405.500 How are violations of this part determined for recipients other than individuals?

A recipient other than an individual is in violation of the requirements of this part if the Director of National Drug Control Policy determines, in writing, that—

(a) The recipient has violated the requirements of subpart B of this part; or

(b) The number of convictions of the recipient's employees for violating criminal drug statutes in the workplace is large enough to indicate that the recipient has failed to make a good faith effort to provide a drug-free workplace.

§ 1405.505 How are violations of this part determined for recipients who are individuals?

An individual recipient is in violation of the requirements of this part if the Director of National Drug Control Policy determines, in writing, that—

(a) The recipient has violated the requirements of subpart C of this part; or

(b) The recipient is convicted of a criminal drug offense resulting from a violation occurring during the conduct of any award activity.

§ 1405.510 What actions will the Federal Government take against a recipient determined to have violated this part?

If a recipient is determined to have violated this part, as described in § 1405.500 or § 1405.505, the Office of National Drug Control Policy may take one or more of the following actions—

(a) Suspension of payments under the award;

(b) Suspension or termination of the award; and

(c) Suspension or debarment of the recipient under 21 CFR Part 1404, for a period not to exceed five years.

§ 1405.515 Are there any exceptions to those actions?

The Director of National Drug Control Policy may waive with respect to a particular award, in writing, a suspension of payments under an award, suspension or termination of an award, or suspension or debarment of a recipient if the Director of National Drug Control Policy determines that such a waiver would be in the public interest. This exception authority cannot be delegated to any other official.

Subpart F—Definitions

§ 1405.605 Award.

Award means an award of financial assistance by the Office of National Drug Control Policy or other Federal agency directly to a recipient.

(a) The term award includes:

(1) A Federal grant or cooperative agreement, in the form of money or property in lieu of money.

(2) A block grant or a grant in an entitlement program, whether or not the grant is exempted from coverage under the Governmentwide rule 21 CFR Part 1403 that implements OMB Circular A–102 (for availability, see 5 CFR 1310.3) and specifies uniform administrative requirements.

(b) The term award does not include:

(1) Technical assistance that provides services instead of money.

(2) Loans.

(3) Loan guarantees.

(4) Interest subsidies.

(5) Insurance.

(6) Direct appropriations.

(7) Veterans' benefits to individuals (*i.e.,* any benefit to veterans, their families, or survivors by virtue of the service of a veteran in the Armed Forces of the United States).

§ 1405.610 Controlled substance.

Controlled substance means a controlled substance in schedules I through V of the Controlled Substances Act (21 U.S.C. 812), and as further defined by regulation at 21 CFR 1308.11 through 1308.15.

§ 1405.615 Conviction.

Conviction means a finding of guilt (including a plea of nolo contendere) or imposition of sentence, or both, by any judicial body charged with the responsibility to determine violations of the Federal or State criminal drug statutes.

§ 1405.620 Cooperative agreement.

Cooperative agreement means an award of financial assistance that, consistent with 31 U.S.C. 6305, is used to enter into the same kind of relationship as a grant (see definition of grant in § 1405.650), except that substantial involvement is expected between the Federal agency and the recipient when carrying out the activity contemplated by the award. The term does not include cooperative research and development agreements as defined in 15 U.S.C. 3710a.

§ 1405.625 Criminal drug statute.

Criminal drug statute means a Federal or non-Federal criminal statute involving the manufacture, distribution, dispensing, use, or possession of any controlled substance.

§ 1405.630 Debarment.

Debarment means an action taken by a Federal agency to prohibit a recipient from participating in Federal Government procurement contracts and covered nonprocurement transactions. A recipient so prohibited is debarred, in accordance with the Federal Acquisition Regulation for procurement contracts (48 CFR part 9, subpart 9.4) and the common rule, Government-wide Debarment and Suspension (Nonprocurement), that implements Executive Order 12549 and Executive Order 12689.

§ 1405.635 Drug-free workplace.

Drug-free workplace means a site for the performance of work done in connection with a specific award at which employees of the recipient are prohibited from engaging in the unlawful manufacture, distribution, dispensing, possession, or use of a controlled substance.

§ 1405.640 Employee.

(a) *Employee* means the employee of a recipient directly engaged in the performance of work under the award, including—

(1) All direct charge employees;

(2) All indirect charge employees, unless their impact or involvement in the performance of work under the award is insignificant to the performance of the award; and

(3) Temporary personnel and consultants who are directly engaged in the performance of work under the award and who are on the recipient's payroll.

(b) This definition does not include workers not on the payroll of the recipient (*e.g.,* volunteers, even if used to meet a matching requirement; consultants or independent contractors not on the payroll; or employees of subrecipients or subcontractors in covered workplaces).

§ 1405.645 Federal agency or agency.

Federal agency or agency means any United States executive department, military department, government corporation, government controlled corporation, any other establishment in the executive branch (including the Executive Office of the President), or any independent regulatory agency.

§ 1405.650 Grant.

Grant means an award of financial assistance that, consistent with 31 U.S.C. 6304, is used to enter into a relationship—

(a) The principal purpose of which is to transfer a thing of value to the recipient to carry out a public purpose of support or stimulation authorized by a law of the United States, rather than to acquire property or services for the

Federal Government's direct benefit or use; and

(b) In which substantial involvement is not expected between the Federal agency and the recipient when carrying out the activity contemplated by the award.

§1405.655 Individual.

Individual means a natural person.

§1405.660 Recipient.

Recipient means any individual, corporation, partnership, association, unit of government (except a Federal agency) or legal entity, however organized, that receives an award directly from a Federal agency.

§1405.665 State.

State means any of the States of the United States, the District of Columbia, the Commonwealth of Puerto Rico, or any territory or possession of the United States.

§1405.670 Suspension.

Suspension means an action taken by a Federal agency that immediately prohibits a recipient from participating in Federal Government procurement contracts and covered nonprocurement transactions for a temporary period, pending completion of an investigation and any judicial or administrative proceedings that may ensue. A recipient so prohibited is suspended, in accordance with the Federal Acquisition Regulation for procurement contracts (48 CFR part 9, subpart 9.4) and the common rule, Government-wide Debarment and Suspension (Nonprocurement), that implements Executive Order 12549 and Executive Order 12689. Suspension of a recipient is a distinct and separate action from suspension of an award or suspension of payments under an award.

PARTS 1406–1499 [RESERVED]

FINDING AIDS

A list of CFR titles, subtitles, chapters, subchapters and parts and an alphabetical list of agencies publishing in the CFR are included in the CFR Index and Finding Aids volume to the Code of Federal Regulations which is published separately and revised annually.

Material Approved for Incorporation by Reference
Table of CFR Titles and Chapters
Alphabetical List of Agencies Appearing in the CFR
List of CFR Sections Affected

Material Approved for Incorporation by Reference

(Revised as of April 1, 2008)

The Director of the Federal Register has approved under 5 U.S.C. 552(a) and 1 CFR Part 51 the incorporation by reference of the following publications. This list contains only those incorporations by reference effective as of the revision date of this volume. Incorporations by reference found within a regulation are effective upon the effective date of that regulation. For more information on incorporation by reference, see the preliminary pages of this volume.

21 CFR (PART 1300 TO END)
DRUG ENFORCEMENT ADMINISTRATION, DEPARTMENT OF JUSTICE

21 CFR

National Institute of Standards and Technology
Computer Security Division, Information Technology Laboratory,
100 Bureau Drive, Gaithersburg, Maryland 20899-8930

Federal Information Processing Standard 140-2: "Security Requirements for Cryptographic Modules," dated May 25, 2001 as amended by Change Notices 2 through 4 dated December 3, 2002 and Annexes listed below:.	1311.02, 1311.08; 1311.30; 1311.55
Annex A to FIPS Publication 140-2 ("Security Requirements for Cryptographic Modules"): "Approved Security Functions," dated September 23, 2004	1311.02, 1311.08; 1311.30; 1311.55
Annex B to FIPS Publication 140-2 ("Security Requirements for Cryptographic Modules"): "Approved Protection Profiles," dated November 4, 2004	1311.02, 1311.08; 1311.30; 1311.55
Annex C to FIPS Publication 140-2 ("Security Requirements for Cryptographic Modules"): "Approved Random Number Generators," dated January 31, 2005	1311.02, 1311.08; 1311.30; 1311.55
Annex D to FIPS Publication 140-2 ("Security Requirements for Cryptographic Modules"): "Approved Key Establishment Techniques," dated February 23, 2004	1311.02, 1311.08; 1311.30; 1311.55
Federal Information Processing Standard 180-2: "Secure Hash Standard (SHS)," dated August 1, 2002 as amended by Change Notice 1 dated February 25, 2004.	1311.02; 1311.08; 1311.30; 1311.55
Federal Information Processing Standard 186-2: "Digital Signature Standard (DSS)," dated January 27, 2000 as amended by Change Notice 1 dated October 5, 2001.	1311.02, 1311.08; 1311.30; 1311.55

Table of CFR Titles and Chapters

(Revised as of April 1, 2008)

Title 1—General Provisions

Title 2—Grants and Agreements

287

288

Title 5—Administrative Personnel—Continued

Chap.

LIV   Environmental Protection Agency (Parts 6400—6499)

LV   National Endowment for the Arts (Parts 6500—6599)

LVI   National Endowment for the Humanities (Parts 6600—6699)

LVII   General Services Administration (Parts 6700—6799)

LVIII Board of Governors of the Federal Reserve System (Parts 6800—6899)

LIX   National Aeronautics and Space Administration (Parts 6900—6999)

LX   United States Postal Service (Parts 7000—7099)

LXI   National Labor Relations Board (Parts 7100—7199)

LXII   Equal Employment Opportunity Commission (Parts 7200—7299)

LXIII Inter-American Foundation (Parts 7300—7399)

LXIV   Merit Systems Protection Board (Parts 7400—7499)

LXV   Department of Housing and Urban Development (Parts 7500—7599)

LXVI   National Archives and Records Administration (Parts 7600—7699)

LXVII Institute of Museum and Library Services (Parts 7700—7799)

LXIX   Tennessee Valley Authority (Parts 7900—7999)

LXXI   Consumer Product Safety Commission (Parts 8100—8199)

LXXIII Department of Agriculture (Parts 8300—8399)

LXXIV Federal Mine Safety and Health Review Commission (Parts 8400—8499)

LXXVI Federal Retirement Thrift Investment Board (Parts 8600—8699)

LXXVII Office of Management and Budget (Parts 8700—8799)

XCVII Department of Homeland Security Human Resources Management System (Department of Homeland Security—Office of Personnel Management) (Parts 9700—9799)

XCIX   Department of Defense Human Resources Management and Labor Relations Systems (Department of Defense—Office of Personnel Management) (Parts 9900—9999)

Title 6—Domestic Security

I   Department of Homeland Security, Office of the Secretary (Parts 0—99)

X   Privacy and Civil Liberties Oversight Board (Parts 1000—1099)

Title 7—Agriculture

SUBTITLE A—OFFICE OF THE SECRETARY OF AGRICULTURE (PARTS 0—26)

SUBTITLE B—REGULATIONS OF THE DEPARTMENT OF AGRICULTURE

I   Agricultural Marketing Service (Standards, Inspections, Marketing Practices), Department of Agriculture (Parts 27—209)

II   Food and Nutrition Service, Department of Agriculture (Parts 210—299)

III Animal and Plant Health Inspection Service, Department of Agriculture (Parts 300—399)

Title 12—Banks and Banking—Continued

Title 13—Business Credit and Assistance

Title 14—Aeronautics and Space

Title 15—Commerce and Foreign Trade

Title 16—Commercial Practices

Title 17—Commodity and Securities Exchanges

Title 18—Conservation of Power and Water Resources

Title 19—Customs Duties

295

Title 24—Housing and Urban Development—Continued

Chap.

XII   Office of Inspector General, Department of Housing and Urban Development (Parts 2000—2099)

XX   Office of Assistant Secretary for Housing—Federal Housing Commissioner, Department of Housing and Urban Development (Parts 3200—3899)

XXV   Neighborhood Reinvestment Corporation (Parts 4100—4199)

Title 25—Indians

I   Bureau of Indian Affairs, Department of the Interior (Parts 1—299)

II   Indian Arts and Crafts Board, Department of the Interior (Parts 300—399)

III   National Indian Gaming Commission, Department of the Interior (Parts 500—599)

IV   Office of Navajo and Hopi Indian Relocation (Parts 700—799)

V   Bureau of Indian Affairs, Department of the Interior, and Indian Health Service, Department of Health and Human Services (Part 900)

VI   Office of the Assistant Secretary-Indian Affairs, Department of the Interior (Parts 1000—1199)

VII   Office of the Special Trustee for American Indians, Department of the Interior (Parts 1200—1299)

Title 26—Internal Revenue

I   Internal Revenue Service, Department of the Treasury (Parts 1—899)

Title 27—Alcohol, Tobacco Products and Firearms

I   Alcohol and Tobacco Tax and Trade Bureau, Department of the Treasury (Parts 1—399)

II   Bureau of Alcohol, Tobacco, Firearms, and Explosives, Department of Justice (Parts 400—699)

Title 28—Judicial Administration

I   Department of Justice (Parts 0—299)

III   Federal Prison Industries, Inc., Department of Justice (Parts 300—399)

V   Bureau of Prisons, Department of Justice (Parts 500—599)

VI   Offices of Independent Counsel, Department of Justice (Parts 600—699)

VII   Office of Independent Counsel (Parts 700—799)

VIII   Court Services and Offender Supervision Agency for the District of Columbia (Parts 800—899)

IX   National Crime Prevention and Privacy Compact Council (Parts 900—999)

Title 28—Judicial Administration—Continued

Title 29—Labor

Title 30—Mineral Resources

Title 31—Money and Finance: Treasury

Title 31—Money and Finance: Treasury—Continued

Title 32—National Defense

Title 33—Navigation and Navigable Waters

Title 34—Education

299

Title 41—Public Contracts and Property Management—Continued

Chap.

301 Temporary Duty (TDY) Travel Allowances (Parts 301-1—301-99)

302 Relocation Allowances (Parts 302-1—302-99)

303 Payment of Expenses Connected with the Death of Certain Employees (Part 303-1—303-99)

304 Payment of Travel Expenses from a Non-Federal Source (Parts 304-1—304-99)

Title 42—Public Health

I Public Health Service, Department of Health and Human Services (Parts 1—199)

IV Centers for Medicare & Medicaid Services, Department of Health and Human Services (Parts 400—499)

V Office of Inspector General-Health Care, Department of Health and Human Services (Parts 1000—1999)

Title 43—Public Lands: Interior

SUBTITLE A—OFFICE OF THE SECRETARY OF THE INTERIOR (PARTS 1—199)

SUBTITLE B—REGULATIONS RELATING TO PUBLIC LANDS

I Bureau of Reclamation, Department of the Interior (Parts 200—499)

II Bureau of Land Management, Department of the Interior (Parts 1000—9999)

III Utah Reclamation Mitigation and Conservation Commission (Parts 10000—10010)

Title 44—Emergency Management and Assistance

I Federal Emergency Management Agency, Department of Homeland Security (Parts 0—399)

IV Department of Commerce and Department of Transportation (Parts 400—499)

Title 45—Public Welfare

SUBTITLE A—DEPARTMENT OF HEALTH AND HUMAN SERVICES (PARTS 1—199)

SUBTITLE B—REGULATIONS RELATING TO PUBLIC WELFARE

II Office of Family Assistance (Assistance Programs), Administration for Children and Families, Department of Health and Human Services (Parts 200—299)

III Office of Child Support Enforcement (Child Support Enforcement Program), Administration for Children and Families, Department of Health and Human Services (Parts 300—399)

IV Office of Refugee Resettlement, Administration for Children and Families, Department of Health and Human Services (Parts 400—499)

2801al

Title 45—Public Welfare—Continued

Title 46—Shipping

Title 47—Telecommunication

Title 48—Federal Acquisition Regulations System

Title 49—Transportation

Title 50—Wildlife and Fisheries

CFR Index and Finding Aids

Alphabetical List of Agencies Appearing in the CFR
(Revised as of April 1, 2008)

Agency	CFR Title, Subtitle or Chapter
Administrative Committee of the Federal Register	1, I
Advanced Research Projects Agency	32, I
Advisory Council on Historic Preservation	36, VIII
African Development Foundation	22, XV
Federal Acquisition Regulation	48, 57
Agency for International Development	22, II
Federal Acquisition Regulation	48, 7
Agricultural Marketing Service	7, I, IX, X, XI
Agricultural Research Service	7, V
Agriculture Department	5, LXXIII
Agricultural Marketing Service	7, I, IX, X, XI
Agricultural Research Service	7, V
Animal and Plant Health Inspection Service	7, III; 9, I
Chief Financial Officer, Office of	7, XXX
Commodity Credit Corporation	7, XIV
Cooperative State Research, Education, and Extension Service	7, XXXIV
Economic Research Service	7, XXXVII
Energy, Office of	2, IX; 7, XXIX
Environmental Quality, Office of	7, XXXI
Farm Service Agency	7, VII, XVIII
Federal Acquisition Regulation	48, 4
Federal Crop Insurance Corporation	7, IV
Food and Nutrition Service	7, II
Food Safety and Inspection Service	9, III
Foreign Agricultural Service	7, XV
Forest Service	36, II
Grain Inspection, Packers and Stockyards Administration	7, VIII; 9, II
Information Resources Management, Office of	7, XXVII
Inspector General, Office of	7, XXVI
National Agricultural Library	7, XLI
National Agricultural Statistics Service	7, XXXVI
Natural Resources Conservation Service	7, VI
Operations, Office of	7, XXVIII
Procurement and Property Management, Office of	7, XXXII
Rural Business-Cooperative Service	7, XVIII, XLII
Rural Development Administration	7, XLII
Rural Housing Service	7, XVIII, XXXV
Rural Telephone Bank	7, XVI
Rural Utilities Service	7, XVII, XVIII, XLII
Secretary of Agriculture, Office of	7, Subtitle A
Transportation, Office of	7, XXXIII
World Agricultural Outlook Board	7, XXXVIII
Air Force Department	32, VII
Federal Acquisition Regulation Supplement	48, 53
Air Transportation Stabilization Board	14, VI
Alcohol and Tobacco Tax and Trade Bureau	27, I
Alcohol, Tobacco, Firearms, and Explosives, Bureau of	27, II
AMTRAK	49, VII
American Battle Monuments Commission	36, IV
American Indians, Office of the Special Trustee	25, VII
Animal and Plant Health Inspection Service	7, III; 9, I
Appalachian Regional Commission	5, IX

305

307

Agency	CFR Title, Subtitle or Chapter
Secretary of Labor, Office of	29, Subtitle A
Veterans' Employment and Training Service, Office of the Assistant Secretary for	41, 61; 20, IX
Wage and Hour Division	29, V
Workers' Compensation Programs, Office of	20, I
Labor-Management Standards, Office of	29, II, IV
Land Management, Bureau of	43, II
Legal Services Corporation	45, XVI
Library of Congress	36, VII
Copyright Office	37, II
Copyright Royalty Board	37, III
Local Television Loan Guarantee Board	7, XX
Management and Budget, Office of	5, III, LXXVII; 14, VI; 48, 99
Marine Mammal Commission	50, V
Maritime Administration	46, II
Merit Systems Protection Board	5, II, LXIV
Micronesian Status Negotiations, Office for	32, XXVII
Millenium Challenge Corporation	22, XIII
Mine Safety and Health Administration	30, I
Minerals Management Service	30, II
Minority Business Development Agency	15, XIV
Miscellaneous Agencies	1, IV
Monetary Offices	31, I
Morris K. Udall Scholarship and Excellence in National Environmental Policy Foundation	36, XVI
National Aeronautics and Space Administration	2, XVIII; 5, LIX; 14, V
Federal Acquisition Regulation	48, 18
National Agricultural Library	7, XLI
National Agricultural Statistics Service	7, XXXVI
National and Community Service, Corporation for	45, XII, XXV
National Archives and Records Administration	2, XXVI; 5, LXVI; 36, XII
Information Security Oversight Office	32, XX
National Capital Planning Commission	1, IV
National Commission for Employment Policy	1, IV
National Commission on Libraries and Information Science	45, XVII
National Council on Disability	34, XII
National Counterintelligence Center	32, XVIII
National Credit Union Administration	12, VII
National Crime Prevention and Privacy Compact Council	28, IX
National Drug Control Policy, Office of	21, III
National Endowment for the Arts	2, XXXII
National Endowment for the Humanities	2, XXXIII
National Foundation on the Arts and the Humanities	45, XI
National Highway Traffic Safety Administration	23, II, III; 49, V
National Imagery and Mapping Agency	32, I
National Indian Gaming Commission	25, III
National Institute for Literacy	34, XI
National Institute of Standards and Technology	15, II
National Intelligence, Office of Director of	32, XVII
National Labor Relations Board	5, LXI; 29, I
National Marine Fisheries Service	50, II, IV, VI
National Mediation Board	29, X
National Oceanic and Atmospheric Administration	15, IX; 50, II, III, IV, VI
National Park Service	36, I
National Railroad Adjustment Board	29, III
National Railroad Passenger Corporation (AMTRAK)	49, VII
National Science Foundation	2, XXV; 5, XLIII; 45, VI
Federal Acquisition Regulation	48, 25
National Security Council	32, XXI
National Security Council and Office of Science and Technology Policy	47, II
National Telecommunications and Information Administration	15, XXIII; 47, III
National Transportation Safety Board	49, VIII
Natural Resources Conservation Service	7, VI

311

List of CFR Sections Affected

All changes in this volume of the Code of Federal Regulations that were made by documents published in the FEDERAL REGISTER since January 1, 2001, are enumerated in the following list. Entries indicate the nature of the changes effected. Page numbers refer to FEDERAL REGISTER pages. The user should consult the entries for chapters and parts as well as sections for revisions.

For the period before January 1, 2001, see the "List of CFR Sections Affected, 1949–1963, 1964–1972, 1973–1985, 1986–2000" published in 11 separate volumes.

315

2004

List of CFR Sections Affected

2005

21 CFR

70 FR
Page

Chapter II

1300.01 Regulation at 68 FR 41228
confirmed.................................22591
(b)(45) added.............................25465
(b)(4) revised.............................74656
1301.13 Regulation at 68 FR 41228
confirmed.................................22591
1301.17 (c) redesignated as (d); new
(c) added..................................25465
1301.27 Added.............................25465
1301.28 Added.............................36342
1301.71 Regulation at 68 FR 41228
confirmed.................................22591
1301.72 Regulation at 68 FR 41228
confirmed.................................22591
1301.74 (c) revised.........................47096
1301.76 (b) revised.........................47097
1304.04 (a) revised.........................25466
1304.11 Regulation at 68 FR 41228
confirmed.................................22591
1304.22 Regulation at 68 FR 41229
confirmed.................................22591
1304.22 (c) revised...........................293
1304.26 Added................................293
1304.33 (c) and (d)(1) introductory
text revised..................................294
1305 Added; eff. 5–31–05.................16911
1305.08 Regulation at 68 FR 41229
confirmed.................................22591
1306.04 (c) revised.........................36343
1306.05 (a) revised...........................294
1306.05 (a) revised.........................35343
1306.07 Heading and (a) revised;
(d) added..................................36344
1307.11 Regulation at 68 FR 41229
confirmed.................................22591
(c) added..................................25466
1307.12 Regulation at 68 FR 41229
confirmed.................................22591
1308.13 (f) revised.........................74657
1308.14 (c)(51) added.......................16937
1308.15 (e) added.........................43635
1308.21 (a) revised.........................74657
1308.33 (a) revised.........................74657
1310 Authority citation re-
vised...294
Temporary exemptions.................5925
1310.03 (c) revised...........................294
1310.04 Technical correction............295
1311 Added; eff. 5–31–05.................16915
1313 Temporary exemptions..........5925

2006

21 CFR

71 FR
Page

Chapter II

1300 Technical correction.............60609
1300.01 (b)(4)(xxiii) and (liv) re-
vised.......................................60427
1300.02 (b)(28) and (29) revised;
(b)(31) removed; (b)(32), (33) and
(34) redesignated as (b)(31), (32)
and (33); new (b)(34) through
(37) added; interim....................56023
1301 Authority citation re-
vised.......................................51112
1301.12 (b)(3) revised.....................69480
1301.13 (e)(1) revised.....................51112
1308 Policy statement....................10835
Regulation at 71 FR 10835 con-
firmed......................................61877
1308.13 (c)(5) through (13) redesignated as (c)(6) through (14); new
(c)(5) added...............................51116
1308.34 Policy statement...............51997
1309 Authority citation amend-
ed...51114
Technical correction...................60609
1309.11 Revised.............................51114
1309.12 Revised.............................51114
1309.71 (a) revised; interim............56023
1310 Technical correction.............60609
1310.02 (b)(12) added......................60826
1310.04 (f)(1)(ii) revised; in-
terim.......................................56024
(f)(2)(i)(H) and (ii)(J) added...........60826
1310.05 (f)(2) revised; interim.........56024
1310.12 (c) table amended..............60826
1310.14 Removed; interim..............56024
1310.15 Removed; interim..............56024
1310.16 Added; interim..................56024
1314 Technical correction.............60609
1314 Added; interim......................56024

2007

21 CFR

72 FR
Page

Chapter II

1300.01 (b)(21) revised...................67852
1300.02 (b)(12), (13) and (25) revised; interim............................17406
(a)(28) added; interim..................20046
(b)(28)(i)(B) revised; interim.........37448
1306.12 Revised.............................64929
1306.14 (e) added...........................64930
1308.12 (d)(5) added.......................24533
(b)(1) table revised.......................54209
(b)(1) correctly amended..............69618

317

319